A River in Spain

To Juan

A River in Spain

Discovering the Duero Valley in Old Castile

ROBERT WHITE

I.B.Tauris Publishers
LONDON · NEW YORK

Published in 1998 by I.B.Tauris & Co Ltd
Victoria House, Bloomsbury Square, London WC1B 4DZ
175 Fifth Avenue, New York NY 10010

In the United States and Canada distributed by St Martin's Press,
175 Fifth Avenue, New York NY 10010

ISBN 1 86064 360 4

A full CIP record for this book is available from the British Library
A full CIP record for this book is available from the Library of Congress

Library of Congress catalog card: available

Printed and bound in Great Britain by WBC Ltd, Bridgend,
Mid Glamorgan

Contents

Maps

Photographs

Foreword

The author, Robert White, has asked me to prepare an introductory note to his book about the Duero River on its passage through the provinces along its course.

Such a request could only be met with a warm reception and acceptance on my part, given that he has chosen a topic so intimately related to our land as is the Duero River. The Duero drains the most extensive river basin in the country, flowing from the Sierra de Urbión between Burgos and Soria through provinces of our Autonomous Region such as Soria, Burgos, Valladolid, Zamora and Salamanca and forming the frontier of the sister nations of Spain and Portugal.

It is laudable that for Mr White, as a foreign scholar, this subject has taken on such great interest and relevancy and that he has written of it with a focus and perspective worthy of the highest praise.

The author explores in great detail, along with the strictly geographical aspects, those of a historic, artistic and religious character that have defined over the centuries all that is meant by the Duero River. These elements constitute the very essence of our region. Mr White dwells particularly on the cultural and religious factors that evolved the length and breadth of the river as it winds its way past the most important provincial capitals and towns of our region.

The bulk of the book is devoted to detailed descriptions of the districts of Castilla marked by the Duero on its passage through them. The reader will find much information of great interest about the regions and towns along the river, interwoven with notable historical events, important background material, and the cultural and religious influences contributed by other peoples that have come to define our national essence. The Muslim conquest, Islamic Spain, the reconquest, the National Unity forged by the Catholic kings, modern Spain, are all themes that the author develops. He also analyses different monuments and architectural styles: Visigothic, Mozarabic, Romanesque, Mudéjar, Gothic, Renaissance and baroque.

With this book, the reader has the opportunity to cross the Castilian steppe with its earthen villages, its people and its cities whose cultural heritage has achieved international renown. Through its pages, carried along by the author's creative inspiration, the reader can relive the monumental past, both the secular and the religious, that evokes profoundly important concepts deeply rooted in the souls of our people, Castilian and Leonese.

The text of the work is done with great care and enriches the store of writing about tourism in our Autonomous Region, emphasizing as it does the scope of the artistic and historical heritage of our land.

We congratulate the author and the publisher for their happy collaboration to produce this book. The itineraries are well-written and comprehensive, of great intrinsic interest, described in a rigorous and disciplined style that will enhance the reader's pleasure.

Juan José Lucas
President of the Council of Castilla y León

Preface

A River in Spain grew out of many motor trips through the Duero valley over a period of more than two years when I lived in Madrid, a happy turn of events having enabled me to make the move from New York. I had visited Spain several times before, but this was an opportunity to tour at leisure and observe in depth.

From early in my stay, my friend and I began spending almost every weekend in one or another provincial capital or small town. Because it is so lovely, so interesting and so accessible from Madrid, we came to concentrate on the valley of the Duero River which drains the heartland of the ancient kingdoms of Castilla and León. We rarely if ever saw foreign tourists, except in the obvious places such as Segovia or Salamanca, which leads me to believe that this book may be useful.

I have written this for the traveller who wants to leave the main roads and explore the countryside. Much of what is interesting in the Duero valley is hidden away in small towns or villages whose churches and castles bear witness to an earlier and grander existence.

For centuries, the Duero marked the embattled frontier between Christians and Muslims in Spain. Along its course deeds great and vile were done, while castles and towns, churches and monasteries rose, flourished and decayed. Many ancient towns are now bustling modern centres ready to meet the next century; others slumber in the shadow of their past glories. In some villages, only a handful of aged citizens remain, still watched over by their well-worn churches and crumbling castles.

This book reflects my interest in medieval history and Romanesque architecture and the experiences we had as we wandered about. There are gaps. We never managed to get to the source of the Duero in the mountains of Soria Province, we did not do justice to the northern fringes of the valley and we were unable to cover the segment of the river that flows through Portugal. But we did enough and saw enough to want to recommend to others the riches this part of Spain has to offer.

Our enjoyment was due in large measure to the many Spaniards – custodians, guides, village priests, passers-by, local citizens – who showed us their treasures and provided us with information. To one, Don Pablo Sainz Casado, parish priest of Sotosalbos (Segovia), special thanks. His enthusiasm for the ancient churches in his charge inspired us to look further and from our trips of exploration this book ultimately emerged.

Thanks also to the directors of the Spanish Tourist Offices in New York and London, Ignacio Vasallo and Antonio de la Morena, to Pilar Vico of the New York office, and to D. Dionisio Miguel Recio, Director General of Tourism for the Autonomía de Castilla y León, all of whom were most encouraging and helpful.

The persistent optimism of Patricia Haskell, my agent and friend, kept me going when publication seemed a distant possibility at best.

I am most grateful to Iradj Bagherzade at I.B.Tauris who first expressed interest in the book and guided me through the long process of refining the manuscript until it was fit for publication.

And finally, thanks and then some to my friend Juan Punchin whose assignment to Spain enabled me to live there and learn enough to write this book and whose navigational and linguistic skills proved invaluable on this as on many other occasions.

Spelling and Spanish Words

In general, I use the Spanish spelling of proper (Spanish) names. I also employ a number of common Spanish words with which the reader should, I think, become familiar. These names and words are often encountered along the route.

Recognizing, however, that Fernando and Isabel, Carlos V and Felipe II may not rest on the eye as comfortably as Ferdinand and Isabella, Charles V and Philip II, I have switched to the English spelling of the names of monarchs. Why English should alter Isabel, a perfectly manageable name, to Isabella, I am not certain. It is perhaps a truncation of Isabel la Católica.

On the first occasion in each chapter where I use a Spanish word, it is italicized. Thereafter it appears in normal print. All such words are in the Glossary.

I should note that the modern Autonomía (Autonomous Region) of Castilla y León was established only in 1983 in accordance with the Spanish Constitution of 1978. León and Castilla la Vieja or Old Castile (as opposed to Castilla la Nueva or the modern Autonomía de Castilla-La Mancha) had separate historical developments though united under the same crown from 1230. When the autonomous regions were established after 1978, Old Castile lost Cantabria and Logroño (La Rioja) which went their own autonomous ways.

Introduction: Some Practical Considerations

To travel comfortably in Spain, a man should have a good constitution, two good servants, letters of credit for the principal cities, and a proper introduction to the best families.

While these elements may be useful now for a comfortable journey, they were deemed essential by Joseph Townsend who travelled in Spain in 1786 and 1787; his book from which this quotation is taken was published in London in 1791. Matters have eased a great deal since then.

The itinerary in this book is arranged from east to west, keeping close to the Duero valley, and from time to time wandering up tributaries to places of special interest. It begins in the mountainous province of Soria, in the north of which the Duero rises, and ends where the wide-open spaces of the meseta come up against the rugged mountains of Portugal. Our last view of the Duero will be as it turns west and flows into Portugal to become the Douro.

Maps and Roads

With a good road map, you can mix and match these itineraries as you please. The *Mapa de Carreteras, España y Portugal* (Almax Editores) is especially useful. The Cruz Roja Española's *Gran Atlas de Ciudades, Carreteras y Puestos de Socorros* is more detailed in some respects, but does not show secondary and tertiary roads as clearly as does the other one. (*Puestos de Socorros* are Red Cross stations.) The Michelin *Motoring Atlas to Spain and Portugal* (ring-bound) is also very good, but is not quite as detailed as the others.

Turespaña publishes brochures on each province which contain maps of the province and plans of the capitals. These are available at Spanish National Tourist Offices abroad. Tourist Information Offices in Spanish towns have local maps and lists of the opening hours (*horario*) of monuments and are staffed by pleasant and helpful people.

Six major national highways (*carreteras*) radiate out of Madrid. Secondary roads, even tertiary and most local ones, are good and well signposted. The traffic returning to Madrid on a Sunday evening or at the end of a holiday along any road can be awful; try to avoid those times. Petrol stations are plentiful, though it is always wise to fill up if you are intending to drive really deep into the country.

Where speed limits are posted, it is a good idea to obey them. Traffic fines are horrendous and there are electronic devices on key roads to bag the unwary.

Hotel and Restaurant Guides

For detailed information on hotels and restaurants, the Red Michelin is indispensable. Also valuable and with more local listings (including hostals) are the annual *Guía de Hoteles* of Turespaña or the *Guía del Viajero* of Plaza & Janés. The latter is particularly useful on restaurants. They are in Spanish, but are easy enough to follow and are available at all Madrid's main bookstores. Both may tell you more than you need to know, however, if you are planning a trip of limited scope.

Paradors are, of course, a Spanish institution and some of them are indeed marvellous, beautiful adaptations of old castles, palaces and monasteries. Turespaña has a booklet in English called *Visiting the Paradors* and each parador has available free booklets listing addresses and telephone numbers of the others.

Provincial capitals have a good choice of hotels and there are comfortable and often charming small hotels or hostals in such places as El Burgo de Osma (Soria); Aranda de Duero, Santo Domingo de Silos and Covarrubias (Burgos); Sepúlveda (Segovia); Tordesillas, Medina del Campo and Medina de Rioseco (Valladolid); and Toro (Zamora).

Hotels hold reservations only until 6 p.m., so if you suspect that you will arrive late, tell them when you make the reservation.

It is wise in towns of any size to reserve your table for dinner at the better restaurants. This is especially true for the evening meal on Friday and Saturday and the afternoon meal on Sunday. On Sundays, Spanish families pour into local restaurants and three if not four generations gather round the table, the *abuela* (grandmother) at one end, often rocking the cradle with the latest addition to the family. Madrileños enjoy getting out into the country on weekends and country restaurants can fill up.

We never picnicked on any of our expeditions. For one thing, it is a relief to get out of the sun for a while. Secondly, the number of bars offering *tapas* in even small towns renders picnics unnecessary, although you may want to check out the offerings before committing yourself. Some bars have more interesting offerings than others. Tapas are small bits and dishes of food which can come in tremendous variety. They are made on the premises and are almost always delicious. Bars are also useful sources of information. Posted therein are notices of local happenings: bullfights, football matches, festivals and the like. By following up on such notices, we witnessed the crowning of a *vendimia* (grape harvest) queen and the initial stages of construction of the 'Biggest Paella in the World' at Rueda (Valladolid) and attended an *encierro*, a sort of amateur bullfight in which both bulls and fighters are young and untried, at Pozáldez (also Valladolid).

Spanish

It is of course helpful to know Spanish, not only to ask directions but to understand the answers. People are enormously friendly and helpful when asked about their local sights, but they are not likely to speak English. In fact, remarkably few people do speak English in these parts, even in hotels, but don't let that discourage you.

Visiting Sites; Hours

Spanish towns and with them monuments tend to close down from 2 to 4 p.m., more or less. The uninhabited torpor into which a Spanish town can sink of an afternoon, especially on weekends, is astonishing. Village churches and places off the beaten track present something of a challenge. You must ask who has the key. If not the local priest (*párroco*), there is always a custodian (*custodio/a*) who will be pleased that you have taken an interest and proud to show off the building in his or her charge. These often elderly people may have held the key for years and are very knowledgeable.

You can usually get into a church and explore before mass and after, although afterwards you must be quick as the priest or sacristan may be anxious to close up and go about his affairs. An appeal for time and his indulgence sometimes works, but not always. Whether or not you manage to get inside, you should walk all the way around a church, wherever possible, so that you do not miss anything.

My final tip relates to open doors. Always go in an open door at first passing. There is no telling what treasure may lie within, and by the time you come back, the door may be closed and you will have missed it. A gentle push may also be rewarding. We saw the marvellous cloister at San Cugat de Vallès near Barcelona at an hour when it was supposed to be closed simply because the door, though shut, was not latched.

Part One
The Background

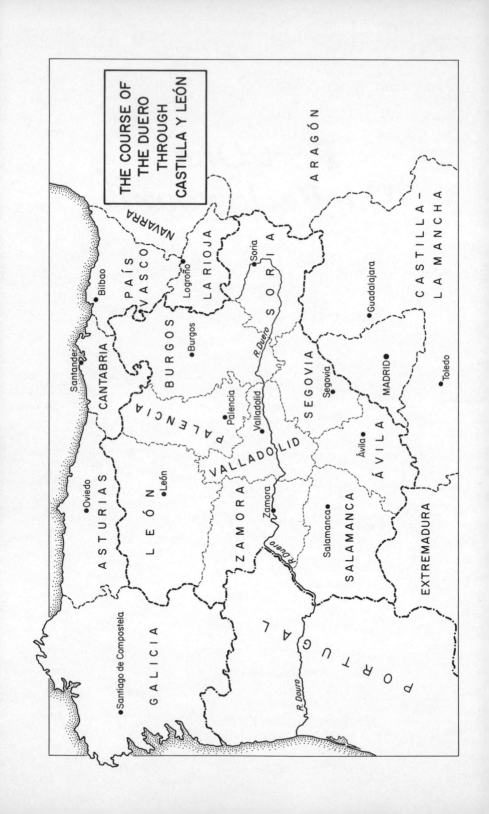

THE COURSE OF
THE DUERO
THROUGH
CASTILLA Y LEÓN

ARAGÓN

NAVARRA

PAÍS VASCO

LA RIOJA

SORIA

CASTILLA-LA MANCHA

• Bilbao

• Logroño
• Soria

BURGOS

• Guadalajara

CANTABRIA

• Burgos

R. Duero

SEGOVIA

• Santander

MADRID •

• Toledo

PALENCIA

VALLADOLID

• Palencia

• Valladolid

Segovia •

• Oviedo

ÁVILA

ASTURIAS

LEÓN

• León

VALLADOLID

• Ávila

ZAMORA

• Zamora

Duero

SALAMANCA

Salamanca •

EXTREMADURA

GALICIA

PORTUGAL

• Santiago de Compostela

R. Douro

1

The Setting

The Landscape

The Río Duero rises in the Sierra de Urbión in the north of Soria Province, the easternmost of the nine provinces that comprise the modern Autonomía (Autonomous Region) de Castilla y León. From the pine forests and mountains of Soria, the river loops east, south and then west for 855 km (535 miles). It flows through the provinces of Soria, Burgos, Valladolid and Zamora, turns south to form the boundary between Spain (Salamanca Province) and Portugal, then passes into Portugal and, as the Douro, drops steeply and swiftly to the Atlantic.

The Duero is not particularly deep, but steep bluffs line most of its northern bank and it thus presents a modest natural barrier in the flat *meseta*, as the high plateau of central Spain is known. The Christian kings advancing south against the Muslims in the 9th and 10th centuries saw this advantage and erected on the bluffs a chain of fortresses, among them Aranda de Duero, Roa, Peñafiel (south of the river), Simancas, Tordesillas, Toro and Zamora.

Tributaries of the Duero drain the other provinces of Castilla y León: the Pisuerga, Valderaduey, Cea and Esla drain Palencia and León to the north; the Duratón, Cega, Eresma, Adaja and the Tormes drain Segovia, Ávila and Salamanca to the south. The Duero basin thus encompasses most of the territory of the ancient kingdoms of Castilla and León. It is not a large area: some 94,150 sq. km (36,350 sq. miles), less than three-quarters the size of England, smaller than New York or Pennsylvania.

The Autonomía comprises 19 per cent of the national territory and contains just over 2.5 million people, about 6.8 per cent of the Spanish population. It was not always thus. From the 13th to the 16th centuries, the population of Castilla and León amounted to two-thirds or more of the population of the entire peninsula. In 1900 it still accounted for 12.4 per cent.

The basin forms a rough triangle with its highest point in Soria, in the northeast, from where it slopes westwards towards Portugal and the Atlantic. It is defined on the north by the Cordillera Cantábrica that separates Castilla and León from the steep green valleys and the rain and coastal fogs of Asturias and Cantabria. To the south and east rises the Sistema Central, a series of ranges which include the Sierra de Gredos and the Sierra de Guadarrama, west and north of Madrid, that separate Castilla la Vieja from Castilla la Nueva (La Mancha, the former kingdom of Toledo). These two mountain chains are tied together in a tangled sort of way by the mountains on the northern and eastern borders of Soria.

Passes through the Sistema Central are few. On the eastern flank are river valleys along which now runs the N-II highway from Madrid to Zaragoza. This was the route of the Roman road, the main passage for Muslim armies into the eastern Duero basin and the link between the Muslim states of Toledo and Zaragoza. It was guarded by fortresses at Atienza, Sigüenza and Medinaceli. The Somosierra Pass (1,445 m/4,735 feet) threads through the mountains north of Madrid (where the N-I to Burgos now runs) and was guarded for the Christians by Sepúlveda. The present road from Madrid to Segovia runs over the Navacerrada Pass (1,860 m/6,100 feet), but that would have been a difficult march in olden days. Further west, Ávila watches over the declivity between the Sierra de Guadarrama and the Sierra de Gredos along which armies could march down to Toledo, or vice versa. And finally, Salamanca commands the approaches to Extremadura.

The meseta ranges in elevation from 600 to 900 metres (roughly 2,000–3,000 feet), making it the highest region in Europe after Switzerland. Winter can be as cold as summer is hot. The weather in winter is tricky. January and February days can be beautiful, but there are also bad spells and morning ground fog can make driving difficult. November and December, March and April, are often cloudy and rainy. Snow can be a problem in higher altitudes. We slithered

off an icy road near Palencia one December Sunday after being hit
by a sudden snow storm and had to be rescued by a farmer and his
tractor. A good adventure as it turned out, but not to be recommended for the traveller with limited time. As for spring, blizzards
are not unheard of even in late April.

The period from mid-June to mid-August can be extremely hot.
The hottest time of day is from 3 to 6 p.m., with temperatures
exceeding 100°F or 40°C. I am not sure that I would go as far as
Laurie Lee who wrote of the heat as 'the brass-taloned lion which
licks the afternoon ground ready to consume anyone not wise enough
to take cover',[1] but he was walking across the meseta in 1935 and in
July at that.

Even intrepid travellers in cars need to retire from the field on
occasion, to seek shelter in a cool pool or restaurant. The heat is
very dry, which helps. Spain is located at the westernmost edge of
the European time zone and thus stays light in the summer until
after 10 p.m.

The Castilian landscape is unforgettable. The vistas are immense,
breathtakingly immense at times, the meseta rolling on and on to
distant mountains. In places, the land is so flat that one loses all
sense of distance to the horizon. Valleys provide marvellous views as
you suddenly reach the edge and make your way down and across,
and up the other side – often with a gaunt castle occupying a strategic
bluff.

In the early spring when the wheat and barley are coming up, the
traveller is treated to landscapes mottled with different shades of
green and brown, the furrows of the plough adding texture to the
scene. Poppies, brilliant red, appear along the roadside and spread
through the newly green fields. As June passes, the valleys remain
reasonably green while the fields of wheat and barley turn yellow in
the advancing heat of summer, not just a plain yellow, but an
extraordinary golden yellow. Whatever the colours, their intensity is
heightened by the floods of light that pour down on the land from a
cloudless sky. It is a marvellous spectacle.

There is a fine description of the meseta in the 1936 novel *Mary
Lavelle* by the Irish writer Kate O'Brien who first went to Spain in
1922. Mary is travelling by train from Bilbao to Madrid.

The land was blond, unbrokenly; its fairness stretched without pause or hurry to meet a sky so far away and luminous as to be only in the most aerial meaning blue. There were undulations, there were valleys; but within this spaciousness the breaks they made were like sighs which alleviate meditation; hamlets were so buff of roof and wall as almost to be imperceptible in the great wash of gold; roads made lonely curves across the quiet and bridges of pale stone spanned shallow rivers.

Acres of sunflowers, grown for their oil, with their bright yellow faces resolutely turned towards the rising sun, add vivid splashes of colour. Stands of pine and eucalyptus provide soothing green and variety. Vineyards have been important since at least the 14th century, some much earlier. We will see those of the Ribera de Duero, stretching from Langa de Duero in Soria Province to Zamora, and others in the Tierra del Vino south of the Duero in Zamora and Valladolid Provinces.

The Duero basin was still heavily forested in early medieval times. The subsequent deterioration has been variously blamed on the clearing of land that accompanied the Christian reconquest from the Muslims and its resettlement in the 9th to the 12th centuries; the importance of the wool trade to the Castilian economy from the 13th century and the consequent emphasis on pasturage for sheep; and the steady population growth which brought new land under cultivation at the expense of woodland and common land. The causes were many; the results disastrous and all too evident. Since the 1960s, governments have pursued an aggressive reforestation policy.

Unfortunately, forest fires are a terrible scourge. The aridity and the prevalence of pines, eucalyptus and other combustible growth make for a lethal combination.

Cereal production has dominated the meseta for centuries, though in recent years the importance of agriculture overall has declined sharply. Once tied to the land, the population has shifted into industry and services or has decamped from the meseta altogether in search of a better life. The period 1960–75 saw a massive outward migration. Madrid and the industrial belts on the north and east coasts as well as opportunities abroad have attracted tens of thousands of people. The sparseness of the population is a striking feature of the Castilian landscape.

The seeming emptiness of the meseta is also a function of population distribution patterns which in Castilla and León are quite different from those in the coastal provinces of the north or in Galicia or Portugal where one is rarely out of sight of a house. Here, people are gathered tightly into towns and little villages. They appear quite suddenly ahead, a cluster of houses gathered in a protective fold in the landscape ('like crocks of earthenware in the soil' as V. S. Pritchett observed)², marked by the tall keep of a castle or a church tower.

Sheep are a common sight, though in recent years cattle raising has expanded. (Don't look for fighting toros; they are raised in Extremadura and Andalucía.) Transhumance, the seasonal movement of great flocks of sheep north and south between summer and winter pasture, has been practised in the peninsula since prehistoric times. By the 13th century, with the reconquest of vast new lands for Christian settlement and with a burgeoning population in northern Europe to stimulate demand for woollen cloth, nobles, bishops and abbots and the military orders went into the business of raising sheep. It was easier than tilling the soil, which took manpower they did not have.

The availability of new grazing land coincided with the introduction from North Africa in the 13th century of the merino sheep, known for its fine white wool. The merino made Castilla and León the centre of medieval European wool production. The routes over which the sheep migrated seasonally north or south are called *cañadas*, an element of place-names to this day. One still sees flocks with their shepherds and dogs moving across the landscape. In the spring, the shepherd may have a lamb or two tucked under his arm, just born on the march.

You will frequently see little signs by the side of the road reading *Coto privado de caza*. These denote private hunting preserves owned by clubs or individuals. You do not see much wildlife afoot in Spain. There are many birds – quail, partridge, pheasant and assorted small birds in the fields, hawks and vultures soaring expectantly overhead and, of course, storks on their church towers – but not many animals. One sees rabbits and the occasional fox, but deer and wild boar are far from the beaten track. Bears still exist, but as a protected species in remote mountainous regions.

Storks merit special mention. These wonderful birds build enormous nests to which they return year after year and they build them almost exclusively on churches. The birds summer in North Africa, returning to Spain in December–February. They are a marvellous sight, especially at sundown when they soar around getting ready to settle down for the night. They make odd clattering sounds with their long beaks. The villagers love them and take care no harm befalls them.

Spain was exporting wine even in Roman days, but not until the reconquest was well established did the vineyards expand. The influence of Cluniac and Cistercian monks from France was a key factor. The phylloxera plague in 1898 wiped out the Spanish vineyards and vintners had to begin again, with French help.

There are vineyards all over Castilla y León with three major areas – *Denominaciones de Origen* (DOs) – along the Duero: the Ribera de Duero stretching from near Peñafiel to Valladolid and including the smaller Ribera de Burgos around Aranda de Duero, the Rueda DO southwest of Valladolid, and that of Toro. The premier vineyard in Spain, perhaps, is the Vega Sicilia at Valbuena de Duero, originally planted in 1864.

A cooperative was established for the Ribera de Duero in 1927 and reorganized in 1970 with headquarters at Peñafiel. Another group was organized in 1980, with its headquarters at Pesquera de Duero. The DO of the Ribera de Duero was established in 1982.

The Rueda area has been producing white wines since the Middle Ages when they provided them to the court at Valladolid. The area is riddled with caves burrowed into the limestone hills. In the 1970s, the Marqués de Riscal people from La Rioja were seeking a new source of white wine and settled on Rueda. The business developed fast and prospered and in 1980 Rueda was awarded DO status.

Toro reds were also famous in the Middle Ages and the area was developed anew after 1975. It received DO status in 1987.

The Urban Scene

For many decades the Duero was the embattled frontier between Christianity and Islam. By the end of the 10th century, the Christian kings stood firmly on the river; by the end of the 11th, Toledo had fallen and the Tajo (Tagus) reached.

Without repopulation, however, the reconquered lands could not be held and tamed. The kings thus promoted the establishment of towns and villages, encouraging settlers from northern Spain and beyond the Pyrenees as well as refugees from the Muslim south. The new settlements were granted generous *fueros* (municipal charters). The monarchs and the towns needed each other's support and the towns fiercely defended their rights and liberties against aristocratic and royal encroachment. Churches and monasteries arose, the latter playing a vital role in bringing the land back under cultivation.

The ancient towns and villages of the Duero have lost precious parts of their heritage to war and to 19th- and 20th-century developers. Some have decayed and are semi-abandoned, but almost all have preserved to some degree treasures from their past which are 'worth the detour' and even 'worth the trip'. The old core, the *casco antiguo*, is embedded in a bustling modern town. Modern Spaniards love their towns and if you cannot find that church and are blundering around in circles, ask anyone for directions. Young or old, they almost always know and are proud to point the way.

Spaniards are, by and large, much attached to their native towns. It is no coincidence that the word *pueblo* means village or town as well as people. Wrote Gerald Brenan in his classic study *The Spanish Labyrinth*: 'Every village, every town, is the centre of an intense social and political life ... [and] a man's allegiance is first of all to his native place, or to his family or social group in it, and only secondarily to his country or government.'[3] This is no doubt less true now than it was when he wrote in the 1940s, but the feeling persists none the less.

Towns exhibit certain consistent patterns, dating from the Middle Ages. These may have been obscured by modern accretions and the destruction wrought by the development frenzy of the 1950s and beyond, but they can usually be discerned.

It is easy, most of the time, to orient yourself once you have penetrated the modern quarters into the casco antiguo or *centro histórico*. There is always the Plaza Mayor and on it are typically the principal church or cathedral, the *ayuntamiento* (town hall), possibly the palace of the former lord, and other public offices including the Guardia Civil. Look for signs indicating 'Centro Ciudad' or 'Plaza Mayor'.

Many old towns stand on rocky spurs with the modern sector spread out in less cramped quarters below, so it is usually sensible to head uphill to reach the historic centre. Going up can be exciting, and the effort is usually rewarded. The thing to do is persevere – but not past the point of wisdom.

Whether the town was founded on a Roman site or on virgin ground, it usually grew up around a strategically-placed castle or an important monastery or church. Settlers gathered according to their origins in *barrios* around their *parroquias* or parish churches. Artisans and tradesmen settled in their own quarters according to their lines of work. The local gentry built their houses along one or more of the main streets; many impressive portals emblazoned with *escudos* (coats of arms) have survived, though the mansions behind may have been transformed beyond recognition. Muslim inhabitants, left over after the reconquest, lived in *morerías* around their mosques and the Jews in *juderías* around their synagogues. All were surrounded by a stout wall.

This pattern of specialized districts of like people, or of people pursuing the same trade, was of course common to western Europe and shares certain characteristics with Muslim towns. Muslim towns in Spain, however, have a street pattern and an organization, or lack thereof, quite distinct from those of Christian towns. In Toledo or Córdoba, for example, you will find a maze of streets with no discernible order. The so-called Plaza Mayor in Toledo is barely noticeable as such.

Each town controlled the countryside beyond its walls and by the 13th century many towns had developed what in effect were municipal *señoríos* (lordships). The *alfoz*, as it was known, consisted of gardens, orchards, vineyards, fields of grain, grazing lands and woodlands. The alfoz could also include villages and key defensive zones, thanks to royal or noble donations.

There is something almost organic in the way villages in Castilla and León emerge from the soil. Depending on location and availability of material, houses are of stone or brick, of rammed earth or adobe. Occasionally, a timber framework is filled with one or another of these materials. Outer walls are covered with plaster and a lime whitewash, frequently renewed.

In really agricultural villages, livestock still live below, the family above. The tumbledown condition of many ancient villages attests to the draining away of the population to urban centres or to the development of more modern types of housing, usually of brick. But where the old houses have been reasonably maintained, or restored, the effect can be strikingly warm and neighbourly.

Most of the Castilian towns on our itinerary declined from their medieval importance and prosperity during the 17th century and by the 18th many were in an advanced state of decay. The appalling damage wrought by the French armies during the Peninsular War of 1808–13 added further to the ruin. Traveller after traveller in the 19th and early 20th centuries wrote of the wretched condition of the cities. Decay, ruin and desolation are constant themes.

A revival of sorts began in the late 19th century, but it was not until the middle of the present century that at least some of these ancient towns, long lost in slumber in the depths of the meseta, began to recover in any real sense.

After the stagnation of the Civil War and the Second World War years, the 1950s saw the economic recovery which led to the booming Spain of the 1970s and 1980s. Valladolid and Burgos have become vibrant industrial centres, followed by smaller centres such as Aranda de Duero and Palencia. Even so, only thirteen towns in the Autonomía de Castilla y León have more than 20,000 inhabitants: the nine provincial capitals (of which León, Burgos and Valladolid have over 100,000), plus Aranda de Duero (Burgos), Medina del Campo (Valladolid), Miranda de Ebro (Burgos) and Ponferrada (León).

They, along with Madrid and the coastal industrial towns, have attracted thousands from the countryside. With the exception of the towns noted above, most municipalities in Castilla y León have lost population since the 1960s. The number of places with fewer than one hundred inhabitants increased six-fold between 1960 and 1985. Soria Province has suffered particularly heavy losses; the provincial map is freckled with places of ten inhabitants, or none. We shall visit at least one such, Caracena, south of El Burgo de Osma, but we shall also see many villages seemingly occupied only by the elderly. There is nothing to hold the young who have drained away down the new roads to distant cities.

The *alcalde* (mayor) of a village in Palencia Province, noting that there were only a few elderly residents left in the village, said ruefully that there would soon be no one to elect or be elected the next alcalde.

The Plaza Mayor The centre of virtually all towns in Spain is the Plaza Mayor on which stand the cathedral or principal church, the ayuntamiento or, in larger towns, the *casa consistorial* (town hall or council) and often the prefecture of police or the Guardia Civil.

Shops, offices, public buildings, restaurants and cafés, depending on the size of the town, occupy the remaining space. The sides of the square are usually arcaded, providing shelter from the elements. In older towns, the Plazas Mayores may be surrounded by wooden balconies and were (still are, in some places) used for bullfights. They can be absolutely charming if not downright beautiful. Happily, there are almost always cafés with outdoor tables to enable the traveller to rest and take in the local scene.

The Plaza Mayor evolved from the market places which began to develop in northern Spain as the reconquest got under way in the 10th and 11th centuries. The repopulation of the Duero lands followed, but it was a long time before commerce and trade revived. Barter and exchange were the usual means of conducting what trade there was; money came only later.

From al-Andalus, Muslim Spain, came textiles and other items of Muslim manufacture, carried north by traders of all faiths. Gradually, local artisans began making goods to meet local demand. Barter trade developed between town and country. Markets took shape, the first documented example being in the town of Cea (in the Tierra de Campos between Palencia and León) in 951.

The late 11th century saw a general economic revival in western Europe accompanied by a steady increase in population that persisted into the 13th century. In Spain, the Duero was reached and secured; Toledo fell to Alfonso VI in 1085 and huge tracts of land were opened up for settlement and exploitation.

Organized markets now became a necessity. Only the king had the authority to establish them. They were important sources of revenue for the crown and the kings were able to reward towns for their support by chartering markets. Markets were usually held weekly, on a day fixed by the charter. Regulations protected merchants and customers; schedules of tariffs were posted. Weekly markets are still held in most towns and villages.

Simple weekly markets soon proved insufficient to serve growing populations. In major towns which produced goods in sufficient variety and quantity to satisfy daily requirements, an area was set aside for their sale on a permanent basis. Thus was born the *azogue* or *azoguejo* (from the Arabic *al-suq*, market or bazaar).

The two types of market eventually merged into the Plaza del Mercado which occupied a central position in the town, convenient to all. The Plaza del Mercado also provided a suitable setting for public ceremonies and spectacles.

The transformation of the Plaza del Mercado into the Plaza Mayor began with Ferdinand and Isabella at the end of the 15th century. The Plaza Mayor was, of course, the principal square, distinguished by two purposes lacking in other squares: it served the townsfolk as a commercial and civic centre and it reflected the commercial and political power of the town or the monarchy. This latter in particular was in the minds of Ferdinand and Isabella when in 1480 they decreed the erection of public buildings in each town, edifices suitable for the exercise of political power. Town halls – ayuntamientos or, in larger centres, casas consistoriales – arose on the old Plazas del Mercado which now became Plazas Mayores dedicated to commerce, to the display of political power and to diversion and relaxation.

This led in turn to an architectural tidying up of what were often irregular spaces. The edges of the Plaza Mayor were aligned and buildings were made to toe those lines. Façades were often erected anew to achieve homogeneity. The final stage in the process was the creation of entirely new Plazas Mayores, designed from scratch as expressions of royal or civic pride. The first built was at Valladolid after the fire of 1561 destroyed the ancient Plaza del Mercado. The Plaza Mayor in Madrid came along in 1617; that of Salamanca in 1733. The architecture was intended to reflect the power of the city, civil order, sobriety and propriety, all those virtues so dear to the hearts of Charles I and Philip II, the first Habsburg monarchs of a Spain that was the leading power of Europe.

We will see many Plazas Mayores on our trip, grand and humble. A few are overpowering, many are charming, almost all are worth sitting in for a while to watch the world go by.

Notes

1. Laurie Lee, *As I Walked Out One Mid-summer Morning* (London, 1969), p. 61.
2. V. S. Pritchett, *The Spanish Temper* (New York, 1954), p. 41.
3. Gerald Brenan, *The Spanish Labyrinth* (Cambridge, 1990), p. ix.

2

A Historical Review

The towns and villages, churches and monasteries, castles and palaces along the Duero valley did not just happen; they were created in response to specific historic developments. Some background history may therefore be useful to the traveller.

The following review is strictly limited in scope and time, focusing on the early medieval history of the Duero valley and on subsequent periods when the valley was the scene of important events.

Ancient and Roman Spain

The Iberian peninsula has long been subject to foreign intrusions. Celts moved across the Pyrenees early in the first millennium BC to occupy the north and west, mingling gradually with the native Iberians of the south and east to form a Celtiberian population. Their settlements were scattered throughout the Duero basin and have left notable archaeological traces. (One of the most famous sites, Numancia, near Soria, is described on pages 101–2.)

In the far south, Phoenician traders founded Gades (Cádiz) around 800 BC; Greeks colonized the east coast in the 7th and 6th centuries; the Carthaginians settled future Andalucía from the 6th century on.

Carthage expanded its empire in the Iberian peninsula after its expulsion from Sicily by Rome at the end of the first Punic War

(241 BC). Hannibal took Helmantike (Salamanca) in 220 BC and brought the Vaccaei tribe of the middle Duero at least temporarily under Carthaginian control. He launched his invasion of Italy from Spain in 218, setting off the second Punic War which ended in the loss of the peninsula to Rome by 207. Carthaginian footprints have long since vanished from the Duero region.

Over the next two centuries, the Romans brought Hispania under centralized control. They were not gentle about it. Roman cruelty and duplicity, the ineptitude and venality of many generals and proconsuls, set off frequent tribal revolts. The best organized were the Lusitanian War (155–138 BC), led by the brilliant tribal commander Viriathus, and the first (181–179 BC), second (153–151 BC) and third (143–133 BC) Celtiberian Wars, the last of which ended with the terrible siege and destruction of Numancia by Scipio Africanus, conqueror of Carthage.

Another serious revolt broke out in 79 BC during the civil wars in Italy between Sulla and Marius. Quintus Sertorius, a talented Roman officer, rebelled in Hispania and, leading a mixed native and Roman force, almost succeeded in creating an independent state but was treacherously slain in 72 BC. Pompey had been sent to deal with him and in his mopping-up operations proved himself to be every bit as brutal as his precursors.

Julius Caesar first held office in Hispania in 61 BC. Later, having fallen out with Pompey, he returned in 49 BC to clear the country of his rival's adherents. Not until the time of Augustus, who came to Hispania to campaign in 26 BC, was the peninsula at long last pacified and a reasonably normal administration instituted. Caesar conquered Gaul in a decade; Hispania took the Romans two centuries.

The Spanish calendar was reckoned according to the Era of Caesar Augustus (ERA), beginning in 38 BC. Only in 1384 did Juan I of Castilla bring the Spanish calendar into line with the rest of the West. ERA 1138 (or MCXXXVIII) on an inscription thus translates to AD 1100.

Hispania's attraction lay in its immense mineral and agricultural wealth that Rome exploited to the hilt. The peninsula had gold, silver, lead, tin (plus access to the tin of Britain), copper, iron and mercury and mica (the only supplies then known). In agriculture, Hispania produced the three primary products of the ancient world: wheat, olive oil and wine. These along with fruit and vegetables, honey, beeswax, pitch, flax and linen, esparto grass, livestock and wool were exported to Italy.

Once pacified, Hispania was a fairly civilized place. Pliny the Elder held office there in AD 73, returning to Italy in time to perish below Vesuvius. Hispania enriched Rome with a number of literary and philosophical figures: the Senecas, father and son, Lucan, Martial and Quintillian among them. The 2nd-century emperors Trajan and Hadrian were born in Hispania as was their 4th-century successor Theodosius I.

Above all, Romanization meant urbanization. Towns spread across the peninsula, endowed with the usual complement of public buildings, theatres and aqueducts. The connecting network of roads facilitated the dissemination of Roman law, language and culture. Spain has some impressive Roman remains – theatres, bridges, roads, aqueducts and mines – that bear witness to more than a half millennium of rule. (The aqueduct of Segovia is, of course, one of the most famous sights in Spain; see page 158.)

The diffusion of Latin, perhaps Rome's most important legacy to the peninsula, opened the doors not only to Roman law but also, in time, to the Roman liturgy. The first explicit references to churches in Hispania appear in the late 2nd-century writings of Irenaeus, bishop of Lyon, and Christianity was firmly established in towns by the end of that century. It may have been introduced by Greek traders; Spanish troops serving in North Africa, a Christian stronghold, may also have imported the new faith. In his Epistle to the Romans (15:24), St Paul even promised to go to Spain to preach. By the 4th century, Christianity was flourishing. Bishop Hosea of Córdoba was spiritual adviser to Emperor Constantine I and presided over the Council of Nicaea in 325. By the end of the 4th century, monasticism had also taken root in the peninsula.

Jewish traders and merchants came along with the Phoenicians and Greeks, establishing colonies in the coastal cities at least as early as the 6th century BC. By Roman times, they were well established.

The Roman order in Hispania began to decay in the 3rd century. Industry and agriculture declined, political instability and civil strife took their toll; the first barbarians crossed the Pyrenees in 262. By the end of the 4th century, the imperial frontiers had collapsed in earnest, admitting the Germanic hordes who swept across Gaul and into Hispania.

Contingents of Vandals, Suevi and Alans crossed the Pyrenees in 409 and in a few years what was left of the imperial government had lost control of most of the peninsula. Roman rule lingered on in northeastern Spain, but the last outposts went down before a Visigothic attack in 475.

Visigothic Spain

In 415 Emperor Honorius engaged the Visigoths to rid Hispania of assorted barbarian invaders. This they did – and took over. The Visigoths' capital was originally at Toulouse, in southern Gaul, but in 507 they were soundly defeated by Clovis, founder of the Frankish kingdom, and transferred their operations to Hispania save for an enclave north of the Pyrenees centring on Narbonne. King Leovigild (569–86) made Toledo his capital. The main area of Visigothic settlement was between the Pisuerga, the upper Ebro and the Duero, tapering down to Toledo. The lands north of the Duero were long known as the Campo Gótico. This region contains all but one of the five extant Visigothic churches.

Fusion of the Visigothic military aristocracy and the Hispano-Roman population was hampered initially by the Visigoths' stubborn adherence, shared by all Goths, to the Arian creed which rejected the full divinity of Christ and his relationship with the Father as defined by Catholic Trinitarian orthodoxy. Church councils at Nicaea (325) and Constantinople (381) condemned Arianism, but this did not seem to trouble the Goths.

A milestone in relations between the Visigothic aristocracy and their subjects, therefore, was the conversion of Reccared I (586–601) to Catholicism. The formation of a united people was yet further advanced under Chindasuinth (642–53) and Reccesuinth (653–72) who promulgated a new territorial code of law equally binding on both the Gothic and Hispano-Roman populations. It remained in effect for generations.

Spain was now thoroughly Christianized. The episcopal hierarchy had represented administrative continuity and order as Roman institutions decayed and the Visigoths kept the Roman church organization reasonably intact. Toledo had become the leading see by the end of the 7th century and the successive Councils of Toledo, fourteen in the 7th century alone, were crucial in the development of spiritual and secular law. Pre-eminent were two bishops of Sevilla, San Leandro (c. 584–601) and his brother and successor San Isidoro (601–36), considered one of the most learned men of his time in Europe, and Braulio, bishop of Zaragoza (631–51).

The Jews, concentrated for the most part in the cities of the south and east coasts, continued to play an important role in trade and commerce. Once the Visigoths embraced Catholicism, however, the kings began to enact increasingly harsh anti-Jewish measures. By the second half of the 7th century, religious uniformity was perceived as the necessary underpinning for a strong national state and, as was to happen with equal ferocity a millennium later, Jews were ordered to conform or be expelled from the body politic.

The Visigoths were never able to create a strong hereditary monarchy. Kings followed each other in rapid succession, with real power being held by the bishops and the magnates. Nevertheless, by the end of the 7th century, Spain was ruled by its own now native kings and exhibited greater signs of political and cultural cohesion than any contemporary state in western Europe including Anglo-Saxon Britain and Merovingian Gaul.

It is interesting to note that Gothic German left virtually no trace in the Spanish language nor, unlike the Angles, Franks, Burgundians and Lombards, did the Visigoths give their name to the land they had conquered. The concept of 'Hispania' was too strong.

The Muslim Conquest

The Arabs had been advancing across North Africa for some seventy years before reaching Tangier in 708. Spain was the obvious next step. Encouraged by the weakness of the Visigothic kingdom, the governor of North Africa, Musa ibn Nusayr, dispatched a force across the straits in 711 under Tariq ibn Ziyad who gave his name to Gibraltar – Jabal Tariq, the Mountain of Tariq. The last king of the Visigoths, Roderic, fell in battle, Tariq and Musa led two columns northwards and by 715 most of the peninsula was in their hands.

Tariq and his men were Berbers. The Berbers of North Africa had resisted the Arab advance and by 711 were only superficially Islamicized. Bitter dissension between Arabs and Berbers and rivalries among various Arab tribes were to cause havoc in the newly conquered realm, now known as al-Andalus.

To later generations of Christian Spaniards, this humiliating defeat – as surprising perhaps to the invaders as to the invaded – had somehow to be explained by tales of treachery or by the decadence of the Visigoths who were punished for their sins. The reconquest of the Visigothic realm was to become an almost sacred duty for the rulers of the Christian Spain that gradually arose from the ruins.

Most of the Hispano-Gothic nobility threw in their lot with their new masters. The bulk of the Christian population had no choice but to carry on, pursuing their trades and cultivating their lands, often adopting more productive methods from the Arab settlers who followed the armies and brought new crops and new technology. Not only agriculture prospered; the 9th and 10th centuries saw a revival of urban life in al-Andalus. Old Roman towns such as Toledo, Córdoba and Sevilla rose to new levels of prosperity and new towns were founded.

Initially, the Muslim rulers were reasonably tolerant of their Christian and Jewish subjects, their worship and their customs. Nevertheless, increasing numbers of Christians from all classes found it expedient to convert to Islam, hoping to better their lot. Their later disillusionment at remaining second-class citizens would cause serious unrest.

In contrast to the Christians, very few Jews abandoned their faith. Their communities continued to prosper in all major cities while Jewish savants made important contributions to literature and science. The Jewish doctors of al-Andalus were renowned in western Europe. Not until the arrival of the fanatical Almoravids from North Africa at the end of the 11th century and of the even more fanatical Almohads sixty years later did life become seriously difficult for Jewish communities.

Christians who remained in their faith were called *Mozárabes* (from *musta'arib* meaning Arabicized, one who adopts Arab customs). As the Muslim rulers grew more militant and intolerant, thousands of Mozarabs made their way north to the Christian lines. Their impact on the cultural and religious life of the rude Christian north was enormous and they provided the rationale and the impetus for the reconquest (*la Reconquista*) of the peninsula from the Muslims.

The Muslim armies washed over the Duero valley and penetrated to the north coast, but the Arabs were not happy with cold damp mountain country and were really more interested in the warm coastal plains of southern France. In the allocation of lands after the conquest, the Duero valley and Galicia went mainly to the Berber contingents. Friction with the dominant Arabs brought about a massive Berber revolt in the early 740s and the Arabs were expelled from the basin. The Berber rebels were finally defeated near Toledo and retired to their homelands in North Africa. Famine in mid-century further exacerbated the situation, with the Duero valley being particularly hard hit. The resultant depopulation of the zone aided the Christian revival.

The Christian Revival

While most of the Christian population remained in situ after the Muslim conquest, many found it impossible to reconcile their faith with the status of being Muslim subjects. These 'men of higher rank or of more generous sentiments', wrote William H. Prescott in his classic study of the reign of Ferdinand and Isabella, 'retreated behind those natural fortresses of the north, the Asturian hills and the Pyrenees, whither the victorious Saracen disdained to pursue them.'[1] The Asturians, Cantabrians and Basques who anciently inhabited the mountain fastnesses of these coastal lands had never submitted fully to Roman or Visigothic rule.

In 718 (or 722) a Visigoth noble named Pelayo (d. 737) inflicted a sharp defeat on a Muslim force near Covadonga, some 50 miles east of the present town of Oviedo. This battle, much embellished by legend, occupies an almost mythical place in Spanish history. Pelayo's victory came to be seen as the first step in the Reconquista which was to end triumphantly for the Christians with the fall of Granada to Ferdinand and Isabella in 1492. The famous battle received scant notice in Arab sources, however, and the first known mention of Covadonga in Christian sources comes in a chronicle of 883.

Myth and legend played a powerful role in investing the Reconquista with divine sanction. The Virgin Mary was said to have appeared at Covadonga to inspire her warriors. Further sanctity adhered to the Christian cause with the mid-9th-century discovery in Galicia of the alleged tomb of the Apostle St James the Great, Sanctus Iacobus, Santiago.

The groundwork for the discovery had been laid some years earlier by an influential Asturian churchman named Beato de Liébana

(d. 789) who first promoted the legend that St James had preached the Gospel in Spain and had taken the land under his protection. Beato corresponded with the court of Charlemagne, was a fierce fighter against heresy and in about 776 compiled and edited an extremely important book, his *Commentaries on the Apocalypse* or the Book of Revelations of St John the Divine, that would be copied and recopied in monastic scriptoria for centuries to come and to which this book refers frequently.

Prior to Beato, St James is first linked with Spain in two manuscripts of the 7th and mid-8th centuries and then in an Asturian hymn of the 780s. The first mention of the apostle being buried in Spain comes in a French source of about 865. Tradition put the discovery of the tomb between 818 and 842 in the reign of Alfonso II (791–842) who founded a shrine at Compostela.

By the late 9th century, when the Asturian monarchy was making a conscious effort to emulate the vanished Visigothic court of Toledo and to link its legitimacy to that of its Christian precursor, Alfonso III (866–910) needed a powerful saint of his own to bolster his kingdom's prestige.[2] He built a splendid new church at Compostela and was a generous donor.

Another layer was added to the legend with the reputed appearance of Santiago mounted on a white stallion at the mid-9th-century battle of Clavijo (south of Logroño in La Rioja), thus ensuring victory to the Christians and earning for the warrior saint the sobriquet of *Matamoros* or Moor-Slayer. Santiago led and protected his Spaniards throughout the long struggle with the Moors and when the Moors were finally vanquished the spirit carried on into the New World. In 1541 the saint is said to have appeared in Mexico where he helped stave off a major Indian attack on Guadalajara.

It is doubtful that Pelayo or his son-in-law Alfonso I ever thought in terms of the Reconquista as such. The expansion of the tiny new Christian state was driven by several reasons including population growth and consequent land hunger, for people and for livestock, and the influence of a military class who wanted action. The growing pilgrimage traffic to Santiago de Compostela from the 9th century brought yet more settlers from beyond the Pyrenees.

Not until the second half of the 9th century did the idea of the Reconquista take firm shape, spurred in part by the thousands of Mozarabs, including monks, migrating north from al-Andalus. In

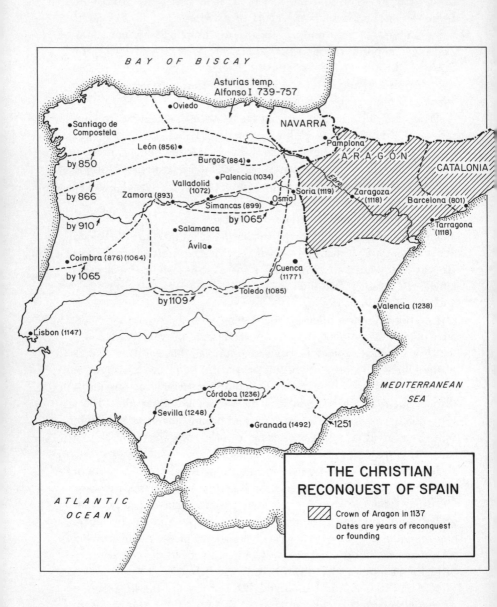

BAY OF BISCAY

Asturias temp.
Alfonso I 739-757

•Oviedo

NAVARRA

•Santiago de
Compostela

Pamplona

ARAGON

CATALONIA

León (856) •

Burgos (884) •

by 850

•Palencia (1034)

Soria (1119)

Zaragoza
(1118)

Barcelona (801)

by 866

Zamora (893)•

Valladolid
(1072)

Osma

Tarragona
(1118)

Simancas (899)

by 1065

by 910

•Salamanca

•Coimbra (876) (1064)

Ávila•

by 1065

Cuenca
(1177)

Toledo (1085)

by 1109

Valencia (1238)

•Lisbon (1147)

MEDITERRANEAN
SEA

Córdoba (1236)

Sevilla (1248)•

ATLANTIC
OCEAN

•Granada (1492)

1251

**THE CHRISTIAN
RECONQUEST OF SPAIN**

Crown of Aragon in 1137
Dates are years of reconquest
or founding

time, these sentiments were given direction and force by the Church. The Reconquista became a divinely sanctioned mission. Centuries of military action against the Moors were to shape Castilian and Spanish character and history from generation to generation. Once the Moors (and Jews) were expelled from Spain, the Reconquista turned inwards to extirpate any trace of heterodoxy. The purity of Catholic Spain had to be preserved, at all costs.

The Advance to the Duero (8th to 11th Centuries)

The Kingdom of Asturias A rapid succession of governors, Berber revolts and famine seriously weakened al-Andalus. Pelayo (718–37) and Alfonso I (739–57) were thus able to establish their new kingdom without undue interference. Alfonso brought the north coast and Galicia under his control, creating an organized state in an area which had known neither Roman rule nor political unity nor, for that matter, Christianity. He also pushed over the mountains into the northern Duero basin where he established a defensive frontier.

The ruin and abandonment of the Duero towns, the sparseness of the population and the scant human resources at his disposal decided Alfonso to create a *tierra de nadie*, a no-man's-land buffer zone in the valley, and thus it remained for more than a century. The main Muslim lines ran from Coimbra on the Atlantic coast through Toledo and Guadalajara to Zaragoza and Pamplona.

Christians and Muslims pegged their respective frontiers on defensive military positions. Place-names are significant. In the north and along the Duero many town names stem from the Roman *castrum* (military camp), *castel* and *castello*. Further south one find names from the Arabic *qasr* (castle) and *qal'at* (fortress). Both sides used the term *atalaya* for watchtowers, many of which still stand on rocky crags.

In 756, the twenty-five-year-old Umayyad prince 'Abd al-Rahman reached Córdoba from Damascus, one of the few of his family, caliphs since 661, to escape massacre in 750 at the hands of the 'Abbasid clan of Baghdad. The realm he founded was to last more than 250 years and lift Córdoba to the first rank of western European cities.

'Abd al-Rahman I (756–88) was too preoccupied with domestic affairs to pay much attention to the weak kings who succeeded

Alfonso I in Asturias. His son Hisham I (788–96), however, was an avid campaigner and his armies attacked Asturias again and again, so battering the little realm that one king, Bermudo I, abdicated and retired to a monastery.

Bermudo's successor, Alfonso II (791–842), was a man of sterner stuff and in his unprecedentedly long reign put the Christians on the march again. He was assisted by disorder in the south which kept Amir al-Hakam I (796–822) fully occupied. Alfonso II established his court at Oviedo and was the true founder of the Asturian monarchy. Working in his favour were the steady growth of a settled population, with all that that meant for agriculture and the revival of commerce, and an influx of Mozarabs from al-Andalus who brought with them culture and skills far superior to those of the crude north.

Ordoño I (850–66) and his son Alfonso III, the Great (866–910), took advantage of continuing unrest in al-Andalus to expand south over the mountains. León, the ancient camp of the Roman Seventh Legion, was occupied in 856, placing the Christians firmly in the Duero valley. Other conquests included Astorga 854, Porto 868, Coimbra 876, Zamora 893, Simancas and Dueñas 899 and Toro 900. Burgos was founded 884.

The repopulation of the Duero basin began in the second half of the 9th century as settlers inched south from the Cantabrian mountains down the river valleys. Repopulation was a deliberate royal policy; without a settled population the new territories could not be held or the Reconquista sustained. The kings issued *fueros* or municipal charters to newly founded towns that set out the rights and obligations of the inhabitants. The terms were favourable to the settlers whose strengths and support the kings needed and laid the ground for the considerable personal and civic liberties that they enjoyed for centuries. Protected by the new towns, agricultural settlers fanned out over the land. Fields of grain, vineyards and pasture for flocks of sheep began to replace the wooded landscape.

The pioneering settlers had no easy life, however. Fields and towns had been devastated by years of Muslim attacks; monasteries had been sacked and looted. The epic legends which now began to take shape preserved the memory of those hazardous times when 'knights and counts and even kings tethered their horses inside their palaces, even in their rooms', so they could spring quickly into action in case of sudden attack.[3]

Ordoño I and Alfonso III encouraged Mozarabs from al-Andalus to come north; the monks among them refounded monasteries wrecked by Muslim attacks or founded new ones that were sources of learning in a rude and violent world and played an important role in expanding cultivation. Among those in the Duero basin (and on our itinerary) were San Pedro de Arlanza, San Sebastián de Silos and San Cosme y San Damián in Covarrubias (all in Burgos Province) and San Salvador de Tábara (Zamora). Episcopal sees swept away by the Muslim invasion were re-established and churches began to rise again in the land. The Mozarab monks argued that the Asturian kings were true heirs to the Visigothic kingdom and had a sacred duty to recover the lost realm.

The Kingdom of León Ordoño II (914-24) moved his court to León, which now gave its name to the kingdom. To the east emerged the county of Castilla, named for the castles built to defend the kingdom from attack from east and south. Farther east yet, in the valleys of the Pyrenees, the kingdom of Navarra and the county of Aragón began to take shape and still further east, on the coast, the counties of Cataluña.

The aggressive actions of Ordoño II and the counts of Castilla, who fortified such Duero towns as Zamora, Simancas, San Esteban de Gormaz, Osma and Clunia, triggered a response from al-Andalus. The remainder of the 10th century was dominated by strong Muslim rulers. 'Abd al-Rahman III (amir of Córdoba since 912 and self-proclaimed caliph 929-61) and al-Hakam II (961-76) savaged the Christian lands repeatedly. In the summer of 920, 'Abd al-Rahman took San Esteban de Gormaz and Osma and went on to rout the kings of León and Navarra near Pamplona.

Ramiro II (931-51) inflicted two such serious defeats on 'Abd al-Rahman in 939 at Simancas and Salamanca that the caliph never took the field against the Christians again. Ramiro and the new count of Castilla, Fernán González (c. 930-70), pressed south of the Duero into the valley of the Tormes to take Ledesma and Salamanca, and Fernán González crossed the Duero in the east to occupy Sepúlveda in 940 and then Atienza.

The death of Ramiro II ushered in a calamitous time of troubles in León with weak kings and powerful magnates feuding to the end of the century. Fernán González made himself virtually independent in Castilla and meddled busily in the struggles in León, but al-Hakam was able to retake San Esteban de Gormaz and Atienza and the count had also to abandon the Duero fortress of Gormaz. To bolster the Muslim position, al-Hakam moved his military command forwards from Toledo to Medinaceli in 946 and in 965 began to rebuild Gormaz into the stupendous fortification that is still an awesome sight today.

The end of the century was dominated by Almanzor (Arabic: al-Mansur, the Victorious), the strongman (976–1002) who overshadowed al-Hakam II's weak successor and wrought havoc across the Christian lands. A child, Ramiro III, sat on the throne of León and a new count, García Fernández, governed in Castilla. García Fernández precipitated hostilities by taking Gormaz in 978. Almanzor moved north, smashed a Christian force near Atienza, besieged Ramiro III in Zamora and routed a hastily gathered force of Castilians, Leonese and Navarrese. The count of Castilla abandoned Sepúlveda and Atienza and retired north of the Duero; Simancas fell and León was barely saved.

In 988 Almanzor struck again: Coimbra was levelled, León and Zamora ravaged, Osma was taken. In 995 he captured Count García near Medinaceli and took him to Córdoba to die. Almanzor launched the greatest raid of his career in 997, sweeping through Portugal to the shrine of Santiago de Compostela. Alfonso III's church was destroyed, the doors carried away and the bells hung in the Great Mosque in Córdoba. There they remained until 1236 when Fernando III captured the city and returned them to Santiago on the backs of Muslim prisoners.

Although Almanzor caused the Christians much anguish and wrought an enormous amount of damage, by the time of his death in 1002 he, like Caliph 'Abd al-Rahman III before him, had made no permanent gains. The Duero strongholds had changed hands repeatedly, but at the beginning of the 11th century the Christians still stood firmly on the Duero frontier, ready to move forwards once again.

The Duero valley towns of the 9th and 10th centuries, despite their strategic importance, were small centres whose inhabitants, great and humble, sought primarily to survive. Within their walls lived a population of military men and settlers who made their living from the soil. Most towns were under the protection of counts or bishops.

Commerce was rudimentary, though gradually shopkeepers, artisans and itinerant merchants appeared to satisfy the slowly expanding needs of the growing population. In the year 1000, León had probably a thousand inhabitants, others even fewer.

The Advance to the Tajo
(11th Century)

The End of the Caliphate The Umayyad caliphate of Córdoba quickly followed Almanzor to its end. A series of weak princes disputed the throne until the last of them was deposed and the caliphate abolished in 1031. The son of the unfortunate Count García Fernández, Sancho Garcés (995–1017), had what was doubtless the enormous satisfaction in 1009 of helping to sack Córdoba where his father had died. He had been called in by Berber rebels against the caliph. His price was the retrocession of the Duero strong points seized by Almanzor.

In the place of the caliphate of Córdoba arose petty city-states, the *taifa*s (from an Arabic word meaning faction or swarm). These coalesced into ten or so, of which Sevilla was the most important. Castilla recovered the Duero fortress towns on its borders and the stage was set for further Christian advances.

The Ascendancy of Navarra Through judicious marriages, the rulers of the little Pyrenean kingdom of Navarra managed first to acquire the county of Aragón to the east and in 1029 the county of Castilla to the west. Sancho el Mayor (1000–35), of Navarra and Aragón, thus became the ruler of a solid block of territory in north central Spain. Yet another marriage brought the kingdom of León to his son and successor in Castilla, Fernando I, when Bermudo III, the last of the ancient line of Pelayo, fell in battle against Fernando, his brother-in-law, in 1037.

Sancho is important because he opened up his kingdoms to cultural influences from France. A movement for monastic reform was sweeping Europe and Sancho invited monks from the Benedictine abbey of Cluny to reform the monasteries in his realm. He was a generous patron of the pilgrimage to Santiago de Compostela, founding monasteries, inns and hospitals along the way. The influx of settlers and travellers from beyond the Pyrenees stimulated the growth of new towns, the spread of commerce and an intellectual revival.

Navarra was never again to play a significant role, however. Aragón absorbed it from 1076 to 1134 and in 1234 it was inherited by the first of a long series of French noble houses. Navarra south of the Pyrenees was finally annexed by Ferdinand, husband of Isabella, in 1512.

The Ascendancy of Castilla Sancho divided his realm among his four sons, of whom Fernando I of Castilla (1035–65) concerns us here. The ascendancy in Christian Spain now passed to Castilla. Fernando had to concentrate on repairing the ravages made by years of warfare to his kingdom, the boundaries of which now rested well south of the Duero on the line of the Sistema Central. Rather than trying to impose his will on the taifa rulers of the south by military force, Fernando hit on the happy notion of squeezing tribute from them as security against Christian aggression. In short, a protection racket. Though disorganized politically, the taifas were rich, profiting from the booming trade of North Africa and from the gold from the interior of the continent. Their tribute constituted a major source of revenue for the north.

Fernando was not averse to military action, just cautious in the use of limited resources. There was no way he could repopulate and hold any new large-scale conquests. Nevertheless, in the east he retook the fortresses of Gormaz and Berlanga in 1060 and cleared the lower Duero valley to the Atlantic by his capture of Coimbra in 1064. He died the next year, after a campaign to Valencia.

On the eastern flanks of Castilla, however, a serious threat remained at Zaragoza where a local Muslim dynasty controlled a solid block of land from Soria to the Mediterranean. In addition, far to the south, deep in the Sahara, a new danger was brewing, but of this the princes of Spain had as yet not a clue.

With the welcome return of peace under Fernando I, the rich lands of the Duero valley experienced a boom. Agriculture prospered and the increased economic and commercial tempo gave new life to towns restored in the 10th century, such as Zamora and Osma, and led to the foundation of new towns, such as Valladolid.

After all the energy invested by Sancho el Mayor and Fernando in consolidating their kingdoms, it seems perverse that they would deliberately divide them among their sons. Centrifugal forces were still at work, however, and local traditions and loyalties were too strong to admit of permanent union. On his death in 1065, Fernando left Castilla and the tribute from Muslim Zaragoza to his eldest son, Sancho II; León and the tribute from Toledo to his second, Alfonso VI; and Galicia and Portugal with the tribute from Badajoz and Sevilla to the third, García. To his daughters Urraca and Elvira went respectively the Duero towns of Zamora and Toro.

The arrangement soon fell apart. Sancho wanted everything. He drove Elvira from Toro in 1071, teamed up with Alfonso to oust García from Galicia and finally turned on Alfonso and seized León in January 1072. Alfonso was taken prisoner, but escaped and fled to the protection of the amir of Toledo.

The rest of the story is related in the chapter on Zamora (see pages 248–9). In brief, Urraca stood firm for Alfonso and, in a stunning reversal that soon became the stuff of legend, Sancho was slain before the walls of Zamora in 1072. Alfonso was now supreme. One would have thought his own experiences would have made him more sympathetic, but when brother García returned from exile in Sevilla to claim his kingdom Alfonso clapped him into prison where he died some eighteen years later.

Alfonso VI and the Conquest of Toledo   Alfonso VI (1065/ 1072–1109) was now the most powerful ruler in the peninsula. Taking advantage of the chronic disorder in the taifa kingdoms, he exacted ever greater tribute payments, meddled constantly in their affairs and campaigned far to the south. The great prize, however, was the city of Toledo, ancient capital of Visigothic Spain and the paramount episcopal see. It surrendered to Alfonso on 6 May 1085.

This momentous event established the Christian frontier on the Río Tajo (Tagus River) from which it never retreated despite temporary reverses. Further, it opened up enormous new tracts for colonization and shifted the centre of power from León and Burgos to the south. To hold on to these new conquests, however, was a daunting task. The mixed population of Muslims, Jews and Mozarabs was culturally quite different from that north of the Sistema Central. Toledo's population of some 28,000 was more than the population of the towns of León and Castilla combined.

Alfonso VI simply did not have the manpower to occupy the

space. Thus it was that in the next century the international military orders, the Templars and Hospitallers, and the home-grown Order of Calatrava as well as monasteries and great secular lords acquired huge tracts to exploit. They turned to raising sheep, which was a great deal easier than trying to bring the land under cultivation and protect it from Muslim raids.

Even before 1085, Alfonso had set in motion the repopulation of the trans-Duero region. About 1078 he settled Cuéllar, Fuente el Olmo de Iscar, Coca, Olmedo, Medina del Campo and perhaps Arévalo, thus forming a solid wedge south of the Duero which could be backed up by the Duero fortresses of Peñafiel, Valladolid and Tordesillas. This in turn made feasible the refounding of Segovia, Ávila and Salamanca as frontier fortresses. His chief architect in this task was his son-in-law Raymond of Burgundy.

There was no dearth of settlers. They came from all the lands of northern Spain to this new frontier where they could settle as free men and bring the land, deserted for centuries, back under cultivation. Advancing south of the Duero, they mingled with the survivors of Almanzor's campaigns and with Mozarabs and Jews fleeing worsening conditions in al-Andalus. The fall of Toledo also meant the absorption of many Muslims who declined to retreat with their defeated rulers. These were the *Mudéjares* (from the Arabic *al-muta'akhkhirun*, those who stay behind) whose many contributions to the evolving Spanish cultural mix included the style of architecture that bears their name.

The Advance to Andalucía (12th and 13th Centuries)

The Almoravid Years, 1090–1147 Alfonso VI did not enjoy his new conquests in peace for long. The taifa rulers, driven to desperation by the king's exactions and the fall of Toledo, called for help, with some misgivings, from a fanatic Berber confederacy which had swept up from the Sahara and overrun Morocco by 1084. The Almoravids (from *al-murabitun*, the men of the *ribat*, the monastic fortress they founded near the mouth of the Senegal River) landed in Spain in 1086 under Yusuf ibn Tashufin and promptly inflicted a severe defeat on Alfonso.

Trouble in Morocco called Yusuf back to Africa, but first-hand exposure to the taifa rulers convinced him of the ease with which he could make their lands his. He returned in force in 1090 and swiftly overran al-Andalus. In the place of the squabbling taifa rulers, a new Muslim power now confronted the Christians.

These were the years of the Spanish hero Rodrigo Díaz de Vivar (c. 1043–99), El Cid. His fascinating saga touches our itinerary only in the vicinity of San Esteban de Gormaz (Soria) and is duly noted there (see pages 121–3). His exploits in the service of both Christian and Muslim rulers culminated with his rule as independent lord of Valencia (1094–99). Around his life grew up the epic *Cantar de Mio Cid.*

In the face of this new threat, Alfonso appealed to France, to the Burgundian abbey of Cluny (Abbot Hugh of Cluny was uncle to Alfonso's queen, Constance of Burgundy), and to the papacy. He was rewarded with, among other stalwarts, several members of the Burgundian ruling family, two of whom married his daughters and stayed on to play prominent roles. Raymond married Urraca while Henry was wed to Teresa who received (northern) Portugal as her dowry.

Cluny and the papacy favoured Alfonso who had granted a generous annual gift to the abbey and had adopted in 1080 the Roman liturgy for his kingdom in place of the ancient Mozarabic liturgy. By this time, the Christian struggle against the Moors in Spain had come to be seen as something of a crusade, and papal blessings and heavenly rewards were offered to those willing to take the field.

Leo IV in 848 was the first pope to offer salvation for those who died in defence of the Cross. Two years previously his city and his church had been sacked by Arabs. Subsequent popes made similar appeals in the face of the threats posed by Muslim raiders. The justification for holy war was much debated in western Europe at this time and holy war against the Muslims came to be perceived as a worthy outlet for society's military energies. Pilgrimages were increasingly popular and pilgrims had to be protected. The age of the Crusades was about to dawn.

The Reconquista was not an isolated phenomenon in Europe. In 1072, thirteen years before the fall of Toledo, the Normans of southern Italy, with papal blessing, had conquered Palermo in Sicily which had been in Arab hands for 241 years. Fourteen years after Toledo, in 1099, Jerusalem fell to the warriors of the first Crusade.

There had been an earlier precedent, albeit an unfortunate one, in Spain. When Ramiro I of Aragón was slain in battle with the Moors in 1063, there were calls for vengeance. Pope Alexander II promised indulgences for all who fought in Spain and a large French force was assembled. The Christians took the fortress of Barbastro, northeast of Zaragoza, in 1064, but their treacherous slaughter of the populace, contrary to solemn undertakings, so enraged the amir of Zaragoza that he massacred the Christians in Zaragoza, suspended his tribute payments to Fernando I of Castilla and retook Barbastro eight months later.

A dismal pattern of behaviour on the part of crusaders was thus established. The Spanish, who lived in close proximity to the Muslims and genuinely admired their culture and their products, tended to be more tolerant. Except in times of actual war, the two sides co-existed more or less peaceably. El Cid spent several years in the service of the amir of Zaragoza fighting against Christian princes and, in the constant competition of princes for power and survival, religion never stood in the way of an expedient alliance. The French and others more distant from the front lines took a harsher view.

Meanwhile, the Almoravids were mopping up the taifa kingdoms. They failed to take Toledo, but they overran the lands to the south. Al-Andalus was a unified Muslim state again. The tributes paid to the Christian kings by the taifa rulers were cut off, causing a serious financial crisis in the north.

The deaths of Raymond of Burgundy in 1107 and of Alfonso's only son Sancho in 1108 in battle, aged ten, presented the king with a desperate succession problem. He finally selected his cousin Alfonso I, the Battler, of Aragón and Navarra (1104–34) as husband for the widowed Urraca. When the king died in 1109, Urraca succeeded and she and Alfonso were wed.

The marriage was a disaster and the kingdom slid into disorder as the royal pair and their partisans feuded across the length and breadth of the Duero valley. Alfonso gave up in 1114 and retired to Aragón. Urraca appears to have been a tough and wily woman who managed to juggle all contenders for power reasonably successfully as well as stave off the Almoravids. She was fortunate in the un-wavering support of Bernard, archbishop of Toledo since 1085, a Burgundian, a Cluniac and a formidable fighter.

One persistently troublesome element was her half-sister Teresa

who was determined to secure Portugal as an independent kingdom
for her son, Alfonso Henriques. He did in fact assume the royal title
in 1139 and Urraca's son Alfonso VII was obliged to recognize
Portugal's independence.

The Almoravids took Zaragoza from its Muslim dynasty in 1110,
seized a few Duero fortresses and raided up through Portugal. Alfonso
the Battler, free of Urraca, struck back and took Zaragoza in December 1118 with French assistance. This was a tremendous victory,
disposing once and for all of the dangerous northern salient of Islam
that had threatened Christian Spain for generations. It also opened
up the Ebro valley for conquest, a process completed when the count
of Barcelona took Tortosa in 1148 and Lérida the next year.

Urraca died in 1126, to be succeeded by Alfonso VII Raimúndez
(1126–57), her son by Raymond of Burgundy. The Battler died in
1134 of battle wounds. He left no issue; the magnates of Aragón
dragged his brother Ramiro from a monastery and married him to a
French lady who obligingly produced a daughter. The infant was
betrothed to Ramón Berenguer IV, count of Barcelona, in 1137 and
thus it was, when Ramiro abdicated and returned to his cell, that
Aragón and Cataluña were united.

The Almoravids, meanwhile, had succumbed to the delights of
civilized living in al-Andalus and their state disintegrated into a new
group of taifas barely sixty years after their arrival. Alfonso VII,
campaigning to the south, was even able to occupy Córdoba briefly
in May 1146. In that very month, however, the Almohads, a new
Muslim menace, landed from Morocco and soon swept away the
petty Muslim rulers.

Notwithstanding this new danger, Alfonso VII divided his kingdom
between his two sons. León and Castilla were again separated, not to
be reunited for another seventy-three contentious years. The rulers
of the two lines squabbled with each other and with the kings of
Portugal, Aragón and Navarra and in more serious moments fought
the Almohads.

The Almohad Years, 1147–1232 The Almohads (*al-muwahhidun*,
believers in the unity of Allah) represented a second generation of
Berber puritans. After eliminating the taifa rulers, they crossed the
Sierra Morena and in 1195 resoundingly defeated Alfonso VIII of
Castilla (1158–1214). In the face of this peril, dynastic rivalries were

patched up (somewhat). Pope Innocent III, the Spanish bishops including Ramón Jiménez de Rada, the fiery archbishop of Toledo, the military orders and the nobility all clamoured to renew the struggle. In response to Christian attacks, the Almohad caliph landed in Spain in May 1211.

In June 1212, the Christian host moved south from Toledo, the Castilians marching behind Alfonso VIII, the men of Aragón led by Pedro II, those of Navarra under Sancho VII and contingents from León and Portugal, whose kings, however, were fighting each other. Passing through the Sierra Morena, they reached the village of Las Navas de Tolosa where battle was joined on 16 July. The Christians won an overwhelming victory. The shattered caliph died in Marrakesh a few months later. Within twenty years, the Almohad empire ceased to exist. The embroidered flap from the caliph's tent hangs to this day in the chapter house of the royal monastery of Las Huelgas in Burgos, while the pass through the mountains which now carries the N-IV from Madrid to Sevilla is still known as the Desfiladero de Despeñaperros, the Defile of the Overthrow of the Dogs. Alfonso VIII survived the great victory by only two years.

His often troublesome cousin and son-in-law, Alfonso IX of León (1188–1230), is notable for two major accomplishments. In the first year of his reign, he summoned a meeting of the royal council at León that enacted a set of laws which has been compared to England's Magna Carta of a quarter-century later. The king guaranteed the security of his subjects' persons and property and pledged a full and fair hearing at his court for anyone accused of a crime.

In addition, Alfonso summoned the towns of the realm to send representatives to León. This is the first time in European history that towns were represented on a royal council. They had become too important as supporters of the monarch and providers of revenue to be ignored. The royal council, the Curia Regis, evolved into the Cortes, summoned at the king's discretion. Its lineal descendant is the modern Cortes or parliament of Spain.

The Almohads reached the height of their power in the last years of the 12th century. Their repeated attacks recovered much of the southern territory conquered by Alfonso VII, but only temporarily. They never took Toledo nor did they manage to make a permanent dent in the Christian lines.

Alfonso IX's son Fernando III succeeded his mother to the crown of Castilla (1217) and his father to that of León (1230); the kingdoms were now permanently united. The Corteses of the two realms continued to meet separately for another century and it took many years for the differences between the two peoples to erode. They may not have done so entirely even today. In parts of Castilla one often sees the 'León' blacked out on signs reading 'Autonomía de Castilla y León' and the reverse in parts of León.

Fernando III took Córdoba in 1236 and Sevilla in 1248, while Valencia fell to Jaime I of Aragón in 1238. Fernando died in 1252 (and was canonized in 1671). Muslim Spain was now confined to the kingdom of Granada which was slowly whittled away until Ferdinand and Isabella put an end to it in 1492.

Religious Developments (11th to 13th Centuries)

The imprint of religion on the face of medieval Spain is strikingly evident in the Duero valley. Churches, cathedrals and monasteries constitute the principal architectural legacy from those early years. An aside on religious developments may thus be useful.

Churches were the creation of communities. They ranged from parochial churches built to serve the needs of settlers in villages and the districts of towns to the great urban cathedrals. Civic pride in growing towns demanded imposing churches. When the community could afford it, these were rebuilt and remodelled over the years to reflect the latest styles: Gothic, Renaissance, baroque. By contrast, monasteries were usually rural phenomena, though towns did develop around some of the earlier ones.

As the Christian reconquest got under way in the Duero basin in the 9th and 10th centuries, religious life began to recover from the destruction of the Muslim invasion. Much of the impetus came from Mozarabs whom the kings encouraged to migrate north from al-Andalus. The monks and craftsmen among them brought intellectual and practical skills that stimulated the development of the Christian states. The monks saw themselves as torch-bearers for the vanished Visigothic realm and impressed on the Asturian kings that the restoration of Christian Spain was a sacred duty.

The early Spanish church had developed largely independent of Rome. Its Mozarabic liturgy, dating from pre-Visigothic times, was codified by San Isidoro, bishop of Sevilla, in the early 7th century. Not until the 11th century did religious influences from western Europe began to penetrate the peninsula in any serious way.

The Muslim campaigns of the 10th century set development back again, but with the collapse of the caliphate in 1031 the revival resumed. The cathedrals of El Burgo de Osma, Valladolid, Palencia, Zamora, Ávila and Salamanca date from this period. Consolidation of the Christian kingdoms provided the opportunity for a reform of religious life along western European lines, a reform inspired and guided by the Burgundian abbey of Cluny.

The Benedictines of Cluny The comprehensive Rule for the organization of monastic life in western Europe set down by St Benedict, founder (c. 530) of Monte Cassino, had long stood as the ideal standard, but monastic practices in the real world often fell short.

In an age of deep faith and real apprehension about the life to come, kings, nobles and other wealthy sinners were prepared to contribute handsomely to monasteries in return for prayers for their souls. Monks were spiritual warriors, fighting to save those souls and to defend the realm against the powers of darkness. All this took prayer, endless rounds of prayer, and ritual.

And money. From an apprehensive and demonstrably sinful laity riches and estates poured in, with the inevitable results. By the end of the 9th century, monastic corruption had become widespread and the time for a spiritual revival was nigh.

The abbey of Cluny in Burgundy was founded in 910 by William the Pious, duke of Aquitaine, with the aim of reviving the Rule of St Benedict. Central to that Rule was a balanced regimen of prayer, study and manual labour under the discipline of an organized communal life. The daily ritual of divine services, rigidly prescribed, was fundamental to the worship of God through whose intercession alone men could be saved.

We have seen that Sancho el Mayor of Navarra, Aragón and Castilla invited Cluniac monks to reform the monasteries under his rule. A council convened by his son Fernando I in 1055 enjoined all monasteries in the realm to adopt the reformed Benedictine Rule. Under his son, Alfonso VI (1065–1109), Cluny's pre-eminence in the peninsula was assured. Constance of Burgundy, niece of Hugh, Abbot of Cluny 1049–1109, became Alfonso's second wife in 1079 and in her train marched the monks of Cluny. Alfonso needed help against the Almoravids and Cluny could generate support from the French nobility and the papacy. The king and his magnates donated Spanish monasteries to Cluny and provided generous financial support.

The papacy had long been disturbed by the persistence in Spain of the Mozarabic rite. Pope Gregory VII (1073–85), a former Cluniac monk, brought immense pressure to bear on the peninsular rulers to adopt the Roman liturgy. Alfonso VI knew full well that the Mozarabic rite was rooted deep in the hearts of his people. The French monks and clerics who swarmed into the peninsula were greatly resented. But Alfonso desperately needed foreign help against the Almoravids and, in the end, he gave way. The Roman liturgy was imposed in 1080 and ten years later a council at León forbade the use of the Visigothic script in ecclesiastical writings, ordaining instead the use of the Carolingian hand.

Small bands of adherents did, of course, continue to worship in their way. In the 15th century, Cardinal Cisneros permitted Mozarabic worship in a chapel at the west end of Toledo Cathedral, where it continues to this day.

The Cluniacs were, however, too much of this world, with vast estates and wealth, and they played a highly visible political role. In Spain they were identified with the suppression of the Mozarabic rite, they occupied many of the best clerical and monastic positions and they were often hated landlords.

The erosion of the Cluniac position coincided with the population expansion and economic revival that marked western Europe in the 11th century. New ideas were abroad and between 1075 and 1125 new religious orders appeared. The reform movement had two broad streams. One led to the increased isolation from the world and devotion to prayer adopted by the Cistercians, the other to practical service to the community, the approach taken by the Augustinians and Premonstratensians. In the 13th century came the Franciscans and Dominicans whose friars abandoned contemplation and the cloister for active preaching and ministering in the market place to the needs of an increasingly urban population.

The Cistercians The Cistercians took their name from the monastery of Cîteaux, founded in 1098 in Burgundy. The real founder of the Order was St Bernard of Clairvaux (1091–1153) who believed passionately in a return to original Benedictine principles. In contrast to Cluniac practices, St Bernard emphasized private meditation, manual labour and avoidance of the outside world. He vigorously opposed what he viewed as the excesses of Romanesque architecture with all those monsters and fabulous beasts mixed in with biblical themes. Display and ornamentation, he held, only distracted from the contemplation of God. His beliefs are reflected in the simplicity of Cistercian architecture. Cistercian buildings thus have a distinctive beauty and some of the best examples in Europe are preserved in the Duero valley.

The Cistercians founded their houses in remote, uncultivated regions. Manual labour was restored as an essential part of the monks' routine, but since they could not themselves do all the work of tilling fields and tending livestock as well as discharge their liturgical duties, they began early on to recruit lay brothers. They thus introduced into their communities farmers, shepherds, masons, millers, weavers and the like who provided the Order with a disciplined labour force that enabled it to bring undeveloped lands into production and to turn its back on the world.

Alfonso VII founded thirteen Cistercian abbeys in Castilla between 1132 and 1157, including Moreruela (Zamora); Alfonso VIII added six more between 1158 and 1214, including Sta María de Huerta (Soria). All told, some sixty Cistercian monasteries were founded in Spain, most of them north of the Duero.

Eventually, however, the Cistercians too slipped from their original simple and austere moorings. They were too successful at agriculture, stock breeding, milling and mining. Wealth poured in; the abbots became rich and powerful. They did not intend it, but they were part of the world despite themselves.

The recruitment of lay brothers became increasingly difficult as the 13th century drew to an end. The Black Death in the mid-14th century took an awful toll. By the beginning of the following century, the Cistercians had become just one of many monastic orders, and a reactionary one at that. New orders, particularly the Franciscans and Dominicans, had arisen in response to new, largely urban, needs.

The Secular Church The secular clergy are so called to distinguish them from the regular or monastic clergy who follow a Rule (*regula*).

Some of the ancient Visigothic bishoprics that had been swamped by the Muslim invasion slowly reappeared as the reconquest gathered speed. In the Duero valley, the bishoprics of León, Palencia, Segovia and Osma were brought back to life and, somewhat later, Zamora, Ávila and Salamanca.

The bishops of these sees came from the great families of the realm, accustomed to wealth, power and responsibility. Their churches and cathedrals owned vast lands, had their own courts and received income from rents and tithes. They were far-reaching in their ambitions and jealously protective of their rights. They sat in the inner councils of the king. They led their men into battle.

Even as late as the 15th and 16th centuries, there were warrior prelates. Cardinal Pedro González de Mendoza, archbishop of Toledo, fought at Toro in 1476 for Ferdinand and Isabella against Alfonso V of Portugal. Cardinal Francisco Jiménez de Cisneros, confessor to Queen Isabella, archbishop of Toledo, regent of Castilla and then of Spain, raised, financed and led an army to North Africa in 1509 to capture Oran. The exploits of the battling Bishop Antonio de Acuña of Zamora during the Comunero rising in 1520–21 are related in the itinerary under that town (see pages 249–50).

True holiness was thus seen as the preserve of the regular clergy. The Cluniacs and Cistercians had carried the banners of reform and, though they stumbled, they were perceived as being less tainted with secular concerns. As Georges Duby puts it, up to around 1130 'the abbots had precedence over the bishops, and the monks triumphed everywhere, for they were holier, and the services they rendered to God were of distinctly higher quality'.[4]

Nevertheless, the appeal of monasticism had begun to fade by the end of the 12th century. The great day of monasteries had passed and the initiative in learning, literature and art departed from the cloister into secular hands. The 13th century saw the rise of the great French Gothic cathedrals at Burgos, Toledo and León. A new spirit was abroad in the land.

Then, too, the monasteries had never catered to the daily spiritual needs of the people. Through all these centuries, villagers and towns-folk sought succour in their churches. The church bells marked the passage of time, summoned the people in times of peril and called them to rejoice in times of celebration.

The churches made major contributions to education. In the 12th century, *escuelas episcopales* or cathedral schools were established at Palencia, Salamanca, Valladolid, Osma and Segovia. From these arose the *escuelas generales* or universities, the first founded at Palencia about 1210. A few years later came that at Salamanca. The curriculum consisted of the classic quadrivium (arithmetic, geometry, astronomy and music) and trivium (grammar, logic and rhetoric) – the seven liberal arts.

Let us now return to the political narrative.

Castilla and León (13th to 15th Centuries)

Alfonso X and His Successors Alfonso X el Sabio (1252–84) gathered around him scholars of all faiths. Everything interested him: literature, history, law, science. His enthusiasm for recently rediscovered Roman law led him to attempt to impose a uniform code of law superseding the rights and privileges of the towns as embodied in their ancient fueros. This threat united the towns, the aristocracy and the Church against him and resulted in his virtual deposition by the Cortes of Valladolid in 1282 in favour of his son Sancho IV. The king died two years later, reasonably frustrated one imagines.

In 1273, Alfonso chartered the *Mesta*, an organization of the great sheep-owners of Castilla. Sheep raising had been important in the peninsula for centuries and the conquest of Toledo opened up vast new lands for pasturage. The merino sheep with its thick, high-quality wool was brought to Spain from North Africa in the 13th century. The privileges sold to the Mesta brought the monarchy badly needed income and kings were to squeeze the Mesta for cash for centuries.

By the 14th century, the textile industries of northern Europe were clamouring for Castilian wool and by the following century wool was central to Castilian trade and prosperity. Monarchs favoured pastoral interests at the expense, many allege, of other sectors of the economy and of the land itself. The Mesta was abolished only in 1836.

Another cause for Alfonso's unpopularity was his relentless effort to get himself elected Holy Roman Emperor, an effort which cost the Castilian treasury dearly. In the end (1273), he lost out to Rudolf of Habsburg whose distant descendant was to become Charles I of Spain, and then Emperor Charles V, with even more disastrous results for the Castilian treasury.

For seventy-five years after Alfonso X's death, Castilla endured almost incessant civil war. Kings died young, to be succeeded by minors who required regencies that were fiercely contested by members of an extensive royal family. An attractive figure amid the turmoil was María de Molina, herself of royal stock, the widow of Sancho IV (1284–95), who from her base in Valladolid served as regent, intermittently, for her son Fernando IV (1295–1312) and her grandson Alfonso XI (1312–50) and tried to keep things together.

One of the more interesting figures of the age, and in the end a rather sympathetic one, was Don Juan Manuel (1281–1349). This statesman, schemer, rebel and scholar was the grandson of Alfonso X, the nephew of Sancho IV and the first cousin of Fernando IV. Fernando III and Alfonso X each left a brood of children. The royal family into which Juan Manuel was born was thus, for the first time in the dynasty's history, a large one. It was also a quarrelsome one, with the younger sons and their heirs all angling for position and power. The death of his father, lord of Peñafiel (Valladolid), when he was barely two years of age forced Juan Manuel to grow up fending for himself, and he did so very effectively.

He was an enthusiastic and not always helpful meddler in the chaotic politics of his day. The turmoil provided ample scope for ambitious junior members of the royal family and the restless nobility to jockey for position. On the death of María de Molina in 1321, Juan Manuel came to power as co-regent with a cousin until Alfonso XI was declared of age in 1325, aged fourteen.

Juan Manuel betrothed his daughter Constanza to Alfonso, but the young king broke off the engagement, shut Constanza up in Toro castle and married the daughter of the king of Portugal whose help he needed against the Moors. Enraged, Juan Manuel turned to Aragón, but its king declined to get involved. Juan Manuel was finally persuaded to pledge his loyalty to Alfonso XI in 1329, but he remained suspect.

Alfonso XI treated his Portuguese wife badly. Her father, greatly annoyed, struck an alliance with Juan Manuel by the terms of which his son Pedro was to marry Constanza, by now released from Toro. The marriage was unhappy; Pedro fell madly in love with Inés de Castro, one of Constanza's ladies-in-waiting, and the unhappy Constanza died in 1345.

The lord of Peñafiel busied himself with the tangled dynastic affairs of Aragón, Portugal and Castilla for several more years, but in the end, after uprisings in 1333 and 1336, Alfonso XI made peace with him and other fractious nobles.

Don Juan Manuel was now in his mid-fifties. It was time, he decided, to devote himself to study. He held ideas unusual for his era. Discussing the wars between Christians and Muslims, he wrote that no one should be compelled to accept religion 'because involuntary and forced services do not please God'.[5] The flowering of the knightly ideal in Spain in the 14th century came late, after victory over the Muslims had been assured. Before this time, a tough nobility had spent its time fighting, with no leisure or inclination for refinements. Juan Manuel now gave thought to the role of the Christian knight and to the social and moral issues of the day.

His most famous work (1335) is *El Conde Lucanor* in which he drew on earlier traditions in poetry and verse, including Arabic and Jewish, to create the first novel in Castilian. Count Lucanor, a young noble, turns for advice on various issues to his counsellor Patronio who answers with tales, each containing a moral and reflections on human nature. *El Conde Lucanor* inspired many comparable works and it remains a standard of Spanish literature. It had influence beyond Spain; one tale inspired Shakespeare's *The Taming of the Shrew*.

We will meet this interesting man again when we reach his castle of Peñafiel at the eastern extremity of Valladolid Province (see page 184ff).

Once he came of age in 1325, Alfonso XI actually managed to bring order to his distracted kingdom, but then came famine and, in 1348, the Black Death. The plague raged for two years, carrying off the king and thousands of his subjects. Once established, plague broke out repeatedly to the end of the century and throughout the 15th century. Burgos, Palencia, Valladolid and the Tierra de Campos north of the Duero were especially hard hit. Some 20 per cent of the population is estimated to have perished.

Alfonso XI was succeeded by Pedro, the Cruel (1350–69). His murderous attacks on his family, particularly on his illegitimate brothers, brought on yet another civil war that was fought up and down the Duero valley and ended with Pedro's murder by his half-brother, Enrique de Trastámara. The contending parties called in foreign assistance which only exacerbated the situation. Pedro allied himself with Edward, the Black Prince, Duke of Aquitaine, son of

Edward III of England. Enrique called on Charles V of France who dispatched the warrior Bertrand du Guesclin with a swarm of mercenaries temporarily unemployed thanks to a truce in the Hundred Years' War between England and France. The stage was set for the last dynasty of medieval Spain.

In the meantime, as the front lines of the Reconquista moved further south, more and more settlers arrived, commerce and trade expanded and so did the population. By the end of the 13th century, the population of Castilla had reached 3.5 to 4 million, some two-thirds of the population of the entire peninsula. The plagues were devastating, but by the end of the 15th century the population had bounced back to 4 or 5 million.

León and Burgos now had some 8,000 to 10,000 inhabitants; Salamanca and Valladolid 15,000 and 25,000 respectively. Trade fairs appeared in the 12th century; that at Valladolid, authorized in 1152, was one of the earliest. Towns had become important; they generated revenues and controlled trade and commerce. There was a down side, however. They were too important to remain outside the grasp of royal power and from 1325, under Alfonso XI, the crown began to assert its authority. The process was assisted by the expanding burgher class which profited from trade and usually staunchly supported the crown.

The Trastámara Kings, 1369–1474 The five kings of the Trastámara line reigned for little more than a century from the accession of Enrique II over the corpse of his half-brother Pedro the Cruel to the death of Enrique IV in 1474. The Trastámara liked the Duero valley and they and their friends and foes appear frequently on our itinerary. Segovia, Valladolid, Medina del Campo, Arévalo and Tordesillas were particularly favoured by the royal family.

Unfortunately for the peace of the realm, the new kings were obliged to reward those who had supported them in their bid for power and in their struggle to consolidate their rule. Grants of extensive crown properties cut into the ability of the kings to raise revenues. Towards the end of the period, the powerful and fractious nobility, which included ambitious members of the royal family itself, was out of control and the power of the monarchy was severely eroded.

On Enrique II's death in 1379, his son Juan I (1379–90) succeeded.

By this time, it was obvious that the unwieldy feudal council of magnates and town representatives was quite inadequate for the needs of the state. In 1385, therefore, Juan summoned a Cortes to Valladolid that took the important step of creating the *Consejo Real* (Royal Council) of Castilla. The initial composition of the council reflected tradition: four churchmen, four nobles and four town burghers. Two years later, Juan substituted for the burghers four *letrados*, men with university training, bright, ambitious, but usually of humble birth, owing their advancement to their abilities alone. The steady move towards technical competence was further reflected in a royal decree of 1459 that brought the number of letrados to eight, reducing the churchmen and nobles to two each.

In 1388, Juan concluded peace with John of Gaunt, Duke of Lancaster, who agreed to drop his claims (by marriage) to the Castilian throne. In honour of the pact, Juan created his son Prince of Asturias, thus emulating the title Prince of Wales borne (since 1301) by the heir to the English throne. The title is carried today by Don Felipe, son and heir of King Juan Carlos I.

Juan I also reformed the Spanish calendar, bringing it in line with the rest of western Christendom. Prior to 1384, dates were reckoned by the Era of Caesar Augustus, thirty-eight years in advance of the normal Christian era.

The minority of Juan's son Enrique III (1390–1406) – married as a boy to Catherine of Lancaster, daughter of John of Gaunt – saw the most terrible massacre of Jews in the history of Spain. *Juderías* (Jewish quarters) had long existed in most towns. Jews were prominent in finance, science, medicine, commerce and agriculture. They were considered the direct subjects of the king and often paid handsomely for his protection.

The portents had not been good. Edward I expelled the Jews from England in 1290; Philippe IV followed suit in France in 1306; the Cortes of Valladolid in 1293 and of Toro in 1371 enacted harsh anti-Jewish decrees. The Dominican friars had been stirring up trouble against them for years. In the recent civil war the Jews had backed Pedro the Cruel whom Enrique de Trastámara accused of being a Jewish puppet. There were serious attacks on juderías in Segovia, Valladolid and Ávila.

The pogrom of 1391 began in Sevilla and soon swept Castilla and Aragón. Thousands were slain and juderías plundered. Under threat of martyrdom, more thousands converted, which only sowed the seeds of future persecution.

Freed from the constraints of being legally Jews, the *conversos*, as they were known, charged ahead in their chosen pursuits, marrying into the upper ranks of the aristocracy and moving into top positions in Church and government. They were never trusted by the 'Old Christians' and the winkling out of allegedly crypto-Jews became the chief task of the Inquisition. Jewish communities did survive down to 1492 in Castilla and León, but after the events of 1391, conversion (at least nominal) became the most common choice of the beleaguered.

Juan II (1406–54) succeeded at the age of two; his reign was not only one of the longest in peninsular history, it was one of the most disastrous. A cultivated and literate man, Juan cared little for the chores of government, but this was no time to be a dilettante. In 1412, his uncle Fernando was elected king of Aragón on the extinction of the ancient line of the counts of Barcelona. Fernando was succeeded in 1416 by his son Alfonso V, a man of immense competence and energy, who had three ambitious and troublesome brothers: Juan, who married the heiress of Navarra and in 1425 inherited that kingdom (and became Juan II of Aragón in 1458), Enrique, master of the Order of Santiago, and Sancho, master of the Order of Alcántara.

The brothers meddled constantly in the affairs of Castilla. Don Enrique actually broke into the palace at Tordesillas and seized the person of Juan II in 1420; the king's release was engineered by Álvaro de Luna, his favourite. For three years, Juan of Navarra controlled the government of Castilla. At length, the combined forces of the king, the prince of Asturias and de Luna routed the rebels at Olmedo, south of Valladolid, in May 1445.

De Luna was ultimately driven from power by the weak and ungrateful king, largely at the instigation of his second wife, Isabel of Portugal, and was executed in Valladolid in 1453. Juan II, an utter failure and knowing it, died a year later.

He was succeeded by his son by his first wife, Enrique IV, *el Impotente* (1454–74). The nobility ran rampant, Enrique twisted and connived between factions; the situation was soon out of control. In 1464, the queen, Juana of Portugal, gave birth to a daughter, known as Juana 'la Beltraneja' after her reputed father, the king's then favourite, Beltrán de la Cueva. The nobility lined up in hostile factions, one supporting little Juana, the other supporting Don Alfonso, son of Juan II by Isabel of Portugal. A rebel group of nobles meeting in Ávila actually proclaimed Alfonso king in 1465, but he died three years later at age fifteen.

The young prince's death thrust his sister Isabella to centre stage. After the most convoluted series of agreements, betrayals and reversals, Isabella succeeded to the throne on Enrique's death in 1474. Five years earlier, she had secretly married Ferdinand of Aragón, son and heir of the aforementioned Juan II of Aragón. Her accession was opposed by Alfonso V of Portugal, betrothed to la Beltraneja, but he was defeated by Ferdinand near Toro in 1476. Juan II of Aragón died in 1479; his son succeeded as Ferdinand II (1479–1516), ruling over Castilla as Ferdinand V.

Ferdinand and Isabella

Castilla and Aragón were now united, though the union did not become final until the succession in 1516 of Ferdinand and Isabella's Habsburg grandson Charles I to both kingdoms after the unhappy reign of their daughter Juana (1504–6) with her feckless husband Philip of Habsburg, king in Castilla as Felipe I.

Their emblems, Isabella's bundle of arrows (*flechas*, the F for Fernando) and Ferdinand's yoke (*yugo*, the Y for Ysabel), appear frequently in Duero valley towns. Isabella was born, married, proclaimed queen and died in the Duero valley. The couple are depicted kneeling in prayer on the tympanums of churches and monasteries; their portraits adorn many a medallion.

They were the last of the ancient line of Spanish monarchs, both direct descendants of Sancho el Mayor (d. 1035), and in 1492 they carried the Reconquista to a successful conclusion with the capture of Granada. For their pains, Pope Alexander VI rewarded them with the title 'los Reyes Católicos', the Catholic Kings.

Their reign was devoted to the pacification of the country which, by dint of their overwhelming personal authority, plain hard work and continuous travel, was brought under firm control. To be Spanish was now to be Catholic; there was no room for, nor need to tolerate, other beliefs. Isabella instituted the Inquisition in Castilla in 1480 as the instrument to root out heretics and non-believers. The Jews were expelled in 1492; Isabella decreed in 1502 that all Muslims must submit to baptism or leave the kingdom. The Moriscos, descendants of the converts, were expelled in 1609.

Their regime was highly centralized. The nobility was brought to heel. The aristocracy and clergy ceased to be summoned to attend the Cortes. The tendency to entrust the direction of affairs to university-trained letrados was accelerated. The sole task of the Cortes was to vote funds requested by the monarchs; it initiated no laws. Town representation, once considered so important, was now confined to two delegates from each of eighteen towns, fully half of them in the Duero basin: Ávila, Burgos, León, Salamanca, Segovia, Soria, Toro, Valladolid and Zamora. The monarchs sent out agents to all towns to administer justice and ensure that the royal will was done.

The Catholic Kings had a tragic family life. Their only son Juan died in 1497, aged nineteen; their eldest daughter Isabel, Queen of Portugal, died the following year. Isabel of Portugal's infant son Miguel, who was accepted by the Corteses of Aragón, Castilla and Portugal as rightful heir, died in 1500. The succession thus fell to Juana who had already exhibited ample signs of severe mental instability.

She and her husband, Philip of Habsburg, succeeded Isabella in 1504, but Philip died in 1506 and Juana, completely unhinged now, had to be put away. Ferdinand, still king of Aragón, took over Castilla till his death in 1516, when he was followed in both kingdoms by his Habsburg grandson Charles.

Spain from 1516

The Habsburgs (1516–1700) The purpose of this historical overview has been to describe developments in, or that affected, the Duero valley. By the end of the 15th century, the Duero had long ceased to be central to political affairs. During the reigns of Charles I (1516–56; d. 1558), better known as Emperor Charles V, and his son Philip II (1556–98), Spain became a European power and dominated the stage for a century. What little political clout remained in the Duero valley vanished when Philip II transferred the court from Valladolid to Madrid in 1561, a move that became permanent in 1606.

The following pages provide an overview of political developments on the national scene while keeping a focus, however episodic, on the Duero valley. In general, its history from the mid-16th century to the mid-20th was grim.

The seventeen-year-old Charles and his Flemish advisers met with a hostile reception on their arrival in Spain in September 1517. Their arrogance and the king's pursuit of the imperial crown (which he achieved in 1519), requiring huge subsidies from the Cortes of Castilla and increased taxation, resulted in a rebellion of the towns. The Comunero Revolt of 1520–21 was led by Toledo, but all the Duero towns participated. After a bitter struggle, the movement was crushed near Toro in April 1521 and its leaders executed. The Duero towns were stripped of their last vestiges of political importance. (The revolt is covered at greater length in the chapters on Valladolid and Zamora provinces.)

Charles and Philip forced Spain into an exhausting struggle to defend Catholicism in Europe. When Philip's policies drove the Protestant states of the Netherlands, the richest possession of the crown, to revolt in 1567, the full burden of financing the war against the Dutch fell on Castilla. The Habsburgs could never obtain any significant financial support from the lands of the crown of Aragón. At the same time, Spain was leading the struggle in the Mediterranean against the Ottoman Turks.

Habsburg international ambitions impoverished Castilla. Philip was bankrupt by 1575 and bankruptcy was declared repeatedly thereafter in the 16th and 17th centuries as expenses far exceeded revenues the embattled crown was increasingly unable to collect.

The wool trade and the treasure from America enabled Castilla to support the new Spanish empire for a while. During most of the 16th century the country produced enough food (the cereals of the Tierra de Campos in particular) and goods to meet the demands of a growing population and those prodigious consumers of goods: crown, Church and aristocracy.

Despite the flood of treasure from the New World, however, the money went everywhere except into the treasury. Bullion flowed into the hands of foreign banks and creditors. The towns of the Duero valley are full of extravagantly decorated religious and secular buildings built by the aristocracy during those years. Today, driving across the Tierra de Campos, enormous churches loom up in the distance, with now decaying villages at their feet. Architects and artists flocked to Spain from abroad in search of lucrative commissions.

In the end, Spain's outmoded, inefficient and protected industries, including the woollen mills of Segovia and Ávila, could not compete in the international market to which the country now belonged. Four outbreaks of plague in the second half of the 16th century added to the country's woes. Philip III (1598–1621) took his country into the terrible Thirty Years' War (1618–48) in Germany which brought a French invasion, internal rebellion and the loss of the Dutch Netherlands (the United Provinces). In 1609 he expelled the Moriscos, the descendants of Muslims forced to convert to Christianity by Ferdinand and Isabella, thus crippling agriculture.

Thrice more in the 17th century plague struck, carrying off perhaps 600,000 people. Valladolid, Ávila and Segovia were especially hard hit. European wars, emigration to America and recurrent famine reduced the population to the point where some parts of the Duero valley were all but abandoned. Not until the middle of the 18th century did the Castilian population return to 1600 levels.

The Habsburg line in Spain died out with the pathetic near-idiot Charles II (1665–1700) by whose reign Spain's predominance in Europe was at an end and Castilla was impoverished.

The Bourbons, 1701–1808 The dying Charles II named Philip, duke of Anjou, grandson of Louis XIV and the Infanta María Teresa, his sister, as his heir. Philip V entered Madrid in February 1701 (aged seventeen, the same age as Charles I when he arrived in Spain), touching off the War of Spanish Succession or the first Peninsular War (1702–13). In Spain, fighting took place largely in Aragón and Cataluña; the Duero valley was barely affected directly. The war ended with the loss to Spain of the Spanish Netherlands (modern Belgium) and its remaining possessions in Italy.

At least Spain was now relieved of the burden of supporting and defending an empire. Population growth resumed and conditions even improved somewhat under the first three Bourbons: Philip V (1701–46) and his sons Ferdinand VI (1746–59) and Charles III (1759–88). Philip V completed the centralization of Spain; the ancient rights of Aragón and Cataluña were swept away and the laws of Castilla were imposed across the board.

Charles III was a man of common sense, keen to improve science, commerce, communications and agriculture. Agricultural reform was desperately needed. All 18th- and 19th-century travellers testify to the poverty and ignorance of rural Castilla. The famous cities of old were in wretched decay, many villages abandoned. (See, for example, the books cited in the Bibliography by Joseph Townsend, who travelled through Spain in 1786–87, and Richard Ford who was there in 1831–32.) Charles III founded factories turning out luxury goods (such as the glassworks at La Granja near Segovia), but only a tiny proportion of the population could afford them and certainly not the peasants whose purchasing power was nil. Charles was faced with a solid wall of entrenched political, religious and economic interests which succeeded in frustrating any attempts at reform.

The inadequacy of transportation in the Duero valley added to the region's woes. The rivers are generally useless for navigation and produce had to be carted out to domestic and international markets on the backs of mules or by slow wagon trains. Charles III thus set afoot the digging of the Canal de Castilla in the Tierra de Campos. Construction of this quite astonishing enterprise went on into the 19th century and the network still exists, but its intended role was eventually usurped by railways and now, of course, by trucks. Valladolid was connected by rail to Palencia by the mid-19th century and to Madrid, Burgos and the north coast by 1870.

Charles III was succeeded by his son, the cloddish Charles IV (1788–1808; d. 1819) who with his unpleasant wife María Luisa of Parma and their brood of children and relatives may be seen cruelly depicted by Goya on a huge canvas in the Prado. Some of the children are attractive, but the adults are a smug, self-satisfied-looking lot. By 1800, reform was out and ignorance reigned. While the king and the prince of Asturias, Ferdinand, were busy loathing each other and the queen was busy cuckolding the king with her favourite and the chief minister, Manuel Godoy, the storm was gathering that would soon blow them all away.

The Peninsular War, 1808–13 So massive was the destruction wrought in the Duero valley, and in the rest of Spain, by Napoleon's armies and so violent the Spanish national reaction that it cannot be skipped over. There is scarcely a town entry in any guidebook that does not refer to the damage caused by the French armies during those terrible years.

Napoleon was determined to bring Spain and Portugal into his coalition against England. With the cooperation of the craven Spanish court, he sent his troops across Spain into Portugal in 1807. A year later, he packed the Bourbons into exile and put his brother Joseph on the throne. To Napoleon's surprise, however, spontaneous uprisings broke out across the country and in short order the French faced a savage popular rebellion. The conflict is known in Spain as the *Guerra de Independencia*, the War of Independence, and it gave us the term 'guerrilla warfare'.

One of the most famous incidents of the war's early years was the popular uprising in Madrid on 2 May 1808. The rebellion was crushed by Marshal Murat using mounted Egyptian Mamluk troops, the first time that Moorish soldiers had appeared on Spanish soil for generations. Not the best way to win Spanish hearts. Goya's painting in the Prado brilliantly captures the swirling scene of Moors with curved sabres drawn as of old wading into the crowd.

The British government sent Sir Arthur Wellesley to Portugal. Napoleon himself was forced to come to Spain, entering Madrid in December 1808. It took a herculean effort under appalling circumstances to oust the invaders. For his bloody 1809 victory at Talavera, southwest of Toledo, Wellesley was created Viscount Wellington and Baron Douro (the Portuguese for Duero). Not until June 1812 when Napoleon invaded Russia, however, was Wellington able to leave his Portuguese redoubt and launch a major attack. By this time, guerrilla warfare had reached such a pitch that the French were in desperate straits. They took revenge by retaliating savagely against persons and property.

In July 1812 Wellington defeated Marshal Marmont at Salamanca and advanced to take Valladolid and then Madrid. The allies reached Burgos, but the French were still too strong and Wellington decided reluctantly to withdraw again to Portugal.

He advanced to Salamanca once more in May 1813. A second force crossed the river in Portugal and came along the north bank of the Duero to surprise a French army just east of Toro. By early June the whole Anglo-Portuguese army was across the river and King Joseph had fallen back on Burgos.

For the final attack, Wellington assembled his troops at Toro and pushed north to Burgos and his decisive victory at Vitoria on 21 June 1813. In two months, the French were cleared from Spain. The wreckage of the terrible struggle remained for years and is remarked on by all 19th-century travellers.

The 19th and Early 20th Centuries The history of the Duero valley and indeed of all Spain from the early 19th to the mid-20th centuries is an almost unrelieved tale of economic distress, social upheaval and civil strife. Once restored to the throne, Ferdinand VII (1814–33) instituted a brutally reactionary regime, sweeping away not only the reforms enacted in 1812 by the liberal Cortes of Cádiz, which tried to represent the nation during the Peninsular War, but those of his grandfather Charles III as well. For a clue to this man's sly, treacherous character, look at Goya's paintings of him in the Prado. (That Goya managed to get away for years with portraying the royal family as accurately as he did is perhaps a measure of their denseness and smug sense of superiority. He finally gave up on Ferdinand's Spain and went into exile in 1824.)

Political power passed from privileged hand to privileged hand more as a result of coups (*pronunciamientos*) by generals than any true elective process. Spain went through the ousting of Queen Isabella II (1833–68; d. 1904), Ferdinand's daughter, whose accession at the age of three touched off the revolt of her uncle Don Carlos and two civil wars (1833–39, 1872–76); an Italian monarch, Amadeo of Savoy (1870–73); the First Republic with four presidents in twelve months (1873); the restoration of the Bourbons with Alfonso XII (1874–89); the failed dictatorship of Miguel Primo de Rivera (1923–30); the flight of Alfonso XIII (1889–1931; d. 1941) in the face of a dramatic swing to the Left in the 1931 elections; and the Second Republic (1931–39) that went down in the flames of the Civil War.

All this was set against the background of a society increasingly polarized between the obstinately obdurate Right and the ever more radical Left and of military disasters that left the army bitter and resentful (the Spanish–American War of 1898 and the catastrophe in Morocco in 1921).

The towns of Castilla and León lay in ruins after the Peninsular War. Travellers' accounts of the wreckage in mid-century are cited in the itinerary. In the depths of the meseta, despite the overwhelming importance of cereal production which accounted for over 50 per cent of all arable land in Spain in 1900, the peasantry was steadily beaten down to subsistence level when not turned into landless labourers.

The Liberal government of Juan Álvarez Mendizábal that took office in 1835 faced a serious financial crisis. To raise cash, the government decreed the disentailment (*desamortización*) of ecclesiastical properties. These had always been targets for monarchs seeking funds to tide them over rough patches, but this constituted a complete sweep. Mendizábal's goal was to generate funds for the state and, not incidentally, to develop a new class of free peasant proprietors who would vote Liberal.

The state did realize handsome short-term profits from the sale of the sequestered Church and monastery holdings in 1835–36, but most properties were snapped up by land-owners, townsfolk and speculators who leapt at the low prices. The intended peasant beneficiaries were unable to compete and were only pushed further down into misery. Most of the new land-owners were, of course, absentee.

The desamortización decrees were also disastrous for Spain's architectural heritage, as we shall see repeatedly in the Duero valley. Many monastic buildings degenerated into farms when they were not used as quarries by locals who lost no time in righting the wrongs of centuries of abuse by monastic landlords. Some monasteries disappeared entirely; a few found private owners and have come down to the present day reasonably intact. Others have more recently been saved and restored by loving hands.

The lot of the peasantry worsened with a later government's decision to sell (between 1855 and 1867) the common lands on which for centuries villagers had hunted, pastured sheep and collected timber and firewood. Revolts broke out, but protest was useless.

There was massive migration to Latin America, Madrid and the industrial coastal areas of the north and east. Some 1.5 million Spaniards migrated between 1896 and 1913. Left behind were the landless and subsistence farmers 'submerged in the introspective world of the *pueblo*, the only contact with a wider world provided by the returned conscript, the tax-collector, or the occasional pedlar'.[6]

At the turn of the century, writes one historian:

> The primitive cereal cycle – drought and poor harvests, high prices bringing marginal land under the plough, overproduction, and low prices leading to withdrawal of land from cultivation – was still in full flow and relatively safe from interference from the state authorities who sent the army and the *guardia civil* when the peasants had the effrontery to publicise their misery and disaffection.[7]

The population of Spain remained predominantly rural well into the 20th century. Only eleven towns had more than 100,000 inhabitants in 1931; none was in Castilla or León. The poverty of the chronically undernourished peasantry affected the towns at whose markets they could not afford to shop.

Many towns had never been able to recover from the Peninsular War. As late as 1927, V. S. Pritchett found Benavente (Zamora) in ruins: 'Every piece of beautiful architecture is decaying and rotting beyond hope, pock-marked and putrescent with neglect. The ancient arcades, bent on their cracked and drunken pillars, still give an air of dignity and some character to the town; but it looks more like a straggling herd of bespattered cattle in a market place.'[8] Benavente is now, I hasten to add, a most attractive and bustling town.

The Civil War and Its Aftermath In the elections of February 1936, the Popular Front, which combined the parties of the Left, won a resounding victory over the Right and took office. Faced with the radicalism of the new government, the army and the most conservative elements in society decided it was time to act. General Francisco Franco raised the flag of rebellion in July 1936, purportedly to save Spain from atheism, liberalism and communism.

The ground had been well prepared and insurgents in the Duero valley quickly seized control of Burgos, Valladolid, Salamanca, Palencia, Zamora and Ávila. The rural population was profoundly conservative, Catholic and generally apolitical. Franco advanced north from Andalucía; Toledo fell in September 1936. By March 1937 his Nationalists had gained control of a broad arc of territory south, west and north of Madrid. Castilla and León were solidly within the Nationalist zone.

Franco established his military headquarters at Salamanca in the autumn of 1936; Burgos was his capital from August 1937 until the fall of Madrid in March 1939. The thirty-five years of Franco's Spain had begun.

The Civil War years brought no relief to the meseta. True, Castilla and León produced the wheat the Nationalists needed to survive, but this advantage held only until the absorption of semi-starving regions of the Republic led to shortages and rationing. The 1940s and early 1950s were the 'years of hunger', marked by bread lines, inadequate diets and rampant tuberculosis. Deaths from malnutrition and disease soared and adverse weather conditions in 1945–46 brought drought and the lowest cereal harvest of the century. Recovery began only after the 1953 treaty with the United States provided economic (and military) aid and a newer generation of politicians was able to introduce some modest reforms in the rigid Franquista system.

The economy took off in the 1960s and 1970s as industry and manufacturing boomed, drawing yet more people from the meseta. Between 1950 and 1976, the percentage of people living off the land fell from 50 per cent to 21 per cent of the total population.[9] Madrid, Barcelona, Valencia, Bilbao and Zaragoza took their thousands, but there was a limit to their absorptive capacities and thousands more went overseas or to the labour-hungry markets of western Europe.

The boom did indeed lift the country out of the stagnation of the Franco years, but at a cost. Developers ran amok. Ancient walls came down, decayed historic buildings fell to bulldozers to be replaced by buildings of often staggering banality and acres of monotonous flats enveloped the old town centres. The thousands from the countryside had to be housed.

Happily, public opinion turned and ran the other way before all was lost. One can only admire the work of salvation and restoration undertaken by many hands. The government of the Autonomía de Castilla y León has contributed immensely to the rescue in recent years with financing from local, national and international sources. Private organizations and individuals have also played a vital role.

The Present Franco was, of course, succeeded on his death in 1975 by King Juan Carlos I, grandson of Alfonso XIII. The transition to a genuinely democratic government was not entirely smooth – witness the attempted coup by an army faction on 23 February 1981 – but modern, democratic Spain is now without question an active and valued participant in European and international affairs.

Valladolid and other industrial centres notwithstanding, Castilla and León remain predominantly agricultural, the vast fields of grain reaching to the horizon, rich vineyards and the Duero valley bursting with crops.

How the meseta works is often a puzzle to the outsider. One sees vast fields, ploughed in season, sprouting, thick with grain and then harvested, but the villages appear empty of life. Though tractors and other mechanical devices abound, signs of prosperity that would have been absent not too many years ago, one seldom sees anyone actually working. The stillness of the open meseta seems rarely disturbed by any bustle. The centuries of emigration have taken their toll.

To the casual traveller, most towns and villages seem reasonably prosperous, with new buildings and blocks of brick flats. Deep in the country and in the mountains one does find villages all but abandoned, but even there, those houses which are occupied sprout TV antennae.

And throughout are the ancient churches, señorial mansions, palaces and castles, some decayed beyond redemption, some well preserved, many recycled for contemporary use, that bear witness to the long and fascinating history of León and Castilla.

Notes

1. William H. Prescott, *The History of the Reign of Ferdinand and Isabella* (Philadelphia, 1873), Vol. I, p. 7.
2. Richard Fletcher, *Saint James's Catapult* (Oxford, 1984), pp. 57–68 passim.
3. Max Aub, *Manual de Historia de la Literatura Española* (Mexico City, 1966), Vol. I, p. 30, quoting from *The Chronicle of San Juan de la Peña* by Pedro IV of Aragón.
4. Georges Duby, *The Age of the Cathedrals: Art and Society, 980–1420* (Chicago, 1981), p. 62.
5. Joseph F. O'Callaghan, *A History of Medieval Spain* (Ithaca, 1975), p. 511.
6. Raymond Carr, *Modern Spain, 1875–1980* (Oxford, 1986), p. 33.
7. Juan Lalaguna, *A Traveler's History of Spain* (New York, 1990), p. 153.
8. V. S. Pritchett, *Marching Spain* (London, 1928), p. 214.
9. Lalaguna, *A Traveler's History*, p. 210.

3

Architectural Notes

A brief review of architectural developments in medieval Spain as they affected the Duero valley may be useful to set the buildings on the itinerary into the proper context.

I highly recommend a visit to the Museo Arqueológico in Madrid (on Calle de Serrano, next to the Plaza Colón). The museum's exhibits cover art and architecture of all periods of early Spanish history: Celtiberian, Roman, Visigothic, Muslim and Romanesque.

Celtiberian remnants are confined largely to museums, though the scant windswept ruins of the town of Numancia (Soria) are on our route. Roman bridges (Salamanca), the Roman arch at Medinaceli (Soria), the Roman theatre at Clunia (Burgos) and the stupendous aqueduct at Segovia require no analysis. I thus begin with the Visigoths.

Visigothic

A few Visigothic churches have survived in whole or in part. Except for Sta Comba de Bande in Orense Province in Galicia, they are to be found north of the Duero in the Campo Gótico, the principal area of Visigothic settlement. Nuestra Señora de las Viñas in Quintanilla de las Viñas (Burgos), San Juan de Baños in Baños de Cerrato and the crypt of Palencia Cathedral (Palencia) and San Pedro de la Nave (Zamora), are on the itinerary.

Visigothic churches are solidly built of ashlar, finely cut and dressed blocks of stone, fitted together without mortar. The *arco de herradura* (horseshoe arch) is used throughout, and the apses are square or rectangular.

The Romans used the horseshoe arch as a decorative device and it had appeared in Syria and Persia as early as the 3rd century BC. The Visigoths probably became familiar with it and the square apse in their early sojourn in the east. They also introduced what became a typical Spanish detail, the *ajimez*, a pair of very narrow twin horseshoe windows, the two lights separated by a tiny column.

Not only were their apses square, but when there were, say, three of them, they were not contiguous but separated one from another. Later generations often remodelled the churches to provide for contiguous apses, but traces remain at San Juan de Baños (Palencia) and San Pedro de la Nave (Zamora).

The presence of a Syrian merchant colony at Narbonne in southern France, the Byzantine occupation of the southeastern coast of Spain in the 6th century and the traffic of pilgrims from Spain to the shrine of St Simeon Stylites (built end of 5th century) near Aleppo doubtless helped diffuse these design elements.

The Visigoths decorated their churches with sculpted bands of circles enclosing animals, birds, floral and leaf designs and abstract geometric patterns. Cable borders, spirals, rosettes, Maltese crosses and stars were favourite devices. These show up particularly well at Quintanilla de las Viñas and San Pedro de la Nave. Capitals, often trapezoidal with flat faces, are imaginatively carved with saints and biblical figures. San Pedro de la Nave has the best examples on our itinerary.

Muslim

The principal area of Muslim settlement was, of course, Andalucía and it is there that the most beautiful examples of the Muslim architectural heritage can be found. The only significant Muslim remains in the valley of the Duero are fortresses, most of which were remodelled by later lords. The most spectacular is the enormous castle of Gormaz (Soria).

The Muslim penchant for geometric surface decoration, bright tiles, mosaics, coloured marbles, tracery in stone or plaster, however, had a lasting effect on architecture in Spain. So did the ajimez, the horseshoe arch and the lobed or cusped arch that they made their own. The *alfiz*, the square moulded frame around windows and portals that you see so frequently, is another import from the ancient Middle East. The best single collection of these elements in the Duero valley may be seen in the former palace of Alfonso XI and Pedro the Cruel at Tordesillas, now the Convent of Sta Clara, but any number of buildings ancient and modern demonstrate the persistence of Muslim influences.

The Muslim heritage inspired two styles of architecture unique to the Iberian peninsula, the *Mozarab* and the later *Mudéjar*. The Mozarab style flourished very early; the Mudéjar came into its own towards the end of the 12th century.

Mozarab

The Mozarabs were Christians who adopted the language, dress and customs but not the religion of their conquerors. From the 9th century, thousands moved to the Christian north. They introduced oriental elements, both Arab and Byzantine, into northern Spain.

The Mozarab churches on our itinerary are San Miguel in Almazán (the cupola) and the hermitage of San Baudelio de Berlanga in Soria Province and San Cebrián de Mazote and Nuestra Señora de la Asunción in Wamba in Valladolid. Horseshoe and lobed or cusped arches are among their distinguishing features. The chapels of Mozarab churches are often horseshoe in floor plan as well.

Romanesque

The dates for the emergence of Romanesque architecture (an originally somewhat pejorative term coined early in the 19th century to describe what preceded Gothic) vary by decades depending on the expert and the country, but the movement was certainly well under way before the year 1000. In Spain it came late and stayed late.

It had been preceded in western Europe by the Carolingian revival. When in 800 Charlemagne was crowned emperor of a revived and Christian Roman Empire, a suitable architecture was needed. Roman models abounded. Carolingian builders took elements from Roman architecture and reinterpreted them to suit the tastes and needs of their imperial patrons and of a Christian society. The successful adaptation of models and materials from various sources, Christian and non-Christian, was to be a hallmark of Romanesque architecture.

Romanesque architecture developed largely in response to the needs of the monastic communities that dominated religious life in Europe from at least the 10th to the 12th centuries. Gothic was the architecture of the more urbanized culture of the 12th century which gave rise to the great cathedrals.

Romanesque in Spain The First Romanesque or Lombard style reached Cataluña from northern Italy in the 10th century. Early churches there are solidly constructed, unadorned save for exterior pilasters and blind arcading, and devoid of sculptural decoration. Heavy tunnel vaults are supported by massive piers. The tall square towers stand detached from the church proper. Almost the only example of the Lombard style in the Duero valley is the church of La Anunciada outside Urueña (Valladolid).

The 10th-century kings of León had too much to do consolidating and defending their lands against Muslim attacks to do much building. Not until the death of Almanzor in 1002 and the collapse of the caliphate itself in 1031, allowing the repopulation of the Duero valley, was it possible to turn to serious building.

The Second Romanesque style percolated into Castilla and León from France along the pilgrimage route to Santiago de Compostela and in the baggage of monks from the abbey of Cluny in Burgundy who were encouraged to come to Spain by the 11th-century kings Sancho el Mayor of Navarra and his son and grandson Fernando I and Alfonso VI of Castilla. Along the same route merchants, settlers, adventurers and certainly masons and sculptors trooped into the peninsula. Once the new style did appear, the Spanish embraced it and were loath to let it go. Romanesque lingered in Spain longer than anywhere else in Europe. The extraordinarily rich legacy of Romanesque in the Duero valley is the principal purpose of this book.

The Pantheon of the Kings in Leon (1063) is held to be the first full-fledged example of the Second Romanesque. The earliest churches on our itinerary are San Miguel of 1111 and slightly later Sta María del Rivero in San Esteban de Gormaz (Soria), San Pedro de Arlanza of about 1080 (Burgos), El Salvador in Sepúlveda of 1093 and nearby San Frutos of about 1100 (Segovia) and the five churches in Zamora built in the late 11th or early 12th century.

VAULTING The outstanding contribution of Romanesque builders was in the development of vaulting. The Romans had employed barrel or tunnel vaults. These were used in early Romanesque churches, but stone vaults were heavy, required massive walls to counteract their thrust, restricted the size of the church and precluded windows. Heavy transverse ribs were one answer to the weight problem. Cumulative experience produced even better solutions.

When side aisles were added it became desirable to separate them from the nave not by ponderous walls pierced by openings but by arcades carried on piers or columns. Bays were thus created, the segments of the church through which you move down the centre axis.

Square bays and the square crossing of the transept and the nave could be roofed by groin vaults that were in essence the simple intersection of two barrel vaults. The weight of the vault was carried down via the corners to massive piers instead of resting solely on the walls of the church.

Groin vaults did not suffice, however, to cover the rectangular spaces created when a narrow transept crossed a wide nave or when the width of a bay was less than that of the nave. In such cases, the intersecting tunnel vaults were of different dimensions and heights, and the intersections awkward to construct.

Builders, experimenting, found that pointed arches lifted the vault over a narrow space up to the highest point of the wider intersecting barrel vault. Pointed arches also exerted less lateral thrust than round arches and permitted a better distribution of the weight of the vault down through the ribs and arches to the piers and the ground. Signs of this process of experimentation can be seen at Zamora Cathedral which has the first pointed arches in Spain.

RIBBING Ribs were the next development. Two ribs were thrown diagonally across the area to be vaulted, crossing in the middle, and the four intervening triangles filled in with lighter material. The weight of these quadripartite vaults rested on the angles. Yet another step was to make the surfaces between the ribs concave so that the ribs carried even more of the weight. This phenomenon, too, first appears at Zamora. Buttresses counteracting the thrust of the vault were first attached to the exterior of the church or concealed in the walls; not till the advent of Gothic did they begin to fly.

Another solution was to re-create a square by combining two bays so that their joint width was equal to that of the nave. Doubling up bays resulted in sexpartite vaults; two ribs crossing in the middle plus a third rib straight across the nave between the two intermediate pillars.

Ribbed vaults permitted higher and wider churches and so distributed the stresses that walls could be opened up by windows.

Ribs and transverse arches had to be supported. The result was the articulated or composite pier. To the basic pier or heavy column were added subsidiary shafts that typically carried (a) the main transverse arch across the nave, (b) the ribs of the nave vault, (c) the arches of the arcade to the left and right, and (d) the ribs and arches of the bay vault in the aisle.

Churches As the repopulation of the Duero valley got under way in the 11th and 12th centuries, churches began to rise again. These *parroquias* (village churches) have survived in amazing numbers and constitute a fascinating legacy of the Romanesque.

They were small affairs, with a single nave and a semicircular apse, although the Visigothic rectangular apse continued to appear in the earliest examples. Walls were thick, consisting typically of two faces of dressed stone filled with rubble, designed to support the heavy stone vaulting.

The *cabecera* (apse) was usually built of finer and more durable materials than the rest of the building and was covered with a half-dome stone oven vault. There are many early Romanesque churches where only the cabecera has survived the centuries. Wooden nave roofs were common in the beginning, though these soon gave way to more fireproof stone barrel or tunnel vaults, often supported by simple transverse arches.

Windows were tiny. Indeed, the Spanish aversion to light in churches is characteristic even of cathedrals, though the situation improved with the advent of Gothic.

Exteriors were severely plain. In time, the walls were articulated in various ways. Attached columns rose the height of the cabecera, dividing it into three or more panels. A row of corbels or eave brackets ran around the walls just below the roof, an echo of earlier timber roofs. (A common Spanish term for sculpted corbels is *canecillos* from the stem *can* meaning the butt end of a beam.) Below these blind arcades, windows, decorative carving and horizontal courses further defined the surface.

Towers stood in front of the church or to one side, or over the crossing. The earliest ones were detached from the main building although most of these were incorporated subsequently; see Vera Cruz in Segovia and El Salvador in Sepúlveda (Segovia) among many examples.

The interiors were bright with colour. Sculptures were polychromed. Interior walls were plastered and painted with depictions of the Holy Family, the saints and scenes from the Scriptures. They were hung with bright textiles, often adorned with tiles, and filled with hanging lamps. Very little of this survives. You may see fragments of plaster and colour but, for the most part, you will see only the bare walls.

Where fragments of fresco have survived it has often been due to the walls having been whitewashed with lime in the Middle Ages to protect – the citizens hoped – against the ravages of plague. Valbuena de Duero (Valladolid), San Justo (Segovia) and Sta María la Mayor in Arévalo (Ávila) offer good examples of such frescoes, brought to light only in recent years.

Churches being dynamic elements in their communities, they were often altered by later generations to suit changing styles. The results were not always happy, particularly in the 17th and 18th centuries. Modern restorers face difficult problems in deciding what to save and what to remove to get back to the original. Much sensitive work has none the less been done to stabilize decaying ancient structures and to bring them back to a semblance of their original state. One can only be grateful to those Spanish institutions public and private and to those individuals who have invested so much time, money and skill in an enormous task.

Pilgrimage Churches In northern Spain and southern France a new type of church developed as a specific response to the needs of the thousands of pilgrims who headed for the Galician shrine of Santiago de Compostela. The rebuilding of that church after its destruction by Almanzor commenced in about 1075, slightly later than the pilgrimage church of St Sernin in Toulouse which it closely resembles. No pilgrimage church is on our itinerary, but its main features were widely adopted.

To accommodate the crush of faithful, side aisles were added to the long broad nave. These either ended in chapels flanking the *capilla mayor*, the central apse containing the main altar, or were continued around the sanctuary, forming an ambulatory that allowed for more chapels and altars to hold saintly relics. People believed in the efficacy of relics. The relics *were* the saints who interceded with God on behalf of the faithful and provided protection and prestige. Early in the 9th century, ancient decrees were revived requiring every altar to incorporate a relic. Trade was brisk. Spain, whose experience with Muslim conquerors had produced any number of martyrs, was particularly attractive to relic hunters.

When the nave and side aisles were the same height, there was no space for the gallery or triforium and the light-admitting clerestory, the two stages above the arcade so characteristic of Gothic. At Santiago the nave is higher than the aisles thus making room for a gallery which runs all the way around the church, but the nave vaults spring from the top of the gallery and there are no windows.

The *coro* (choir), where the daily services are chanted, was originally located in the central apse. By the mid-12th century, this area had come to be reserved for the capilla mayor, dedicated to the high altar. The coro was moved west into the nave and was later enclosed to separate the clergy from the worshippers.

The uninterrupted view down the nave to the altar that is so characteristic of most western European cathedrals is usually absent in Spain. It has been said that the Spanish, accustomed to endless vistas out of doors, prefer to have their ecclesiastical vistas more confined.

Monasteries The period from the 10th to the 12th centuries was the heyday of monasticism in western Europe. Monasteries were not only centres for prayer and repositories of sacred relics, they were also centres of learning and their abbots often played significant political roles. Monks from the powerful abbey of Cluny in Burgundy came to Spain in the 11th century, summoned by the kings of Navarra and Castilla to reform the monasteries in their realms. (See pages 39–43, 'Religious Developments'.)

Liturgical demands had architectural consequences. As in the case of pilgrimage churches, aisles were added, terminating in apsidal chapels, and transepts were extended to accommodate yet more chapels which were needed for saintly relics and to provide altars for the monks to say masses.

Cluny developed a coherent organization for monasteries. The chapter house, library, refectory, kitchen, store rooms, dormitories and lavatories were linked directly with the abbey church. The out-buildings – hospital, inn, workshops, granaries and so on – were set apart. There was no single format; the rough scheme could be adapted to local circumstances. The abbots of Cluny were more interested in conformity in discipline and liturgy than in architecture. They were also interested in magnificence, wherein lay the seeds of their downfall.

Monastic life centred round the cloister which from early in the 11th century became a principal element in the monastic complex. Thus originated those 'architectural marvels, various in style, which continued to appear up to the 16th century, with their wealth of works of art, their sculptured columns and capitals, their fountains, gardens and trees, their views framed in Gothic arches, and the peaceful rhythm of their secluded galleries providing a shield from worldly troubles.'[1] Some still maintain their gardens, others have a single great cypress, some are a bit scruffy and in need of care, but they are all oases of calm.

Sculpture Sculpture is one of the most fascinating aspects of Romanesque churches; there are countless wonderful examples in the Duero valley. The period saw the first extensive use of sculpture on the exterior of buildings since Roman times.

Sculpture on portals appeared first in 11th-century Cataluña. The earliest dated lintel sculpture in Europe (1020–21) is at St Genis-des-Fontaines, south of Perpignan, an area long within the Catalan orbit. Should you pass that way, this charmingly primitive little piece is worth a detour. It depicts Christ in a mandorla supported by angels and flanked by six bowling-pin-shaped apostles, each sheltered under a little horseshoe arch.

The tympanum over the main portal was the earliest focus of

sculpture, from where it spread to the flanking jambs, the capitals of columns and the corbels under the eaves. The capitals in the cloisters gave sculptors unlimited scope for invention. Some of the most delightful bits of sculpture appear on the columns flanking the apse windows and on the corbels. The latter were favoured for grotesqueries and inventive indecencies.

The purpose was to make Christian history and precepts intelligible to a largely illiterate population. Scenes from the Old and New Testaments predominate, though references to classical antiquity appear. Events in the life of Christ, the saints and the Virgin Mary occupy the most prominent places.

The sculptors drew inspiration from contemporary life as well. Capitals provide glimpses into the daily activities of all classes of society, high and humble alike. You frequently see knights clad in full chain mail jousting or participating enthusiastically in such biblical events as the Slaughter of the Innocents, a favourite topic.

The animals, monsters and fabulous beasts teeming on capitals and corbels are quite extraordinary. They derive from a wide range of sources, including the Middle East, transmitted by sculptors from many lands, Christian and Muslim. It is not uncommon in 11th- and 12th-century churches to find depicted men with turbans and Muslim garb; examples can be seen at San Miguel in San Esteban de Gormaz (Soria).

The artists were masters at adapting their themes to the space available. It is amazing how much they could get onto one or two faces of a capital and how cleverly they managed to compress events to make them fit.

'El Románico Porticado' Early Romanesque churches in what is now the province of Segovia and adjacent areas of Burgos and Soria provinces were often built with a portico or arcaded gallery, a feature unique to these parts. The gallery is usually on the south side, occasionally extending around the west end and very occasionally (San Martín and San Millán in Segovia) around the north side as well. They served an important civil function, enabling the town dignitaries to gather to discuss the issues of the day in a protected spot that got the sun even in winter. 'El románico porticado' is the term Carlos Lafora uses in his book on the subject.

Prototypes are found further north, with Mozarab San Miguel de

Escalada (León) of 913 being a notable example, but the style caught on in the general area of Segovia Province. The two earliest known galleries, from the early 12th century, are at San Miguel in San Esteban de Gormaz (Soria) and El Salvador in Sepúlveda (Segovia).

Galleries typically have seven arches. Seven was a mystical number. It appears throughout the Book of Revelations, a mystical and prophetic work that had great influence in the early Middle Ages. Illuminations in extant copies of Beato de Liébana's *Commentaries on the Apocalypse* depict the seven churches of Asia to which St John addressed his letter from Patmos as an arcade of seven horseshoe arches separated by slender columns. The seven arches of the typical Segovian portico were presumably inspired by the same tradition, if not by these very illuminations.

Mudéjar

Mudéjar architecture came into its own at the end of the 12th century, flourishing simultaneously with Gothic. The Mudéjares were Muslims who remained in their places as the Reconquista rolled over them. The repopulation of the Duero valley resulted in a huge demand for churches and buildings and Mudéjar artists and craftsmen were readily at hand. They were skilful potters, carpenters, bricklayers, metal workers and weavers, experts in moulding and carving plaster, and they put their skills to work for their new Christian lords. They worked largely in brick, a medium with which the East had long been familiar.

Mudéjar builders thus created an instantly recognizable style peculiar to Spain. Wall surfaces are beautifully articulated with complex patterns picked out in plain or glazed brick, tile, ceramic plates and little columns. The horseshoe arch, the intricate plasterwork, the splendid *artesonado* (coffered wooden) ceilings, the twin-windowed ajimeces and a host of decorative details are marks of their style which flourished from the 12th to the 16th centuries.

In the Duero basin, good examples survive in Zamora Province at Toro (San Lorenzo and San Salvador); in Valladolid Province at Arévalo (Sta María la Mayor, San Martín and La Lugareja), Madrigal de las Altas Torres (San Nicolás de Bari) and Peñafiel (San Pablo); in Segovia Province at Olmedo (San Andrés, San Juan, San Miguel and La Trinidad) and Cuéllar (San Andrés and San Martín);

and in Soria Province at Andaluz and a number of smaller parroquias.

Among secular buildings, the 14th-century palace of Alfonso XI
and Pedro the Cruel at Tordesillas is notable; its remaining Mudéjar
elements are incorporated into the Convent of Sta Clara. There are
splendid brick castles at Coca (Segovia) and Medina del Campo
(Valladolid).

The Mudéjar style reached its apogee in the 14th century. In the
15th, it began to be overshadowed by Hispano-Flemish Gothic and
suffered a setback when the Muslims were expelled from Spain. But
it remained as an undercurrent, contributing its subtle bit to Spanish
architecture of the Renaissance and beyond. In time it was fully
incorporated into the Spanish architectural canon. Las Ventas (1934),
Madrid's bullring, is a splendid example and there are countless
public and private buildings all over Spain in the Mudéjar style.

Gothic

Early or Proto-Gothic (12th Century) The Gothic style began
with the rebuilding of the abbey of St Denis outside Paris about
1137. The emphasis of Gothic is, of course, on the vertical: pointed
arches, pillars and composite shafts reaching upwards to the multiple
ribs of the soaring vaults, flying buttresses and the addition of one if
not two courses (triforium and clerestory) above the arcades of the
nave. Above all, Gothic invokes the image of light streaming in
through vast expanses of stained glass, a development made possible
by lighter ribbed vaulting and buttresses that eliminated the need for
heavy solid walls.

The first hints of Gothic in Spain appear in the churches of the
Cistercians who in the 12th century supplanted the Cluniacs on the
cutting edge of monasticism. Northern Spain has perhaps the finest
collection of Cistercian houses extant; more than half of the original
sixty survive in whole or in part.

The conquered territories were being resettled; economic activity
was quickening. Builders of the 12th century were open to new
techniques. They recognized that the stability of a building depended
on the balance between the downward and outward thrust of the
roof and vaulting and the restraining thrust of the internal arches
and external buttresses. As the century progressed, the Cistercians

made increasing use of pointed arches, ribbed vaults, light vaulting materials and composite pillars with attached shafts to support the added rib work.

These advances can be seen at Cistercian foundations such as Moreruela (Zamora) of the mid-12th century and slightly later Sta María de Huerta (Soria) and also in the cathedrals of Ávila, Zamora and Salamanca, all begun in the second half of the century.

St Bernard, founder of the Cistercian Order and a strict proponent of simplicity in all things, developed a master plan for monasteries that included features such as the rigid separation of lay brothers – who provided the labour the monks needed to carry out their many enterprises – from the choir or regular brothers. The quarters of the lay brothers and their refectory were in the west range of the cloister. The quarters of the choir brothers stood on the east range; their refectory, flanked by the kitchen and the calefactorium (warming room), stood to the south. Cistercian abbeys were always built in a valley over or near a stream that provided water for the kitchens, the infirmary and the latrines.

A stairway led down from the choir brothers' dormitory to the east end of the church. The lay brothers entered the church at the west end. The two communities were kept separate even inside the church, which was usually aisleless and divided into three transverse segments by walls, screens or steps. The church was intended solely for the use of the monks. Visitors got no further than the vestibule.

The emphasis on simplicity meant the disappearance from capitals and portals of the biblical scenes and the animals real or fabulous of the Romanesque. Sculpture was forbidden in 1124 along with illuminations in manuscripts. Towers went in 1157 and any existing stained-glass windows were ordered replaced in 1182. The beauty of Cistercian buildings thus lies in the pure architectural aesthetic.

The original Cistercian plan stipulated a simple rectangular apse with an altar table. As demand for altars increased, the Cistercians added two or three flanking chapels in each arm of the transept. The model of a square east end with a rectangular central chapel and flanking transept chapels was common to all Cistercian churches to Bernard's death in 1153.

On our itinerary, the original model can be found at Sta María de Huerta (Soria) where the polygonal central chapel opens directly on to the transept and is flanked by two rectangular chapels on either side.

Eventually, the Spanish Cistercians returned to the chevet model, an ambulatory around the apse with contiguous radiating chapels. At Moreruela, seven rounded chapels radiate from the ambulatory, with a small rectangular transept chapel on either side. These additional chapels were not to house the relics and statuary of the pilgrimage churches, which St Bernard despised, along with chevets, but to answer the spiritual needs of the monks by giving them increased access to altars.

The vaulting of the apse also changed. The semicircular Romanesque apse was covered by a simple oven vault. The vault of a square or polygonal apse had to be supported by ribs.

Classic Gothic (13th Century) By the end of the 12th century, the influence of the Cluniac and Cistercian monasteries had begun to wane. Bishops took the place of abbots as builders and patrons. They often came from powerful noble families. They built churches for public worship and the display of pomp and wealth – their own and the community's – not for an enclosed monastic community.

The Gothic style entered Spain in force in the reign of Fernando III (1230–52), conqueror of Córdoba and Sevilla, with the construction of the French Gothic cathedrals at Burgos (begun 1221), Toledo (1226) and León (1255). Here all the basic Gothic elements finally appeared in Spain. But they had no imitators. They were imposed on Spain by French influence and the style remained alien, though elements were copied. The cathedral at El Burgo de Osma (Soria), for example, shows clear affinities with Burgos.

The conservative nature of the Spanish and, quite possibly, their desire to avoid the dazzling light that floods the country led to the continuation of Romanesque forms long after Gothic cathedrals had been built. As we have seen, the pointed arch was introduced in the early 12th century, but Spain continued to employ round-headed arches until well into the 13th.

'It is rather characteristic of the Spanish,' wrote Bernard Bevan somewhat sharply,

> that, although [Spain] had welcomed these French innovations and adopted them in her secular cathedrals, she made no attempt to act upon the new building principles involved, the most fundamental of which was the substitution of a horizontal for a vertical thrust. Walls

remained as massive as ever, windows remained small and often round-headed, and flying buttresses were not even attempted. For more than two hundred years Spain had learned to build as if beauty depended upon weight. Romanesque suited her climate and her temperament.[2]

Sculpture also took new strides with Gothic. Sculptors looked to the visible world for inspiration in modelling bodily features and clothing instead of to the symbolism of the Romanesque. Scenes from the life of Christ or of the Virgin supplanted Old Testament scenes, monsters and grotesqueries.

The work of Master Mateo, creator of the Pórtico de la Gloria at Santiago de Compostela (1168–88), influenced such men as Master Fruchel who worked on Ávila Cathedral and San Vicente. The influence of the workshop of sculptors that evolved at Burgos Cathedral radiated throughout Castilla. Sculptures of the Burgos school enriched the cathedrals of Ávila and El Burgo de Osma and the colegiata at Toro.

Fourteenth-century Castilla was distracted by civil war and the Black Plague. The main focus of architectural activity moved to Aragón which was in these years expanding its Mediterranean empire.

Hispano-Flemish (15th and 16th Centuries) Not until the 15th and 16th centuries did cathedral building in Castilla resume: Sevilla, the largest Gothic cathedral in the world (begun in 1402; virtually completed by 1520), the New Cathedral at Salamanca (1513) and Segovia (1525). This late Gothic flowering was due in part to the arrival from the Netherlands and the Rhine valley of a talented group of architects, sculptors and painters. Treasure was pouring in from the New World; wealthy patrons, lay and ecclesiastic, abounded.

Close commercial ties (the wool trade in particular) with the Netherlands and Burgundy had existed at least since the reign of Juan II of Castilla (1406–54) when the trade fair at Medina del Campo was at its peak. Juan II surrounded himself with a newly ennobled gentry who aped Burgundian ways and many Spaniards travelled to Burgundy.

The connection was strengthened later in the century when Juan II's daughter Isabella and her husband Ferdinand married their daughter Juana to Philip of Habsburg. Their son Charles succeeded as ruler of the Netherlands and Burgundy in 1506, ten years before he became king of Spain.

Juan de Colonia (d. 1481) arrived in Burgos from Cologne about 1440. He and his son Simón (d. c. 1511) worked principally at Burgos Cathedral, still abuilding after 200 years. Simón did the façade of Sta María in Aranda de Duero and the lower portion of that of San Pablo in Valladolid.

The sculptor Gil de Siloé (d. c. 1501), from Antwerp, reached Burgos about 1480 and soon established his reputation as a worker in wood and alabaster, especially for retablos. The marvellous tombs of Juan II and Isabel of Portugal and their son Alfonso in the Cartuja de Miraflores in Burgos are his. The design of the façade of the Colegio de San Gregorio in Valladolid has been attributed to him. His son Diego (c. 1495–1563), sculptor and architect, was prominent in the development of the Castilian Renaissance.

Another centre of Flemish sculptors and architects developed in Toledo where Juan Guas (c. 1430–96), originally from Brittany but trained in Brussels, arrived in around 1440. He was a leading exponent of the new Hispano-Flemish style. Much of his life was devoted to Toledo, but he worked at Ávila Cathedral from 1471 and the next year he was in Segovia supervising the construction of the Monasterio del Parral, one of the first buildings in the Hispano-Flemish style. Another early work is the cloister of the old cathedral of Segovia (1472–91), moved to the new cathedral in 1524. In Segovia he was also responsible for the west front of Santa Cruz.

For the powerful Mendoza clan he built first the castle of Manzanares el Real, north of Madrid, and then (1480–83) the palace of the dukes of the Infantado in Guadalajara, perhaps his masterpiece. The façade, blending Flemish and Mudéjar styles, is covered with a regular pattern of decorative stone projections. This treatment inspired the diamond-shaped stone surface decoration of the Casa de los Picos in Segovia and the shells on the Casa de las Conchas in Salamanca.

In 1487 Juan Guas was working in Valladolid under the eye of Bishop Alonso de Burgos. The magnificent cloister and chapter of San Gregorio have been attributed to him. One of his hallmarks is the raised tribune carrying the coro and spanning the nave at the west end of the church.

Egas Cueman (d. 1495) came to Toledo from Brussels around 1445. His sons Antón (active early 16th century) and Enrique Egas (d. 1534), trained under Juan Guas and became noted architects.

Enrique succeeded his teacher as master of works at Toledo and held the same post at Granada. He also built the royal hospital at Santiago de Compostela (1501–11), now the splendid Hotel Reyes Católicos.

Juan Gil de Hontañón (c. 1480–c. 1531), from Cantabria, was one of the most prominent native architects in the Hispano-Flemish tradition. He was master of works at Salamanca (1513–26), Sevilla (1513–17) and Segovia (1525–26), carrying on the Gothic tradition as the Renaissance arrived in Spain. His son Rodrigo (c. 1500–77) succeeded him at Segovia and rose to even greater prominence.

Another native son was Juan de Alava (c. 1480–1537) whose masterpiece was San Esteban in Salamanca, begun in 1524. He was one of the team who planned the New Cathedral. Alava enjoyed the patronage of Alonso III de Fonseca, Archbishop of Santiago de Compostela, but that prelate's taste eventually shifted to the new Italian Renaissance and he came to favour the work of Alonso de Covarrubias and Diego de Siloé.

The work of these men is known as National Gothic. It reflected native Spanish characteristics rather than being simply imposed as was the French Gothic of the 13th century and reached its peak with the cathedrals of Salamanca and Segovia. 'Neither can vie with Seville in mere size,' wrote Bevan, 'but their towering clustered columns, their wonderful reticulated vaulting, and their majestic proportions make of them a glorious *finale* to Gothic Spain.'[3]

Renaissance

Late Gothic/Early Renaissance Transition Experts disagree about the proper labelling of buildings in the period between the last clearly Gothic works and the arrival in Spain of full-blown Italian Renaissance styles. The most obvious characteristic of the early period was the reassertion of the Spanish love for surface decoration.

Isabelline A peculiarly Spanish coda to National Gothic was the Isabelline style of which Juan Guas and Simón de Colonia were notable exponents. Façades were lathered with naturalistic carving embedded in much lacy ornamentation. Doors and windows were particular foci of attention. Curved arches and other devices frame groups of figures. Medallions with the busts of Ferdinand and Isabella are common, as are their shields and emblems. The façade of Sta María in Aranda de Duero is the first example on our itinerary; the façades of San Pablo and San Gregorio in Valladolid and of Salamanca's New Cathedral are striking examples. The Spanish loved ostentation and ornamentation and by the 16th century plenty of money was available to enable the rich to indulge their tastes.

Plateresque It was an easy transition from Isabelline to Plateresque, generally considered to be the first phase of the Renaissance in Spain (first half of the 16th century). The name derives from the work of silversmiths (*plateros*) that the style was supposed to resemble. It featured purely surface decoration, unrelated to any structural requirements: intricate geometric patterns, imaginative arches and pierced stone tracery. Salamanca is a treasury of Plateresque art; see in particular the façade of the university (1520s). The soft stone of which much of the city was built lent itself to elaborate carving. Enrique Egas, Alonso de Covarrubias and Diego de Siloé were among its practitioners.

The Renaissance Proper Sevilla Cathedral was completed in the first half of the 16th century and work was begun at Salamanca and Segovia on the last Gothic cathedrals built in Spain. Meanwhile in Italy, a full century earlier, Brunelleschi (1377–1446) had launched the Renaissance with the dome of Florence Cathedral (1420–36). The first of the High Renaissance architects, Bramante (1444–1514), completed his life and work a year after the cornerstone was laid for Salamanca Cathedral.

The revival of classical models that distinguished the Renaissance represented a sharp break with the evolution from Roman to Romanesque to Gothic. The architects of the Italian Renaissance took the rounded Roman arch, pediments, the correct use of columns and pilasters and the three classical orders of capitals established by the ancient writers and adapted them in new ways. Rounded rib vaults and more massive effects came to replace the lightness of Gothic.

The Spanish were more cautious. Besides, they were not comfortable with the austere grandeur that was Rome; they wanted embellishments. Europe's architectural enthusiasms had always taken time to reach the peninsula. Bramante and the others did exert influence, but it was long in coming. Part of the problem lay in politics.

Castilla bordered on anarchy under Juan II (1406–54) and Enrique IV (1454–74). There was no time for building. As it happened, however, a branch of the Aragonese royal house had ruled Sicily since the late 13th century. Thus it was that Ferdinand of Aragón, husband of Isabella, had direct experience ruling Aragón's Italian domains.

Spaniards became familiar with Italy. Many prominent men held important posts there as Charles I (Emperor Charles V) and Philip II consolidated Spanish rule. Italian styles and craftsmen soon made their appearance in Spain. Tombs sculpted by Italians became fashionable. Young Spanish artists went to Italy to observe and study. Prelates travelled continually and were in a position to admire and import new ideas as well as sculpture and painting. From cathedrals the new style spread to episcopal palaces, hospitals and universities founded by ecclesiastics and then to the palaces and town houses of the lay nobility.

The first signs of the classical Renaissance in Spain appeared in Valladolid at the Colegio de Santa Cruz under the patronage of Pedro González de Mendoza, Cardinal-Archbishop of Toledo. Santa Cruz was begun in 1486 as a Gothic building, but in 1490 Lorenzo Vázquez took it over and completed it in the Renaissance style. Vázquez followed this in 1492–95 with the palace of the dukes of Medinaceli in Cogolludo (Guadalajara) which is about as Italian-Renaissance-looking as you can find.

A new generation of architects awaited. Alonso de Covarrubias (c. 1488–1570), pupil of the Egas brothers, began as a decorative sculptor, turning to architecture in 1534. He was only twenty-four when he was invited to join the conclave of masters at Salamanca in 1512 to review plans for the New Cathedral. In 1534, he succeeded Enrique Egas as master of works at Toledo Cathedral. From his Plateresque work of the early 16th century, Alonso developed into a leading member of the first generation of Renaissance architects.

Diego de Siloé (c. 1495–1563), son of Gil, also began as a sculptor. He spent several years in Italy absorbing the Renaissance and returned to Burgos in 1519 to construct the Escalada Dorada (Golden Stair) in that city's cathedral. In 1529 he was taken up by Archbishop Fonseca and put to work in Salamanca.

Rodrigo Gil de Hontañón (c. 1500–77) was the most prolific architect of his day. He began in the Hispano-Flemish tradition of his father, but about 1533 turned to the Italian Renaissance. He worked with his father Juan at Salamanca and Segovia, succeeding him about 1526 as master of works at Segovia, a post he held off and on until 1540 when construction stopped. The chapter called him back in 1560. He returned to Salamanca as master of works in 1538 and worked on the Palacio de Monterrey and the Fonseca Colegio del Arzobispo.

In Valladolid he was responsible for the chapel of La Magdalena and the monumental portal of San Benito. About 1540 he designed the church that still stands in Mota del Marqués (Valladolid) and the next year he was master of works at Palencia Cathedral. His mark can be found throughout Castilla.

Juan de Herrera (1530–97) was the leading exponent of classical Renaissance architecture. His enduring monument is Philip II's monastery at San Lorenzo de El Escorial. Philip was devout and austere and Herrera was his man. The Herreran style was too formal and cold for Spanish taste, however, and although it continued to enjoy royal favour, it had few takers elsewhere. There are virtually no examples in the Duero valley, save for Valladolid Cathedral which was built in part to Herrera's plans. The church at Santo Domingo de Silos (Burgos), begun in 1755 by Ventura Rodríguez, is in the Herreran tradition.

Baroque

Not even the Escorial could weigh down the Spanish penchant for elaborate decoration for long. The late 17th century saw the revival of the complicated design tradition that had been stored away in the Spanish architectural attic. The Baroque had arrived and its main practitioners in Spain were the Churriguera family who specialized in huge gilt and polychromed retablos. This tradition strongly influenced their architecture.

The first major commission of José Benito (1665–1735), the eldest of three brothers, was the retablo (1693) in the church of San Esteban in Salamanca, his native town. This launched the style that was to bear the family name. José's only other work in the Duero valley was at Segovia Cathedral. The patio of the Colegio de Anaya and the Colegio de Calatrava in Salamanca were the work of Joaquín (1674–1724).

The third brother, Alberto (1676–1750), did not take up

architecture seriously until after the deaths of the other two. His triumph is the Plaza Mayor in Salamanca, begun 1733. There were other commissions in Salamanca, but Alberto then resigned as chief architect of the cathedral and occupied himself with smaller works, including the façade of the parroquia in Rueda (Valladolid).

Baroque is not to everyone's taste. We were amused at the reaction of Señora Munda, the elderly lady who has held for over thirty-five years, and I hope still does, the keys for Santa María de Sandoval, a Cistercian monastery near León. The apse of the otherwise austere church contains a huge and very ornate retablo which Señora Munda dismissed with a contemptuous wave of her hand; 'Ese barrocco!' ('That Baroque!'), she sneered.

Rejas and Retablos

Spanish churches are distinguished by two striking features: *rejas*, the ornate wrought-iron screens that close off chapels, and *retablos*, the often monumental constructions that fill the apse behind and above the altar. One sees them everywhere and a few details may therefore be useful.

Rejas *Rejería* began in the Romanesque period with rather simple screens and came to full flower with Gothic. It was made possible by technical advances in metal working and was driven by the proliferation of chapels containing holy relics and art works of great value requiring protection but which at the same time needed to be visible to the faithful. The 14th century saw the first true rejas, but it was in the second half of the 15th century that the art really took off.

Rejas can be extraordinary works of art. Not only are the verticals beautifully worked, but the crowns display remarkable scroll work, angels and putti, kings and queens, escutcheons of donors and so forth. They can be enormous, spanning the width of the nave in some cathedrals. Large or small they contribute mightily to the majesty of Spanish cathedrals.

Retablos Perhaps even more notable are the glowing retablos that rise behind and above the altar at the rear of the apse. Most are of wood, but they can be of marble or even alabaster. The definitive work on the subject seems to be *Behind the Altar Table: the Development of* *the Painted Retablo in Spain, 1350–1510* (University of Missouri, 1989) by Judith Berg Sobré on which I have drawn for the remarks that follow.

In the 12th and 13th centuries, the apses of Spanish churches were often decorated with painted scenes, centring on a Christ figure in the vault. There were also elaborate altar frontals consisting of richly painted or carved panels focusing on Christ or the local patron saint.

Changes in architecture and liturgy doomed both these art forms. The smooth surfaces of the Romanesque apse gave way to the articulated surfaces of the Gothic that made them difficult to paint. The altar was moved eastwards against the rear apse wall so that the priest now stood between it and the congregation. The coro was moved westward into the nave, thus opening up a clear area before the apse that now called for embellishment.

Something free-standing was required. From reasonably simple decorated shields behind the altar evolved soaring works of art to fill the entire apse. The retablo has three sections: the base, the main body and the surrounding frame known as the *polvoguardos* or dust catcher (they do not seem to work very well).

The base, similar to the predella of Italian altar pieces, depicts Christ and/or saints. The main body of the retablo usually focuses on two or three large paintings or sculptures of Christ, the Virgin and so on, flanked by vertical rows of paintings of the life of Christ, the Virgin or the saint to whom the church is dedicated. The polvoguardos range from relatively simple to anything but, and in later Gothic retablos elaborate pinnacles and fretwork often surmount the main figures.

The finest painters and sculptors of the day worked on retablos. Many remain in their original settings, though the trouble in most churches is getting enough light to see them. Look for the coin box which turns on the illumination or wait, as some do, for someone else to deposit the coin.

I have dealt above mainly with religious architecture. Let us now turn to another type of building.

Castles

A survey in the 1960s listed 2,538 castles in Spain.[4] They include simple *atalayas* or watch towers, enormous hilltop fortresses such as

Gormaz, strongholds of the meseta such as Montealegre or Torre-lobatón with their high walls and enormous keeps and great late medieval castle-palaces like the Alcázar in Segovia and the Fonseca castle at Coca. They crown improbable crags, command the heads of fertile valleys, guard strategic passes or loom up protectively from the vastness of the meseta.

Castles were often built on the sites of previous fortifications, a strategic position being just as attractive to the Muslims or Christians as to the Celtiberians or Romans. Because they were built and rebuilt according to the tastes of the current owner or to meet changing military imperatives (gunpowder and heavy artillery, for instance), the earliest structures have been largely obliterated, discerned only by the expert. Gormaz, a 10th-century Muslim rebuilding of an earlier fortress, retains horseshoe portals and other obvious signs of Muslim ownership, but it is an exception.

Castles usually consist of three basic elements: the outer line of defensive walls and towers; the walls, towers and gates of the inner precinct; and the inner precinct itself, dominated by the *torre de homenaje* (keep) and containing living quarters, store rooms, the armory and the lord's treasury. There was always a chapel or, in the larger castles, a separate church. Between the outer and inner walls was a parade and exercise ground for the garrison, the *plaza de armas*, where people and livestock of the vicinity could take refuge in times of trouble.

Around and below the battlements ran a walkway shielded by a wooden gallery. The battlements protected the archers and, when carried forwards on corbels to form machicolations, enabled the defenders to dump on the besiegers and made it difficult to use scaling ladders.

Some spectacular defences were developed. Towers were originally square, but it was soon realized that round ones were less vulnerable to hits and battering rams. You also see triangular towers and other shapes.

Castles built on rocky outcrops conform, naturally, to the shape of the site. They are therefore often long and narrow as at Berlanga, Peñafiel and Peñaranda de Duero. The seamless blending of castle wall with sheer natural rock face can be awesome and made scaling virtually impossible.

Castles of the flat meseta are rectangular in plan, with towering walls of often immense thickness and the huge keep astride one wall of the inner precinct as at Fuensaldaña, Torrelobatón and Villalonso. Moats with a sloping glacis prevented attackers from getting directly at the main walls.

Some towns grew up at the feet of castles, but castles were occasionally built expressly to control towns, such as the Alcázar in Segovia. Not infrequently in times of civil strife the town would fall or defect to the besiegers, leaving the garrison holed up in the castle which thus had to be well provisioned. Heroic stories tell of castles held against long sieges when the townsfolk had opted for the other side. The keep was designed to be the last point of defence, but once matters got that far, it was probably too late.

Colonel T. E. Lawrence, he of Arabia, on being told that a certain crusader castle in the Holy Land could be held by one man, remarked that, even so, it could be besieged by two, one on either side of the entrance.

The keep gradually evolved from a primitive defence post to the residence of the lord, with two or more floors connected by wooden stairs or corkscrew stairs built into the thickness of the walls. At Peñafiel the floors have been restored; in most castles you now look straight up to the sky from the bottom of the tower. Windows were confined to the uppermost storeys and even then tended to be narrow slits.

By the 14th and 15th centuries the primitive lodgings of earlier years had given way to abodes of reasonable comfort and even luxury, more fortified palaces than defensive castles. The Moors had been dealt with, warfare had become the monopoly of the crown and those nobles who were so inclined could turn to other pursuits. Some even took up culture and from the 15th century libraries begin to appear.

The Trastámara period (1369–1474) witnessed the growth and enrichment of a new nobility who, especially in the reign of the weak Enrique IV (1454–74), virtually captured the monarchy. Their new power was reflected in castles and strongholds such as Peñafiel, Coca, Cuéllar and Berlanga de Duero. The Trastámara nobility forsook uncomfortable and windy crags and established themselves in towns. Many of their urban palaces are on our route.

Strong kings made repeated efforts to destroy the castles of the more fractious nobles. Ferdinand and Isabella ordered the demolition of many castles and forbade the construction of new ones, but by that time castles were becoming outmoded anyway. During the 16th century, many were transformed into elegant palaces such as Coca, Cuéllar, Segovia and Simancas.

Furthermore, as urban populations grew, the castle on its crag outside town became less able to control matters. The increase in commercial and mercantile activity and the importance of urban revenues for the crown called for more efficient municipal organization and government than the old lord in his castle could provide or was capable of providing regardless of where he lived.

In the 16th century, Philip II ordered an inventory of the castles of the realm and, though it was never finished, the picture that emerged was bleak. The huge arks had become fair game for contractors or local villagers needing basic construction material. Owners were often glad to sell. Not until this century were serious efforts made to preserve and restore this incredible patrimony. The Asociación Española de Amigos de Castillos now keeps an eye on things and presents awards to the best conservation efforts. It is a colossal and expensive task and it is impressive to see what has been done and what is being done.

Notes

1. Frederick Rahlves, *Cathedrals and Monasteries of Spain* (London, 1966), p. 73.
2. Bernard Bevan, *A History of Spanish Architecture* (London, 1938), p. 76.
3. Ibid., p. 130.
4. Carlos Sarthou Carreres, *Castillos de España* (Madrid, 1992), p. 26.

Part Two
The Itinerary

The traveller who journeys into the countryside to seek out the villages, towns, churches, monasteries and castles of the Duero valley will find it a fascinating and rewarding experience.

The towns were founded, or refounded, by kings and nobles who had just wrested the land from the Muslims. Many villages have histories equally as long as that of the towns, if more obscure. The warrior kings of the 9th, 10th and 11th centuries encouraged settlers from the north of Spain and beyond the Pyrenees to come to the Duero valley, repopulate the land and secure the frontiers. Without these settlers, these farmers, shepherds, traders, artisans, warriors and monks, the newly conquered lands could not have been held.

Much has happened here. There is much to explore.

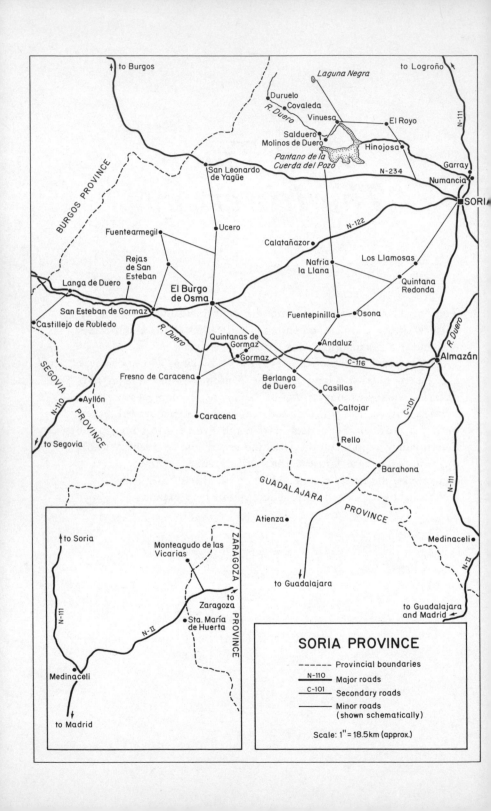

to Burgos

to Logroño

Laguna Negra

Duruelo
Covaleda
R. Duero
Vinuesa
El Royo

Salduero
Molinos de Duero
Hinojosa

N-111

Garray

Pantano de la Cuerda del Pozo

N-234

Numancia

SORIA

San Leonardo de Yagüe

BURGOS PROVINCE

N-122

Ucero

Calatañazor

Fuentearmegil

Nafria la Llana

Los Llamosas

Rejas de San Esteban

Quintana Redonda

Langa de Duero

El Burgo de Osma

San Esteban de Gormaz

Fuentepinilla

Osona

R. Duero

Castillejo de Robledo

SEGOVIA

Quintanas de Gormaz

Andaluz

R. Duero

Almazán

Gormaz

C-116

N-110

PROVINCE

Fresno de Caracena

Berlanga de Duero

Casillas

Ayllón

Caltojar

C-101

to Segovia

Caracena

Rello

Barahona

N-111

GUADALAJARA

Atienza

PROVINCE

Medinaceli

N-II

ZARAGOZA

to Soria

Monteagudo de las Vicarias

to Zaragoza

to Guadalajara

N-111

N-II

Sta. María de Huerta

PROVINCE

to Guadalajara and Madrid

Medinaceli

N-II

to Madrid

SORIA PROVINCE

- - - - - Provincial boundaries

N-110 ―――― Major roads

C-101 ―――― Secondary roads

――――― Minor roads (shown schematically)

Scale: 1" = 18.5km (approx.)

4

Soria Province

This lovely mountainous and wooded province seems to be completely off the foreign tourist track, though it is a popular destination for the Spanish who escape the summer heat in its resorts and lakes. The Spanish are enthusiastic hikers and campers and this is a fine region for such activities.

Approaches

1. From Madrid via the N-II   There are two alternatives: a. The town of Soria is 225 km (140 miles) from Madrid by the N-II, the main highway eastwards to Zaragoza and Barcelona. The N-II sweeps around the south side of GUADALAJARA, a town that suffered greatly in the Civil War. On its north side is the Palacio del Infantado, built in the 1480s by Juan Guas for the Mendoza dukes of the Infantado. It was the first palace in Spain influenced by the Italian Renaissance and the treatment of the external wall surfaces inspired the Casa de Picos in Segovia and the Casa de las Conchas in Salamanca. The palace has a fine inner court; it is now a museum.

The N-II jogs north to cross the southeastern tip of Soria Province on its way to Zaragoza. Just past Medinaceli (see below), the N-111 branches off the main highway and heads straight north to Soria through a mountainous landscape, thickly wooded once past Almazán.

b. An equally scenic route is the C-101 that leaves the N-II just beyond Guadalajara. Some 42 km (26 miles) beyond the turn-off, as the road swings around a mountain spur overlooking the valley of the Río Henares, the ruined castle of JADRAQUE comes into view on its solitary crag. It was built in the 15th century by the dukes of Osuna. The ninth duke was a friend and patron of Goya who painted him and his family several times. The C-101 continues north past Atienza (worth a pause for its old Plaza Mayor), enters Soria Province and joins the N-111 at Almazán.

2. From Madrid via the N-I Another approach, only slightly longer (240 km/150 miles), is via the N-I, the Burgos highway. After crossing the Sierra de Guadarrama and emerging on to the plains of Segovia Province, take the N-110 (right) to El Burgo de Osma and on to Soria. It is a lovely drive, with the mountains on your right, through several interesting towns.

3. From the north A short distance south of Burgos, the N-234 branches left off the N-I and runs straight, more or less, to Soria.

The N-111 from Logroño (La Rioja) follows the gorge of the Río Iregua and is another good route. In the distance on the left, before you plunge into the gorge, is a lofty crag surmounted by a castle topped by a Cross of Santiago. That is Clavijo below which, in the mid-9th century, took place the battle in which Santiago (St James) is first alleged to have appeared on his white horse to spur on the Christians to victory over the Moors.

History

The western portions of the present province were retaken from the Moors and repopulated in the 11th century following the capture of Toledo in 1085 by Alfonso VI of León and Castilla. The town of Soria fell to Alfonso I the Battler of Aragón, Alfonso VI's son-in-law, in 1119, following his capture of Zaragoza. These Aragonese conquests eliminated the main Muslim salient north of the Tajo (Tagus) River.

Alfonso repopulated Soria with settlers from Castilla and Aragón. Pockets of Muslims remained in Soria, Almazán, Calatañazor and Medinaceli. These were the *Mudéjares* ('those who stayed behind') who were permitted to continue their pursuits as artisans, tradesmen and farmers. In addition, from his 1125–26 campaign to Valencia and

Andalucía, Alfonso brought back thousands of *Mozárabes*, Christians who had lived for centuries under Muslim rule, to help repopulate the Sorian lands. It was thus a rich mix of settlers who established themselves in small villages and towns in the Duero bend.

Before visiting the town of Soria, however, let us stop at Medinaceli and then continue towards Zaragoza to visit a very important site, the monastery of Huerta, on the border with Aragón.

Southeastern Soria Province

Medinaceli The old town of Medinaceli, 154 km (96 miles) from Madrid, sits high on a bluff overlooking the valley of the Río Jalón. Its Roman past is attested to by the triple-gated Roman archway, the only one in the peninsula.

After the Arab conquest, Medinaceli became a powerful Muslim fortress, from 946 the headquarters of the northern command of the caliphs of Córdoba. Medinaceli and the nearby towns of Atienza and Sigüenza (Guadalajara Province) guarded the main Muslim lines of communication from Toledo to Zaragoza and the eastern meseta via the Henares and Jalón river valleys. Count Fernán González of Castilla made some progress in reconquering the area, but Christian plans were severely set back by Almanzor's victory over the Christian allies below the walls of Medinaceli in 995. Count García Fernández of Castilla was taken prisoner and died in captivity either at Medinaceli or Córdoba. Almanzor himself died here in 1002, much to the relief of the Christians.

The three towns were still Muslim strongholds at the end of the 11th century, but the end was nigh. Alfonso VI took Medinaceli in 1104, twenty years after he had captured Toledo. Atienza and Sigüenza held out until 1124 when they were taken by the forces of Queen Urraca.

Medinaceli is worth visiting for its old stone houses which have been beautifully restored, almost too much so. The ruins of an ancient castle can be visited in a pleasant stroll across fields. On the Plaza Mayor stands the palace of the powerful de la Cerda family, descendants of the eldest son of Alfonso X el Sabio and for many years claimants to the throne of Castilla. They were created counts of Medinaceli in 1368 and dukes (by Isabella) in 1479. The town is a riot of roses in June.

Santa María de Huerta The exceptionally fine Cistercian monastery of Sta María de Huerta stands just south of the N-II, almost on the border of Zaragoza Province. Alfonso VII founded the original house near Almazán in 1144; the monks moved to the present site in 1162. The church was begun in 1179; the main buildings were completed by 1184. Romanesque though it still is, Cistercian architecture foreshadowed the Gothic style and at Huerta pointed arches and sexpartite vaulting appear throughout.

Standing on the border between Castilla and Aragón, the canny abbots managed to secure privileges and lands from both crowns. Monks have inhabited Huerta continuously except for the period 1835–1930. Damaged during the years of abandonment after the dissolution of the monasteries in 1835–36 and the wars of the 19th and 20th centuries, it has been remarkably well restored and is perhaps the most complete example of a Cistercian monastery in Spain. The arrangement whereby the cloister and monastic buildings lie to the north of the church rather than to the south is unusual.

The complex dates from different periods. One enters first the cloister added in the 17th century, a rather austere structure. Parallel to its north passage is the refectory of the lay brothers whom the Cistercians recruited to work their lands and man the workshops, a 12th-century building and thus one of the earliest parts of the complex. The entrance to the refectory is through the monumental 13th-century kitchen, with an enormous canopied fireplace in the centre. The room is pure Romanesque, with five stout pillars marching down the center to divide it into two aisles and to support the strongly vaulted ceiling.

East of the kitchen is the original cloister. The lower storey dates from the 13th century and shows distinct signs of Gothic, while the Plateresque upper storey was added in the 16th century. Typically Renaissance medallions depict heads of royalty, monks and ordinary folks. The combination of the two styles works rather well.

A fine portal off the north aisle of the cloister gives entrance to the 13th-century refectory of the choir brothers (so called to distinguish them from the lay brothers), a marvellous long room, with strong Gothic elements, terminating in a wall with four round-headed windows below and two twinned above, each surmounted by a little rose window. The rose window at the opposite (entrance) end is partly blocked by the upper storey of the Plateresque cloister. Tall niches separated by slender columns break up the surface of the wall.

At the far end, on the right, stairs in the thickness of the wall lead to the pulpit from which appropriate texts were read during meals. A handy slide for passing food connects the kitchen and the refectory.

The 17th-century stairway to the right of the monks' refectory leads to the upper floor where the monks' quarters are located, along with the 18th-century sacristy. From the south side of the upper loggia you enter the raised tribune at the west end of the church, with carved walnut choir stalls and the organ, from which you can look down into the church proper. As in all Cistercian churches, stairs for the choir brothers lead down into the church from their quarters. The choir brothers and the lay brothers were kept rigidly apart.

The church, begun in 1179, is in the typically austere Cistercian style. Recent restoration has stripped it of later accretions, though an enormous 18th-century *retablo* remains in the *capilla mayor*. Note the arrangement of the apse. The church is in the shape of a Latin cross with five chapels opening off the crossing: the polygonal capilla mayor flanked by two rectangular chapels off each of the transept arms. This arrangement differs, as you will see, from that at the Cistercian monastery of Moreruela near Zamora which has an ambulatory with seven semicircular radiating chapels.

Monteagudo de las Vicarias A little further east on the N-II, crossing a corner of Zaragoza Province, the road to the left leads north to this picturesque small town. En route are the photogenic ruins of the castle of RAYA. Monteagudo was one of the lordships bestowed by the victorious Enrique II de Trastámara on the French mercenary Bertrand du Guesclin after Enrique had slain his half-brother Pedro el Cruel in 1369. The present castle with mighty towers along its curtain wall dates from the 15th century. The town has good walls, a fine gate, a church and great views.

Soria

'Soria fría, Soria pura, cabeza de Extremadura' ('Soria the cold, the pure, head of Extremadura') sang the poet Antonio Machado (1875–1939) who lived there early in this century. At 1,050 m (3,445 feet), Soria is the second highest provincial capital in Spain (after Ávila),

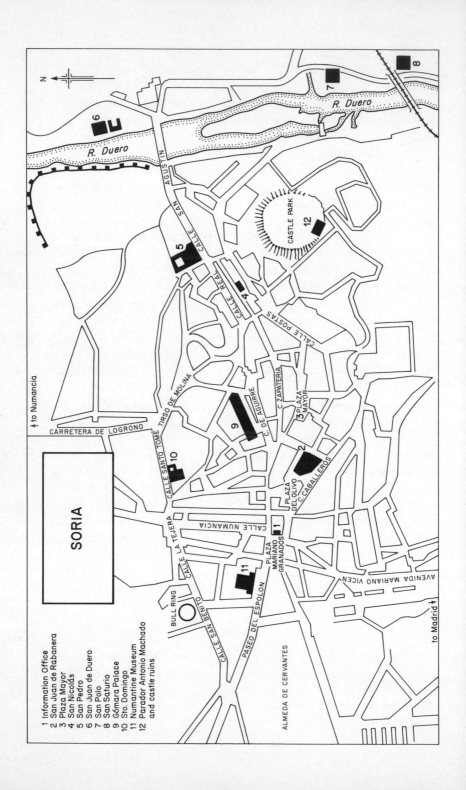

SORIA

1 Information Office
2 San Juan de Rabanera
3 Plaza Mayor
4 San Nicolás
5 San Pedro
6 San Juan de Duero
7 San Polo
8 San Saturio
9 Gómara Palace
10 Sto. Domingo
11 Numantine Museum
12 Parador Antonio Machado
  and castle ruins

N

R. Duero

R. Duero

↑ to Numancia

CARRETERA DE LOGRONO

CASTLE PARK

CALLE SAN AGUSTIN

CALLE REAL

CALLE POSTAS

CALLE SANTO TOMÉ

TIRSO DE MOLINA

C. DE AGUIRRE

C. ZAPATERIA

PLAZA
MAYOR

PLAZA
DEL OLIVO

C. CABALLEROS

CALLE NUMANCIA

PLAZA
MARIANO
GRANADOS

BULL RING

CALLE LA TEJERA

CALLE SAN BENITO

PASEO DEL ESPOLON

ALMEDA DE CERVANTES

AVENIDA MARIANO VICEN

↓ to Madrid

1
2
3
4
5
6
7
8
9
10
11
12

which explains the cold. The purity comes from its blue skies, the sparkling quality of its clean mountain air and the unblemished lineage of its ancient families. It was the 'cabeza' or head of Extremadura because of its exposed position on the eastern flanks of Castilla, confronting the Moors of old.

History The settlers brought in by Alfonso I of Aragón after his conquest of the town in 1119 grouped themselves in *barrios* (neighbourhoods) around their own parochial churches or, in the case of the Mudéjars, their mosques in the *morería* (Moorish) quarter.

Soria had one of the most important Jewish communities in Castilla, dating from at least the 12th century. The *judería* lay next to the castle (where the parador now stands) and extended down the hill towards town, thus emphasizing, as in so many Castilian towns, the close ties between the Jewish community and the king under whose protection they lived and by whom they were regularly squeezed when a little ready cash was needed.

Soria commanded the passage of the Duero between Navarra and Castilla. Alfonso thus granted it extensive lands and it became a stronghold against both the Muslims to the south and the designs of the neighbouring Christian states of Navarra and Aragón. Alfonso's brother and successor ceded Soria to Alfonso VII of Castilla in 1136.

The town did not attract any special attention until 1163. Alfonso VIII of Castilla (1158–1214) had succeeded to the throne at the age of three, not a good age to be a king in 12th-century Spain. His uncle Fernando II of León (1157–1188) initially showed remarkable restraint and actually protected the boy and his rights, but intrigues swirled and early in 1163 Fernando tried to seize the young king who was at the time in Soria. Forewarned, a local noble, Pedro Núñez de Fuente Armegil, spirited Alfonso to safety in San Esteban de Gormaz, whence he was taken to Ávila. The king remained ever grateful to Soria, granting it extensive privileges and building churches, some of which remain to this day.

Soria stood at the head of the most easterly of the *cañadas* or routes over which flocks of sheep moved from summer pastures in the mountains to winter pastures in the south. Wool was thus an important factor in Soria's prosperity. As early as the 12th century, the weavers of Soria had formed a guild to defend their economic interests.

Twelve noble families came eventually to control Soria; their *escudos* (escutcheons), can be seen all over town.

In the civil war between Pedro I the Cruel (1350–69) and his bastard half-brother Enrique de Trastámara, the future Enrique II (1369–79), Soria was captured by Enrique's ally, the French knight Bertrand du Guesclin. A lull in the Hundred Years' War between England and France had unleashed thousands of mercenaries on the French countryside and when Enrique appealed to Charles V of France for help against Pedro, the king eagerly responded (1367) by sending du Guesclin with as many mercenaries as he could round up. Enrique rewarded him with the lordships of Soria and Almazán.

When peace was restored, after Enrique himself slew Pedro in du Guesclin's tent, the French captain resided in Soria as lord of a considerable *señorío*. When Charles V named him Constable of France in 1370, he sold his señoríos back to Enrique II and went home.

In the general stagnation that afflicted Castilla from the 16th century, the population of Soria shrank from 5,000 to 3,000. In 1808, during the Peninsular War, it was sacked by Marshal Ney. In 1831, the English traveller Richard Ford found Soria, population about 5,000, 'a dull place, inhabited by agriculturalists'. He noted also the fertile pasture lands around Soria on which grazed 'hungry flocks, which produce much and excellent wool'.[1]

The population had recovered to some 7,000 by 1900 and by 1920 it stood at 8,000. Along with the rest of Castilla (and indeed Spain), Soria profited from the boom that began in the 1950s. Its population is now around 35,500. This has had a predictable effect on the urban fabric and there has been some disastrous modern construction. Sad to say, Soria is not the only town in Spain that has destroyed parts of its architectural heritage in recent years.

A Tour of the Town Soria's main sights can easily be covered on foot. From the Tourist Information Office at the end of the Alameda de Cervantes, a pleasant park between the old and new towns, there are two possible routes. One is the Calle de Collado on the left, an attractive and lively old street with señorial houses emblazoned with escutcheons, that leads down to the Plaza Mayor. Or, you can take Calle de Ramón y Cajal on the right to an irregular plaza with the *Diputación* (provincial seat) on the right and, ahead, the church of San Juan de Rabanera of about 1200.

Medinaceli (Soria) This Roman triple arch of the 2nd or 3rd century AD is the only one of its kind in Spain and is all that remains of Roman Ocilis, the future Muslim fortress town of Medinaceli. Its precise purpose is unclear. Positioned at the very edge of a steep scarp, its use as a triumphal entrance would have been rather awkward.

Sta María de Huerta (Soria) Sta María de Huerta is one of the most complete Cistercian monasteries in Spain. Construction began in 1179 and continued for centuries. The upper storey of the Claustro de los Caballeros (shown here) was superimposed on the original 13th-century cloister in the 16th century.

Castle of Raya (Soria) The ruins of the castle of Raya stand between Sta María de Huerta and the fortress town of Monteagudo de las Vicarias on the borders of Castile and Aragon. It was one of several such strong points guarding the frontier between the two kingdoms.

Hinojosa (Soria) This is a typical agricultural village of the Upper Duero, one of many founded during and after the 11th century as the Christian reconquest gained pace. Its 15th-century castle was held by an opponent of Isabella in her struggle for the Castilian throne. When the prize was finally hers, she wasted no time in seizing the castle.

← **Calatañazor (Soria)** The arcaded main street of this ancient town is lined with half-timbered houses. The street shown here appears in Orson Welles's *Chimes at Midnight*, surely one of the most exciting events for centuries in Calatañazor's history.

→ **Calatañazor (Soria)** The shattered remains of the town's castle look out over the Valle de Sangre, where, legend has it, the terrible Almanzor, scourge of the Christians for a quarter of a century, finally met defeat in 1002. The battle is almost certainly fictitious, but the Muslim warrior did die later the same year in Medinaceli.

↓ **Nafria la Llana (Soria)** Agricultural villages of the Duero bend, such as this, were founded during the Christian repopulation of the region from the 11th century on. Like most, it has a Romanesque church, this one from the 12th century.

Andaluz (Soria) Andaluz was settled by Mozarabs, Christian refugees from al-Andalus, Muslim Spain, early in the 11th century. Its principal church, San Miguel Arcángel, dates from the 12th century. The typically Segovian gallery or portico on the south side originally ran around the east and west ends of the church, but much of it was obliterated by later construction, including the tower.

Almazán (Soria) The church of San Miguel, in this ancient Muslim fortress town of Almazán situated where the Duero River turns west and starts its long run to the Atlantic, was built before 1200. It is Almazán's most important monument. Its beautifully constructed apse and octagonal tower make a particularly attractive ensemble. The cupola of San Miguel covers a dome the ribs of which form an eight-pointed star exactly like those in the Great Mosque of Córdoba, suggesting that the church was built by Christian refugees from the Muslim south.

SAN JUAN DE RABANERA Walk around to the east end of San Juan to see the fine *cabecera*. Fluted pilasters rise the height of the building dividing the drum of the apse into four panels. A horizontal course about one-third of the way up ties them together. This is surmounted by two decorated windows in the two central panels and by even more beautifully embellished pairs of blind windows in the two flanking panels. The rosettes and other carved details are neat and crisp.

The main (west) portal was brought in 1908 from ruined San Nicolás (13th century) further down the hill towards the Duero. The handsome doorway has four archivolts resting on columns; the capitals are carved with scenes from the New Testament (left) and the miracles of San Nicolás (right). In the tympanum appears San Nicolás flanked by priests.

This is Saint Nicholas of Myra, in southwestern Turkey, whose relics were stolen in 1087 by men from Bari in southern Italy. He gradually metamorphosed into Santa Claus.

The elegant south portal is now sealed. You enter the church through the west portal. The single nave interior is in the shape of a Latin cross, rather rare in these parts. Its main interest is the dome over the crossing, a hemisphere of Byzantine inspiration erected on an octagon formed by building four graceful masonry fans across the corner angles of the square crossing. The transverse arches of the nave rest on attached columns with good capitals.

THE PLAZA MAYOR Down the hill behind San Juan is the Plaza Mayor with a nice lion-guarded fountain, the *ayuntamiento* (town hall), other public buildings and several good restaurants. Soria celebrates the festival of its patron saint on 24 June. Everyone in town, young and old, turns out to party in the Plaza Mayor. The *verbena*, as such parties are called, starts late, towards midnight. They are great fun.

SAN NICOLÁS Behind the Plaza Mayor, the Calle Real drops down towards the river, passing the ruins of 13th-century San Nicolás from which came the portal at San Juan de Rabanera. By the 19th century the church was derelict and much of it was taken down, saving only the apse with slender columns and graceful blind arcading, reminiscent of San Juan de Rabanera.

SAN PEDRO The Calle Real eventually joins the Calle del Obispo

Agustín. On the left is the Concatedral de San Pedro. The original Romanesque church was replaced in 1152 by a larger structure that collapsed in 1520. The present Renaissance church dates from 1520–73. The spacious interior has massive columns, ribbed vaults and splendid retablos. Over the rather ornate south portal is San Pedro himself.

Of the original Romanesque church, only three sides of the cloister remain. The entrance to the cloister is to the left of the main building, down a short alley. It is a lovely place, with rounded arches supported by pairs of columns resting on a low wall. Best preserved is the north gallery. The charm is heightened by pots of bright geraniums between each pair of columns.

SAN JUAN DE DUERO At the foot of the hill beyond San Pedro a stone bridge crosses the Duero and a short distance to the left, resting quietly among the trees at the river's edge, is San Juan de Duero. Its origins are obscure. It seems likely that it was built in the 12th century, soon after the reconquest of Soria by Alfonso I of Aragón, and subsequently came into the possession of the Order of the Hospital of Saint John of Jerusalem, more commonly known as the Hospitallers, founded in the Holy Land during the first Crusade.

Of the ancient monastic complex, only the church and the roofless 13th-century cloister remain. The cloister is unique in Spain. Four different styles of arcading are represented and the styles change not at the corners but in the middle of each side. The northwest angle has regular rounded Romanesque arches supported by double columns resting on a low wall. On the northeast, the Gothic pointed arches are supported by clusters of four columns. The southeast angle has the most unusual pattern of all: interlocked pointed arches, slightly bulging, resting on solid square fluted piers. The arches of the southwest angle are also slightly pointed and interlocked, supported by double columns. The capitals contain a wealth of carving.

Interlocking arcades appear in caliphate architecture both free-standing (as, for example, in the Great Mosque of Córdoba and the Aljafería in Zaragoza) and, more often, as blind arcading. Romanesque builders adopted the latter and used it frequently, attesting once again to the influence Islamic Spain had on the arts of northern Spain.

The chief interest of the church lies in the baldachins on either side of the apse, each sheltering an altar. They are square structures, each side a rounded arch resting on quadruple column clusters. The baldachin on the right has a conical roof; that on the left, a dome.

It is supposed that they were connected with rites practised by the Hospitallers in the East; they are certainly oriental in flavour. The capitals are marvellous. Among the scenes depicted are (under the cone) the Judgment of Solomon (with Solomon tugging pensively on his beard), the Slaughter of the Innocents, the Annunciation, the Nativity and the Adoration of the Magi; and (under the dome) the Beheading of John the Baptist by two chaps in full-length chain mail, griffins, centaurs and dragons.

Note that the horseshoe triumphal arch before the sanctuary is slightly pointed, an odd touch. The vault and second arch behind it follow suit.

Tucked in among the trees at the river's edge, San Juan de Duero must have been a pleasant retreat for its community. The monastery had been abandoned by the end of the 18th century and was not declared a national monument worthy of preservation till 1882.

SAN SATURIO   Downstream from San Juan and on the same side of the river, a road through an arch leads to the hermitage of San Saturio. Just inside the arch, to the right, is the 13th-century Templar church of SAN POLO which passed to the Hospitallers after the suppression of the Templars in 1312. It is on private property.

Saturio was a noble Goth who exchanged his possessions for a life of contemplation and retired to the cave grotto over which his shrine was later built. Stairs lead up to an 18th-century sanctuary. You may not find it very interesting, but it offers a fine view of the Duero and the walk along the gently flowing river is soothing.

PALACIO DE GÓMARA   Returning across the bridge and climbing the hill to the centre of town, we find the 16th-century Palacio de los Condes de Gómara with a marvelous façade of 1592. The central portal is surmounted by a sumptuous escutcheon supported by two *maceros* (mace bearers). The building houses government offices but, if the portal is open, go in. The courtyard is most impressive.

SANTO DOMINGO   The next major sight in Soria is the church of Santo Domingo, on the north side of the city. Several streets from the centre of town climb the hill and converge on the square in front of the church.

The principal (west) façade is one of the finest Romanesque creations in the country. The central portal is the main attraction, but the whole ensemble is a triumph: two rows of blind arcades surmounted by a handsome rose window. Most of what one sees was undertaken on the orders of Alfonso VIII (1158–1214) who remodelled an earlier church in gratitude to Soria for protecting him against the machinations of his uncle Fernando II of León.

Alfonso and his queen, Eleanor Plantagenet, daughter of Henry II of England, are represented by statues flanking the top of the arched portal. The arrangement of the façade below the central gable, two storeys with blind arcading, echoes the influence of Poitiers in west central France. Eleanor's mother was Eleanor of Aquitaine whose lands included Poitiers, so such influence is not surprising.

The four deeply recessed archivolts of the portal are abuzz with activity. In the tympanum appears the God the Father, seated, with Christ on his lap, flanked by four angels. On the right stands the Virgin and on the left, St Joseph (perhaps). The innermost archivolt depicts the twenty-four Elders of the Apocalypse with their various musical instruments. The second is given over to the Slaughter of the Innocents, a favourite topic of the age; it appears frequently but seldom in such loving detail as here. The third contains scenes from the infancy of Christ: the Annunciation, the Dream of St Joseph, the Adoration of the Shepherds and of the Magi, the Flight into Egypt, and so on. The three men with crowns tucked into bed are the Three Kings to whom the angel appeared in a dream directing them to avoid Herod and go home by another route. On the outer band are scenes from the Passion of Christ and the Resurrection. A decorative band of floral design surrounds the whole. Note also the capitals of the columns of the portal and of the lower blind arcade.

The twenty-four Elders of the Apocalypse are noted in the Book of the Revelation of St John the Divine, or the Apocalypse, the final book of the New Testament, which was as important in early medieval Spain as the four Gospels since it was taken to predict the triumph of Christianity over the forces of evil (a.k.a. Muslims). The Elders occupy a prominent place on the main portals of many churches in Spain, usually lined up along one of the archivolts, on either side of Christ, sometimes looking straight ahead, often chatting with each other. Revelation says they had harps, but carving twenty-four harps was presumably a rather boring task so Romanesque sculptors used their fertile imaginations and gave them a multitude of instruments.

What with one thing and another, construction of the main body of the church went on into the 16th century. The nave arches and vaults are pointed in good Gothic style; massive transverse ribs support the nave vault. The capilla mayor is 16th century, with a baroque retablo. The façade is the glory of the church, so do not feel badly if the door is locked.

The Upper Duero

The source of the Río Duero lies in the Sierra de Urbión, part of the mountain system separating Soria from the valley of the Río Ebro, La Rioja and the ancient kingdoms of Navarra and Aragón. The mountains run up to over 2,000 m (6,500 feet).

The eastward loop of the Duero embraces many agricultural villages of ancient foundation with early Romanesque churches. Their number reflects a grander era and a greater population than now exists. The fields continue to produce the grain that has sustained the population for centuries, but many villages are depopulated, some almost abandoned. Their churches, testimony to the great faith that sustained their creators and congregations in the years of testing, have been rescued from total decay only in this century. One can only marvel at what has been done in Spain to restore or at least to stabilize these precious relics.

Such was the building boom beginning in the 12th century that local craftsmen, often monastery trained, were soon in short supply. There is ample evidence that stone masons and sculptors travelled from place to place. Sorian Romanesque is distinguished by its strong Mudéjar flavour, very apparent in the sculptured capitals of rural churches.

Numancia Taking the N-111 (towards Logroño) north of Soria, the first stop is the hilltop site of this town of the Celtiberian Arevaci whose doomed resistance to Roman might has been commemorated in the Spanish adjective *numantino* which refers to a basically hopeless struggle, however heroic, against overwhelming odds.

The brutality of Roman rule during the 2nd century BC occasioned repeated revolts among the native inhabitants. The last of three Celtiberian Wars broke out in 153 BC and the Romans did not do well. The capitulation of C. Hostilius Mancinus, the Roman commander, with some 20,000 men to no more than 8,000 Numantinos has been characterized as 'perhaps the bitterest disgrace in the whole of Roman military history'.[2] The Senate decided this would not stand and dispatched Publius Cornelius Scipio Aemilianus Africanus, destroyer of Carthage in 146 BC, to the scene. Numancia was invested and besieged for a year before falling in 133 BC. The end was unpleasant.

There is not much to see on the windswept ridge save some tumbled walls and, in season, masses of wild flowers, but lovers of lost causes will find it evocative. Traces of Scipio's camps can still be found on the ridges around Numancia.

Garray The village stands just below the ridge of Numancia where the Duero turns abruptly west. Just over the bridge and up the hill to the right is the ERMITA (HERMITAGE) DE LOS SANTOS MÁRTIRES. The martyrs in question were an Italian quartet whose fame reached Garray early in the 13th century when the church was built, around 1230. It was about the last Romanesque church built in the region. Of the original fabric only the cabecera and the south portal remain. These two elements often survive because they were constructed of stouter materials than the body of the church.

The south portal and the corbels above it and around the exterior of the apse are notable. The tympanum bears a large and wonderfully crisp rosette, a burst of leaves, surrounded by others slightly smaller and different in design. A band of blind interlocking arches, reminiscent of San Juan de Duero, surrounds the tympanum. Other detailing includes human and feline heads. Assorted creatures occupy the capitals of the columns flanking the three archivolts of the portal, carved with geometric designs. Storks have nested in the little bell tower and a fine view of the Duero valley spreads out before you.

Towards the Source of the Duero Returning to Soria, take the N-234 west, turning north at Toledillo. The road runs through fields of grain, green in the spring, yellowing as the summer sun grows more intense. The huge wedge-shaped Pico Frentes to the west dominates the southern flank of the Duero valley and to the north mountains loom in the distance.

Across the Duero is Hinojosa with a photogenic 15th-century castle. Its lord backed the wrong contender for the succession to Enrique IV (d. 1474) and the castle was confiscated by Isabella when the throne was finally hers. The road passes through El Royo, an attractive town of stone houses, and skirts the northern end of the huge Pantano de la Cuerda del Pozo (Reservoir of the Well Rope) with more serious mountains to the north.

This open country is grim in the winter. Soria is one of the coldest provinces in Spain. It is largely pastoral land, deserted when the flocks move south for the winter months. An old pastoral song sighs: 'Triste y oscura queda la sierra; ya se van los pastores a la Extremadura' ('Sad and dark lies the sierra; already the shepherds have gone to Extremadura').

Summer and winter resorts have now sprung up to cater to the Spanish love of the outdoors. Vinuesa is a pleasant resort and jumping-off place for the mountains to the north and west. Some 20 km north, following a road that winds among pine forests, rushing streams, campsites and hikers, is the LAGUNA NEGRA, a lovely lake, green rather than black, with steep cliffs on three sides and set about with pine forests of a peculiarly Japanese look.

Leaving Vinuesa, the road follows a wooded valley with the little Duero on the left. Molinos de Duero is a prosperous-looking town with a number of señorial mansions emblazoned with escutcheons and a 16th-century church topped by an enormous storks' nest. Salduero is a charming village with a line of stepping stones across the stream that is the Duero here. Beyond Duruelo de la Sierra a serious effort is required to hike along the slender thread of the Duero up into the Sierra de Urbión. Lumbering is important in these parts and the little towns are businesslike and prosperous.

The Soria–Almazán–Burgo de Osma Triangle

The triangle formed by the N-122 (Soria–Burgo), the N-111 (Soria–Almazán) and the C-116 (Almazán–Burgo) has much to offer the diligent explorer.

Calatañazor From Molinos de Duero, a local road runs south, crossing the N-234, to the N-122 which runs west and south from Soria. Just to the west stands Calatañazor, a wonderful village. The name derives from the Arabic Qal'at al-Nusur, Castle of the Vultures, which still soar in these parts, but the history of the town goes back at least to Roman times. The approach is dramatic: a narrow road peels off the N-122, rounds a cliff, and ahead is the village on a rocky spur crowned by a ruined castle and girt with crumbling walls. At the foot of the crag is the ERMITA DE LA SOLEDAD with fine carved corbels beneath the eaves of the apse. Note the bearded man with angrily clenched teeth.

You can drive up into the village and all the way to the castle, but it is more interesting to walk from La Soledad. The road winds up below the steep cliffs and through a gate, along a street of crumbling houses with wooden arcades, past the 16th-century SANTA MARÍA with its Romanesque west portal and a small museum, and finally to the shattered ruins of the castle.

Legend has it that in the broad valley below, in 1002, took place the battle in which the dread Almanzor, strongman of the decaying Umayyad Caliphate of Córdoba and the scourge of Christian Spain, was at last defeated, after which he retreated south to Medinaceli to die. The battle is almost certainly fictitious, but the valley is still known as the Valle de la Sangre, the Valley of Blood.

The medieval air of Calatañazor persists to this day, despite the electric lines and lights, but even they can be dealt with. The most excitement in centuries, no doubt, came in 1966 when Orson Welles arrived to film *Chimes at Midnight.* He was looking for a medieval setting for his film, based on Shakespeare's character Falstaff, and all he had to do was take down the electric poles. How the great man found Calatañazor, I can only guess; Fernando Rey had a part in the film, which may have had something to do with it.

Nafria de Llana Just east of Calatañazor, the first road right (south) off the N-122 leads to this rather dispirited little village which, however, boasts a church from the first half of the 12th century described by Sr Enríquez de Salamanca as 'one of the most elegant examples of the rural Romanesque of Soria'.[3] As usual, the apse, built of carefully hewn and dressed blocks of stone, has survived better than the main body of the church. It is outstanding. Stout rounded shafts crowned with good capitals rise the height of the apse, dividing it into three panels, each of which contains a window with rounded arches resting on colonnettes with well-carved capitals. From the corbels under the eaves peer a rogues' gallery of faces. People and actions of the mundane world were often depicted on corbels, occasionally very graphically.

Nafria de Llana is but one of a number of picturesque villages in the area whose semi-deserted state attests to the flight of the rural population to less arduous and more rewarding environments. Their fine churches bespeak a grander history than is now apparent. Try casting the mind back to the 12th century when settlers were swarming to a still perilous frontier to clear the land, build their houses and raise their parish churches, meanwhile protected by those men in chain mail depicted on so many church capitals.

Osona At Fuentepinilla, you have two choices. The first, if you are heading back to Soria, is to turn northeast to Osona. Its church stands at the top of a lane leading past simple dwellings decked out with bright flower gardens. The mid-12th-century portal is the main attraction. The block containing the doorway stands forwards from the mass of the building, thus emphasizing the four rounded archivolts and the line of nine heads on the corbels. The decorative detail of stars, leaves and cords on the archivolts, especially the raised star-like projections on the outer archivolt, is striking. The human and animal heads under a neatly carved band beneath the eaves are well preserved. On the right, above the arch, is a curious relief of a bishop(?) in a sarcophagus.

Los Llamosos Further along, 3 km past Quintana Redondo, is Los Llamosos with reportedly the oldest church in the province (first quarter of the 12th century) after those of San Esteban de Gormaz. NUESTRA SEÑORA DE LA ASUNCIÓN has Mozarab features including a horseshoe portal with lightly decorated archivolts. A deep porch shades the portal, however, and a locked gate impedes access. We asked an elderly lady sewing outside her house who had the key. The priest, she said. When does the priest come? 'Viene cuando quiere' ('He comes when he pleases'). The church reportedly has a fine 14th-century *artesonado* ceiling.

Most of these village churches do not have their own priest

(*párroco*). One priest makes the rounds of a number of villages. Usually, however, someone in the village holds the key and he or she is pleased to show visitors around. If an absent priest has the key, you can get in only when there is a *culto* (service): Saturday evenings or Sunday mornings. You can often visit a church just before or just after a mass without disturbing anyone, but be quick. The priests or sacristans are wont to slam the door and lock it right after the service and hurry on their way.

Andaluz Returning to Fuentepinilla, the road south leads to a particularly interesting church in the village of Andaluz, a short distance north of the Duero. As its name implies, it was settled by Mozarab settlers from al-Andalus early in the 11th century. The original of its *fuero* (charter) of 1089 is preserved in the cathedral of El Burgo de Osma.

The more scenic approach, however, is from the south, from the Almazán–Burgo de Osma road (C-116). Crossing the Duero via a modern bridge, with an ancient precursor just downstream, Andaluz appears ahead on high ground, surrounded by its fields. Clearly visible, rising above the village, is the church of SAN MIGUEL ARC-ÁNGEL with an arcaded gallery on the south side. This is the first example on our itinerary of the galleried churches so characteristic of Segovia Province and adjacent areas. Of the original church, only the gallery, part of the south wall with portal and a few other fragments remain.

The gallery has eight arches and an entry on its south side and two arches at the west end. It dates from the middle of the 12th century and originally extended around the east and west ends of the church. Subsequent modifications left only two arches of the west gallery and obliterated the east gallery entirely. The columns are short and squat, the capitals and bases massive, with generous wall space above and below. The capitals are varied, with mainly floral motifs. There is a nice touch in the gallery east of the entry arch where three single columns alternate with two quadruple, perhaps reflecting the rhythm of the main portal. On the capital of the single column at the west end is a nervous-looking fellow with a big head between two four-footed creatures.

The portal, inside the gallery, is a noble one, with five nicely rounded archivolts, three plain, separated by bands of chequerboard

design, and two resting on columns with a rounded moulding. Above
the portal and to the left is an inscription, topped by a feline of
some sort, that gives the date of the church's completion as ERA
1152 or AD 1114.

Almazán This town, on the N-111 south from Soria, takes its
name from an Arabic word meaning fortified. It occupies a commanding site on a bluff on the south bank of the Duero where the
river turns sharply west to commence its run to the Atlantic. A
pleasant park has been laid out along the north side of the river,
affording a good view of the church of San Miguel, the walls and the
Palacio de Altamira. Crossing the river, look for the street up to the
right that passes through the Puerta de la Villa and into the Plaza
Mayor. There are often places to park below the gate. Everything in
town can be reached in an easy walk.

This ancient fortified frontier town was formerly an important
Muslim strongpoint, captured, but not for long, by Alfonso VI in
1097, and finally in 1128, nine years after he took Soria, by Alfonso
the Battler of Aragón who ordered it to be repopulated. An extensive
Mudéjar community remained. After passing with Soria to the crown
of Castilla, Almazán played an important role in the war between
the faiths. It occupied a strategic site and was always, and still is, an
important communications hub. It is now a bustling and prosperous
town of some 6,000 inhabitants.

Almazán's principal sight is the church of SAN MIGUEL that
dominates the Plaza Mayor. If the church is not open, the key (an
enormous one) is at the office of the Policía Municipal, under the
arcade to the right.

San Miguel dates from before 1200, but only the apse and first
two bays of the nave are original. Until the restoration work of a
few years ago, the exterior was cluttered with structures that had
been tacked on, including the 18th-century portico that still shelters
the south entry portal and does not seem to fit very well.

One can now admire San Miguel from several angles. From the
plaza and from the slope below the church are particularly good views
of the lovely cabecera and, rising behind it, the octagonal brick cupola
on its stone drum. On the left is a round staircase tower. The cornice
of tri-lobed arches around the apse and that of round-headed arches
around the drum of the cupola make for a particularly nice effect.

Inside, the cupola is especially notable. Eight ribs, grouped in four parallel pairs, cross to make an eight-pointed star with an octagonal space in the centre, above which rises the lantern. Light shines in through eight round windows between the ribs; an unusual feature. The star arrangement is identical to the cupolas adjacent to the *mihrab* (prayer niche) in the Great Mosque of Córdoba. This feature, proof positive of the presence of artisans from al-Andalus, appears in a few other churches in Castilla; this is a particularly fine example. We will see another in the Talavera chapel off the cloister of the Old Cathedral of Salamanca.

The square chancel and the apse are skewed slightly to the right of the main axis, a peculiarity which has generated some debate. The church of San Andrés in Toledo is similarly arranged and its priest advanced the theory that it reflects the portrayal of Christ on the Cross with his head lolling to the right.

To the left of the chancel, in the apse at the end of the north aisle, is a sarcophagus with a frontal depicting the murder of Thomas Becket, Archbishop of Canterbury, by several fully armoured knights, one of whom has run the unfortunate prelate through with a huge broadsword. Thomas met his end in 1170 and was canonized in 1172; his cult spread swiftly in Spain.

Across the square, to the right as you exit San Miguel, stands a former palace of the Mendoza family, now the PALACIO DE ALTAMIRA. Its loggia overlooks the river valley. Straight across the square is a bar with reasonably good tapas where the crowd gathers on Sunday morning after mass before dispersing to their homes.

Almazán has other churches and a stroll to the far end of town will take you to the (restored) Puerta del Mercado where a good stretch of wall remains. Beyond the gate, a narrow lane disappears into the open country, much as it must have done in the 12th century.

Rello Heading south, take the rural road 101 that forks right after the petrol station at the southern side of Almazán as far as Barahona. Barahona was the headquarters of the caliphal commander Ghalib who marched from here in 975 to rout the besieging Christians at Gormaz.

At Barahona, a small road to the right leads to Rello. The crumbling village with its crumbling castle sits on a spur formed by a bend in a tributary of the Duero. The approach is dramatic: the road runs through a green and pleasant valley and suddenly Rello looms grim and stark high above you. The road clambers up to the main wall, thrown across the spur from side to side. It is pierced by two gates, one of which is angled in proper military fashion and surmounted by a fierce if eroded eagle.

There seems to be no firm evidence as to the date of this castle and circuit of walls, or whether it served the Muslims as a strongpoint between the fortresses of Medinaceli and Gormaz or rose in response to the interminable wars between Christian kings and nobles in later years. Portions of the fortifications, including the tower, date from before the 15th century, restored and modified in the 16th.

Whatever its dates or history, Rello is a most unusual survival. We shall see only one place comparable, the walled village of Urueña in the meseta west of Valladolid. There is little to recommend Rello save the view and the sense of abandonment, but they are worth a stop and a stroll through the ancient streets.

Caltojar Caltojar is next, with early-13th-century SAN MIGUEL, well restored. The apse has a splendid double cornice of arches below the eaves. The south portal has a fine strong diamond-pointed motif on the outer of five archivolts and a double-arched doorway with an interesting central column.

San Baudelio de Berlanga Just beyond Caltojar, a signposted lane to the left leads to the extraordinary ERMITA DE SAN BAU-DELIO, invisible from the road. The building, a solid cubical mass with no external adornment, stands in a remote valley described up to this century as being wooded with oaks, but is now virtually treeless. A visitor early in this century describes it thus: 'The chapel lies away from the road, accessible by a cattle track; the scent of bruised thyme and lavender is strong ... Halfway up [the hillside] it crouches, brown like a rabbit, rough, dark stone-built, the little square apse projecting under its own gabled roof.'[4]

It was built probably towards the beginning of the 12th century (though some authorities posit an 11th-century date) over a hermit's cave dating possibly from Visigothic times. San Baudelio was a 4th-century French martyr. The rude exterior, reflecting the troubled and dangerous times in which the hermitage was built, hides (or hid) an astounding series of frescoes painted not long after the building was completed.

On entering, the first thing that strikes the eye is the massive central column rising to eight ribs that spread out like palm fronds to support the roof. A horseshoe arch opens left into the small sanctuary. On the right is a tribune raised on columns and under the tribune is a low opening that gives access to the hermit's cave. All arches are horseshoe. Access to the tribune now is via an outside stair; from it you can see the small frescoed chapel built into the top of the central column, a curious feature.

Throughout the building are traces of the now vanished frescoes. There were two cycles: the upper was devoted to scenes of the life and death of Christ, the lower to secular scenes such as falconry and the hunt. Of the lower cycle two animals remain in situ, bulls perhaps, head to head. Only shadows and vague outlines bear witness to the remainder.

The hermitage was rediscovered late in the last century and was declared a national monument in 1917. Word of the find spread. In 1921 the agent of one Gabriel Dereppe, a New York lawyer, appeared on the scene and persuaded the owners of the property, residents of the neighbouring village of Casillas, to sell him the contents.

When it became known that the frescoes were being removed there was an outcry, followed by a desperate effort to annul the sale. The matter was carried to the highest court in the land which in 1925 ruled that the owners were quite within their rights to sell and the buyer was quite within his rights to remove his property. And so early in 1926 the work of transferring the frescoes to canvas was resumed and the paintings were transported out of Spain. The files of the Museum of Fine Arts in Boston contain photographs showing them mounted and hanging in Mr Dereppe's living-room in New York.

The frescoes were subsequently acquired by four museums in the United States: the Boston Museum of Art (the Last Supper and the Three Marys at the Sepulchre); the Cloisters of the Metropolitan Museum in New York (the Healing of the Blind Man and the Raising of Lazarus, the Temptations of Christ and a lanky camel); the Cincinnati Art Museum (Mary Magdalen and Jesus in the Garden, San Nicolás and an ibis, all from the sanctuary, and a falconer); and the Indianapolis Museum of Art (the Entry into Jerusalem and the Marriage at Cana). The Cincinnati Museum has mounted its frescoes in a replica of the sanctuary.

Negotiations between the Metropolitan Museum in New York and the government of Spain concluded in 1957 with the exchange of the apse from the ruined church of San Martín de Fuentidueña (see Segovia Province, page 175), now at the Cloisters, for six frescoes from the secular cycle. These, on display in the Prado Museum, include a mounted hunter with three dogs and two rabbits, a second mounted hunter in pursuit of a deer whom he had just struck with an arrow, a warrior with shield and lance and an elephant carrying a castle on its back.

Much scholarly debate has swirled around the paintings and suggested dates range across the 12th century. Given the sharp difference in subject matter between the religious upper register and the secular lower, some experts have seen the hands of at least two different artists at work at different times. Though many contemporary scholars hold that the entire ensemble was the work of one artist or of one 'studio', the Prado suggests that the building may have been a hunting lodge prior to being converted to a church. The two cycles do seem quite distinct in both subject matter and manner of execution.

The frescoes closely resemble a cycle of paintings in the small church of Vera Cruz in Maderuelo (Segovia), also now in the Prado in the same room with the San Baudelio frescoes. Stylistically, the secular paintings have been linked with Sassanid (3rd to 7th century Iranian) antecedents and the religious with Byzantine, and the hermitage has been called the most Muslim church in Spain.

Returning to the main road and turning left, we pass Casillas where live presumably the descendants of those who sold the San Baudelio frescoes to Dereppe's agent. It is a place without charm.

Berlanga de Duero Ahead, on a high ridge, appears the mighty castle of Berlanga de Duero, guarding the confluence of two small rivers and, just beyond, the line of the Duero. Although the present castle dates from the 15th and 16th centuries, Berlanga was a powerful Muslim fortress in its day and, with Gormaz to the west, constituted the principal Muslim strongpoints on the Duero line facing the Christian fortresses at Osma and San Esteban de Gormaz. It changed hands several times, being taken by Fernando I about 1060, by Alfonso VI twenty-five years later, and finally by Alfonso the Battler of Aragón in the early years of the 12th century. Alfonso VI granted it for a time to El Cid.

Here rested one night, according to the epic *Cantar de Mio Cid*, the daughters of El Cid after they had been beaten and abandoned by their wretched husbands, the cowardly infantes de Carrión. They were rescued and taken to San Esteban de Gormaz (see below) from where they made their sad way back to their father.

The existing outer wall with its many towers – the only wall remaining of several which once encircled the castle – dates at least in part from the 13th century. The corner angles of the castle itself are secured by formidable round towers and the mighty *torre de homenaje* (keep) rises from the inner precinct.

Once the castle ceased to play a role on the fighting frontier, Berlanga and its environs were erected into a señorío held by leading families of the realm. These included the Velasco dukes of Frías in whose favour Charles V raised the lordship to a marquisate in 1529. Below the castle stand the imposing ruins of the Renaissance Velasco palace, reduced to its present sad state by the French during the Peninsular War. The young sons of François I of France, exchanged for their father after his capture by Charles V at Pavia (Italy) in 1525, were held in the castle for several months in 1528.

The Puerta de Aguilera with an elegant pointed arch gives access to the town. The street leads past the fine early-16th-century COLEGIATA DE STA MARÍA DEL MERCADO and down to the pleasant arcaded Plaza Mayor. Sta María is a hall church, designed to enable as many people as possible to see the altar. This concept was an important shift away from monastic churches where services were for the clergy or the brethren. It was built in 1526–30 for the constable of Castilla, who owned the castle. The lofty space is notable for its huge cylindrical columns, graceful ogival vaults, truncated *coro* (choir), and, to the left of the entrance, the double tomb of two bishops.

Outside, on the wall facing the Plaza Mayor, a plaque honours Fray Tomás de Berlanga (d. 1551), discoverer in 1535 of the Galapagos Islands, one of those tidbits of information you stumble across from time to time in Spain. Fray Tomás went early to the New World and was named bishop of Panamá in 1534. His tomb is in the church.

Gormaz Beyond Berlanga, pick up the C-116 and turn towards El Burgo de Osma. Shortly after crossing the Duero, take the road left to Quintanar de Gormaz. Ahead, on top of a long ridge, appears

Berlanga de Duero (Soria) A key Muslim fortress on the Duero line, Berlanga fell to the Christians in the early 12th century and was held for a time by El Cid. The present castle dates largely from the 15th and 16th centuries, though the outer walls are from the 13th. Here, in 1528, the young sons of Francis I of France, including the future Henry II, were held hostage for some months.

San Baudelio de Berlanga (Soria) This remote hermitage, built by the early 12th century, once had wonderful frescoes that were removed from the church in the 1920s and are now to be found in museums in the United States and Madrid. This fresco of two bulls is the only one to survive *in situ*.

↑ **Gormaz (Soria)** Built by the caliph of Córdoba in the third quarter of the 10ᵗʰ century to anchor the Muslim defences on the Duero line, Gormaz was contested for many years, falling finally to the Christians in 1059. It was held for a time by El Cid and passed to some of the most powerful families of Spain.

← **Gormaz (Soria)** This view through a Muslim horseshoe arch in the walls of Gormaz shows fields in the Duero valley east of the castle.

→ **Gormaz (Soria)** The Duero river is seen winding through fields east of the castle in this view from the heights of Gormaz.

← **El Burgo de Osma (Soria)** Originally a Roman town (Uxama), Burgo later became a Visigothic bishopric. After the Muslims were beaten back, the bishopric was refounded early in the 12th century. A Gothic cathedral replaced the original Romanesque one in the 13th century. This is a view of one of the old gates of the town, and the bridge over the Ucero River, with the 18th-century tower of the cathedral.

↓ **Caracena (Soria)** Now all but deserted, this mountain village features the church of San Pedro whose wonderful capitals in the gallery depict jousting knights, monsters in combat and much more. Caracena is typical of many mountain villages that have seen their young drain away to the towns and cities.

San Pedro de Arlanza (Burgos) The Benedictine monastery here was founded in 912; the present church was begun in 1080. The view is down into the nave; later monastic buildings lie to the right. The complex suffered severely after the dissolution of the monasteries in the 1830s when the locals hauled away tons of stone.

Santibáñez del Val (Burgos) The 11th-century Mozarabic chapel of Sta Cecilia stands just beyond the village on a bluff by a stream. As with all such early churches, it has a square apse, this one adorned with a curious window in the shape of a Greek cross carved from a single block of stone.

the stupendous mass of the CASTILLO DE GORMAZ, one of the largest castles in Europe.

The road forks just beyond Quintanar de Gormaz. To the left, you descend to the Duero and a stone bridge, from the other side of which are fine views of the castle. The right fork, to El Burgo de Osma, takes you to the turn for the castle. The road climbs up through the tiny village of Gormaz on the steep slope below the castle to a parking area just below one of the gates.

The Celtiberians and then the Romans fortified the site, but the present castle was built by the Caliph al-Hakam II of Córdoba between 961 and 976. It occupied a pivotal position on the Duero facing the Christians. Fernán González, count of Castilla (c. 930–70), held Gormaz briefly before losing it again to the Moors and it changed hands a number of times during the struggles of the 10th and 11th centuries. In 975 the caliph's army under Ghalib, coming from Barahona, defeated the combined forces of León, Castilla and Navarra beneath its walls.

Gormaz fell finally to Fernando I in 1059 thus allowing the incorporation of this section of the Duero basin into Castilla. Alfonso VI granted it to El Cid in 1081 and in succeeding centuries it was held by some of the great families of Castilla.

A huge, many-towered wall, some 2,400 feet or almost half a mile in circumference, surrounds the top of the ridge. At the northern end are the ruins of the keep and other buildings comprising the *alcázar*, heavily rebuilt by Christian victors and feudal lords. Among the gates is a fine horseshoe arch through which the Duero can be seen winding through the green valley and the broad fields.

In the summer the sun hammers down from a cloudless sky and all is sere and brown below. In the winter, beneath a lowering sky, the frigid wind tears around the ramparts and the winter wheat sprouts green in the fields below the hill. Gormaz is always impressive, with sweeping views over the river, the fields and the hills in all directions. It would have to have been a very close-to-the-ground Christian to escape detection from those walls.

On the way down, spare a moment for the little church of San Miguel de Gormaz, built probably in the middle of the 11th century after the Muslims had been cleared from the zone. Note the horseshoe arches of the walled-up portal. This now largely deserted village was once a place of considerable extent and importance.

Western Soria Province

By now the mountains are falling back from the valley and the river itself is settling down for its long run to the Atlantic as it approaches the meseta, the central Castilian tableland. The land through which we have passed was largely reconquered from the Muslims by Alfonso I of Aragón in the early 12th century. Western Soria Province was recovered in the 11th century following Alfonso VI's conquest of Toledo in 1085. Cultural influences from Castilla predominate, most importantly the galleried churches so common to Segovia. With El Burgo de Osma we reach an important cultural centre in its own right.

El Burgo de Osma   The town stands slightly north of the Duero on the Río Ucero. The N-122 (Soria to Aranda de Duero) cuts through the town; the cathedral, marked by its huge 18th-century tower, and the quiet old quarter with an arcaded Calle Mayor (High Street) lie south of the highway.

Coming from Gormaz, and bearing right under the cliffs along the Río Ucero, keep an eye out for the imposing tower of the cathedral. Just as you come abreast of it, a road slips over an old bridge and through a gate into a square dominated by the south side of the cathedral. The fountain at the top of the square is topped by a fat pineapple (or is it a pine cone?).

On the right is a row of somewhat dilapidated arcaded houses belonging to absent and uninterested heirs of the original owners who want too much money for them. A couple have been fixed up already, but the last time we were there the centre of the row was shielded from view by tall hoardings behind which one or two houses had been razed to the ground. It is unclear what will replace them; a passer-by said there had been a huge *polémica* (argument) over the issue, but the developer won.

El Burgo de Osma derives its name from the Roman Uxama Argelae, previously a town of the Arevaci (as was Numancia). Its scant ruins are nearby. Uxama backed the wrong side in a revolt against Rome and was sacked by Pompey in 72 BC after a heroic resistance. It recovered its fortunes and was the seat of a Visigothic bishopric from the late 6th century.

Alfonso I of Asturias is said to have taken it in 746, but it sank

out of sight in the deserted buffer zone that Alfonso created along
the length of the Duero valley. The ruined stump of the castle rises
on a hill just south of town. It looks like an arduous climb. There
was probably an Arab fortification up there from the 8th century;
the present structure dates from the 10th.

Osma was first repopulated in 912, below the citadel. An important
link in the Christian defences of the Duero valley, it was bitterly
contested for two and a half centuries. Caliph 'Abd al-Rahman III
sacked it in 920; Ramiro II of León was besieged here in 933;
Almanzor seized it in 989. It passed finally into Christian hands in
the time of Alfonso VI, a century later.

Among later lords of the señorío was Álvaro de Luna, all-powerful
minister of the weak Juan II and virtual ruler of Castilla for twenty
years before his fall and execution at Valladolid in 1453. An important
guest within the castle walls in the fall of 1469 was the seventeen-
year-old Infante Don Fernando of Aragón, en route through hostile
territory to meet and marry Doña Isabel of Castilla. William Prescott
tells the story.

> As he [Juan II of Aragón] could spare neither the funds nor the force
> necessary for covering his son's entrance into Castile, he must either
> send him unprotected into a hostile country already aware of his
> intended enterprise [the marriage to Isabel] and in arms to defeat it,
> or abandon the long-cherished object of his policy at the moment
> when his plans were ripe for execution. ...
>
> It was at length determined that the prince should undertake the
> journey, accompanied by half a dozen attendants only, in the disguise
> of merchants, by the direct route from Saragossa ... Ferdinand
> assumed the disguise of a servant, and, when they halted on the road,
> took care of the mules, and served his companions at table. In this
> guise ... they arrived, late on the second night, at a little place called
> the Burgo, or Borough, of Osma, which the count of Trevino, one of
> the partisans of Isabella, had occupied with a considerable body of
> men-at-arms. On knocking at the gate, cold and faint with travelling
> ... they were saluted by a large stone discharged by a sentinel from
> the battlements, which, glancing near Ferdinand's head, had wellnigh
> brought his romantic enterprise to a tragic conclusion; when his voice
> was recognized by friends within, and, the trumpets proclaiming his
> arrival, he was received with great joy and festivity by the count and
> his followers.[5]

Alfonso VI entrusted the task of refounding the episcopal see to Pierre de Bourges, subsequently San Pedro de Osma, who chose a site across the Ucero for his new church. San Pedro, bishop of Osma 1101–9, was a monk from the Burgundian abbey of Cluny who came to Sahagún in the company of Constance of Burgundy, wife of Alfonso VI. His tomb of 1258 is one of the glories of the cathedral. The town (Burgo) grew up around the church, eventually supplanting Osma.

A prominent later inhabitant of the Romanesque monastery was Domingo de Guzmán (d. 1221), founder of the Dominican Order. While a canon of the cathedral chapter, he decided to devote himself to the apostolic life of preaching. He accompanied his bishop on a trip to Europe and ultimately dedicated himself to the suppression of the Albigensian heresy in southern France. Domingo was canonized in 1234.

One of the long line of distinguished bishops of Osma was Juan de Palafox y Mendoza (1600–59), a member of the Council of the Indies from 1626, bishop of Puebla in Mexico and Viceroy of Mexico in 1642. Returning to Spain, he ended his days as bishop of Osma 1653–59. He was a learned man and the books that he left behind in Mexico form the nucleus of the collection housed now in the splendid Biblioteca Palafox in Puebla.

Entering the town from the east, on the right stands the former (1555) UNIVERSITY OF SANTA CATALINA with an elaborately worked portal. It is now a secondary school, having been until recently the headquarters of the Guardia Civil. The courtyard is worth a quick look.

Parking is available a few steps farther on. From behind the hotel diagonally across the street, the arcaded Calle Mayor runs past some nice old mansions and the Plaza Mayor. The northern side of the Plaza Mayor is occupied entirely by the handsome early-18th-century HOSPITAL OF SAN AGUSTÍN. The episcopal palace has a fine portal, framed in a giant *alfiz*, that square frame around doors and windows that is so dear to the Spanish heart.

The principal sight in El Burgo de Osma, however, is the CATHEDRAL. The present early Gothic structure was begun in 1232 to replace the Romanesque church. Of that original fabric, the cloister and a few other pieces lasted until the rebuilding of the cloister in 1510–15. Recently uncovered, having been walled up for 400 years, are two double windows that opened to the cloister from the old *sala capitular*. Each consists of a pair of arched openings framed in a blind arch. The capitals, particularly those of the two central columns, are wonderfully inventive: scenes from the infancy of Christ on the left and of the Passion on the right. Other fragments of the Romanesque cloister are visible around the corner.

The sala capitular holds the 1258 sarcophagus of the saint. It also preserves one fine capital from the original church showing that favourite of subjects, the Slaughter of the Innocents, depicted in blood-curdling detail. The sarcophagus rests on the backs of four patient lions. San Pedro lies comfortably on top. There is marvellous carving on its sides: the poor and helpless (including an unfortunate woman being trundled along in an ox cart); secular drinking scenes; bishops rising from their tombs; the Flight into Egypt. The original polychrome is in remarkable shape and the faces are beautifully worked.

The bishop's shroud, now in the cathedral museum, is an embroidery of Persian workmanship. This fragment and other such (most notably the dazzling display of textiles from the royal tombs that can be seen at Las Huelgas, Burgos) attest to the commercial links between the Christian and Muslim states and the esteem in which Christian prelates and princes held Muslim crafts and workmanship.

The cathedral stands at the threshold of the Gothic style that had already begun in Spain at Burgos in 1221. The spacious interior has a lofty nave and two lower side aisles; windows in the nave admit generous light. The builders used the quadripartite vault throughout. The apse consisted originally of the capilla mayor flanked by two chapels on either side. In the 18th century, the second chapel in from each side was broken through to make room for an ambulatory and other dependencies, including a round chapel with a lofty dome beyond the ambulatory. Chapels were also added to the south aisle.

The interior fittings, including the choir stalls, are mostly 16th-century work and there are later additions. The retablo of the capilla mayor is magnificent, a 1554 work of Juan de Juni (see pages 198–9). In the cathedral museum are manuscripts, books, paintings and miscellaneous items of some note. A lively three-generation sculpture of St Anne, the Virgin and the Christ child is especially appealing.

Of major interest among the cathedral's manuscript holdings is a copy of Beato de Liébana's *Commentaries on the Apocalypse*, or Book of Revelation of St John the Divine, copied in a monastery in Sahagún (León) in 1086. Beato was an 8th-century Asturian abbot, a fervent propagandist for St James, who compiled his great work in about 776. One of the illustrations depicts the seven churches of Asia, to which St John addressed himself, by means of seven horseshoe arches. This conventional representation, which appears in several other copies of the *Commentaries*, is said to have inspired the idea of the seven-arched galleries in Segovian churches.

The cathedral is a most interesting building and is in the hands of priests who are devoted to it. Almost too devoted. They can also be a bit brusque, doubtless the result of too many tourists. To see anything other than the spacious and noble interior, you must take a tour led by one of these enthusiastic clerics who will show you absolutely everything. Depending on the size of the group that has gathered, the time of day and your persistence, you may or may not see all there is to see, but it is certainly worth bearing through one tour.

Outside again, the fine pointed arch of the glorious south portal is deeply recessed in a rounded archway at the end of the stumpy south transept. Above, separated from the lower part by a balustrade, is a rose window enclosed in a Gothic arch set in another rounded arch. A 15th-century Christ occupies the central column, below a frieze of the Apostles. Lady saints, the twenty-four Elders of the Apocalypse and angels adorn the archivolts.

Three splendid figures stand on either side of the portal. On the left are Moses (with Commandments) and an Annunciation with the Archangel Gabriel and the Virgin. On the right are the Queen of Sheba chatting with Solomon and a lady variously identified. These sculptures of around 1300 are said to be by the same hands that were responsible for the south portal of Burgos cathedral. The lintel above the portal depicts the Death of the Virgin, with angels and apostles, another beautiful piece of work.

The cathedral tower, which dominates the little town at 72 m (235 feet), was built in the 18th century.

Ucero El Burgo de Osma is a good base for expeditions. To the north, a few miles up the valley, is the village of Ucero, dominated by a fine castle. The bishops of Osma acquired the castle and its rich valley lands early in the 14th century. The road crosses the river over a stone bridge in the middle of town.

The most dramatic approach to Ucero is from the north, on the road to Burgo from San Leonardo de Yagüe (on the Burgos–Soria N-234). The road crosses high wooded land and then suddenly plunges in a series of hairpin turns to the valley of the Río Lobos with fine views of the castle and the valley.

A kilometre north of Ucero, the main road turns right to begin its climb out of the valley, while a track left leads into the Parque Nacional de Cañón de Río Lobos. Along the river are picnic and camping sites. The road is barred after 2.7 km and the early-13th-century ERMITA DE SAN BARTOLOMÉ DE UCERO, spectacularly situated beneath the sheer wall of the canyon, must be approached on foot. It is perhaps the latest Romanesque church in Soria Province and is all that remains of the Templar monastery of San Juan del Otero. The hermitage is in the form of a Latin cross, a notion from Cataluña and Aragón not often found in Castilla (but note San Juan de Rabanera in Soria).

Return to Burgo by a more circuitous route across the country west of the river. The village of Fuentearmegil is the birthplace, no doubt, of that valiant knight Pedro Núñez de Fuente Armegil who in 1163 spirited the child king Alfonso VIII of Castilla away from the clutches of his uncle Fernando II of León.

Berzosa Reachable either from this direction or directly from Burgo de Osma (10–12 km) is the village of Berzosa with its *parroquia* (parish church) of SAN MARTÍN on a hill in the centre. The original Romanesque church was much altered in the 17th century, but it preserves its 11th-century south portal and mid-12th-century gallery.

The archivolts of the portal rest on three columns on either side, with curiously primitive capitals. The inner two on the left have feline beasts of some sort while on the right are two scenes. In one, an angel holds the reins of a horse whose rider has a cross in his right hand; in the other, two couples are holding hands and doing whatever your imagination decides. Above the portal is a cornice with sculpted corbels.

The rather heavy gallery of seven arches has quadruple column clusters to support the arches; the complex capitals have various designs, including more felines. The gallery offers fine views over the rolling farm country. It is worth while wandering around on these country roads to get a sense of the rural life.

Caracena Another outing from El Burgo de Osma – not recommended in rainy weather, given the road – takes you south about 30 km via Fresno de Caracena to this remote mountain village. Approaching from below, the very ruined castle is visible on the right, the church of San Pedro stands tall in the middle, and Sta María and other ancient bits and pieces are on the left. The population of Caracena now numbers about a dozen and can all gather easily in the sadly decrepit main square.

Park in the square and climb up the hill to SAN PEDRO, go around the corner and behold! – a superb gallery on the south side with the regulation seven arches, plus one on the east end, and marvellous capitals. Knights joust while pages stand in attendance; there is a Resurrection; a seven-headed hydra is locked in combat with another monster; and animals, birds, people and floral motifs cover other capitals. The graceful columns are doubled, except for those flanking the entry portal which are quadruple. The one to the right of the entry is twisted for some reason. (One sees these twisted columns not infrequently.) San Pedro dates from the first half of the 12th century.

It is a short walk to STA MARÍA of which the only notable part is the lovely slender window in the apse. The opening is flanked by colonnettes with birds and animals on the capitals that support a rounded arch with a braid design. Above that is a curious sort of vine cluster. An ominous crack runs down the apse wall and across the window.

The ruined but still impressive castle of Caracena dates originally from the 12th century. The señorío was held by various important figures, including Alfonso Carillo de Acuña, nephew of the archbishop of Toledo, who acquired the castle in 1491 and completely rebuilt it. The present decay and isolation of Caracena make it difficult to grasp that this was once a vital place, important enough to support two churches and a castle.

Returning towards El Burgo de Osma, you pass again through Fresno de Caracena. The road from there to Gormaz provides one of the best approach views to that great castle.

Just south of the Duero on the road to Burgo de Osma is the village of Navapalos. According to the *Cantar de Mio Cid*, it was here that El Cid crossed the Duero with the knights who had chosen to follow him into the exile.

Rodrigo Díaz el Vivar (c. 1040–99) took service as a young man with the future Sancho II of Castilla. When Sancho was murdered in 1072, he switched allegiance to Alfonso VI. In 1081 he and Alfonso had a falling out and the king exiled him from Castilla.

The earliest version of the *Cantar* that has come down to us is a 14th-century copy of an original possibly of 1207 (these dates are not universally accepted) now in the Biblioteca Nacional in Madrid. It opens as Rodrigo and his followers leave Burgos and turn for the last time to see their abandoned homes, 'their eyes brimming with tears' ('De_los sos ojos tan fuertemientre llorando'). Passing San Esteban de Gormaz, they filed through the village of Alcubilla de Marqués that still stands just south of the N-122 between Osma and San Esteban de Gormaz. It then marked the limits of Castilla. They rested the night in Figueruela, somewhere in the vicinity of Fresno de Caracena. Beyond lay Muslim territory where Rodrigo was to make his career for three years in the service of the amir of Zaragoza. He came to be called 'El Cid' from the Arabic meaning leader.

San Esteban de Gormaz A dozen kilometres or so west of El Burgo de Osma the Ducro is reached again at San Esteban de Gormaz, another major frontier fortress and the site of two important churches. It lies just south of the N-122 that now detours around the town. Of the ancient castle, probably begun by Muslims in the 10th century, nothing remains but a long sweep of wall with a single doorway, poised improbably on a rocky outcrop. Traces of Roman settlement have been found.

San Esteban's castle and bridge at a strategic river crossing made it one of the gates of Castilla. It changed hands repeatedly in the 10th and 11th centuries, not being taken definitely for Christendom until 1054. Alfonso VI granted the castle to El Cid in 1087.

To San Esteban de Gormaz, according to the *Cantar de Mio Cid*, were brought the two daughters of El Cid after they had been beaten, robbed and abandoned by their husbands, the cowardly infantes de Carrión. These haughty and pusillanimous lords were nephews of Pedro Ansúrez, founder of Valladolid, and joined El Cid on the Valencian front in the hope of picking up some booty.

For the most mercenary of reasons, they asked for and won the hands of El Cid's daughters. He was honoured by the attentions of this high-born pair, though mistrustful of their true intentions. Treated with scorn and derision for their cowardly behaviour on the battlefield, the infantes determined to go home. Having decided that they had married beneath them, they laid a dastardly plot. They camped one night in the forest of Corpes (west of San Esteban), dark and gloomy, the lair of wild beasts, and passed the night with their wives in their arms, showing them, according to the *Cantar*, every sign of love. The next morning, however, the infantes sent ahead the baggage train and their retainers and then beat and robbed their hapless brides. They fled, leaving the women senseless and half naked, their garments and flesh torn and bloody.

The girls were found by their cousin who had come after them, suspecting the worst of the infantes. He brought them to safety in San Esteban de Gormaz. The people of San Esteban had always been good folk, says the *Cantar*; 'greatly they lamented the deed and pressed upon the daughters of El Cid meats, bread and wine. And here they remained till they felt themselves restored.'

In due course, their cousin escorted them back to their father in Valencia, stopping the first night at Berlanga, the second at Medinaceli and the third at Molina where, it is worth noting, they were courteously received and given aid by the amir. The two girls eventually married well; the infantes got their comeuppance at the court of Alfonso VI where they were hauled before the king and the outraged Cid.

With the conquest of Toledo in 1085, the population of San Esteban de Gormaz, a mix of Castilians, Mozarabs from the south and Jews, could get on with their lives and tend to the growing prosperity of the town based, as usual in these parts, on agriculture and livestock. From these days have come down to us the two parish churches of San Miguel and Santa María del Rivero or Ribero.

SAN MIGUEL This church has been dated 1081, which would make it the oldest of the churches in Sorian–Segovian territory, and the arcaded gallery on its south side is the first such in Spain. The date is known because a little bug-eyed fellow on a corbel to the left of the south entrance to the gallery holds a book on which it is written that Master Julián built the church in ERA 1119 [AD 1081]. He was first noticed only in 1957.

Unless, of course, you side with another group of experts who have more recently interpreted the date on the rather deteriorated book as equivalent to AD IIII. In which case, although the gallery continues to hold place of honour as the first in Spain, the church itself comes second to El Salvador in Sepúlveda (Segovia) which was unquestionably built in 1093, but whose gallery is of a later date. In any case, there seem to have been close links between Sepúlveda and San Esteban in the church-building department and there are those who hold that San Miguel is a copy of El Salvador. More of this when we reach Sepúlveda (see pages 169–70).

A flight of stairs leads up to the gallery with its seven rounded arches. A pair of arches gives access to the east end, next to the plain drum of the apse with a nice little window. At the west end is another opening flanked by double columns. The church has been restored in recent years.

The columns, capitals and bases of the gallery are rather heavy, but the fascinating carvings on the capitals indicate clearly that they were the work of Mozarab craftsmen. Carlos Lafora, in his book *Por los Caminos del Románico Porticado*,[6] draws attention to 'the typically oriental representation of pine cones, persons with turbans, and the symbolic figure of a siren with a double fish tail of Sasanid influence, continuing the siren myth of ancient times'. One capital shows a fortress with gates under a caliphal horseshoe arch. The church well reflects the mixed Christian and Muslim population of a frontier town in the 11th century.

STA MARÍA DEL RIVERO On the highest point at the edge of town is Sta María del Rivero, cruder in construction, though slightly later in date, than San Miguel. Only part of the cabecera survives from the original structure, along with the gallery east of the entrance, the five remaining arches on the south side and the two on the east and the battered carved figures on the corbels above them. The clothing and the symbolism attest again to an artist familiar with the Muslim world. The cabecera is divided by tall slender columns into three panels, each with a window. There is a fine view from the church.

Rejas de San Esteban The road to the village turns off right from the N-122 a few kilometres beyond San Esteban. At the entrance to the village, by a ball court, is SAN GINÉS. The arcade of the south gallery has been walled up, leaving only the outer faces of three capitals, the right-hand one of which shows three men (Christ and Apostles?) in a boat.

Further along, up the hill, is more the impressive SAN MARTÍN. Its very fine gallery has the traditional seven arches and a splendid main portal with seven archivolts bearing geometric patterns. The gallery capitals are simple but elegant; the columns are double and, in two cases, quadruple. Another portal opens at the east end of the gallery. The apse is said to contain early-14th-century paintings.

The N-122 follows the Duero's north bank, passing north of Langa de Duero. The tall keep of its vanished castle overlooks the town. Alfonso VI granted Langa to El Cid.

Castillejo de Robledo The village lies about 11 km south of Langa, on a minor road, in a now lightly wooded area which has been identified as the site of the Robledo (oak woods) de Corpes where El Cid's daughters had their sad experience. A ruined Templar castle overlooks the village, jammed into a rocky gorge. The village occupies the westernmost point of Soria Province.

Just at the village, the road turns abruptly right; you carry on straight ahead through the village to a square with a public fountain and a section of stream that has been channelled and provided with broad stone steps where women do their washing. The ruins of the Templar castle loom above, and in front of you is the early-12th-century parroquia.

The church has been much altered, but it retains its elegant original cabecera and splendid south portal. The drum of the apse is divided into three panels by two tall slender columns and the surface is further articulated by two meticulously carved horizontal mouldings, one at the level of the base of the three slit windows, one in each panel and the other at the level of the tops of the capitals of the little columns that flank the windows. Many of the corbels supporting the cornice retain their often amusing carved figures. It is a most pleasing assemblage of details and owes its present condition to sensitive restoration work.

The original south gallery has disappeared, but the bland modern one protects a beautiful 13th-century portal that still preserves some of its original polychrome. The lobes of the second archivolt are still remarkably crisp.

A clamber to the castle is optional. The views are fine.

From Castillejo de Robledo you can drive down a lovely valley some 24 km to Aranda de Duero (Burgos), but then you would miss the monastery of La Vid (also Burgos). It is a very short run from Langa to La Vid, so you can do that first and then return to Langa and take the Castillejo road.

Just beyond Langa, on the N-122, we enter the Province of Burgos.

Notes

1. Richard Ford, *A Handbook for Travellers in Spain* (London, 1966), pp. 1468–9.
2. *Cambridge Ancient History* (Cambridge, 1952), Vol. VIII, p. 321.
3. Cayetano Enríquez de Salamanca, *El ruta románico en la provincia de Soria* (Madrid, 1986), p. 67.
4. Georgiana G. King, *Pre-Romanesque Churches of Spain* (New York, 1924), p. 198.
5. William H. Prescott, *The History of the Reign of Ferdinand and Isabella* (Philadelphia, 1873), Vol. I, pp. 203–4.
6. Carlos R. Lafora, *Por los Caminos del Románico Porticado* (Madrid, 1988), p. 15.

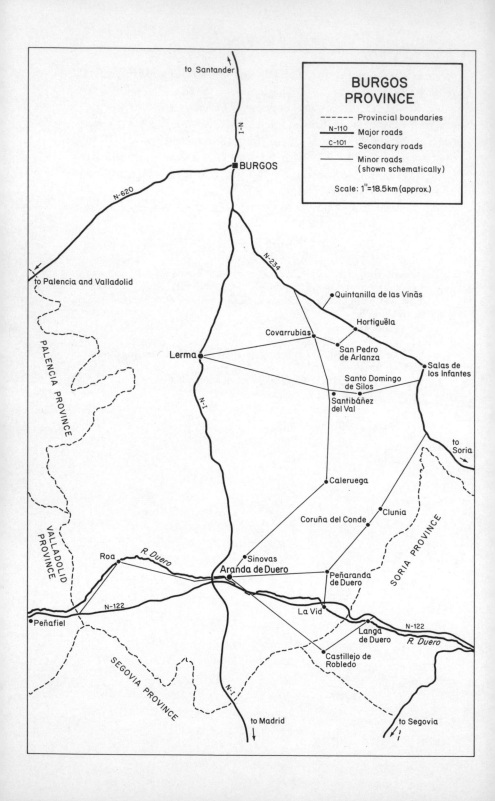

5

Burgos Province (Southern)

Approaches

Access to all points in the province is easy from the main Madrid–Burgos highway, the N-I, that passes through Aranda de Duero, the main town in the southern part of the province. This tour, however, dutifully follows the N-122 along the Duero coming from Soria Province. Outside Aranda, all the sites described lie east of the Burgos highway, accessible by several local roads.

History

The city of Burgos grew up at the foot of a castle built in 884. It and the mountainous north of the province, the heart of the ancient county of Castilla, lie outside the scope of this book. You should, however, visit Burgos for its splendid early (1221) Gothic cathedral, the royal monastery of Las Huelgas, a Cistercian foundation of 1187 for women, and the Cartuja de Miraflores, among other sights.

There were counts in Castilla, even of Castilla, towards the end of the 9th century, subject to the kings of Asturias and then of León. The mountainous nature of the terrain and the distance from court gave these border lords, charged with the defence of the realm from attacks from the east and south, considerable independence. This was consolidated by the famous Fernán González, el Buen

Conde, the Good Count (c. 930–70), who was assisted in his quest for independence by the virtual collapse of authority in León after the death of Ramiro II in 951. The puny kings who filled the last half of the century were no match for Fernán González.

The defeat of Caliph 'Abd al-Rahman III at Simancas in 939 gave the count the opportunity to expand south of the Duero to Sepúlveda (Segovia) and Atienza (Guadalajara), but when al-Hakam II went on the offensive in the 960s the Castilians were thrown back north of the river. The situation worsened with the hammer blows inflicted by Almanzor who captured Count García Fernández, son and successor of Fernán González, in 995 and took him off to die. Not till the death of Almanzor in 1002 and the collapse of the caliphate thirty years later were the counts of Castilla able to consolidate and repopulate their lands in the Duero valley.

La Ribera del Duero

Resuming travel on the N-122, you now enter the Ribera del Duero, one of the most important wine regions of Spain, extending from San Esteban de Gormaz to Valladolid. The region has produced wines for centuries. In addition to vineyards, orchards, fields of grain and vegetables cover the floor and sides of the valley. It is a lovely stretch of river, with bluffs thrusting forwards from the eroded edges of the meseta, punctuating the line of vision westwards.

Santa María de la Vid Just inside Burgos Province, the N-122 makes a jog south of the Duero to the 16th-century monastery of Sta María de La Vid (of the Grape Vine).

In 1147 Alfonso VII bestowed the lands of La Vid on the bishop of Osma who five years later gave them to the Premonstratensian Order to found a monastery. La Vid remained in Premonstratensian hands until the disentailment of the monasteries in 1835. In 1866, the government granted it to the Augustinians who until recently ran it as a seminary. It is now used mostly for retreats.

The original church was considerably altered in 1318, but most of the buildings you now see date from the time of Cardinal Iñigo López de Mendoza, bishop of Burgos and abbot-for-life of La Vid in the early 16th century. The building programme continued into the 17th and 18th centuries.

The cloister was glazed in this century after a particularly bitter winter; the arches have unusual stone tracery. Only fragments remain from the Romanesque cloister. On either side of the portal of the *sala capitular* (chapter house) are two wide blind arches, each with two smaller windows of similar shape that once opened from the sala capitular on to the cloister. Each pair has quadruple columns, twisted a quarter turn, as a central support and is flanked by double columns. The left-hand side is restored and has no ornamentation; the capitals on the right bear leaf motifs. The plain second storey of the cloister was added in the late 18th century.

The 16th-century church is the high point of La Vid. It was actually founded as a funerary chapel by Cardinal Mendoza (d. 1533) and Francisco de Zúñiga y Avellaneda, third count of Miranda (d. 1536) whom we will meet again in Peñaranda de Duero. The cupola over the crossing springs from an octagon made by bridging the corners of the square with graceful masonry fans embellished with bishops and saints. The *capilla mayor* of 1572 has a delicately ribbed half dome behind the triumphal arch of the crossing. Angels and putti hold swags that drape horizontally across the base of the dome.

A beautiful Virgin with Child of the 14th century, with soft 17th-century polychrome, stands on the high altar. She has a faint smile on her very Spanish face and the alert Child gazes expectantly forwards. An arrangement of small mirrors in the frame allow the Virgin's face to be seen in reflected profile. The friar claimed with pride that she was the most beautiful statue in Spain, and he cannot have been far wrong. Behind the altar rises a splendid *retablo* of 1592. The cardinal rests in a tomb to the left of the altar, the count on the right.

An interesting little museum has been installed in rooms off the east side of the cloister. Five Augustinian friars accompanied the explorer Miguel López de Legazpi on the expedition to the Philippines that led to the founding of Manila in 1571. The Augustinians have thus always had an interest in the islands and a number of objects in the museum are of Filipino origin. Note the ivory crucifix with a very oriental-looking Christ.

Aranda de Duero

From La Vid, you soon arrive at this bustling, prosperous industrial town of some 28,000 inhabitants, headquarters of the Pascual milk and dairy products company whose trucks ply the highways of Spain. Aranda also produces pisco in those same black bottles that one knows from Peruvian pisco. Perhaps more important in the drinks department are, of course, the wines of the Ribera del Duero.

Aranda is also famous for its *cordero asado* (roast lamb). Whether it is the lamb itself or the wood-fired ovens, it is absolutely delicious. When you order lamb in Spain, you get just that: very young lamb, not young sheep. A leg (*pierna*) is just enough to feed two people and chops (*chuletitas*) are so small that it takes a heap to make a plateful. An appetizer, cordero asado, mixed salad, dessert, and coffee – a perfect meal!

Aranda was sacked by the Muslims, rebuilt by Ordoño I in 861, and had its share of the disturbances of succeeding centuries. In Aranda, Charles I (the future Emperor Charles V) met for the first time his brother Ferdinand who was leaving Spain, where he had been born and raised, for Austria which he would in time rule. The foreigner Charles, speaking no Spanish and surrounded by Flemish and Burgundian courtiers eager for advancement, was the rightful king; Ferdinand might well have become the focus of a national opposition party.

Coming from the south, the road crosses a bridge over the Duero and bears right before the old town gate to curve around the town. The N-I passes west of town.

STA MARÍA Aranda has managed to demolish almost everything of any historical interest, but it does have the late 15th-century Sta María, reached by going through the aforementioned gate, bearing left and then right. The façade is spectacular. Within a richly carved and ornamented arch, the double doorway (the wooden doors are original) is surmounted by a double tympanum. On the left, Joseph and Mary kneel by the manger from which the cow and the ass are feeding; the Christ child is on the floor. On the right is depicted the Epiphany or the Adoration of the Magi. Above the portal is a Crucifixion, flanked by Christ bearing the cross, and a Resurrection.

The upper part of the façade bears the insignia of the Catholic Kings, Ferdinand (a double ox yoke or *yugo*, the Y for Ysabel) and Isabella (a bundle of arrows or *flechas*, the F for Fernando), plus the arms of Castilla y León and of Aragón and a good bit more. The ensemble is the work of Simón de Colonia (d. 1511) who with his father Juan helped make Burgos cathedral the masterpiece it is. This is the first example on our itinerary of Isabelline Gothic that we will also see flourishing in Valladolid and Salamanca.

The interior is, for want of a better word, noble. A carved stone staircase leads up to the *coro*, elevated on a tribune at the west end. The only time I was actually in the church, mass had just started, the choir was singing away, and I could not inspect more carefully.

SAN JUAN BAUTISTA A short distance northwest of Sta María is San Juan Bautista with an unusual portal: a lofty pointed Gothic arch of nine plain but impressive archivolts with a slight floral design around the outermost. The saint occupies the tympanum. The interior has been completely restored in recent years.

Some 30 km southeast of Aranda is the Pantano de Linares del Arroyo on the north shore of which there is good swimming, just off the road before reaching the bridge. The reservoir is overlooked by the old walled town of Maderuelo. (See pages 172–3.)

Sinovas The village lies just northeast of Aranda, on a road signposted to Santo Domingo de Silos. On the edge of the village in a park stands the church of SAN NICOLÁS DE BARI. The portal is simple but attractive and a modern restoration has spared some of the original carved corbels.

The interior is remarkable for its superb 14th-century *artesonado* ceiling supported by fine painted beams. Or rather part of one, the west end having fallen, the sacristan told us, in the lifetime of his grandparents. Saints and knights, bishops and kings, escutcheons and scenes of daily life cover the surface of this amazing survival. An elegant stone staircase mounts to the tribune at the west end, supported by beams, the ends of which have human faces painted on them save for the two nearest the stair which are bovine heads.

Artesonado ceilings, of which this is the first we have encountered in Burgos Province, are part of the *Mudéjar* legacy. They are made of pieces of wood fitted together to form square or octagonal coffered panels. They can be plain, painted or gilded and are always interesting and frequently magnificent. There are fine examples in the Museo Arqueológico in Madrid.

The Arandilla Valley

At Aranda, the Duero is joined from the northeast by the Aranzuelo and Arandilla, streams that converge some dozen kilometers east of town. An excursion up the Arandilla is worth while. Other than enjoying the scenery, you can visit Clunia, the only Roman site on our itinerary.

Peñaranda de Duero The town, the first stop on this route, is dominated by its mighty castle ruin. The outer walls enclose the top of a long narrow ridge and above them rises the impressive *torre de homenaje* (keep). Peñaranda was an important fortress on the Duero line and a castle stood on the commanding height certainly by the 11th century.

One side of the Plaza Mayor is occupied by the huge block of the 16th-century PALACE of the Zúñiga y Avellaneda family, counts of Miranda and later dukes of Peñaranda. The family held the town and castle from the 14th century, thanks first to Alfonso XI and then Enrique II. The present castle was begun by the first count of Miranda, who also held the castle of Iscar in Valladolid Province that we will visit in due course (see page 220). Francisco, the third count, built the palace as well as (in cooperation with Cardinal Mendoza) the magnificent church we have seen at La Vid. Aside from an fine two-storey patio, the palace boasts an astounding collection of some sixteen splendid artesonado ceilings that are well worth seeing.

Across the plaza stands the COLEGIATA, built in 1605 by Don Francisco de Zúñiga, seventh count and first duke. The portal is adorned with busts and columns from Clunia. The lofty interior is very shabby. According to one local guidebook, the church holds the heart of the count of Montijo, father of the Empress Eugenie of France, that 'is guarded like a reliquary'.

At one side of the Colegiata is a *rollo*. One frequently sees these elaborate Gothic columns in plazas; they usually have arms projecting from the capitals and are topped by a cross. Rollos were symbols of jurisdiction, serving often as pillories for criminals.

The Plaza Mayor gives on to a smaller adjacent square lined with ancient arcaded houses. The view up the arcade on the right is particularly pleasing. The street to the left leads to a pharmacy, La

Botica, that has been run by the Jimeno family since its founding in the 18th century. It is a fascinating little place.

Coruña del Conde Shortly before reaching this next town, you will see on a hillside to the left the isolated ERMITA DE SANTO CRISTO dating from the late 11th or early 12th century. The square apse is a primitive feature from Visigothic times. The apse has blind arcades with battered capitals and, high up, a curious figure in a pleated skirt with its right hand raised. The main portal is also nice. The stones of the hermitage are said to have come from Clunia.

Coruña del Conde is a town of señorial mansions with a ruined castle high on a crag above it. It was an important fortress on the Duero line, destroyed by Caliph al-Hakam II in 963 along with Osma and other towns, and taken again by Almanzor. The castle whose ruins we see began to rise in the 14th century and was held for a while by the Padilla family, whose María (d. 1361) was the passion of Pedro the Cruel. Enrique IV's favourite, Juan Pacheco, marqués de Villena, was another notable owner.

In 1798, according to Javier Bernard's little book on the *Castillos de Burgos*, the appropriately named Diego Marín Aguilera (*águila* = eagle) precipitated himself from the heights of the castle in a flying contraption he had copied from plans by Leonardo da Vinci. It worked well enough to terrify the local populace who promptly destroyed the machine.

Clunia Proceeding further up the Arandilla valley, between Coruña del Conde and Huerta del Rey, a road signposted to Peñalba de Castro goes off to the left. Before reaching that village, another road turns left and climbs to the hilltop, passing the theatre of ancient Clunia on the left.

Clunia was founded as a military post by Tiberius early in the 1st century BC. Later in the century, it became the centre of one of the seven *conventi* or judicial districts of the province of Tarraconensis which sent delegates to the provincial capital at Tarraco (Tarragona).

Here in 68 AD, Servius Sulpicius Galba, the Roman governor of Hispania Tarraconensis, learned of the death of Nero and of his selection by the Senate to succeed him. His reign lasted less than a year.

The remains of Clunia's public buildings, however scant, attest to its importance. The theatre, built into one side of the scarp on which the city stands, seated some 9,500 spectators. Visigothic wars and the Moorish invasion brought decline and ruin.

The site of Clunia was resettled in 912, but later in the century it was sacked by Caliph 'Abd al-Rahman III and then by Almanzor and the population gradually drifted away to nearby Coruña del Conde (the name Coruña derives from Clunia) and other villages.

Visitors may find Clunia a disappointment. Excavations have revealed the ground plans of a number of buildings and the forum, but very little remained above ground. There are a number of fine mosaic floors and the theatre. A Roman bridge crosses the little river below the heights. There is the site itself with views over the valley and fields. And one may think of the elderly Galba starting off on what even he must have known was a journey to an uncertain future.

An Excursion to the North

Fairly close together northeast of Aranda are four places deserving of a visit: the Visigothic church at Quintanilla de las Viñas, the ruined abbey of San Pedro de Arlanza, the charming town of Covarrubias and its Colegiata and finally the important monastery of Santo Domingo de Silos.

Heading north from Aranda, you can either take the N-I to Lerma and turn right on the C-110 following the valley of the Arlanza to Covarrubias or, for deep-in-the-countryside aficionados, go east from Aranda towards Peñaranda de Duero and then follow the rural road north via Caleruega to Covarrubias. The latter is a particularly beautiful drive.

Quintanilla de las Viñas Coming south from Burgos, take the N-234 towards Salas de los Infantes. A well-marked road turns off left from the N-234 to this village that sits a short distance back from the main road, invisible at first. In the middle of the village a sign directs you to the guide whom you pick up at his house. Or he may be already up at the church, on the other side of the village. A guide is necessary to unlock the church. Those I met were very knowledgeable.

NUESTRA SEÑORA DE QUINTANILLA DE LAS VIÑAS or what is left of it – the typically Visigothic square apse and the east side of the transept – stands alone on a ridge commanding a fine view. To the east is the stump of a tower, all that remains of the castle of Lara where may have been born Fernán González, el Buen Conde, the first independent count of Castilla. The counts of Lara were among the earliest Castilian lords to appear on the scene in the 9th century.

The church is built of finely cut blocks of stone, carefully dressed and fitted without mortar in typically Visigothic style. It dates probably from the end of the 7th century, though it was repaired and restored in the 10th at the initiative of the counts of Lara. Excavations have revealed that it had three naves; the original floor plan has been clearly demarcated in front of the remains. The naves collapsed probably in the 14th century.

Around the exterior of the apse run two decorative bands and part of a third of Visigothic motifs: a series of circles made by a continuous running vine, within which are bunches of grapes, flower and leaf designs, spirals, stars, birds and rather oriental-looking animals. These motifs are also common to early Syrian churches. High up on the wall of the apse are letters, perhaps a monogram, that one guide said was that of the Visigothic King Reccesuinth (653–72). It is possible; his father Chindasuinth left traces in Covarrubias.

Within are charming reliefs. A horseshoe arch separates the apse from the transept. Christ appears above the arch, his hand raised in benediction, and to the right and left the impost blocks are carved with depictions of the sun and moon, helpfully labelled SOL and LUNA, each supported by two angels. Other Visigothic carvings are displayed in the sanctuary. The two blocks carved in the same flat relief fashion depicting angels flanking, in the one instance, Christ, in the other, a female figure, may have been the impost blocks of the now vanished arch between nave and transept. Both the church and the view are well worth the detour.

San Pedro de Arlanza Continue eastwards to Hartigüela and turn right for Covarrubias. Around a bend in the valley of the Río Arlanza, the ruins of San Pedro de Arlanza appear against the hillside. This Benedictine monastery was founded in 912 by Count Gonzalo Fernández, father of Count Fernán González, on the site of a Visigothic monastery. The present church dates from 1080;

building continued into the 12th century and beyond. The massive tower is 12th century; the ruined cloister and the buildings with Gothic vaults date from the late 14th and 15th centuries.

About 1250, a monk of San Pedro composed the epic *Poema de Fernán González* to glorify the memory and embellish the history of the Good Count. In niches still visible on either side of the ruined three-aisled nave, near the high altar, rested the tombs of Fernán González (d. 970) and his lady, Doña Sancha, until their removal in 1841 to the colegiata in Covarrubias.

San Pedro suffered fearful damage when the monasteries were dissolved in 1835. The custodian said that the locals carted away load after load of stone, but as late as 1933 a British visitor reported towering heaps of rubble in the nave from the collapsed vaults and arcades.[1] A Romanesque portal is in the Museo Arqueológico in Madrid.

Wall paintings were discovered in 1894 on the second floor of the tower in the northeast corner of the cloister. It may have been the chapter house. They had been plastered over some time in the 18th century and were revealed only when a fire brought down the dome and much of the plaster.

The owner removed them from the walls in the 1920s and offered them for sale. A fierce lion and a coiling dragon are now in the Cloisters (Metropolitan Museum) in New York, an ostrich of imaginative design is in the Fogg Art Museum in Cambridge, Mass., and the remainder, a griffin, a castle and other fragments, are in Barcelona. The Fogg fresco still shows clearly the gouges made to hold the new plaster when the room was replastered. The frescoes look rather Byzantine and date probably from the 13th century.

Covarrubias A few kilometers further along is the pleasant little town of Covarrubias, taken from the Moors and repopulated in the reign of Alfonso III (866–910). In 972, Count García Fernández, son and successor of the Good Count, erected it and extensive territories and rights elsewhere into an *infantado* (royal lordship) for his daughter Urraca.

This pious lady was abbess of the newly-founded dual monastery (for monks and nuns) of SS Cosme and Damián in Covarrubias and remained so until her death around 1032. She was also regent of Castilla (1017–25) for her young nephew García Sánchez, whose assassination in 1029, aged nineteen, threw Castilla into the hands of his brother-in-law, Sancho el Mayor of Navarra. Other infantas followed Urraca as abbesses, including Urraca of Zamora (d. 1103), daughter of Fernando I, whom we will meet in Zamora, and Sancha (d. 1159), daughter of Queen Urraca of Castilla and Raymond of Burgundy.

TORREÓN DE FERNÁN GONZÁLEZ Facing the Plaza Mayor are the *ayuntamiento* (town hall) and arcaded houses including the Hotel Arlanza and a restaurant. Down the hill and around the corner is an irregular open plaza dominated by the massive square, slightly tapering, 10th-century tower called the Torreón de Fernán González. Its massive stone base is possibly Celtiberian. A horseshoe doorway, reached by modern iron steps, gives access to the interior. High up on the topmost floor are three windows on each side, below which are stout stone brackets that probably carried balconies. Across the square are a couple of old timbered houses, bright with flower pots, one of which has been dubbed the Casa de Doña Sancha.

COLEGIATA DE SAN COSME Y SAN DAMIÁN Around the corner, at the edge of town, is the beautiful 15th-century Colegiata de SS Cosme y Damián. It stands on a site once occupied by a Visigothic church founded in 645 by King Chindasuinth and then by an 11th/12th-century church of which a few fragments remain. Presiding over the church and doubling as an enthusiastic and witty guide is a young priest, Francisco Javier Gómez Oña, who has written a lively guide to Covarrubias, *Cuna de Castilla* (Cradle of Castilla).

The church contains several important tombs. To the left of the altar is the plain sarcophagus of Count Fernán González, draped with the flag of Castilla. Opposite lies his countess, Doña Sancha, a princess of Pamplona (Navarra), in a superb 3rd-century AD palaeochristian sarcophagus from Clunia. Behind the altar repose three royal abbesses. A particularly nice tomb on the right includes a panel depicting the Magi presenting their gifts to the Holy Family. High up on the south wall, near the fine rose window, is a 17th-century organ.

In the 16th-century cloister is the tomb of Princess Cristina of Norway who in 1258 married the Infante Don Felipe, brother of Alfonso X. Their father, Fernando III, had named Felipe abbot of Covarrubias in 1248 when he was twenty years of age. Fernando intended him for the archbishopric of Sevilla, but Felipe's inclinations were secular and he gradually backed out of his religious responsibilities to marry Cristina. She died in Sevilla in 1262, aged twenty-eight, and her husband brought her back to lie in the monastery of Covarrubias. Felipe lies far away in Villalcázar de Sirga (Palencia) in an absolutely splendid tomb alongside the equally magnificent tomb of his second wife who wears a very odd headdress which makes her look Pharaonic.

Cristina has not been forgotten. The standards of Castilla-León and of Norway flank the sarcophagus that always seems to have fresh flowers on it, and in a park across from the entrance to the church stands a lovely statue of the young princess, donated by the people of her native town in Norway.

How, you may wonder, did a dashing Castilian prince meet a lovely Norwegian princess in the middle of the 13th century? Alfonso X of Castilla and León (1252–84) spent a great deal of time, effort and Castilian money in an ultimately unsuccessful attempt to secure his election as Holy Roman Emperor. He was casting about Europe for allies. At the same time, King Haakon IV of Norway had just pulled his country together from a bout of anarchy and was looking for support in the south of Europe. Alfonso dispatched an emissary to Norway and an extraordinary deal was struck: Haakon offered his daughter to Alfonso to be married to any one of his four eligible brothers – but Cristina was to choose which one. The young lady arrived in Castilla in suitable style, presumably lined the princes up in a row, and chose Felipe.[2]

The Colegiata museum contains textiles, paintings and the usual religious objects. Its treasure, however, is the astounding triptych of the Kings presenting their gifts to a Christ child who, seated in his mother's lap, reaches out to inspect them. The figures in this masterpiece of carved and painted wood – the Virgin and Child, Joseph, the three Kings and a dog – have wonderfully realistic faces and stances. It is a Flemish work, most probably of the early 16th century, possibly carved in Castilla.

Covarrubias has other old houses and churches and an impressive city gate, built at the command of Philip II to hold in its upper storey the archives of the Council of Castilla, the principal governing body of the realm.

Just upriver and within sight of Urraca's tower is a swimming hole in the bed of the Arlanza. It is a most pleasant spot. The water is cool and clean, and the local youths have rigged up a rope in a tree on the bluff opposite so that they can swing Tarzan-like out over the water and drop in.

The road south to Santo Domingo de Silos crosses a bridge from which there is a good view of the Torreón, the ancient town wall and the Colegiata, but photography is hampered by a large and ugly concrete wall in the river bed. By careful manoeuvring, you can avoid it.

Santibáñez del Val The road continues through lovely country. Make a brief detour to this small village, beyond which, on a bluff overlooking a stream spanned by the remains of a Roman bridge, is the little 11th-century Mozarab chapel of STA CECILIA, much restored. It has a square apse with a low solid tower and a simple four-arched gallery looking out over the fields of grain. A curious window in the apse, in the shape of a Greek cross with lobed ends, was carved from a single block of stone.

Santo Domingo de Silos You enter the town abruptly, passing the monastery complex on the right and coming into a small square with the Hotel Tres Coronas up on a terrace to the left. The entrances to the church and MONASTERIO DE SANTO DOMINGO DE SILOS are down the lane to the right. The lane runs on past a shelter where housewives do/did their laundry, through an old gate and across a bridge into the valley.

The monastery cloister is of great artistic significance. The trick is to see it when it is not jammed with tourists, school children, etc. Immediately after the Gregorian morning mass in the church on a Saturday morning seems to be a good time. There may be younger monks in blue coveralls working in the garden, thus heeding St Benedict's rule that 'Idleness is the enemy of the soul, therefore the brothers ought to be occupied at definite times in the work of the hands, at other set times in holy reading'.

The town stands on the edge of a small valley where monastic communities settled in Visigothic times. On the site of a Visigothic church, Count Fernán González built a new church and monastery in the 10th century, dedicated to San Sebastián. The community adopted the rule of St Benedict in 954. Three 10th-century manuscripts survive from the Silos scriptorium.

Towards the end of the 11th century, the scriptorium produced a copy of Beato de Liébana's famous *Commentaries on the Apocalypse*, now in the British Library. The Silos Beatus was illustrated by one Prior Petrus who added at the end of the text the following statement:

> A man who knows not how to write may think this no great feat. But only try to do it yourself, and you shall learn how arduous is the writer's task. It dims your eyes, makes your back ache, and knits your chest and belly together – it is a terrible ordeal for the whole body. So, gentle reader, turn these pages carefully and keep your fingers far from the text. For just as hail plays havoc with the fruits of spring, so a careless reader is a bane to books and writing.[3]

San Sebastián was destroyed in one of Almanzor's raids. About 1041, Fernando I called upon the future Santo Domingo (c. 1000–73) to found the monastery anew. Domingo had been prior of the ancient Riojan monastery of San Millán de Cogolla, but had had a falling out with the king of Navarra, who wanted to appropriate some monastic property for his own purposes, and had removed himself to Castilla. He remained abbot of Silos till his death, introducing into his new foundation the monastic reforms developed by the Benedictine abbey of Cluny in Burgundy. Nothing remains of Domingo's foundation but the cloister, though even it may actually date from between 1085 and 1100. The upper storey was added in the 12th century and there were later alterations.

The present church dates from the 18th century. Its massiveness, simplicity and noble proportions echo Juan de Herrera's much larger and earlier church of San Lorenzo de El Escorial. The effect is heightened by the rather theatrical lighting the brothers lay on during the service.

The lower cloister has massive corner piers, the faces of which bear the carved panels for which the monastery is famed. The solid rounded Romanesque arches are carried on double columns, except in the centre of each side where there are quadruple columns encasing a slender central column. The capitals present a profusion of fantastic animals, birds, monsters and luxuriant vegetation. There are very few human figures or biblical scenes; two capitals in the west gallery depict scenes from the infancy of Christ and from the end of his life, including the Entry into Jerusalem.

It has been suggested that the sculptors of the Silos capitals may have been Muslim prisoners of war from Andalucía: 'The fantastic animals of Silos have no connection with the demons and phantoms with which Christianity illustrated the terrors of damnation. They are children of another world.'[4] Other experts dispute this explanation, vigorously.

Domingo's original tomb (his remains were moved to the chapel inside the church in 1733) is in middle of the north gallery. In the niche behind is a relief of the saint freeing chained prisoners. Santo Domingo became in time the patron saint of slaves and those who set them free.

Two, perhaps three, artists were at work in the cloister. The first, a contemporary of Santo Domingo,[5] did the east and north galleries and all but the southwest pier panels. The west and south galleries and the southwest pier were the work of another hand, perhaps fifty years later. The galleries have fine 14th-century Mudéjar ceilings supported by painted pine beams (restored on the northeast and east). The panels on the corner piers with their flat elongated sculptures are extraordinary.

You enter the cloister at the southeast corner. On one face of the pier is the Ascension with the Twelve Apostles looking up at a disappearing Christ; on the other, the Pentecost or coming of the Holy Ghost upon the Apostles.

Moving on through the east gallery of the cloister, next is the northeast pier depicting the Descent from the Cross (note how Mary holds Christ's right hand from which the nail has been drawn) and, on the other face, a double scene of the Entombment and the Resurrection.

The northwest pier holds Christ on the road to Emmaus and a crowded scene in which Christ throws his right arm stiffly upwards so that Doubting Thomas can poke his finger into the wound on his side.

With the southwest pier we come to the work of the second artist who worked in a very different style, more rounded and naturalistic. The faces of the pier depicts the Annunciation and the Tree of Jesse.

Much scholarly debate has been devoted to the six panels of the first artist, comparing and contrasting them with works of the same period in France, most particularly at Moissac. There are striking similarities in the flat relief of the figures and the flowing lines of bodies and clothes at both Moissac and Silos. Writes Nikolaus Pevsner: 'The cloister of Santo Domingo de Silos is the most impressive example [of major figure sculpture in Spain]. This style of long, highly stylized figures with small heads, highly expressive gestures, and feet placed as if they were engaged in a ritual dance was taken over in the south of France especially at Moissac about 1115–25.'[6] Leaving these fine points aside, the sculptures of Silos make a remarkable ensemble, to be enjoyed unhurriedly and in peace.

The museum off the cloister is worth a visit, as is the little pharmacy. In the northeast corner of the cloister is a fine Romanesque portal with a horseshoe arch, about all that remains of the south transept of the Romanesque church.

With the dissolution of the monasteries in 1835, the community of Silos was disbanded and the archives and treasury were despoiled. The former abbot remained as custodian until 1857 (when he was made archbishop of Sevilla) and another former monk tried to hold the place together until 1875. The monastery was saved from destruction by French Benedictines from the monastery of Solesmes who were expelled from France in 1880 and were allowed by Alfonso XII to settle at Silos in 1881. The community is now once again entirely Spanish.

Solesmes stands beside the Sarthe River, southwest of Le Mans, and is noted for its work in reviving the Gregorian chant. It is no wonder, then, that Silos is known for the quality of its liturgical chants: perhaps better known than the brothers might wish. A recording of Gregorian chants by the monks rocketed to the top of the Spanish charts in 1993 (and has been followed by others) and the ensuing publicity and interest seriously disrupted the ancient rhythm of life at the monastery. One hopes that the excitement has died down. Sto Domingo is not a place for crowds.

Leaving Silos, you can either go back towards Covarrubias and take the road to Lerma and the N-I or head south through the Yecla Gorge, a mighty piece of work by a rather small river. The road traverses lovely country, awash with poppies in June. Before Caleruega, birthplace of Santo Domingo de Guzmán (d. 1221), founder of the Dominican Order, you can turn off towards Huerta del Rey to visit Clunia, Coruña del Conde and Peñaranda de Duero as described above.

Lerma Those taking the road via Lerma can drive up to the centre of the old town to witness a perfect example of 'Sic transit gloria mundi'. On a vast and dusty square stands the huge decaying palace built for Don Francisco Gómez de Sandoval y Rojas, duke of Lerma, who was the generally incompetent *privado* or chief minister of Philip III from 1598 to his fall in 1618, shortly after he had persuaded the pope to make him a cardinal.

The palace with its four strong corner towers and the accompanying religious foundations was designed by Francisco de Mora (d. 1610), a protégé of Juan de Herrera, architect of the Escorial, and was built 1604–14. It was pillaged by the French in 1808 and used for a while as a barracks, and seems now to have degenerated into a hive of what look like rather squalid apartments.

West of Aranda de Duero

Returning to Aranda de Duero, let us resume our journey westwards. The N-122 cuts straight across country towards Peñafiel and Valladolid while the Duero swings north. The lesser road which follows the south side of the river is more pleasant. It crosses the richly cultivated valley to a nice old bridge over the Duero. The bridge is almost impossible to photograph because of some doubtless useful but very ugly modern gas tanks and buildings.

Roa The town stands high on its ridge ahead of you. Past the bridge, the road climbs up steeply. The collegiate church fronts a small square.

The Romans were in Roa – as good a place for a fortified settlement then as later – as were the Muslims, and it was repopulated in the 11th century. Queen Urraca of Castilla (1109–26) settled here at one point the better to pursue her interminable war against her husband Alfonso the Battler of Aragón.

In Roa on 8 November 1517 died the great Cardinal Francisco Jiménez de Cisneros (1437–1517), archbishop of Toledo and regent of Castilla since the death of Ferdinand the Catholic in January 1516. The cardinal was on his way to welcome the new king, the Habsburg Charles I, who had landed in Asturias in September. Raised in the Netherlands and speaking not a word of Spanish, the seventeen-year-old Charles came to Spain very full of himself and surrounded by Flemish advisers who were equally ignorant of the country. He wanted none of the old Castilian men of power around him and he wrote curtly to Cisneros, dismissing him as regent.

The king was to learn better very soon when he sought funds from the Cortes of Castilla to enable him to buy the imperial electors who, suitably rewarded, chose him as Emperor Charles V (1519).

Roa is now the seat of the regulating council for the Ribera de Duero vineyards Denominación de Origen.

The road runs along the north bank of the Duero, past vineyards on the slopes and cultivated fields on the valley floor, punctuated by groves of ramrod straight poplars. The river hugs the bluffs on the north side of the valley and there are long vistas of fields and headlands. At San Martín de Rubiales the road crosses an old bridge to the south bank and soon rejoins the N-122.

Around a bend is the castle of Peñafiel riding gloriously on its lofty ridge, the effect only slightly marred by the sugar-beet factory, built right at the turn. We have now left the Province of Burgos and have entered the Province of Valladolid.

Notes

1. Walter Muir Whitehill, *Spanish Romanesque Architecture of the Eleventh Century* (Oxford, 1941), p. 203.
2. I owe this information to Mr Leif Mevik, Ambassador of Norway to Spain, to whom I wrote a letter of enquiry.
3. James Snyder, *Medieval Art* (New York, 1989), p. 247.
4. Frederick Rahlves, *Cathedrals and Monasteries of Spain* (London, 1966), p. 81.
5. The dates of the sculptures at Silos are still the subject of debate. Some scholars place them well into the 12th century.
6. Nikolaus Pevsner, *An Outline of European Architecture* (Penguin, Baltimore, 1974), p. 83.

Segovia (Segovia) The Alcazar of Segovia may be the most famous sight in Spain. Its commanding position makes for dramatic views. A castle has stood here since the 11th century; it began to take its present shape under Alfonso X in the 13th century. Isabella of Castile's father, Juan II, built the mighty keep where she was residing when she was proclaimed queen of Castile in 1474.

Segovia (Segovia) The city's Plaza de San Martín is dominated by the tower of the Lozoya Palace and features a statue of Juan Bravo, a leader of the revolt of the towns (Comuneros) against the newly-installed Habsburg king Charles I. After a string of victories, the Comunero cause collapsed and the young Juan Bravo was executed in 1521. The Lozoya tower is one of a number of finely-preserved medieval buildings that surround the square.

Segovia (Segovia) The tower of San Esteban dates from the late 12th/early 13th century. Its fine detailing, especially the slender columns rising the height of the chamfered corners, is effectively highlighted by the building's beautiful tawny gold stone.

Segovia (Segovia) Across the Eresma valley from Segovia stands the 15th-century monastery of El Parral, with its fine view of the Alcázar.

Segovia (Segovia) The Roman aqueduct of Segovia, 128 m. (420 ft.) high as it crosses the square, was built of finely cut blocks, entirely without mortar, and dates probably from the reign of Augustus (27BC–AD14). Damaged in Muslim attacks, it was restored by Isabella. It is seen here from the tower of the church of San Justo, across the square.

Segovia (Segovia) A closer look at Segovia's Roman aqueduct shows clearly the strength of the mighty arches built of unmortared blocks of stone.

Segovia (Segovia) The 12th-century tympanum in the church of San Justo most probably depicts the three Marys at the sepulchre, although there are other interpretations. Traces of the original polychrome have survived. It is an exceptional piece of sculpture.

Segovia (Segovia) This little capital depicting the flagellation of Christ adorns a doorway on the Calle de Velarde not far from the Alcázar.

6

Segovia Province

The N-122 westwards from Peñafiel will be resumed in the next chapter. For now, I want to leave the immediate vicinity of the Duero valley for Segovia Province. The province almost touches the river, but does not quite make it, due most probably to some ancient claim of the kings of Castilla on the *señorío* of Peñafiel that was often held by members of the royal family or their favourites.

The detour is amply justified by the beauty of the Segovian countryside and the richness of its Romanesque legacy. The province is the heartland of the galleried Romanesque churches of which we have seen a few examples already in southern Burgos and western Soria provinces.

The town of Segovia repays several visits. There is a lot to see, it is a pleasant town in which to poke around, it makes a good base for exploring the province and it has good restaurants. A word about the weather, however: at 1,005 m (3,300 feet), Segovia is considerably higher than Madrid and can be a lot colder. That does not mean, however, that it is appreciably cooler in the summer.

Approaches

From Peñafiel, it would be logical to ascend the valley of the Duratón, but since you may well come to Segovia from Madrid and make that your base, let us start off in that city. The most scenic route to Segovia is the highway northwest from Madrid to Colmenar Viejo, then the C-607 to Navacerrada (heavy traffic on weekends and

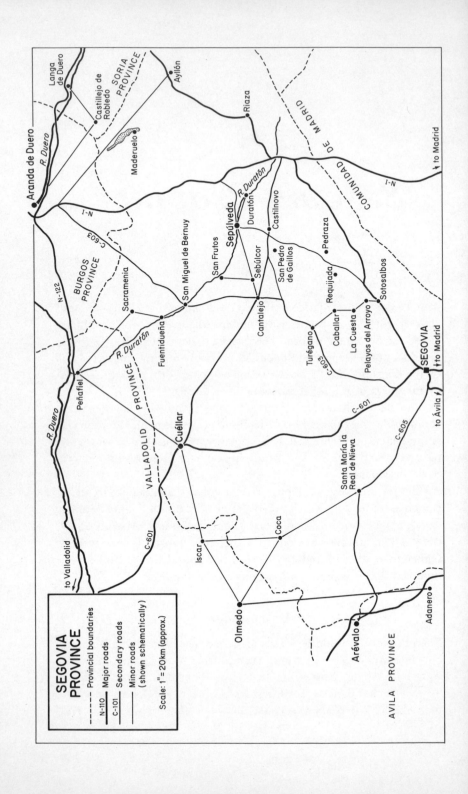

SEGOVIA
PROVINCE

Provincial boundaries
N-110 ——— Major roads
C-101 Secondary roads
Minor roads
(shown schematically)

Scale: 1" = 20km (approx.)

holidays) and the N-601 which climbs over the Sierra de Guadarrama. The descent on the northern flanks of the Sierra, navigating the *Siete Revueltas* (seven hairpin bends), is lovely. The pine forest which cloaks the mountains is at its best with the afternoon sun shining through the reddish trunks of the towering trees.

At San Ildefonso, the road makes a sharp turn left by the gates of LA GRANJA, the palace built by Philip V, first of the Bourbons, in 1735–39 for his second wife, Elizabeth Farnese of Parma. It has fine gardens and a large collection of tapestries, but the palace can be frigid in winter. Philip and his wife are buried in the chapel; he and Ferdinand VI are the only two kings since Charles I/V not buried at the Escorial.

History

Repopulation of the lands south of the Duero, anciently the *Extrema Durii*, began after the victory of Ramiro II of León and Count Fernán González of Castilla over Caliph 'Abd al-Rahman III at Simancas in 939. The caliph retired from the field and for a while the Christians were able to move into the lands south of the river unmolested.

Muslim counter-attacks, in particular the terrible raids of Almanzor, who directed the Cordoban state and armies in the years 976–1002, forced the Christians to fall back. Not until Alfonso VI took Toledo in 1085 could repopulation of this area resume.

The king charged his son-in-law Raymond of Burgundy with the creation of a new line of defence pegged on newly fortified towns such as Segovia, Ávila and Salamanca and designed to contain the fanatic Almoravids who had swarmed into Andalucía in 1090. The new settlers did not find the region totally vacant. There were *Mozárabes*, Christians who had lived under Muslim rule, and *Mudéjares*, Muslims who elected to remain on the lands they had worked for generations. The same situation prevailed across the Extrema Durii from Soria to Salamanca. Protected by the advance of the fighting frontier to the Tajo (Tagus), this mixed population was now able to organize its civil life.

Each fortified town was surrounded by an extensive territory (*alfoz*) of farmland, pasture, woods and villages from which it drew support and sustenance. The settlers were free men whose liberties were guaranteed and protected by the *fueros* (municipal charters) granted them by kings who needed their support to anchor the new conquests. They were farmers and shepherds mainly, with the *villanos caballeros*, men who owned horses and arms, responsible for maintaining the defence system to which all citizens contributed their strong right arms.

Religious life was organized under bishops and around *parroquias* (parochial churches). The new settlers came from all over northern Spain and beyond and the parroquias provided the social and religious glue that held the groups together.

The early churches were presumably rude affairs, the first task being to build houses and bring the land under cultivation. Stone churches came later and the evidence suggests that schools of masons and sculptors worked first in the fortified central towns and then fanned out to the villages.

Of the very earliest churches built after the conquest of Toledo in 1085, only four have survived: El Salvador in Sepúlveda (Segovia) and San Miguel in San Esteban de Gormaz (Soria) and the slightly later priory of San Frutos (Segovia) and Sta María del Rivero also in San Esteban. We have seen the San Esteban churches; we will see the other two. Not until the early 13th century did the main Romanesque church-building boom get under way as a consequence of the renewed repopulation effort undertaken by Alfonso VIII (1158–1214).

Segovia

This town of some 58,000 inhabitants stands just north of the Sierra de Guadarrama. The site is beautiful, especially when there is snow on the mountains and the blue sky is cloudless. Though built on a crag, Segovia lies lower than the surrounding countryside and is thus hidden until you suddenly come upon it. The first sign of the city is usually the tower of the cathedral, peeking up above the fields.

Entering Segovia, you find yourself in the Plaza de Azoguejo (Arabic *al-suq*, the market) which is crossed by that stupendous aqueduct, all that remains of Roman Segobriga.

History Segobriga prospered under the Romans, was the seat of a bishop under the Visigoths, was conquered by the Muslims and reoccupied by the Christians in 1088 under Alfonso VI, following the

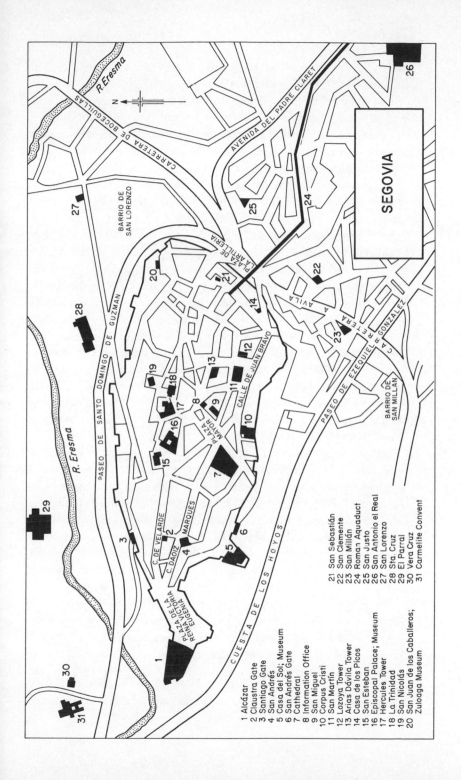

SEGOVIA

1 Alcázar
2 Claustra Gate
3 Santiago Gate
4 San Andrés
5 Casa del Sol; Museum
6 San Andrés Gate
7 Cathedral
8 Information Office
9 San Miguel
10 Corpus Cristi
11 San Martín
12 Lozoya Tower
13 Arias Dávila Tower
14 Casa de los Picos
15 San Esteban
16 Episcopal Palace; Museum
17 Hercules Tower
18 La Trinidad
19 San Nicolás
20 San Juan de los Caballeros;
   Zuloaga Museum

21 San Sebastián
22 San Clemente
23 San Millán
24 Roman Aquaduct
25 San Justo
26 San Antonio el Real
27 San Lorenzo
28 Sta. Cruz
29 El Parral
30 Vera Cruz
31 Carmelite Convent

surrender of Toledo. The walls were completed around 1139. The first bishop was consecrated in 1119.

The new inhabitants, drawn from all over northern Spain and beyond the Pyrenees, settled in *barrios* around their parroquias. It was this collection of parroquia-based barrios that led the 12th-century Moroccan geographer al-Idrisi to describe Segovia as not so much a city as a collection of closely-packed villages.

Segovia had a prosperous Jewish community as early as the 12th century. The *judería* lay on the south side of the walled city, below the present cathedral. The Calle de Judería Vieja and the church of Corpus Cristi, formerly the chief synagogue, mark the spot. In 1412, Catherine of Lancaster, daughter of John of Gaunt, widow of Enrique III, and regent for her son Juan II, ordered those Jews who had survived the frightful pogrom of 1391 to move to the Barrio Nuevo, west of the site of the present cathedral, where the church of La Merced may have been their synagogue.

Segovia figured prominently in the life of Queen Isabella. The closing years of her half-brother Enrique IV's reign were marked by a fierce struggle for the succession between Isabella, who married Ferdinand of Aragón in 1469 against Enrique's wishes, and Juana, either the king's daughter (doubtful) or the illegitimate daughter of his queen (probable). Enrique and Isabella were reconciled briefly in Segovia in December 1473.

Isabella was proclaimed queen of Castilla at Segovia in December 1474. Enrique had kept his treasure in the Alcázar; securing it was a top priority for her while Juana's claims were being championed by the king of Portugal. Ferdinand was in Aragón when Isabella was proclaimed queen and was a mite irked at being left out of the ceremonies, but Isabella was queen and Ferdinand but consort in Castilla, and no matter how much she loved him, which she did, greatly, politics were politics and she was to be mistress in her own house.

Many years later, in 1503, Isabella returned to Segovia with her distracted daughter, the unhappy Infanta Juana, and it was from Segovia in the dead of winter that the queen was forced to dash to Medina del Campo to rescue Juana from her madness, a tale to be related when we reach that town in Valladolid Province (see page 235).

The boom in the wool trade from the 15th century brought prosperity and by 1500 Segovia had 600 textile looms. Plague, drought, famine, foreign wars and emigration to America in the 16th and 17th centuries took their toll and by 1640 only 300 looms remained. By the end of the 18th century, Segovia was but a sad shadow of its former self, its wool and textile industry ruined by government incompetence, high prices and European competition. Joseph Townsend in 1786 noted that from 5,000 families in 1525, Segovia had not 2,000 in his day, 'a scanty population this for twenty-five churches, five parishes ... the cathedral ... and one and twenty convents'.[1] To complete the ruin, in June 1808 during the Peninsular War, Segovia was sacked by the French who also drove off or ate the sheep on which the town's prosperity depended. Richard Ford said he found only 9,000 inhabitants.[2] Less than a century after Townsend's visit, in 1870, another traveller, John Hay, of Boston, estimated the population at 11,000 and noted that the woollen mills which had once employed 14,000 people and turned out 25,000 bolts annually, could manage but 200. 'It has not vitality enough', sniffed Hay, 'to attract a railroad, and so is only reached by a long and tiresome journey by diligence.'[3]

A Tour of the Town ALCÁZAR Since the most famous sight in Segovia, possibly even in Spain, is the Alcázar, let us start there, at the very western tip of the ridge on which Segovia stands. The best view of the fortress is from below, at the point where the Río Eresma meets the little Clamores stream. Another fine view is from across the valley, at the top of the hill past the church of Vera Cruz.

So famous and so spectacular is the Alcázar (Arabic *al-qasr*, castle) that it seems almost churlish to point out that much of it dates from the restoration that followed a terrible fire in 1862. It is said that the fire was started by cadets of the artillery academy that had occupied the castle since 1764 in the hope that they would be transferred to Madrid.

Restoration notwithstanding, the Alcázar is well worth visiting. It has some splendid *artesonado* ceilings, moved in from elsewhere, and the state rooms give a good idea of what life there must have been like.

Alfonso VI built a fortress on the crag in the 11th century, using Moorish foundations of the previous century, but the castle began to assume its present shape only with Alfonso X in the 13th century. This enquiring king conducted astronomical observations here. He is said to have doubted that the sun moved round the earth; a flash of lightning quickly restored him to orthodoxy.

Juan II, who grew up in the Alcázar from the time he became king in 1406 at the age of two, built the massive *torre de homenaje* or keep, with its striking line of bartizan turrets around the top. His daughter Isabella was in residence here when she was proclaimed queen in 1474.

Among distinguished guests was Charles Stuart, Prince of Wales, the future Charles I, who was entertained here in 1623; his curious visit to Spain will be recounted when we reach Valladolid (see pages 199–200). Ford, among many others, notes that Charles dined on 'certaine trouts of extraordinary greatnesse'.[4]

Philip II married his cousin Anna of Austria, his fourth wife, in the Alcázar in 1570. That pious monarch swept away the Moorish decor favoured by his predecessors and gave it over to Juan de Herrera, the architect of the Escorial, to impose his more austere style. And here in 1609 Philip III signed the decree expelling from Spain the *Moriscos*, descendants of those Muslims who had been forcibly converted to Christianity under Ferdinand and Isabella.

BETWEEN THE ALCÁZAR AND THE CATHEDRAL The park in front of the Alcázar gates was the site of the 12th-century Romanesque cathedral, destroyed during the Comunero uprising in 1520 against Charles V.

Just east of the old cathedral lay the Claustra de las Canonjías, home to the officials connected with the cathedral. The two main streets were the Canonjía Vieja, now Calle de Velarde, and the Canonjía Nueva, now Calle de Daoiz, under which ran the prolongation of the aqueduct carrying water to the Alcázar and the adjacent areas. Three gates closed the barrio at night; only one remains, that in Velarde, the Puerta de la Claustra. The other two, one in Daoiz, the other where the two streets converge, were destroyed in 1570 so that the nuptial procession of Philip II and Anna of Austria could reach the Alcázar. The quarter still contains many ancient houses, or at least their façades.

It is a short walk from the Alcázar to the cathedral. The Calle de Daoiz, to the right, is the most direct route; to the left, the Calle de Velarde leads through the PUERTA DE LA CLAUSTRA. Look to the left as you walk through; the capital of the little column flanking a doorway depicts the flagellation of Christ. Further along, on the left, the lintel of an old señorial doorway carries two rather amusing little heads.

The Calle de Daoiz takes you to the Plaza de la Merced. Romanesque SAN ANDRÉS has a lovely 13th-century Mudéjar tower and two remaining apses of the period. To the south of San Andrés is the PUERTA DE SAN ANDRÉS, a splendidly robust medieval gate that once gave access to the judería. The walls on the south side of Segovia have recently been restored and give a good idea what the walled town on its crag must have looked like in its medieval prime.

CATHEDRAL Segovia Cathedral, begun in 1525 on the site of the old judería, was the last major Gothic structure built in Spain. The architects were Juan Gil de Hontañón (d. 1526) and his son and successor Rodrigo (d. 1577), who came here from working on the New Cathedral of Salamanca. Rodrigo remained master of works from 1526 to 1540 when the nave was vaulted; construction then stopped. The chapter invited him to resume his post in 1560, but not till 1620 was the building finished. The interior space is enormous, with three lofty naves, slender cloistered shafts soaring up to the lovely vaults with complex ogival ribs and a remarkable amount of light for a Spanish cathedral. The *rejas*, the gilt wrought-iron screens closing the *coro* and the chapels, are notable. The chevet (apse) has an ambulatory with seven radiating chapels and is supported on the exterior by proper Gothic flying buttresses. A forest of pinnacles adorns the roof.

Of a summer evening, from the cafés in the Plaza Mayor, you can watch dozens of storks slowly wheel about over the cathedral in the gathering dusk and settle down for the night, one by one, each atop a pinnacle, until all are occupied.

The cathedral museum occupies the cloister, which was moved here from the site of the old cathedral in 1524. The cloister was built by Juan Guas who was master of works at the cathedral 1473–91. He also worked at el Parral and Santa Cruz. Juan and Rodrigo Gil de Hontañón are buried near the entrance to the cloister. Along with much else in the museum, one sees the tomb of the Infante Don Pedro, infant son of Enrique II, who fell from a window of the Alcázar in 1366. It is related that his nurse followed him out the window.

PLAZA MAYOR A bandstand occupies the middle of the animated Plaza Mayor and along the sides are cafés that spill out into the arcades in the warm months. The Tourist Office is located under the arcades on the east side. It has good town maps, opening hours of monuments, and other useful information.

In the 12th century, the church of San Miguel stood in the middle of the present Plaza Mayor facing what by the end of the 15th century had become the main plaza. Isabella was crowned queen there in December 1474 and there Ferdinand took the oath the following month to rule as her husband. The church collapsed in 1532. On the other side of San Miguel was the Plaza del Azogue and a large section of the judería.

With the collapse of San Miguel, the city joined the two squares into a stately plaza abutting the advancing cathedral. San Miguel was rebuilt in its present position just off the Plaza Mayor in 1588. With the 17th century came further building; the *casa consistorial* or *ayuntamiento* was completed in the 1620s on the site of the old town council building. The Teatro Juan Bravo was added, as the inscription indicates, in 1917. The square saw a weekly fruit and vegetable market until well into the 19th century.

CORPUS CRISTI By the apse of the present cathedral is the Calle de Judería Vieja which runs past the church of Corpus Cristi, the main synagogue until it was converted to Christian use in 1421. Corpus Cristi was virtually destroyed by fire in 1899. It has been rebuilt, but the loss of the original was a tragedy as it was almost identical to 13th-century Santa María la Blanca in Toledo, that lovely former synagogue. Paintings show the same graceful horseshoe arcades and intricate stucco capitals that can be seen in Sta María la Blanca.

The church is now in the hands of Franciscan nuns, the Clarissas, and you ask for the key at a little window opposite the entry to the convent. The horseshoe arches of the arcades have been reconstructed, but without adornment, the galleries are just façades, and the artesonado ceiling and plasterwork in the apse are modern restorations. All very nice, but totally lacking in resonance; see Sta María la Blanca for a clue as to what has been lost. Plans are apparently afoot to continue restoration work, given the funds. From the pleasant promenade along the walls behind Corpus Cristi one has a good view of the apse and the slender horseshoe-arched windows.

SAN ESTEBAN In the opposite direction, across the Plaza Mayor, bear left past the theatre and, a few steps further along, go left again. The street drops downhill to the Plaza San Esteban, now a car park. It is dominated on the right by the granite façade of the 16th-century Episcopal Palace (which now houses the Museo Diocesano off the 18th-century patio).

On the left soars the superb tower of San Esteban, built in the 12th century (or early 13th) of beautiful tawny gold stone. Its shape and detailing make it a delight to behold. A particularly effective touch is the tall slender columns at the chamfered corners that rise the full height of the tower. The gallery has ten arches on the south side and wraps around the west side. The capitals are rather battered, but interesting.

In 1904 San Esteban had fallen into such disrepair that the tower was pulled down lest it fall. It rather takes the edge off it to realize that what you see is a 20th-century restoration, but it is still magnificent. The interior of the church was thoroughly brought up to date in the 18th century, so don't bother. In fact, the interiors of most of Segovia's Romanesque churches were redone in the 18th century (not a century famed for architectural merit).

We are now in the Barrio de los Caballeros, occupying the high ground north of the present Plaza Mayor and Plaza de San Martín. Here the nobles and their retinues lived in fine mansions grouped around the parroquias of San Esteban, San Nicolás, La Trinidad, San Martín, San Juan, San Sebastián and others now vanished. The kings of the Trastámara line (1369–1474) were fond of Segovia and were often in residence, so the nobility, most of them Trastámara creations, flocked to build their mansions near the court. A great many of these still exist, converted to assorted municipal and private uses. They usually have fine interior courts that can be seen by stepping through the outer portal.

SAN MARTÍN Returning to the Plaza Mayor, take the Calle de Isabel la Católica which turns into Juan Bravo, the busy commercial street in the upper town. You soon reach San Martín. The church is of the 12th century, perhaps 11th, but the tower was rebuilt in the 14th century after a fire. The west portal has four very fine elongated sculptures of prophets and the carved capitals are in better shape than those at San Esteban. The galleries on three sides of the church are at different levels and the arcade of the north gallery has been blocked up by a heavy wall.

Unfortunately, the middle of the three original apses was replaced, probably in the 18th century, by an ugly square apse that is too big and contrasts badly with the original work. The contrast in the otherwise noble interior is all the more striking; it is awful.

San Martín straddles the upper and lower sections of the square that is surrounded by fine señorial mansions of the 14th, 15th and 16th centuries. They have been converted to assorted modern uses. The tall, powerful tower with a band of machicolations near the top is the 14th-century Torreón de Lozoya. At one side of the lower part of the square is a heroic statue of Juan Bravo, one of the principal leaders of the 1520 revolt of the Comuneros, lifting high the flag of rebellion.

Juan Bravo was a member of the minor nobility who received an appointment at court and in 1504 settled in Segovia. He entered the service of Cardinal Cisneros and in 1519 was named regidor of Segovia, an office carrying primarily military responsibilities. In 1520, influenced by Juan de Padilla of Toledo, he joined the Comunero uprising against the new monarch Charles I. He successfully defended Segovia against a royalist attack led by Rodrigo Ronquillo, *alcalde* (mayor) of Zamora, whom we will meet again. Juan Bravo took part in the siege and capture of Torrelobatón and Simancas (Valladolid), but was captured at the final rout of the Comuneros at Villalar, near Toro, in April 1521 and summarily executed.

By this time you will have observed that Segovians are fond of covering the outside of their houses with plaster or stucco stamped with ornamental geometric designs (*esgrafiado*).

CASA DE PICOS Further along the Calle de Juan Bravo, on the left, is the 15th-century Casa de Picos. A later owner added the façade of closely packed stone pyramids that make for remarkable light effects. The inspiration for this façade and that of the Casa de las Conchas in Salamanca came from the Palacio del Infantado in Guadalajara, built in the 1480s by Juan Guas for the Mendoza family.

Before continuing downhill to the Plaza de Azoguejo and the aqueduct, let us return to the Plaza Mayor. Take again the street to the left of the theatre but instead of turning left to San Esteban, turn right.

SANTISSIMA TRINIDAD This 12th-century church, built in the austere Cistercian manner, with a lovely gallery of five arches and a wide portal, was restored in 1986. The two portals are simple and effective.

SAN NICOLÁS Behind La Trinidad, on a small square, is 12th-century San Nicolás retaining its apse and tower. Its portal was removed some years ago to San Juan de los Caballeros (below).

CASA DE HIDALGO Further along, at the angle where the Calle Cronista Lecea coming from the Plaza Mayor meets the street on which you are walking, is this señorial mansion, restored in the style of the 16th century. It houses a small museum of paintings and furnishings of the period.

SAN JUAN DE LOS CABALLEROS Next comes the Plaza del Conde de Cheste, surrounded by señorial mansions with fine portals, emblazoned with escutcheons, and façades covered with Segovian stucco work. Down to the left, following a narrow street between two mansions, lies the Plaza de Colmenares, set about with cypress trees, and the church of San Juan de los Caballeros. This is the oldest (11th century) galleried church in Segovia, though the gallery is of somewhat later date. The church is so named because the Junta de Linajes, the Council of Lineages, used to bury its noble members there.

The church has suffered various reforms and interventions which have not helped it. Even the upper part of the tower appears to be Gothic or so. The gallery consists of nine arches on the south side and three on the west; unfortunately some of them, including the three western ones, have been blocked up which spoils the ensemble. The capitals and carvings on the corbels are interesting, but rather the worse for wear. The principal portal at the west end came from 12th-century San Nicolás and fits rather oddly. Within is the original portal. The church was acquired in 1905 by the ceramicist Daniel Zuloaga (uncle of the painter Ignacio Zuloaga, owner of the castle in Pedraza) who used it as his atelier; it is now a museum.

From the Plaza del Conde de Cheste, you can descend the road to the Plaza del Azoguejo or take a quieter narrow street that passes the little church of SAN SEBASTIÁN with a lovely portal and ends at the top of the aqueduct.

THE AQUEDUCT Stairs descend to the Plaza de Azoguejo. The view is great, especially if the peaks of the Guadarrama range are still covered with snow.

The remaining section of the aqueduct is 813 m (2,670 feet) long and where it crosses the square it is 128 m (420 feet) high. It was probably built during the reign of Augustus (27 BC–AD 14) and brought water from the mountains some 15 km away to the Roman settlement on the heights. It was repaired at the end of the 1st century AD under Trajan. Note the total lack of mortar. Severely damaged in a Moorish raid of 1071, it was restored by Isabella.

By the 18th century, houses had been built against the arches and plans to remove them never seemed to get anywhere. Richard Ford[5] relates how in 1806 the coach of the pregnant wife of the Swedish ambassador overturned amidst the rubble, and the lady miscarried. Charles IV ordered the arches cleared at once, thus exposing the Plaza de Azoguejo for the first time in many years.

Descending to the Plaza de Azoguejo, there is a virtually irresistible camera shot of the tower of San Justo across the Plaza de Azoguejo, framed between the piers of the aqueduct.

The Plaza de Azoguejo used to be a maelstrom of traffic thundering under the arches of the aqueduct and doing it no good. Now, happily, it and several blocks south have been closed to traffic and replaced by a pleasant pedestrian mall. This has made for some fairly circuitous routing to get from one side of the aqueduct to the other, but the gains at least for pedestrians (and the fabric of the aqueduct) have been considerable.

SAN JUSTO A hike up the hill to the late 11th/early 12th-century church of SANTOS JUSTO Y PASTOR is a must. The cult of the martyred brothers attained popularity in 7th-century Spain and their success was assured when Ramiro II defeated Caliph 'Abd al-Rahman III in 939 at Simancas on their feast day.

Their church has recently reopened after some years of restoration. The nave had been a total ruin. The principal treasures are in the apse, wonderful frescoes of about 1220 (or earlier), found only in the 1960s. They were covered over by desperate men of the 14th century and later who, to protect themselves against plague, were wont to whitewash the interiors of churches with disinfectant lime. Many early frescoes have been so preserved.

The paintings cover the biblical ground from Genesis to the Crucifixion and Christ Triumphant. They include, in the apse, a rather odd-looking Christ framed in a mandorla representing the radiance of his glory. He is surrounded by the twenty-four Elders of the Apocalypse in lively converse. Below on the left is the Crucifixion; on the right the Descent.

The scenes on the right wall are the best preserved. In the upper register are depicted the Taking of Christ in the Garden and the Kiss of Judas, with a companion of Jesus whacking off the ear of the soldier (Matthew 26:51). Below are the Three Marys, rather damaged, and three Roman soldiers with swords and shields, attired in the latest 13th-century knightly fashions, hurrying out of the deep window embrasure, rather a clever touch.

The lower register on the left is gone. Above, on the curve of the vault, is the Last Supper. On the vault itself is an Agnus Dei with apostles, saints, angels, and so on.

The scenes on the soffit of the triumphal arch are fascinating. The Creation is in the middle, with birds and fishes still visible though damaged. On the right are Adam and Eve with a serpent that looks like an intelligent moray eel; on the left, figures identified as Cain and Abel. The scenes are wonderfully animated.

On the north side of the nave, a door opens into a room below the tower. The tympanum above it carries a fine relief in extraordinarily good condition, with traces of polychrome. Much of the colour was lost, apparently, when a torrential rainstorm during the recent restoration penetrated the roof and washed down the walls.

Extraordinary also is the apparent lack of agreement on what the scene represents. When I first saw it, just as the restoration was beginning, I was told it depicted the Three Marys at the Sepulchre, with the angel on the right and a bishop (San Justo?) on the left, his crozier rather squashed by the curve of the finely decorated band around the tympanum. Now, however, one is informed that it depicts Saint Helena, the mother of Constantine, with two lady companions discovering the True Cross. The bishop is now Makarios, bishop of Jerusalem in the early 4th century when the Empress Helena was questing for relics. Yes, the lady on the right wears a crown and there is indeed a cross above what I insist on thinking is the tomb (note the winding cloth draped over the side), but the three ladies are carrying jars of unguents and I remain persuaded that the scene shows the Three Marys. There are yet other explanations, but I stick with mine.

In the chapel on the north is an 11th-century crucifix figure with articulated arms known as Sto Cristo de los Gascones. According to legend, it was brought from France in 1088 by a group of Gascon settlers. It is a curious and rather affecting piece, with a long sad face.

The original body of the church underwent major changes, especially when the tower was built. A climb up the tower, which has lost all but two of its windowed storeys, affords a fine view over town and country. The tower has the same tall slender corner columns as San Esteban. San Justo is very worthwhile; don't miss it.

SAN MILLÁN From the Plaza de Azoguejo, take the main street down to the church of San Millán in a plaza on the right. You pass en route early 13th-century SAN CLEMENTE on the left. It has suffered over the years, but if you walk up the left side, you can still see part of the apse and deteriorated corbels. The stairs to the now filled in west portal were presumably lost to street-widening.

Between San Millán and the walls of the upper city lay the *morería* or Moorish quarter into which was gathered the Mudéjar population that remained after the conquest.

The church was built between 1111 and 1126 under the patronage of Alfonso I of Aragón, husband of Alfonso VI's daughter and successor Urraca, who controlled large parts of his wife's kingdom at one time or another during their years of feuding. An earlier church stood on the site of which only the much-restored tower remains. The galleries were added in the 13th century, as was the fourth apse on the north side, adjacent to the tower. The carvings of the portals and the capitals are battered, but worth attention as are the corbels, especially on the north side and around the drums of the apses.

SAN ANTONIO EL REAL Following the aqueduct from the Plaza de Azoguejo in the opposite direction from the walled city you arrive at, on the right, the Monasterio de San Antonio el Real, formerly a hunting lodge of the future Enrique IV who in 1455 ceded it to the Franciscans. Thirty-three years later, they gave it to the Clares, their female counterparts, who have been there ever since. The principal chapel has a superb Mudéjar artesonado ceiling. The portal of the church is a fine example of Isabelline Gothic. The cloister is reputed to be very fine. Check with the Tourist Office for visiting hours.

VERA CRUZ Still outside the walls, below the Alcázar and across the Eresma valley, is the little twelve-sided Church of Vera Cruz (the True Cross). It was traditionally attributed to the Templars, but was probably built by the Order of the Holy Sepulchre. The church was dedicated to the Holy Sepulchre in 1208, but in 1224 Pope Honorius III sent a piece of the True Cross and the dedication was changed.

In the central chapel, also twelve-sided, elevated in the middle of the church, fledgling knights stood vigil before taking their vows. The tower was originally detached, as was often the case in early churches. The three semi-circular apses on the east side are a later addition. Vera Cruz belongs now to the Order of the Knights of Malta.

From Vera Cruz there is a fine view of Segovia across the Eresma valley, with the Alcázar riding high above, and an even better view from further up the hill where one can park by a small church and walk out into the field.

Across the road from Vera Cruz and down the slope stands the 17th-century CONVENTO DE LOS CARMELITAS DESCALZOS (the Barefoot Carmelites) containing the tomb of San Juan de la Cruz (1542–91), mystic, poet, and friend of Sta Teresa de Avila.

EL PARRAL On the hillside in the other direction stands the mass of the Monasterio de El Parral, founded in 1447 by Juan de Pacheco, later marqués de Villena. Pacheco wormed himself into the good graces of the future Enrique IV and the two conspired against the powerful Álvaro de Luna, minister of Juan II of Castilla. When de Luna fell in 1453 and Enrique succeeded his father in 1454, Pacheco came into his own, but while posing as the faithful servant of the king he was really out to enrich himself, which he did quite well.

The monastery was entrusted to the Hieronimite Order (founded in Toledo in 1374) and construction began in 1459. The king was a heavy contributor. The original architect, Juan Gallego of Segovia, was replaced in 1472 by Juan Guas of Toledo who also worked on the old cathedral of Segovia. The deaths of both Villena and Enrique IV in 1474 interrupted work, but the church was finished in 1503. The tower dates from 1529.

Gutted during the Carlist Wars of the mid-19th century, it was long closed for restoration, but is now open, to a degree. Inside the monastery portal (ring for admission) is an arcaded patio, a pool and a fine view of the Alcázar. You are shown the adjacent small cloister, a quiet place with gently rounded arches, but the great cloister can only be glimpsed; it is the abode of the monks.

The visitor is admitted to the church proper through the unfinished portal of Juan Guas. The church is a lofty single nave affair, with fine vaulting and chapels instead of aisles. A raised tribune fills the west end. The main attraction is at the east end where a retablo of polychromed wood (1528) soars up to the vaults above, flanked by the elaborate Renaissance tombs of the marqués-founder (left) and his wife María de Portacarrero (right). The elaborate portal at the right end of the crossing, leading to the great cloister, is also the work of Juan Guas.

In the arms of the crossing hang huge late 16th-century painted canvases in grisaille depicting scenes of the life of Christ. They were found in 1950, rolled up fresh as new, in the Dominican monastery of Santa Cruz nearby.

El Parral may be reached by car, but it is far more pleasant to walk to it through the lovely peaceful park that stretches along the right bank of the Eresma. A path leads down in front of the monastery of Santa Cruz and crosses a bridge. It is particularly lovely in the early morning with the sun striking the towers of the Alcázar high above.

SANTA CRUZ The Convento de Santa Cruz la Real was founded in 1217 by Domingo de Guzmán, founder of the Dominican Order, as his first convent in Spain. It was built on the site of the cave where he established himself. Ferdinand and Isabella set afoot a major reconstruction which included the Isabelline Gothic portal. The tympanum shows the royal pair kneeling on either side of a pietà, with a Crucifixion above in the midst of the usual Isabelline adornments. Juan Guas was probably the architect of the reconstruction.

SAN LORENZO A road that turns off beside the convent leads to the main square of the barrio of San Lorenzo, a charming little corner of Segovia with half-timbered houses and a fine church built on the ruins of a Mozarab structure of which a few elements remain.

It has three imposing apses, a good gallery, a horseshoe portal and a brick Mudéjar tower.

Northeast of Segovia

Between Segovia and the Duero stretches an undulating landscape of great beauty, wooded in part, with fields of grain and pastures cut across by the intensely cultivated valleys of little rivers coming down from the snowy crest of the Sierra de Guadarrama to swell the Duero. The valley of the Duratón is particularly attractive. The region is thick with small villages, many with Romanesque churches worth a visit. It is pleasant to poke around on country roads, the fields, brown, green or yellow depending on the season.

Sotosalbos Departing Segovia on the road to on the road to Soria (N-110), you come first to Torrecaballeros, the church tower of which is occupied in season by three or four families of storks. The N-110 continues across rolling fields, with views of the Guadarrama range on the right.

Off to the left appears the stout square tower of the church at Sotosalbos. The signposted road to the village is just around a bend. This is a wonderful church and if you are lucky enough to find the priest and gain entry, you will be in for a treat. He is a local historian of some renown; his booklet on the history of Sotosalbos gives much information on the church and village. If you can't get in, enjoy the gallery, the carvings on the corbels and the main portal which will keep you busy for some time.

SAN MIGUEL DE SOTOSALBOS The parroquia dates from the 12th century. Its gallery of seven arches, plus the main portal on the south side and another on the east, has nine battered but still legible capitals combining fantastic (monsters), secular (tournament with knights) and religious (Adoration) scenes.

The little figures under the cornice are extraordinary, a profusion of warriors, artisans, apostles, signs of the zodiac, animals, flowers and even a hand of God. Each is nested in a little arch which rests on carved corbels, between which are metopes with further carving. It is an astonishing place. The bold zig-zag carving of the archivolts and windows is also striking.

In the interior, much altered, the rectangular apse is original and preserves frescoes of Christ in Majesty and the insignia of the Evangelists. (These are the angel of St Matthew, the winged lion of St Mark, the winged bull of St Luke and the eagle of St John.) The raised tribune at the west end is made of a portion of the former artesonado ceiling. To the left of the triumphal arch is a 12th-century wooden Virgin with the Child and an apple in her right hand. Both figures look straight forwards with wide, rather anxious expressions. It was found in the church.

In the ground floor of the tower are the sacristy and the museum. Among the treasures of the latter are a little 12th-century Christ, found only in 1966 during restoration work, and another 12th-century polychromed wooden carving of the Virgin and Child. The Virgin wears an odd cap (wool?) pulled over her head. Both look rather grave and gaze past you into – what? It is an oddly moving little piece.

Collado Hermoso The second carving came from the Cistercian monastery of SANTA MARÍA DE LA SIERRA near this next village beyond Sotosalbos on the N-110. It was found in the 1930s in the episcopal palace in Segovia, but had been listed in a 1504 inventory of the monastery.

The monastery, originally a Benedictine foundation of around 1133, affiliated with the Cistercians in about 1212. At some point it was placed under the monastery of Sta María de Sacramenia (see page 176) as a priory and subsequently downgraded to the status of a *granja* or farm. It was suppressed in 1835 (along with other monasteries in Spain) and its holdings sold. The ruins, now a shelter for cows and horses, are buried in the woods on the hillside just south of Collado Hermoso. Enough remains of the vaulting and ribs to make it clearly recognizable as Cistercian. The ruins are overgrown and there were masses of wild flowers when we visited.

To reach it, take the track that goes off right from the N-110 just as you reach Collado Hermoso and carry on to a largish house set a bit back, on the right. Leave the car and walk up the track to the left until ruins and/or animals appear.

Pelayos del Arroyo This tiny agricultural village with a handful or two of inhabitants lies just past Sotosalbos, off to one side of the local road. Its little parroquia of SAN VICENTE stands on the opposite side of the village from the road. The exterior of the apse preserves good carved corbels. The original south door has been protected by the addition of an outer portal. In the apse are faded frescoes of the life of San Vicente. The capital of the column supporting the left side of the triumphal arch is quite unusual, depicting a mounted knight with his dogs bidding farewell to his wife (who wears a wimple) and household.

The frescoes on the south wall are of great interest. The upper panels show scenes from the life of San Vicente, to be read from right to left in the upper row and left to right in the lower. Early in the 4th century, Emperor Diocletian unleashed a particularly savage persecution of the Christians and many were the Spaniards added to the lists of saintly martyrs. The Roman governor of the day was one Dacian and here he is, his name written above him, in the midst of his court condemning Vicente; Vicente broken on the wheel; the raven guarding his body from attack by wild beasts; Vicente dumped into the sea where the fish refused to eat him; Vicente safe on shore. (The medieval section of the Prado has two panels representing Vicente's fate which are worth noting; his calm demeanour throughout his trying ordeals is impressive and, no matter what, he keeps his hands folded over his privates.) Below these frescoes, in an entirely different style, are a centaur with bow hunting a deer with huge antlers, and two knights jousting. Once again, as in San Baudelio (Soria), there is a question of whether the secular paintings indicate a non-religious use for the original structure.

The priest of Sotosalbos holds the key to San Vicente. Mass is said on Sunday morning which is the only time the church is open to the public.

West and north of Sotosalbos are the villages of La Higuera, Tenzuela, Torreiglesias and Peñarrubias, all with churches, but we push on from Pelayos via CABALLAR and LA CUESTA to Turégano. Caballar's church sits on the side of a hill above the villages; its three portals (unusual) are of some interest. The church at La Cuesta sits rather forlornly on its hill with an air of abandon.

Turégano Turégano has a good arcaded Plaza Mayor dominated by its stout castle crowning the hill. The bulk of the castle rises from behind a crenellated curtain wall, with corner towers. Embedded in the castle moat is the 13th-century church of SAN MIGUEL; seldom has the fabric of church and castle been so closely interwoven. Two mighty turrets bracket the three tiers of the *espadaña* (belfry) of 1703. The outer line of walls has been reduced to large fragments; the second line of walls and the castle are in remarkably good shape.

Turégano had been an important Celtiberian stronghold, occupied subsequently by the Muslims. Fernán González, the first independent count of Castilla (c. 930–70), conquered the region and entrusted the repopulation to his son Gonzalo who built a new castle, greatly modified in later centuries. It played a role in the conjugal strife between Queen Urraca of Castilla and her husband Alfonso I of Aragón; in 1123 she gave castle and town to the bishop of Segovia in order to make her peace with the pope.

A 15th-century bishop was responsible for the expansion of the church to its present size and for the castle which encompasses the church. The different construction periods are clearly visible inside the church.

Ferdinand of Aragón stayed in the castle in late December 1474 to collect his thoughts and consider how best to deal with Isabella who had been crowned Queen of Castilla in Segovia while he was tending to Aragonese affairs.

A track leads up to the castle where you can park just outside the main gate. A very pleasant lady custodian (not always there, however) will take you around the church, and show you how to scramble up into the castle. From the roof you get a good idea of the layout and can admire the landscape sweeping away on all sides. The huge wooden doors of the south portal of the church are the 13th-century originals. They were discovered hanging at the west portal, walled up since the rebuilding of the 15th century.

In a tiny cell dug in the massive walls behind the altar Antonio Pérez, lover and co-conspirator of the famous one-eyed Ana de Mendoza, Princess of Eboli, was held for a time after the two had been arrested by Philip II. Or perhaps it was in another room; some doubt he was held here at all, but why spoil a good story?

From Turégano it is an easy run to Sepúlveda, but I want first to go back to the N-110. You can take the C-603 towards Aranda de Duero, but it is a rather dull drive across flat land through scrubby pine woods.

Requijada Continuing past Sotosalbos on the N-110, take the road just beyond La Salceda toward Pedraza. Watch for an isolated little hermitage on the right of the road just before the turn (left) to the village. NUESTRA SEÑORA DE LAS VEGAS has a nice gallery with seven arches and a door, and, inside the gallery, an attractive portal with rosettes.

Pedraza de la Sierra Pedraza is a cheerful walled town with a stout fortified gate guarding its single access, a picturesque Plaza Mayor and an impressive CASTLE. The castle stands on the site of a Muslim fortress. It has had various owners, including the Velasco, created constables of Castilla and dukes of Frías by Ferdinand and Isabella. We have met them in Berlanga de Duero. The castle was purchased in 1920 by the painter Ignacio Zuloaga (1870–1945) and houses a small collection of his works.

François I of France, captured by Charles V at Pavia, near Milan, in 1525, was held here before being removed to Madrid. He was released in exchange for his two sons, including the future Henri II, who remained hostages from 1526 to 1530 and were imprisoned in the tower of Pedraza castle under harsh conditions for the last year and a half. They had been kept at Villalba de los Alcores (Valladolid), but Charles became so annoyed at the French king's failure to raise the necessary ransom money that he decided to tighten the screws on the unfortunate youths.

The arcaded PLAZA MAYOR is charming, though the adjacent church has an undistinguished interior and the tower has been spoiled. Narrow streets and old houses make for good strolling, but on weekends the place is packed with Madrileños come to enjoy the restaurants and the country air.

Off in a field below a sharp bend in the road up to Pedraza are the ruins of NUESTRA SEÑORA DEL CARRASCAL. A little clambering about will get you a good photograph of Pedraza and its walls.

A side road to the right, north of Pedraza, leads to El Arenal (or Orejana); its church has a fine gallery.

San Pedro de Gaillos Taking the main road from Pedraza to Sepúlveda, a fine Romanesque church stands in the plaza of San Pedro de Gaillos. The west end was mutilated, probably in the 16th century, by the erection of a ponderous tower. Only the main doorway to the gallery, two flanking arches on either side and another elegant doorway at the east end remain of the original. The gallery has paired columns with interesting if deteriorated capitals. The interior portal is beautifully decorated with rosettes, stars, spirals, floral and vegetal motifs. The cabecera is a bit heavy, overpowering its three little windows, but the ensemble is well worth the detour.

Castilnovo Not far east of San Pedro, towards Sepúlveda, stands this charming castle set among trees by the edge of a stream. A good view of the rear of the castle may be had from a small road that parallels the stream. Built between the 12th and 15th centuries, it has had several distinguished owners, including Fernando I of Aragón, Juan II's minister Alvaro de Luna, and Ferdinand and Isabella. It is now the headquarters of the Centro Cultural Hispano-Mexicano and is visitable by appointment, I understand. The rear terrace looks like a fine place for cocktails.

Sepúlveda This ancient town is strung out along a high narrow ridge between two streams, the Duratón and the Caslilla. The Romans called it Septem Publica. It endured all the usual ups and downs in the long struggle of the Reconquista, and was taken from the Moors by Fernán González of Castilla in 940. After Almanzor sacked it in 984, it was virtually abandoned. As late as 1065, what was left of the town stood only a few miles from the Moorish frontier.

With the death in 1075 of the amir of Toledo, friend of Alfonso VI, that town fell into hostile hands and Alfonso needed a new frontier fortress. Commanding the approaches to the Somosierra Pass on the principal route between Burgos and Toledo, Sepúlveda saw its fortunes restored. The king granted it a new fuero in 1076, confirming the earlier one of Fernán González. The leaders of the town were able to parlay their strategic importance into favourable concessions and for many years Sepúlveda enjoyed a high degree of autonomy and its citizens great personal freedom, well protected against arbitrary encroachments from the ecclesiastical and lay lords who prowled the land.

The town was sacked by the French in 1808, during the Peninsular War, but the present sad shape of the castle and the disappearance of the main gate are thanks to mid-20th-century developers.

The best approach is from the south, from Pedraza. The road

suddenly swings left and the whole town appears across the valley, spread out on a ridge, the church of El Salvador crowning the highest point. At the bend is a mirador from which you can enjoy the view. The road descends into the valley of the Caslilla, twists around a bit, and heads up the slope to the Plaza Mayor.

The Plaza Mayor occupies an irregular space in the saddle between two ridges. At the west end is the old ayuntamiento, tucked against the scant remains of the castle. At the other end, dealers in pottery spread out their wares.

From the far (east) end of the Plaza Mayor a street leads past San Bartolomé – seemingly always closed but exhibiting nothing particularly noteworthy on the outside – to the top of the ridge and fine views of the town with the Duratón gorge to the north and the valley of the Caslilla to the south.

EL SALVADOR A street leads up from behind the ayuntamiento to stairs to the church of El Salvador. For many years this important church disputed the honour of being the oldest in the region with San Miguel in San Esteban de Gormaz (Soria). A stone in the apse bears the date ERA MCXXXI or AD 1093 and a rereading of the date found at San Miguel now places that church some eighteen years later. The gallery of San Miguel still takes first place, however.

From the foot of a broad flight of stairs, look up at the handsome cabecera of the church, with the gallery on the left and a strong square tower, originally detached, at the northeast corner. The principal entrance for worshippers climbing up from town is at the east end of the gallery, at the top of the stairs.

The gallery runs around the south side and west end, but the arcade of the latter was replaced by a solid wall in the 16th century and now has only a simple door which leads directly to the west door of the church proper. The plain main portal is inside the south gallery. The eight arches of the gallery are arranged in four pairs, each separated by a stout pier. The four slender columns dividing the pairs of arches have either floral capitals or badly eroded scenes.

The lofty body of the single-nave church rising above the gallery presents a pleasing appearance from any angle. The stonework and proportions of the building are very fine. At least one art historian[6] has pointed out the odd contrast between this work, probably by a master from along the Camino de Santiago, and the crudeness of some of the sculpture. Many capitals in the interior carry clearly Visigothic motifs, such as stars and petals within circles. One curious carving to the left of the triumphal arch depicts a fierce beast seizing an unfortunate human by the arm.

The interior has four bays. The nave, barrel vaulted with three transverse arches (matched externally by three buttresses), is unusually high, allowing for windows framed by double arches in the south wall above the roof of the gallery and one in the north wall. The apse is lower than the nave, allowing another window above the triumphal arch. A little arched window also opens at the west end.

Be sure to note the corbels around the apse and the external detailing around the windows.

SAN JUSTO This church stands down the north side of the ridge. It has a reportedly good crypt and a Mudéjar artesonado ceiling; it has been *en obras* (under repair) for years. According to a passing lady, the custodian does not live in Sepúlveda and comes only for funerals. 'Listen for the sound of drums,' she said. The shell of ruined Santiago is nearby.

NUESTRA SEÑORA DE LA PEÑA Following the same street, which begins at the Plaza Mayor between the ayuntamiento and El Paulino restaurant, you can either pass out through one of the massive old gates or follow along to the north side of town where the 12th-century (or early 13th) church of Nuestra Señora de la Peña stands at the edge of the scarp that plunges down to the Duratón.

Over the portal inside the gallery is a fine tympanum with Christ and the four Evangelists surrounded by the Elders of the Apocalypse. Below the figure of Christ in Majesty is a chrismon supported by two angels with, on the left, a knight with lance mounted on a dragon and, on the right, the weighing of souls with San Miguel and the Devil tugging at the scales. Rather crude additions have been tacked on to the original apse and the interior was refashioned in the 18th century with the usual fatal results. The splendid square tower with three tiers of nicely detailed window openings bears an inscription of 1144. The site and the view are striking.

Duratón Continuing out of town and south across the rolling landscape with the Sierra de Guadarrama as backdrop, you shortly reach the village of Duratón with its very fine Romanesque church, LA ASUNCIÓN, visible across the fields to the left as you approach the village.

The gallery has ten arches, six to the west of the portal and four to the east, with another entry arch at the east end. The handsome main portal is lobed, a Moorish touch. The twin columns of the gallery are united by single capitals.

The most interesting, indeed wonderful, capitals are the two depicting the birth and infancy of Christ. One to the left of the portal shows Gabriel(?); the Visitation; the Virgin in bed with two midwives in attendance; and the Child, well swaddled, in the manger apparently being grazed on by the cow and ass. Angels with incense-burners hover above these last two scenes. On the other side is a shepherd in his hood and a king.

A capital on the right side of the gallery shows the Three Kings with a rather regal Mary and Child, while Joseph is around the corner, moping as usual in Spain, his head resting on his hand.

The unusually long cabecera includes the presbytery and apse proper and is articulated with stout buttresses. There are a number of good corbels and window capitals. Remains of a Visigothic necropolis lie about.

From Duratón, go east a bit to the N-I, passing the little church at Sotillo with a nice lobed portal and good corbels, then south (right) a short distance, and pick up the N-110 (right) back to Segovia. It is a pretty drive, but then most are in these parts. Other churches in the vicinity with good portals or other details include those at El Olmo, Castillejo de Mesleón (the other side of the N-I), Perorrubio, Castrocerna and Ventosilla.

Eastern Segovia Province

The N-110 from Segovia meets the N-I, jogs north (left) for a while and then resumes its eastward path towards Soria. It by-passes RIAZA, a popular ski resort, with a good Plaza Mayor – a large oval surrounded by attractive old houses.

Some 20 km beyond Riaza, the huge church of STA MARÍA DE RIAZA looms up on a hill to the right of a bend in the road. It is difficult to gain access to the church to view its fine artesonado ceiling; the key is usually with a priest who resides in Ayllón and comes only for services. Drive up there anyway; the views are superb. The church dates from the 13th to 16th centuries.

Ayllón The N-110 runs straight to the massive gate set in its old walls; you bear left for Soria but, before that, go through the gate to the Plaza Mayor. Just inside is the splendid façade of the PALACIO DE CONTRERAS (late 15th century), its massive door enclosed in an *alfiz*, that square frame of eastern inspiration around doors and windows so beloved of Spanish builders. Above the lintel are two bands of inscription and above that three shields bearing coats of arms.

The arcaded Plaza Mayor could be attractive, with its fountain, but it is a car park. The church at the end of the square retains remnants of its Romanesque past; it has been much built upon. The apse has some good corbels and there is a portal within a curious porch of much later construction. To the right and around the corner is a 15th- or 16th-century church of little apparent interest. The ruins of the Convento de San Francisco, marked by a lofty *espadaña* (belfry), occupy the ridge above the town. It may have been the first Franciscan house in the peninsula.

Maderuelo Some 15 km northwest of Ayllón on the C-114 towards Aranda de Duero is a large reservoir, the Pantano de Linares del Arroyo, in which you can swim. There are beaches on the north side of the reservoir.

On the bluff opposite stands the decayed town of Maderuelo. Just to the left of the narrow bridge across the reservoir, at the very edge of the water (and sometimes in it), is the sad little church of VERA CRUZ, now totally derelict. It was once adorned with 12th-century frescoes, brought to light in 1907. They were transferred to canvas in 1948 and removed to the Prado where they may now be seen in a new and very effective installation in the same room with the frescoes from San Baudelio.

The Prado has created a mock-up of the original chapel. The accompanying text is clear enough and the scenes easily decipherable (mostly), so I will say nothing further other than to remark on scenes on the west wall: the Creation of Adam and the Temptation with Adam and a sinuously curvaceous Eve with That Serpent. Everyone is very blond, including God. The frescoes have stylistic affinities with the paintings from San Baudelio; some experts detect the same hand.

Maderuelo is a walled town, with a stout gate. Entering, you pass Romanesque San Miguel on the left and finally reach Sta María, perched on the edge of the cliff, with horseshoe arches in its side gallery. The reservoir lies below you and the meseta undulates into the indistinct distance.

The drive south, back to the Burgos–Madrid N-I, on a spring day with green fields and snow still on the Guadarrama range, is most pleasant.

We have now reached the eastern limits of the Province of Segovia. Let us go back to Sepúlveda.

The Lower Duratón Valley

The Duratón valley from Sepúlveda to Peñafiel and the Duero offers a particularly lovely and interesting drive. There are several local roads to explore; you never know what you may find. The first stop must be the hermitage of San Frutos, poised at the tip of a long narrow spur formed by a loop in the Duero.

San Frutos To reach the hermitage from Sepúlveda, go south across the Caslilla and turn right on a local road. On your right are views of the Duratón canyon which offers good walks for nature lovers. Beyond Villar de Sobrepeña, the road forks in the middle of a lush green valley; take the right to Villaseca (signposted 'San Frutos'). The road crosses the Duratón, which here runs through a meadow full of stands of trees and picnic spots.

Once over the bridge, a short walk along a path to the right leads to the CUEVA DE LOS SIETE ALTARES (Cave of the Seven Altars), an extremely ancient hermitage dating most likely from Visigothic days when hermits abounded in these parts. A slight climb is required to reach the cave. Visible (albeit dimly) through the grate are altars in horseshoe arched embrasures surrounded by primitive geometric designs cut into the rock face.

Should you be coming up the C-603 from Turégano to Cantalejo, take the road through Sebúlcor to the fork and then the left branch to Villaseca. Dams impound reservoirs in the Duratón gorges and other possible roads may end at flooded gorges or private properties.

Just at Villaseca, an unpaved track goes off to the left across the flat fields 5 km to the hermitage. This track is *not* advisable in wet weather. A huge loop of the Duratón, a hairpin turn, and the hermitage comes into view in its marvellous setting.

San Frutos (d. 715) was a rich youth of Segovia who was inspired by tales of the early Egyptian hermits to retire with his brother and sister to this remote spot. At the time of the Muslim invasion, many Christians took refuge with them. The story goes that Frutos, seeking martyrdom, went out to meet the Moors at the narrowest part of the neck on which his retreat stood. Planting his staff firmly, he ordered the Moors not to pass, whereupon the Lord, always watchful over his flock in those perilous days, produced a miraculous fissure in the rock (*la cuchillada de San Frutos*) leaving the doughty hermit on the safe side.[7] Not for long, though. His wish for martyrdom was soon fulfilled.

In 1076, Alfonso VI donated the existing hermitage to the monastery of Santo Domingo de Silos, whose founder had died but three years before. According to an inscription found on the site, Abbot Fortunio of Silos, successor to Domingo, sent one Michael in the year 1100 to rebuild the hermitage. What I find particularly interesting, given the remoteness of the spot even now, is that the new building was consecrated in the presence of the metropolitan of Toledo, the Cluniac Bernard, an exceedingly powerful figure, installed by Alfonso VI at the head of the Toledan diocese after the taking of the town in 1085.

The church of 1100 had a single nave and a rounded apse. An enlargement in the 13th century added two lateral chapels with apses, of which only the north survives, and the existing west portal. The two galleries are in ruins as are the monastic buildings which were destroyed by fire in the 19th century. A few carved corbels remain.

Further out on the point is a tiny chapel with the now empty tombs of San Frutos and his siblings Santa Engracia and San Valentín who met their martyrdoms at Cuéllar.

The site alone is worth the detour. The gorge, dammed below the hermitage, is filled with greenish water and vultures wheel and turn below you, suddenly riding currents of air to soar high above.

Fuentidueña I suggest you backtrack to Sebúlcor and Cantalejo before heading north on C-603. As the road reaches the Embalse

(Reservoir) de las Vencias, a minor road left goes to Fuente el Olmo while the C-603 veers right to San Miguel de Bernuy. Both villages have Romanesque churches. We proceed straight ahead to the west of the Duratón to Fuentidueña.

For the best view of the fortified town, stronghold of the lower Duratón in the Middle Ages, turn right at the junction at the edge of town (instead of left into town), drive up the hill and look back. The fortifications of the old town enclose a now almost empty enceinte, castle ruins crown the ridge, churches and the modern village stand further down.

Passing through an ancient gateway, make your way uphill past a very battered 16th-century church on the left, and an even more battered monastic layout further along on the right, and turn to park just below Romanesque San Miguel.

SAN MIGUEL The influence of the builders of this splendid church radiated throughout the lower Duratón valley. In common with most Segovian churches, the original 13th-century structure had a single nave, a semicircular apse, a gallery (on the north side, unusually) and portals on the north and west (the west is better preserved). In the 16th century, the sacristy and tower were added on the south side and a transept was created which sticks out clumsily on both sides from the original fabric.

The apse is nicely articulated, with good windows, and it and the nave exhibit a battery of imaginatively carved corbels covering subjects sacred and profane. They are well worth a careful look. You will not have much company. Fuentidueña seems unusually deserted even by Spanish village standards.

SAN MARTÍN Walk up the track, past several Celtiberian tombs, and around the bend to the gaunt ruin of San Martín. The apse is missing; it is in the Cloisters (Metropolitan Museum) in New York. The interior is now a cemetery. The Fuentidueña Chapel room at the Cloisters also contains the museum's frescoes from the hermitage of San Baudelio (Soria) and just outside are the two frescoes from San Pedro de Arlanza (Burgos).

The road into the castle complex is barred, but walk out through the gateway into the fields for a view of tumbled walls and crumbling towers and the Duratón valley below.

From Fuentidueña, our goal is Sacramenia, via minor but perfectly good roads. The drive is soothing: fields and bluffs, tall slender poplars which turn golden in the autumn and flocks of sheep. Depending on your route, you can stop to see churches at Vivar de Fuentidueña (on the river) or at Fuentesoto and Pecharromán further east.

Sacramenia There are two monuments of note here, neither of which, alas, I have visited. The ruins of the church of SAN MIGUEL stand high on a bluff overlooking the village and are reportedly worth the arduous-looking climb. The remains of the MONASTERIO DE STA MARÍA DE SACRAMENIA founded by Alfonso VII in 1141 are on private property ('Coto de San Bernardo') and cannot be visited by the ordinary passer-by.

The monastery was the first Cistercian foundation in Castilla and one of the first in the peninsula. William Randolph Hearst bought the cloister and the refectory in 1925 and had them crated up and shipped to the United States where they sat in a warehouse for thirty years. The stones were finally bought by some Miami developers and re-erected in North Miami Beach as the 'Ancient Spanish Monastery' Museum in 1954.

The story of the sale and removal of the frescoes from the hermitage of San Baudelio in the 1920s has been related on pages 110–11. The 1920s also saw the sale of the frescoes discovered in San Pedro de Arlanza (Burgos), now distributed between American and Spanish (Barcelona) museums, and the sale to Hearst of both the Sacramenia cloister and the choir reja from Valladolid Cathedral (now in the Metropolitan Museum, New York).

Spanish writers tend to be a trifle bitter about this, understandably, but at the time there was nothing to prevent such sales and Spanish owners sold. In the San Baudelio case, opponents fought the sale up to the highest court in the land, but lost. None of this could happen today, of course, but at the time, the preservation of cultural patrimony was not such a hot issue in Spain nor, for that matter, in France.

From Sacramenia, our little road makes its way through the Duratón valley to Peñafiel. I recommend this route because it affords a sudden and very dramatic view of Peñafiel castle riding high on its crag at the head of the valley.

But now we return to Segovia to begin our tour of the western side of the province.

Pedraza de la Sierra (Segovia) Pedraza is a charming old town. The plaza mayor is often the scene of country dances and other performances. The castle once belonged to the painter Ignacio Zuloaga and houses a small collection of his works.

Sepúlveda (Segovia) Originally a Roman settlement, this hilltop town sank into oblivion. after the Muslim invasion. In the 11th century its strategic position made it vital to Alfonso VI in the run-up to his capture of Toledo in 1085. This view from the southeast shows the church of El Salvador, the oldest (1093) in the region.

Sepúlveda (Segovia) A close-up of the church of El Salvador shows the gallery on the south side, a typically Segovian feature. Constructed early in the 12th century this is probably the second oldest such gallery in the region.

Duratón (Segovia) In the fertile valley of the Duratón river lies the village of Duratón and its remarkable church of La Asunción, another 12th-century gem. The gallery is a particularly fine example of the Segovian tradition of galleried churches. The lobed portal is of Muslim inspiration.

Duratón (Segovia) Of the many carved capitals in the lovely gallery of La Asunción, the two dealing with the birth and infancy of Christ are particularly notable. This shows one of the three Kings approaching a very regal, crowned Mary with Christ on her lap. Joseph is on the face of the capital to the right, moping and looking left out as he usually does in Spain. The other capital shows the Virgin in bed, with two attendant midwives, and the Christ child in the manger.

San Frutos (Segovia) In a wide bend of the canyon of the Duratón river stands this isolated hermitage named after an early toiler for the faith who was martyred by the Muslims in 715. He defied the Muslim force that was attacking his sanctuary and the good Lord responded by striking a mighty gash across the spur of rock on which the hermitage stands. It is visible to this day, but it did not long delay the Muslims, alas. The present hermitage was founded around 1100 and enlarged subsequently. Much of the complex has fallen victim to time and fire, but enough remains to make this a most evocative spot to visit.

Northwestern Segovia Province

Two main roads lead north and northwest from Segovia, the N-601 to Cuéllar and Valladolid and the C-605 to Arévalo. We encounter now a very different architectural heritage. This is the region of Mudéjar Romanesque where structures were built primarily of brick instead of stone. When the construction boom of the late 11th and 12th centuries got under way, brick was cheaper and the makings of it more abundant here than stone. The Mudéjar were particularly adept at working in brick and plaster and they put their skills at the service of their new Christian lords and a new style of brick Romanesque emerged.

Cuéllar The N-601 crosses rolling and not particularly exciting country, covered with stands of pine to Cuéllar. This rather drab town does have several fine brick Mudéjar churches, most notably SAN ANDRÉS and SAN ESTEBAN, with characteristic tall rounded apses and blind arcades. The lofty apse of San Esteban is a quite extraordinary composition of blind arcades, rectangles, squares and geometric patterns.

The Celtiberians had an important settlement where the castle now stands; the Romans left no trace. The town was repopulated in the 9th century by the counts of Monzón on behalf of the kings of León, but Almanzor put a stop to that and Cuéllar did not begin to recover till the late 11th century.

Enrique IV stripped his half brother and sister, Alfonso and Isabella, of the lordship of Cuéllar in 1464 and gave it to his favourite, Beltrán de la Cueva, the putative father of the queen's daughter, Juana la Beltraneja. In the war with Juana's betrothed, Alfonso V of Portugal, that followed Enrique's death and Isabella's accession to the throne, Cuéllar was held by the Beltranejistas while the Fonseca family of nearby Coca supported Isabella.

Beltrán de la Cueva is an interesting example of the new nobility created by the later Trastámara kings, in this case, Enrique IV. Starting off as a mere page, he caught the king's favour and soared upwards, accumulating titles and positions along the way. He also seems to have impressed the queen, Juana of Portugal, who in 1462 gave birth to the Infanta Juana whose suspected paternity brought her the nickname of la Beltraneja. She was Isabella's rival for the succession.

As the king came increasingly to mistrust his alleged friend, Juan Pacheco, marqués de Villena (founder of La Parral Monastery in Segovia), he built up Beltrán as a counterweight. Enrique made him Master of the Order of Santiago, and though he lost that honour in a subsequent power play, he led the king's armies against the dissident nobles in 1465–68 and was rewarded by being made duke of Albuquerque. He defeated the rebel nobles at Olmedo (Valladolid) in 1467.

After Enrique and Isabella made peace (albeit briefly) in 1468, the duke retired to his castle at Cuéllar. He seems to have made it up with Isabella, whose side he took in the war of succession against Alfonso of Portugal and la Beltraneja and he also fought in the campaigns against Granada. He died in 1492 after the fall of that city.

Cuéllar had two walled precincts; the walls of the upper town around the castle are the best preserved. You enter through an imposing arch. The castle was remodelled in the 16th and 18th centuries; it is still an impressive sight. Pleasant must have been strolls in the arcaded galleries high up beneath the roof line, commanding views over the country. It is now an educational institution.

A short distance beyond Cuéllar, the N-601 enters Valladolid Province and takes us to Portillo, whose castle we shall visit when we get to that province.

Sta María la Real de Nieva Returning to Segovia, let us take the C-605 to the village which takes its name from the convent of Santa María la Real de Nieva, founded in 1393 by Catherine of Lancaster, daughter of John of Gaunt and Constanza of Castilla, daughter of Pedro the Cruel. Catherine was wed to Enrique III, thus uniting the rival lines of Pedro and his half-brother and assassin, Enrique II. In 1399 she donated the church and its dependencies to the Dominican Order. The convent was under royal patronage and often played host to monarchs.

After the disentailment of 1835, the monastic buildings were converted to various municipal purposes, suffering serious fire damage in 1899 and 1900. The latter destroyed the *retablo* in the *capilla mayor* along with the venerated statue of the Virgin, the miracle-attended discovery of which in 1392 occasioned the foundation of the convent.

The cloister is fascinating. The entrance is via a small door facing the main road and a small car park. Around the corner is the north portal of the church, a striking Gothic ensemble. Restoration work in the 1920s unblocked the arcades of the original cloister and in the 1950s restorers dismantled the 16th-century upper storey, bringing the cloister back to its original splendour. There are some eighty-six capitals and almost all of them are worth a close look.

The best are those depicting daily life in the cloister and the outside world. Monks, all neatly tonsured, sing to the accompaniment of an organ, or lift building stones with a tackle and pulley, or study and so on. There are scenes of ploughing and of jousting and the hunt. There is the Flight into Egypt, an Annunciation and other scenes sacred and profane, including centaurs and lapiths. Angels hold the shields of Catherine and Enrique III. The capitals are, for the most part, remarkably well preserved.

Our last visit to the monastery illustrated perfectly our dictum never to take a locked door as the final answer. It was Saturday morning, the cloister was supposed to be open, but it was locked. We crossed the street to the Ayuntamiento and found a gentleman sitting alone in his second-floor office who, when we enquired, jumped up, got the key and came down and across the street to let us in.

At the entrance to the village of Sta María, a road leads left to Villoslada, 2 km beyond which is an isolated hermitage which preserves its 12th(?)-century apse and south portal. It isn't much, but its survival in the midst of these vast and ancient farmlands is somehow rather moving.

Coca From Santa María a road leads northwest to Coca which has a spectacular CASTLE-PALACE, built entirely of pinkish brick. It is a superb example of Mudéjar work, a rarity in Castilla where castles tend to be of stone.

It was begun around 1448 by Alonso de Fonseca (d. 1473), bishop of Ávila, archbishop of Sevilla, and head of one of the great ecclesiastical families of Castilla who were loyal supporters of Isabella in her struggle for the throne. Enrique IV granted Alonso the señorío of Coca with permission for a market. When Alonso I took up his ecclesiastic career, his brother Fernando succeeded to Coca, but was slain at Olmedo in 1467 by Beltrán de la Cueva. His son Alonso (d. 1505), 3rd lord of Coca, helped King Ferdinand to victory over the Portuguese supporters of Isabella's rival, Juana la Beltraneja, at Toro in 1476.

This Alonso had three half-brothers. Juan Rodríguez de Fonseca

(d. 1524), Isabel's chaplain, was successively bishop of Badajoz, Córdoba, Palencia and Burgos as well as head of the Council of the Indies. (He thought Columbus was crazy to attempt his scheme.)

Alonso II (d. 1512) became archbishop of Santiago de Compostela in 1460 and held various great offices of state, including the presidency of the Council of Castilla. He accompanied the Infanta Catalina on her voyage to England in 1501 to wed Prince Arthur. He was succeeded at Santiago by his illegitimate son Alonso III (d. 1534) who in 1524 was elevated to the see of Toledo (and later named Patriarch of Alexandria). Alonso III was a notable patron of letters and the emerging Renaissance style in architecture, especially in Salamanca where we will meet him again. He was a generous supporter of the Dutch humanist Erasmus, as were others of his class in early 16th-century Spain, until the Inquisition quashed the movement as dangerous to orthodoxy.

The third brother, Antonio 'el Valoroso' (d. 1532), 4th lord of Coca, fought valiantly for his sovereigns at Granada and then distinguished himself during the Comunero uprising by putting Medina del Campo to the torch.

Various members of this illustrious family, who were so much at home in the highest realms of church and state, lie beneath splendid Renaissance tombs in the church of STA MARÍA LA MAYOR, begun in the same style as the castle by the unnumbered Alonso, 3rd lord of Coca. The fine Mudéjar tower belonged to an earlier church.

The castle was restored some years ago to what appears to be pristine condition and now houses a forestry school. From within the deep moat rise up the mighty walls and towers, topped by merlons and turrets. Both the brickwork and the actual construction are exceptionally intricate. The thick layers of mortar between the courses of brick make for a particularly attractive effect.

The castle overwhelms the town, the history of which predates the Romans when it was known as Cauca. It was a town of the Celtiberian Vaccaei and was treacherously taken in 151 BC by L. Licinius Lucullus (ancestor of the man whose life-style gave us his name as an adjective) who massacred the inhabitants. Pompey sacked Cauca again during the war with Sertorius seventy-five years later. The town eventually recovered and prospered and in the 4th century formed part of the estates of the noble Spanish general Theodosius whose son was Emperor Theodosius I the Great (379–395).

Coca preserves brick walls and an impressive gate, as well as the tall Mudéjar tower of vanished SAN NICOLÁS, gaunt and square.

From Coca, it is an easy run to Iscar or Olmedo, both in Valladolid Province. Coca and Cuéllar, along with Segovia to the east and Iscar and areas further west as far as Salamanca, were first repopulated under Alfonso VI around the time of his conquest of Toledo (1085).

We have wandered very close to Valladolid, but we must return to Peñafiel to pick up our route along the Río Duero.

Notes

1. Joseph Townsend, *A Journey through Spain in the Years 1786 and 1787* (London, 1791), Vol. II, p. 117.
2. Richard Ford, *A Handbook for Travellers in Spain* (London, 1966), p. 1226.
3. John Hay, *Castilian Days* (Boston, 1871), p. 176.
4. Ford, *Handbook*, p. 1227.
5. Ford, *Handbook*, p. 1229.
6. Inés Ruiz Montejo, *El Románico de Villas y Tierras de Segovia* (Madrid, 1988), pp. 21 and 25.
7. Walter Muir Whitehill, *Spanish Romanesque Architecture of the Eleventh Century* (Oxford, 1941), p. 228, tells the tale in full.

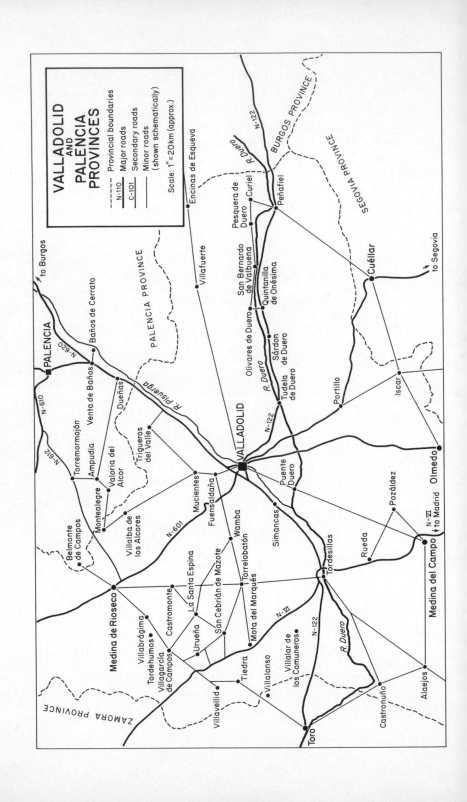

VALLADOLID
AND
PALENCIA
PROVINCES

Provincial boundaries
N-110   Major roads
C-101   Secondary roads
Minor roads
(shown schematically)

Scale: 1" = 20km (approx.)

to Burgos

BURGOS PROVINCE

SEGOVIA PROVINCE

PALENCIA

PALENCIA PROVINCE

ZAMORA PROVINCE

N-620
N-610
N-611

Baños de Cerrato
Venta de Baños
Dueñas
Torremormojón
Ampudia
Valoria del Alcor
Montealegre
Villalba de los Alcores
Belmonte de Campos

Trigueros del Valle
Mucientes
Fuensaldaña

VALLADOLID

R. Pisuerga

Encinas de Esqueva

Villafuerte

Pesquera de Duero
Curiel
Peñafiel

San Bernardo de Valbuena
Quintanilla de Onésima
Olivares de Duero
Sardon de Duero
Tudela de Duero

R. Duero

N-122

Cuéllar

to Segovia

Portillo

Iscar

Puente Duero

Simancas
Wamba
Torrelobatón
Mota del Marqués

N-601

La Santa Espina
San Cebrián de Mazote
Castromonte
Urueña
Villabrágima
Tordehumos
Villagarcía de Campos

Medina de Rioseco

Villavellid
Tiedra
Villalonso
Villalar de los Comuneros

N-VI

Tordesillas
Rueda
Pozáldez
Olmedo

N-VI
to Madrid
Medina del Campo

R. Duero

Castronuño
Alaejos

Toro

7

Valladolid and Southern Palencia Provinces

Approaches

The direct route from Madrid to the city of Valladolid is via the N-VI west to the N-601 which branches off north at Adanero, a distance of about 190 km (120 miles). Even more direct is the A-6 toll (*peaje*) road via the Guadarrama tunnel. As the road drops down the flanks of the Gredos mountains, there are fine views of the meseta stretching away to the north as far as the eye can see. This may not always be far. Morning ground fog in the winter can make driving difficult. You can also reach Valladolid easily from Segovia.

Let us now go back to the Duero valley as we entered Valladolid Province on the N-122.

History

Valladolid Province includes the Tierra de Vino (wine) and the meseta south of the Duero and the Tierra de Pan (bread) and the Tierra de Campos (fields) stretching north of it. I have also included in this chapter part of southern Palencia Province.

The Camino de Santiago, the pilgrimage road to the shrine at

Compostela, cuts across Palencia Province and skirts the northern edges of Valladolid. From this highway of the Middle Ages, influences from beyond the Pyrenees filtered down into the peninsula along with warriors, monks and settlers who made the repopulation of the recovered zones possible. The area north of the Duero between the Pisuerga and Cea rivers was long and hotly contested between the kingdoms of León and Castilla, the older kingdom's upstart rival and eventual supplanter. Strongpoints were established along the Duero at Tordesillas, Simancas and Peñafiel in the 10th century; not until the late 11th was Valladolid founded.

The province contains striking evidence of the wealth that made Castilla mighty once the Reconquista was secured. The wool trade and, in the 16th century, the influx of treasure from the Americas created the huge plazas at Valladolid and Medina del Campo, the extravagantly adorned churches and palaces of the towns and the enormous village churches that loom ahead like beached ships as you cross the Tierra de Campos. The evidence of centuries of outward migration from the land is also striking; the emptiness of the landscape and the paucity of population in many villages are awesome.

EASTERN VALLADOLID PROVINCE

Peñafiel As we enter Valladolid Province from Burgos, the CASTLE OF PEÑAFIEL appears riding high on its ridge, the curtain walls gleaming white in the sun and the keep slightly forwards, like the bridge of a ship. It is one of the better castle views in Spain.

The walls enclose an enceinte 210 m (690 feet) long by 20 m (66 feet) wide and are punctuated by thirty cylindrical towers. The outer and lower walls date from the 11th century; the inner line, of much finer construction, is from the end of the 13th century or a bit later.

The road up is a bit tricky to find; you must go around the back of town and look for signs. There is a parking space just below the fortified entry portal, the only one to break the line of walls. Towering above is the keep, all 34 m (112 feet) of it. Stairs lead to the roof through two high vaulted chambers.

At the confluence of the Duero and the Duratón rivers, the crag was occupied early and formed a key fortress on the Duero line. It was seized by Almanzor; Sancho García of Castilla won it finally for

Christendom in 1013. According to legend, the count plunged his sword into the ground on the summit of the ridge and cried: 'From this time forwards, this will be the most faithful crag of Castilla' ('Desde hoy en adelante, ésta será la Peña más fiel de Castilla'). A good story, but a document of 943 already refers to the castle of 'Penafidele'.

Queen Urraca was besieged here in 1112 by her husband, Alfonso the Battler of Aragón. They did not get along. Alfonso IX turned Peñafiel into a *señorío* for his son the future Fernando III; his son Alfonso X (1252–84) lived here and eventually ceded it to his brother, the Infante Don Manuel (d. 1283). Sancho IV confirmed the grant to the latter's infant son Don Juan Manuel.

Don Juan Manuel's turbulent life in the early 14th century has been dealt with in the historical section (pages 45–6). He fought for power, schemed and rebelled against his king and in the end turned to contemplation and the writing of books, the best known being *El Conde Lucanor*, in his castle of Peñafiel.

After Juan Manuel's death in 1349, Peñafiel reverted to the crown, but in 1367 Pedro I granted it to Juana Manuel, daughter of the late prince and wife of the future Enrique II of Castilla. Their son, Juan I, bestowed it upon his younger son Fernando de Antequera who became king of Aragón as Fernando I in 1412 and passed Peñafiel to his son, the future (1425) Juan I of Navarra and later (1458) Juan II of Aragón.

This turbulent prince spent years conspiring against, when he was not actively fighting, his cousin Juan II of Castilla who besieged Peñafiel in 1429. The possession of Castilian fortresses like Peñafiel and La Mota in Medina del Campo gave the Aragonese branch of the Trastámara family a powerful base in their constant efforts to undermine their cousin of Castilla.

In 1465 Enrique IV, son of Juan II, granted Peñafiel to Don Pedro Girón, Master of Calatrava, in whose family, counts of Urueña and dukes of Osuna, it remained till early in the 19th century. The main structure of the castle dates from this time. We will meet Don Pedro again at Urueña, on the opposite side of the province.

This was a typical example of the widespread alienation of royal domain by the weak later Trastámara kings in favour of the nobility who supported them. Pedro Girón (d. 1466) started out as a page to the future king and soon gathered about him titles and honours, not to mention a lot of property and land, mostly in Andalucía. He even made a bid for the hand of the Infanta Isabella and the king agreed, but Girón died before anything could come of it, much to Isabella's relief.

Peñafiel kept its reputation as a centre of dissent when Pedro's grandson, Juan Téllez Girón (d. 1528), second count of Urueña, supported Juana la Beltraneja, Isabella's rival for the throne. After the defeat of Juana's supporters near Toro in 1476, the count switched sides and became a firm supporter of Isabella and Ferdinand. A descendant was made duke of Osuna; we have encountered the family at Jadraque (Guadalajara) en route to Soria.

Down in town is the former CONVENTO DE SAN PABLO, built as a palace by Alfonso X and given by Juan Manuel to the Dominicans. Here he deposited his beloved books for safekeeping. In the prologue to *El Conde Lucanor* he warns readers that books contain many errors of copying. One letter often looks like another, he says, and careless copying can change the meaning of words and confuse the issues, faults that are then imputed to the author. Therefore, Juan Manuel 'prays those who read any book which has been copied from one that he wrote, [if] they find any faulty word, that they do not put the blame on him but rather consult the very book which Don Juan himself wrote'.[1] He then enumerates the works that he is depositing in San Pablo.

Sad to say, all those works so carefully deposited, doubtless in beautifully written and illuminated manuscripts, have perished and his literary output is now known only through copies, only about half of which have survived.

The church of the former convent has three naves and an extra-ordinary polygonal brick *Mudéjar cabecera* of 1324–40, on a stone basement course, with prominent buttresses separating the wall into panels. The window arches are lobed horseshoes and similar blind arches decorate the buttresses. The Mudéjar work is all the more striking in contrast with the Plateresque apse of the Renaissance chapel built in the 16th century by a descendant of Juan Manuel.

Do not miss the PLAZA DE COSO in the southern corner of Peñafiel, visible from the castle, but harder to find once on the ground; the entrance is through a narrow passageway off the main street, around the corner to the right as you come back into town from the castle. The plaza is surrounded by ancient houses with curious shuttered balconies, and there is a superb view of the castle riding high above.

Curiel Two routes lead from Peñafiel to Valladolid. Both pass through lovely country, the Ribera Vallisoletano (adjective for Valladolid), the heartland of the vineyards of the Ribera de Duero. The north bank road is pleasantly rural; on the south bank is the main N-122.

Cross to the north bank and follow a minor road up a valley to the castle of Curiel, probably one of the oldest in the region, dating from the early years of the 10th century. It may have been built after the defeat of Caliph 'Abd al-Rahman III at Simancas in 939. Its strategic importance declined with the building of Peñafiel, clearly visible south across the Duero.

As you approach up the valley, the enormous rocky mass ahead resolves itself into the castle, though it looks from afar like an integral part of the outcrop. It is accessible only by foot and would be a very tough climb. Below the ridge, where the village now stands, are the remains of a 13th-century castle. During the civil war between Pedro the Cruel and his half-brother Enrique de Trastámara, Curiel often sheltered foes of the king. Enrique imprisoned Pedro's bastard sons here, one for 55 years. Just off the square is the *parroquia* of Curiel with a nice portal.

Later in the 14th century, Curiel passed from royal control when Juan I bestowed it on Don Diego López de Zúñiga whose family converted the castle into a palace that stood intact until the early years of this century when it was destroyed by its owners. Only the main tower and the façade fronting the square remain, along with some of the defence bastions overlooking the valley.

On his hurried and incognito dash from Aragón to join Isabella in 1469, Ferdinand stayed at Curiel after leaving El Burgo de Osma.

Valbuena de Duero From Curiel, take the road to Pesquera de Duero (a wine centre) and San Bernardo where a sign points left to the Cistercian monastery of Valbuena de Duero. (The monastery is at San Bernardo, *not* at the village of Valbuena de Duero, another kilometre or so further.) The monastery, now a partial ruin, was founded in 1143; the church, spacious and cleanly simple in the Cistercian style, dates from 1200 to 1230.

In the sacristy to the right of the main altar are 13th-century paintings of knights and kings and such, seemingly over-restored, but perhaps not. Such secular paintings are rare. They were discovered only a few years ago under layers of plaster.

The cloister is lovely: the lower part dates from the early 13th century while the upper storey is 16th-century Renaissance, making for a striking contrast. The monastic rooms and halls disposed around the cloister according to the standard Cistercian plan include a fine refectory and an awful baroque *sala capitular*. Good views of the exterior and the whole complex may be had from the field behind the church. Further on, at the village of Olivares de Duero, an old bridge crosses the river to Quintanilla de Onésima and we rejoin the N-122. Just to the east, across the river from the village of Valbuena de Duero, are the vineyards of the *Bodega Vega Sicilia* that produce some of the most prized wine in Spain.

Sta María de Retuerta Some 6 km west of Quintanilla is Sardón de Duero, 2 km beyond which is the Premonstratensian abbey of Sta María de Retuerta, founded in 1143. The abbey allegedly has a fine chapter house and cloister, but it is in private hands. We espied them by their pool one hot Sunday afternoon, but decided not to bother them. Judging from the state of the buildings and fields, Retuerta is a prosperous farm.

Next comes Tudela de Duero with a 16th-century church and a pleasant bridge. The N-122 crosses to the north bank of the Duero here and you very shortly enter the outskirts of Valladolid.

Valladolid

This commercial and industrial city and provincial capital stands on the Río Pisuerga a short distance above its confluence with the Duero. With some 346,000 inhabitants, it is the largest town in Spain along the Duero; only Porto at the mouth of the river in Portugal is larger. The city is, among other things, an automobile manufacturing centre, capital of the Ribera de Duero wine industry and the administrative seat of the Autonomía de Castilla y León.

Vineyards had existed in the Duero valley for centuries; they expanded dramatically in the 15th century as population and demand increased. The area around Valladolid and the triangle to the south

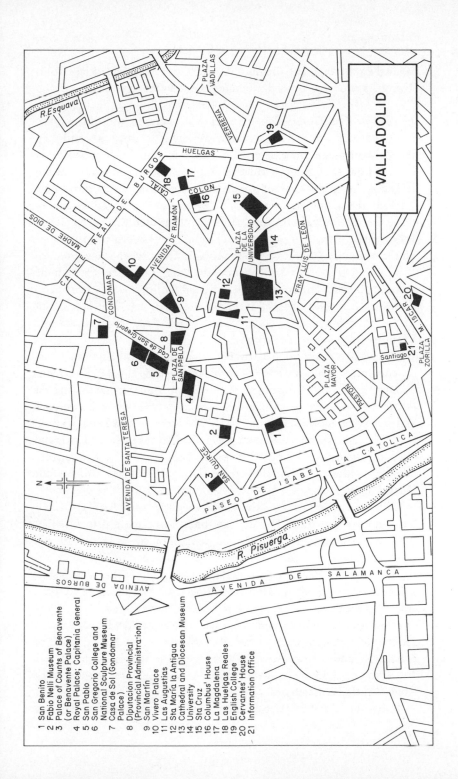

VALLADOLID

1 San Benito
2 Fabio Nelli Museum
3 Palace of Counts of Benavente
  (or Benavente Palace)
4 Royal Palace; Capitania General
5 San Pablo
6 San Gregorio College and
  National Sculpture Museum
7 Casa de Sol (Gondomar
  Palace)
8 Diputacion Provincial
  (Provincial Administration)
9 San Marfin
10 Vivero Palace
11 Las Augustias
12 Sta María la Antigua
13 Cathedral and Diocesan Museum
14 University
15 Sta Cruz
16 Columbus' House
17 La Magdalena
18 Las Huelgas Reales
19 English College
20 Cervantes' House
21 Information Office

formed by Medina del Campo, Arévalo and Madrigal de las Altas Torres have always been particularly suitable for viticulture.

History The Celtiberian Vaccaei were here in the 8th century BC; the Romans settled in the area from the 1st century AD and then the Visigoths had their day. The name of the town is variously derived from Arab sources. Bilad Walid, the Country of Walid, caliph in Damascus at the time of the Muslim conquest, is one possibility.

With the Christian reconquest, agricultural villages took root throughout the region. In 1072, Alfonso VI granted the site to Count Pedro Ansúrez (d. 1119), who founded the town. Pedro was the uncle of the cowardly Infantes de Carrión who married the daughters of El Cid and then beat and abandoned them near San Esteban de Gormaz (Soria). The Ansúrez were an old family, counts of Monzón (north of Palencia) since early in the 10th century. The first count had been a bitter rival of Fernán González for control of these Leonese–Castilian border lands.

The walled town stood between the Pisuerga and Esgueva rivers on the route from Burgos to newly-conquered Toledo, and commanded river valleys running north to Burgos and south to Segovia and Ávila. By 1100, Valladolid had a palace, a market, two churches and a *colegiata* built by Count Pedro. The citizens had been granted the usual liberties and the town was poised to take off. The original town centre was the present Plaza de San Miguel; population expansion in the 12th century brought a shift south to the present Plaza Mayor.

Valladolid soon attracted the attention of the royal family. Alfonso VII authorized a trade fair in 1152, one of the earliest in Castilla. Alfonso VIII annexed it to the royal domain on the death of the last of the Ansúrez in 1208.

His daughter Berenguela married Alfonso IX of León at Valladolid in 1197 and she was crowned queen of Castilla here in June 1217 (in succession to her brother Enrique I who died young), abdicating immediately in favour of her son Fernando III. María de Molina (d. 1321), herself a member of the royal family, wife of Sancho IV and tireless guardian and regent for her son Fernando IV and grandson Alfonso XI, lived here. Her tomb is in the 16th-century Convento de las Huelgas.

Pedro the Cruel (1350–69) married Blanche de Bourbon here in

1353; her unhappy tale is told later in the chapter. During the civil war between Pedro and his half-brother Enrique de Trastámara, his ally, Edward, Prince of Wales, the Black Prince, lived here for four months in 1367, after his famous victory over the Trastámara forces at Nájera (La Rioja). In the end, Valladolid declared for the future Enrique II and the new dynasty thus favoured it.

Whereas by the 14th century most European countries had settled on a fixed capital, the court of Castilla remained ambulatory, moving around between Burgos, Toledo, León, Sevilla and Córdoba, although there was a growing tendency to concentrate in the Burgos–Zamora–Toledo triangle. The peripatetic nature of the court made proper administration of increasingly complex state affairs very difficult.

From early in the 15th century, Valladolid became the favoured royal residence and thus the political centre of the kingdom, a pre-eminence which it retained for two centuries. In 1442, the seat of the Audiencia or Royal Chancery was permanently fixed here.

Catherine of Lancaster, daughter of John of Gaunt, Duke of Lancaster, queen of Enrique III, regent for their son Juan II, died in Valladolid in 1418. She was partially responsible for the fiercely anti-Semitic legislation passed by the Cortes of Valladolid in 1412. As early as 1293 another Cortes here had enacted repressive legislation and the Jewish community, long established, did not fare well in Valladolid. They were accused of having supported Pedro the Cruel in his losing battle with Enrique de Trastámara and in 1369 the *judería* was attacked and its eight synagogues destroyed. The 15th century saw efforts by the community to revive its fortunes, but it was too late. No trace of the judería survives today.

Isabella of Castilla married Ferdinand of Aragón here on 19 October 1469 and it was in Valladolid in 1483 that Ferdinand named Tomás de Torquemada first Inquisitor General.

Ferdinand's successor, Charles, first of the Habsburg dynasty, was only seventeen years of age in 1517 when he arrived in Castilla from the Netherlands where he had ruled since the death of his father Philip I in 1506. After calling on his mother, the unfortunate Queen Juana, at Tordesillas, he entered Valladolid. His first Cortes met in February 1518 and, reluctantly, recognized him as king.

Charles was accompanied by a flock of arrogant Flemish advisers and hangers-on. None of them, the king included, spoke Castilian. The new king's subjects were even more put out by his costly campaign to gain election to the imperial throne on the death of his grandfather Emperor Maximilian I in 1519. Along with the huge cost of this adventure, the imperial crown meant an absentee monarch for long periods. Why should Castilian money and men be wasted on non-Castilian purposes? – a question that was to occur regularly throughout the reigns of 'los Austriacos', as Spain calls its Habsburgs.

All these grievances came together in the Comunero revolt of May 1520, an uprising of the towns, and initially of a segment of the nobility, to defend the ancient institutions and rights of Castilla against the foreigners. Valladolid played a key role in the uprising. In September 1520, the two principal leaders, Juan de Padilla of Toledo and Juan Bravo of Segovia, actually arrested the Regent Adrian of Utrecht (the future Pope Adrian VI) at Valladolid, along with several members of the Royal Council. A few months later, however, in April 1521, the royalists won a decisive victory near Toro and put an end to the Comuneros.

Philip II was born here in 1527; he elevated Valladolid to the rank of *ciudad* or city in 1595. The city experienced a considerable boom in the first half of the 16th century. Nobles and prelates went all out to adorn the city and burnish their reputations with splendid buildings. A fire in 1561 destroyed the area around the Plaza Mayor and in the same year Philip II moved the court to Madrid.

Philip III returned to Valladolid in 1601 at the urging of his minister the duke of Lerma; Philip IV was born here in 1605. But Madrid became the permanent seat of the court in 1606 and Valladolid's years of glory were gone. Observed Richard Ford: 'Thus a position on a fine river, in a rich fertile country abounding in fuel and corn, and under a better climate, was abandoned for a mangy desert.'[2]

Deserted by their lords, the palaces decayed; the great new cathedral was never finished. Plagues in 1596–1602 and other ills reduced the town's population from 40,500 (1591) to 15,000 in the first half of the 17th century and it was devastated by plague again in 1647–52.

Royalty returned, albeit reluctantly, in 1710 during the War of Spanish Succession following the death of the last Habsburg, Charles II. Backed by the British and Austrians, Archduke Charles entered Madrid in September 1710, Philip V, the first Bourbon king, having been forced to withdraw to Valladolid. The allies were not able to hold the capital for long, and Philip was back in Madrid in December.

The 18th century saw something of a revival when the Canal de Castilla opened up Valladolid's hinterland, the rich fields of grain to the north (Tierra de Pan) and the lush vineyards to the south (Tierra de Vino). The new canal, a project of that busy monarch Charles III, enabled produce to reach its natural market.

Nevertheless, Henry Swinburne, who visited the town in 1775, could write:

> Being abandoned by their owners ... [the palaces] are fallen to decay and exhibit a picture of the utmost desolation; the palace of the king is so ruined that I could with difficulty find any body to shew me the spot where Philip [III] had resided. The private houses are ill-built and ugly ... The university is in the last stage of a decline, and trade and manufactures at as low an ebb. It is melancholy to behold the poverty and misery painted in the meagre faces, and displayed in the tattered garments of the common people; the women go quite bareheaded.[3]

Another disaster befell the town during the Peninsular War when it was taken by the French (December 1808). They caused extensive damage, as was their wont. Ford found only 24,000 people there in 1831. Recovery was slow, helped when the railway reached the town in 1860. By the turn of the century, the population was approaching 70,000.

Predominantly agricultural, Valladolid Province entered the 20th century poor and conservative. The depressing economic situation was turned around only in the 1960s and 1970s when the government targeted several neglected regions for development. Valladolid has been particularly successful, attracting investment and industry from abroad. Automobile firms, iron and steel, textile, food processing, engineering and construction companies are flourishing. The city has also drawn in people from the rural districts and the population has tripled in the last thirty years.

A Tour of the City The PLAZA MAYOR is a logical place to start. It is not particularly attractive, with traffic thundering through it, but the arcades help, as arcades usually do, and the balconied houses surrounding it have a cheerful air. Tables and chairs spill out over the sidewalks from cafés and bars. The plaza is exceptionally large, a legacy of its role as a commercial centre in the Middle Ages.

Alfonso VII authorized the holding of an annual fair here in 1152 and it was known as the Plaza del Mercado until the 16th century.

Along with the market activity, bullfights, autos de fe and other popular entertainments, the Plaza Mayor saw some special events. Álvaro de Luna, the fallen favourite of Juan II of Castilla, was executed here in 1453, done in at last by the nobility whose power he had fought for so long to contain and by the urging of the queen, Isabel of Portugal, who deplored his influence over her weak husband. (Despite his fall from grace, de Luna and his wife now lie beneath truly magnificent tombs in a chapel in Toledo Cathedral.) In this square in 1521 Charles I pardoned the remaining Comuneros and in 1559 Philip II presided over the first auto de fe as the Inquisition swung into high gear.

What you see now is the result of the rebuilding of the late 16th century after the fire of 1561, although the most prominent building, the Casa Consistorial, was built 1892–1908 after the demolition of a derelict earlier structure. In the middle is a paved island where Vallisoletanos gather to chat and stroll. In their midst stands a statue of Count Pedro Ansúrez, the city's founder.

This was the first rationally planned and executed Plaza Mayor in Spain, a product of Philip II's passion for order and monumentality. The fire was a disaster and the town council sent off an urgent appeal to the king in Madrid. Philip II responded at once, uncharacteristically – Valladolid was his natal town, after all – making clear his wish to be intimately involved with the work ahead. The city fathers consulted with him constantly, but financial difficulties, rivalries among architects and the vacillations of the king prolonged the rebuilding for some forty years.

Behind the *ayuntamiento* is the arcaded Calle de Cebaderia, down which traffic roars through the Plaza del Ochavo. This rather neat little octagon at the intersection of Cebaderia and Platerías must have been charming before automobiles.

SAN BENITO EL REAL   Turning left and then north (right) past one end of the public market, you see ahead the enormous porch of this monastery. The original monastery, a humbler affair, was founded by Benedictines in 1407. When this became the chief house of the Congregación Benedictina, a grander setting was required and the present Gothic edifice was built between 1499 and 1515. The porch and its octagonal corner tower, which gives the already rather severe church a military air, was one of the last works of Rodrigo Gil de Hontañón (d. 1577).

The richness of San Benito in its heyday can best be judged by visiting the National Sculpture Museum in the Colegio de San Gregorio (see below). Magnificent sculptures and choir stalls, among other treasures, were saved after the dissolution of the monastery in the 1830s and eventually installed in the museum, although major parts of the composition were lost.

To the left is the CONVENTO DE SAN BENITO. This mostly 17th-century structure, in the severest Herreran style (Juan de Herrera, architect of the Escorial) with an imposing but rather cold cloister, now houses offices of the ayuntamiento.

MUSEO ARQUEOLÓGICO Farther along is the 16th-century PALACIO DE FABIO NELLI. Nelli was a banker of Sienese extraction, one of the Italians who became dominant in 16th-century financial circles after the expulsion of the Jews wiped out indigenous financial know-how. The palace now houses the Archaeological Museum.

Depending on your interest in fragments from Palaeolithic to Roman times, the museum is worth a visit for three exhibits at least: a superb bust of a bearded Roman in Room VI and a marvellous bronze faun's head in Room VIII. There are also some fine mosaics from a nearby Roman villa. On the top floor is a rather remarkable early 14th-century fresco from San Pablo in Peñafiel, showing scenes from the life of Mary Magdalen and a Last Judgment.

Just beyond the museum, a gate in an iron fence opens into the COSO VIEJO, the old bullring, now cleverly converted to apartments around a very attractive central garden.

PALACIO DE LOS CONDES DE BENAVENTE The Plaza de la Trinidad, just north of the Coso Viejo, was the heart of the now vanished judería. On the left stands the early 16th-century palace of the counts of Benavente, now the public library of Valladolid and thus alive with students. It has a nice black and white tiled courtyard.

CONVENTO DE SAN PABLO A few steps beyond the Coso Viejo and around the corner is the Plaza de San Pablo, dominated by the spectacular façade of the church of the Convento de San Pablo. The original church was founded in 1276, the year in which the Dominicans first arrived in Valladolid. In 1463 the Dominican Cardinal Fray Juan de Torquemada (d. 1468), uncle of the Inquisitor, decided to rebuild the by then partly ruined structure.

Fray Alonso de Burgos (d. 1499), bishop of Palencia, took over the programme on Torquemada's death, and began adjacent San Gregorio in 1487. 'Fray Mortero' – Brother Mortar, as he was called – engaged Simón de Colonia from Burgos to carry out the works; the façade up to the cornice above the rose window is his, completed around 1497.

This is the first example we have seen since Sta María in Aranda de Duero (Burgos) and Santa Cruz in Segovia, of Isabelline Gothic, characterized by lacy ornamentation spread thickly over the surface along with complicated blind arches and other decorative devices. Busy, but certainly remarkable, and the richness of the decoration is emphasized by the two towers that frame it, unadorned save for the shields of the duke of Lerma, favourite and inept chief minister of Philip III. Lerma acquired the patronage of San Pablo in 1601 and undertook further works of aggrandizement, including the central portion of the façade.

Over the portal is the Coronation of the Virgin, on the right hand of whom, and half again as large, is the kneeling figure of Fray Alonso de Burgos, under the protecting eye of San Juan Evangelista. The flanking shields held by angels originally bore his arms, but Lerma replaced them with his own. The upper portion resembles an altar retablo, with saints, and scenes arranged in panels. The four Evangelists under tri-lobed arches immediately above the portal are the work of Simón de Colonia. The crests of Ferdinand and Isabella appear in the pediment.

The spacious interior, a vast single nave with side chapels instead of aisles, is rather stark. It was trashed by the French in 1809 and the conventual buildings were razed to the ground by Napoleon's orders. According to the story, a gardener killed a French soldier in the convent garden and threw the body down a well. Napoleon was thorough in his revenge; only the church survived.

The tombs that once occupied niches have been removed. The doorway at the end of the south transept is a splendid confection of the early 16th century that originally gave access to the funerary chapel of Fray Alonso. Above the door, the Virgin bestows a chasuble on San Ildefonso (d. 667), bishop of Toledo, who wrote a book defending the perpetual virginity of the Mother of Christ. He was rewarded by the appearance of Our Lady who draped him in a chasuble, a sort of ecclesiastical poncho.

With his customary reticence, Fray Alfonso appears to the right of the central group, on his knees and being helpful. The portal is now blocked; access to the chapel is through San Gregorio around the corner. In the apsidal chapels are sculptures by Gregorio Fernández, the most typical being the dead Christ in the right chapel. Of Gregorio Fernández, more anon.

SAN GREGORIO AND THE SCULPTURE MUSEUM Around the corner to the right of San Pablo is the COLEGIO DE SAN GREGORIO (built 1488–96). The Isabelline Gothic façade has been variously attributed to Juan Guas, to Gil de Siloé and to Simón de Colonia. The saint in question is Pope Gregory I the Great (d. 604). The doorway beneath a richly embroidered ogival arch is flanked by four hairy wild men (*maceros*) and above, in the tympanum, Fray Alonso, on his knees again, presents the church to San Gregorio who is flanked by Santo Domingo and San Pablo.

The upper part of the ensemble (1495) consists of a tree bearing lions holding huge shields with royal escutcheons, along with other figures and heraldic devices. Around the base of the tree, naked children disport themselves.

Inside to the left is the Capilla del Colegio, built (1484–92) by Juan Guas as Fray Alonso's funerary chapel; he lies beneath a slab in the centre. The handsome chamber is decorated in the purest Hispano-Flemish style. The retablo was made by Alonso Berruguete for a church in Olmedo and was brought here in 1932. It has nine exquisitely sculpted panels. The one on the lower left of Christ carrying the cross amid an animated throng of people is especially fine.

Left and right of the altar are gilt bronze statues of Lerma and his wife, curiously and probably not accidentally resembling the statues of Charles I, Philip II and their wives in the church of San Lorenzo de El Escorial.

The adjacent sacristy, the work of Simón de Colonia, contains a recumbent tomb figure of a knight, in polychromed wood. He is sleeping peacefully, in full armour, his long hair tumbled on the pillow. It is a rare survival.

The two-storey cloister of San Gregorio is a triumph of Hispano-Flemish style. Below, graceful spiral columns support rounded, slightly flattened, arches. The upper storey is an extravaganza of lacework in stone. Rather short spiral columns support arches enclosing twinned lights supported by very slender, carved, columns; the upper halves of the arches are like elaborately worked window blinds, pulled halfway down. Around the eaves are marvellous gutter spouts in fantastic shapes: demons, dragons and assorted animals.

At San Gregorio, in August and September 1550 and again in April 1551, before a tribunal convened by Charles I, Fray Bartolomé de Las Casas argued his case for the protection of the New World's Indians against enslavement and the rapacity of the Spanish settlers. When he returned from Mexico for the last time, in 1547, after an unsuccessful stint as bishop of Chiapas, Las Casas took up residence in San Gregorio where he remained for most of the rest of his life.

San Gregorio houses the MUSEO NACIONAL DE ESCULTURA RELIGIOSA, an extraordinary collection of 13th- to 18th-century Castilian sculpture which is not to be missed. It is notable for the works of three great sculptors: Alonso de Berruguete (c. 1488–1561), Juan de Juni (c. 1507–77) and Gregorio Fernández (1576–1636).

The first rooms contain figures by Gregorio Fernández; the Baptism of Christ by John the Baptist and a Pietà are especially notable.

The next rooms contain fragments of the enormous retablo carved in 1526–32 by Alonso de Berruguete for San Benito el Real. The retablo remained in situ, slowly decaying, for some years after the dissolution of the monasteries in the 1830s and the surviving pieces were installed here in the 1930s. Alonso, one of the greatest sculptors of 16th-century Spain, was the son of Pedro de Berruguete (fl. 1477–1504), Spain's first major Renaissance painter. Like his father, Alonso studied in Italy, arriving in Florence about 1504, the year in which Michelangelo unveiled his David.

The grand staircase with huge armorial shields (the fleur de lys) of Fray Alonso de Burgos leads to the upper cloister and the main part of the museum where sit the splendid choir stalls from San Benito, carved 1525–29 by Diego de Siloé and others. Note St Stephen carrying the fatal stones in his cloak and St Peter with a huge triple crown and keys.

The museum is an introduction to the Valladolid school of occasionally rather excessive realism in sculpture. Juan de Juni, born

Jean de Joigny, led the way for realism as opposed to the idealistic approach of earlier artists. A room is dedicated to his works; his Burial of Christ is remarkable in its way. Most effective is a concerned John trying to restrain Mary's grief. The adjacent figure of Santa Ana is a wonderful study of old age.

Juni had a worthy successor in Gregorio Fernández. Agony, blood, gaping wounds, tears – the lot! Everyone has little ivory teeth and glistening eyes. By the reign of Philip III (1598–1621), Spanish sculpture was devoted almost entirely to religious themes. Its aim was to inspire the faithful and Gregorio Fernández was the leading proponent of the school. He was a man of profound religious conviction, noted Richard Ford, whose purpose was to make sculpture 'a means of religious education, for rarely in his hands was it prostituted to monkish hagiology and deception'.[4]

A museum such as this gives one the opportunity to look closely at works of art that are all too often lost in the darkness of Spanish churches and cathedrals. Retablos in major churches can usually be illuminated by dropping a coin in a box, but they are still distant, and getting into the *coro* to look at the often marvellous carving on the stalls is often difficult.

PALACIO DEL CONDE DE GONDOMAR A few steps farther up the street from San Gregorio is the Palace of the count of Gondomar or, from the emblem above the central façade, the CASA DEL SOL. Diego Sarmiento de Acuña (1567–1626) was a loyal servant of the crown and in 1612 Philip III named him ambassador to the England of James I. Don Diego served twice in this post, 1613–18 and 1619–23, and in 1617 was created count of Gondomar. He strove to ease the lot of English Catholics and by dint of persuasion aided by money managed to slow down English privateer attacks on Spanish possessions overseas. He was instrumental in securing the execution (1618) of Sir Walter Raleigh who had been attacking the Spanish in the Caribbean in defiance of his sovereign's orders.

One of his major tasks was to negotiate the marriage of Charles, Prince of Wales, the future Charles I, and the Infanta María Ana, daughter of Philip III. The purpose of this seemingly quixotic scheme was to keep James I from supporting the Protestant states against the Austrian and Spanish Habsburgs on the eve of what was to be the Thirty Years' War and in particular to isolate the Dutch. Philip and his advisers saw James as a restraining influence on the German Protestants. Gondomar persuaded James that a Spanish marriage for the Prince of Wales would be a good idea. From the Spanish point of view, of course, Charles was a heretic and only a conversion would enable such a marriage to take place. The Infanta was particularly unenthusiastic.

When Philip IV succeeded to the throne in 1621, aged sixteen, the twenty-three-year-old Charles was persuaded that the personal touch might prevail where diplomats had failed. In March 1623, therefore, the prince and the Duke of Buckingham arrived in Madrid, after travelling incognito across Europe as John Brown and Tom Smith, would you believe, to conclude negotiations.

There was immense opposition to the scheme at the Spanish court, not the least from the first minister, the Count-Duke of Olivares. In the end, negotiations collapsed and a rather annoyed Charles went home in September to contract, finally, a French marriage.[5] And María? She did not do at all badly. She married her cousin Ferdinand, King of Hungary, later Emperor Ferdinand III, and her portrait by Velázquez hangs in the Prado.

DIPUTACIÓN PROVINCIAL Returning to the Plaza de San Pablo, the building on the left, facing the plaza, with a window niche in the corner, was the palace of the Pimentel family where Philip II was born in 1527. It is now the Diputación Provincial. The entrance foyer has modern *azulejo* (tile) scenes from the Valladolid of Philip's day, including a dramatic depiction of the great fire of 1561. The building has a good courtyard.

CAPITANÍA GENERAL OR PALACIO REAL The classical building across the plaza was built in the early 16th century for Francisco de los Cobos, a young man from Andalucía who rose in the world to become private secretary to Charles I. Cobos sought to create an efficient administration and bureaucracy in Castilla and in the 1540s was responsible for arranging that state papers be deposited in the castle of Simancas (see below) thus creating Spain's first national archive.

Both Charles I and Philip II lived in the palace on occasions. In 1600, the duke of Lerma bought it and promptly sold it to Philip III once he had persuaded that pliant and pious monarch to transfer the court back to Valladolid from Madrid. The unhappy Don Carlos of Verdi opera fame was born here, as was Philip IV. During the Peninsular War, both Napoleon (in January 1809) and Wellington (in July 1812) lodged here. It became the seat of the Capitanía General early in this century. The Renaissance patio with typical portrait medallions in the spandrels of the flattish arches is well worth a look, guards permitting.

SAN MARTÍN The Calle de las Angustias leads southeast past the Diputación Provincial to the heart of old Valladolid. About halfway down the street, tucked off in some narrow lanes that make photography difficult, is the church of San Martín. The fine 13th-century tower is all that remains of one of the oldest churches in the city, demolished at the end of the 16th century and replaced by something of little interest.

PALACIO DE LOS VIVERO In this palace, a couple of blocks or so north of San Martín, Ferdinand and Isabella were married in 1469. The ceremony was performed virtually in secret to avoid any hostile reaction from Isabella's half-brother Enrique IV. The palace has passed through various civic uses and has recently been renovated as the Archivo Histórico Provincial.

It was built by Alonso Pérez de Vivero, an official under Juan II. Don Alonso was accused of disloyalty by the king's favourite, Álvaro de Luna, and was flung to his death from a window of a house in Burgos on Good Friday, 1453. This was the last straw for the anti-Luna party, led by the queen, Isabel of Portugal, who wanted to get rid of the man who had such a hold on her husband. The favourite was stripped of his honours and executed in the Plaza Mayor some months later. Don Alonso also built the castle at Fuensaldaña outside Valladolid (see below).

A later Vivero went to the New World; his son was created marqués del Valle de Orizaba and his son acquired the palace in Mexico City known as the Casa de los Azulejos. It now houses a restaurant of the Sanborn chain in its splendid patio.

NUESTRA SEÑORA DE LAS ANGUSTIAS This church, begun at the end of the 16th century, stands at the lower end of the Calle de las Angustias. The church contains the famous Virgen de las Angustias by Juan de Juni. The seven knives piercing her bosom were added in the mid-17th century.

STA MARÍA LA ANTIGUA At the bottom of Calle de las Angustias a very fine tower comes into view, that of Sta María la Antigua. The late 11th-century church dating from the time of Pedro Ansúrez, founder of Valladolid, was a simple, single nave affair. Population growth demanded larger quarters and in the 13th century a gallery and the tower were added. The tower is particularly graceful and elegant.

The Romanesque church was replaced in the 14th century by the present Gothic structure; only the tower and the north gallery remain. The interior is curiously stubby, with a raised tribune at the west end occupying only the nave, leaving the aisles open. In the apse are two tiers of Gothic stained glass.

STA MARÍA LA MAYOR Across the square between Sta María la Antigua and the Angustia are the scant remains of the original cathedral huddled against the mass of the new one. Sta María la Mayor was built in the late 11th century, also at the orders of Count Pedro, but was largely replaced in the 13th century by a Gothic colegiata.

At Sta María la Mayor, on 3 June 1353, there took place a wedding fated to bring unhappiness to the bride unusual even for those hard-hearted times. When Alfonso XI was carried off by the Black Death in 1350, his fifteen-year-old son Pedro came to the throne under the protection of his mother, María of Portugal, and her confidant and countryman Juan Alfonso de Albuquerque, immensely rich and detested by the Castilians.

By his mistress, Leonor de Guzmán, Alfonso XI had left a bastard brood (including the future Enrique II) and the Queen Mother, after years of humiliation, lost no time in seeing that lady dead, with Albuquerque's assistance. The stage was set for civil strife and the factions, national and international, lined up. It was imperative that the young king be married as soon as possible. The Queen Mother and Albuquerque chose Blanche de Bourbon, niece of Philippe VI of France.

In the meantime, young Pedro was living it up with his chums to the point where Albuquerque decided it was best to settle him down with a nice girl, pending the outcome of negotiations with France. A meeting was arranged between Pedro, eighteen by now, and María de Padilla. The Padilla had been ruined in the civil strife earlier in the century, and María's brother and uncle saw an opportunity to recoup their fortunes. María was lovely and accomplished. Pedro fell madly in love with her and remained so for the rest of her life, politics and his two marriages notwithstanding.

Encouraged by María and the Padilla and by a new-found sense of his own worth and freedom after a season campaigning against the Moors, Pedro began to ignore Albuquerque. By the time Blanche de Bourbon and her French entourage arrived in Valladolid, Pedro was ensconced with María and a young and boisterous court at Torrijos, west of Toledo. His mother's efforts to get him to the altar proved unavailing. Finally, the queen dispatched Albuquerque who read Pedro the riot act on the political consequences of his feckless behaviour: Castilla needed the French alliance and Pedro needed an heir.

So at last the king came to Valladolid in June 1353 and was wed to Blanche. Hours later, he slipped out of town and back to Torrijos. Even María saw the unwisdom of this and persuaded him to return. Back Pedro went to his bride – for two days. As soon as the French delegation went home, Pedro incarcerated Blanche and left for Sevilla. She never saw her husband again. She was executed by his orders at Toledo in 1361, aged twenty-five. María de Padilla died the same year.

Of the four daughters whom María bore to Pedro, two did very well indeed. Constanza married John of Gaunt, Duke of Lancaster, and bore Catherine, wife of Enrique III. Isabel married Edmund of Langley, Duke of York; Edward IV and Richard III of England were her great grandsons.

CATHEDRAL The 13th-century Gothic colegiata endured till the late 16th century when Valladolid was elevated to the rank of a bishopric (it had been suffragan to Palencia). This meant, of course, a proper cathedral.

The present cathedral is not particularly distinguished. Work began in 1527 on a new church to replace the Gothic one. Rodrigo Gil de Hontañón (d. 1577) took over the job in 1536. Following his death, the chapter commissioned Juan de Herrera (d. 1597) to design an entirely new church. Building began in 1582 but by 1595, when it was elevated to cathedral status, it was still a construction site. The dimensions of Herrera's church were similar to those of Sevilla, but only about half the church was ever built.

The court's removal to Madrid in 1606 as well as plagues, famines and various civil disruptions prolonged construction into the 18th century when Alberto de Churriguera (d. 1750) worked on it, and even the 19th when the one tower completed of the four originally planned collapsed (1841) and had to be rebuilt. The lower portion of the façade is by Herrera; the upper by Churriguera.

The interior is immense, classical and cold. A blaze of colour and splendour is provided by the retablo in the *capilla mayor*, the work (1550–62) of Juan de Juni, originally made for Sta María la Antigua. The cathedral is unusual for the absence of a coro in the middle of the nave. It was moved in the 1920s to the east end and the *reja* that enclosed it was, in the words of the label at the Metropolitan Museum in New York, 'no longer needed'. William Randolph Hearst's agents were attentive to such things and, by his bequest, the reja is now at the Metropolitan.

The DIOCESAN MUSEUM is well worth a visit; it has some outstanding works. Gregorio Fernández is represented by a powerful 'Ecce Homo' which makes up for his Archangel Gabriel in the adjacent room. The unfortunate archangel is stark naked with a bulbous little tummy. Two 13th-century sarcophagi depict lines of mourners, some tearing at their cheeks, and chatting Apostles arranged in pairs. There are some very fine choir stalls, statuary of the 13th to 18th centuries and a fragment of the old colegiata cloister with the magnificent Romanesque portal that once connected the cloister with the church. The portal is used as a frame for an impressive sculpted group of about 1500, the Lamentation over the body of Christ.

UNIVERSITY OF VALLADOLID East of the cathedral stands a statue of Miguel de Cervantes who settled in Valladolid in 1603. The first part of *Don Quixote* appeared here in 1605 (Valladolid had had a printing house since 1481). Beset by debt and various other problems, he followed the court to Madrid in 1606 and died on 23 April 1616, the same day as William Shakespeare.

Beyond him is the University of Valladolid, founded in the 14th century. Its monumental façade is the work (1715) of Narciso and Antonio Tomé, brothers and pupils of Alberto Churriguera. Narciso was also responsible for the amazing Transparente in Toledo Cathedral. The present building, behind the façade, was built in the mid-20th century, the old buildings having fallen into disrepair. Other university buildings are scattered all through this part of town.

COLEGIO MAYOR DE STA CRUZ This noble building, now part of the university, was founded in 1483 by Don Pedro González de Mendoza (1428–95), cardinal, archbishop of Toledo, friend and supporter of Isabella in her struggle for the throne, confidant of the Catholic Kings. The building was begun in 1486 in the Gothic style, but in 1490, the cardinal turned it over to Lorenzo Vázquez of Segovia who had trained in Bologna.

Vázquez finished the work in 1492 as the first major Renaissance building in Castilla. The three-storey patio is splendid. The cardinal appears on the tympanum over the entrance, kneeling before Saint Helena, mother of Emperor Constantine and, by tradition, discoverer of the True Cross. Vásquez's next assignment was the palace of the dukes of Medinaceli in Cogolludo (Guadalajara), a perfect Italian Renaissance palace.

LA MAGDALENA Moving along the Calle de Cardenal Mendoza and the Calle de Colón, past a small museum dedicated to Columbus who died in Valladolid in 1506, we come to the church of La Magdalena, built as a family funerary chapel for Don Pedro de la Gasca (d. 1567). The façade with its gigantic family escutcheon was designed by Rodrigo Gil de Hontañón. This flamboyance was wrought for a man who was, by all accounts, a model of tact and humility, qualities that stood him in good stead when he was sent to Peru in 1546 to restore order and bring the rebellious Gonzalo Pizarro to heel. This he did, with great success, returning to Spain in 1550. He subsequently became bishop of Palencia and then of Sigüenza.

COLEGIO DE LOS INGLESES This huge, rather ugly, brick barracks-like structure stands to the south of the Colegio de Sta Cruz. The present building dates from the 1670s, but the college was founded in 1559 by English priests who fled to Spain after the death of Queen Mary and the accession of Elizabeth. Philip II was generous to the foundation, hoping in his obstinate way to train up priests to lead the Catholic restoration in England once that awful red-headed woman was out of the way. There is no particular reason to walk that way unless you just want to look.

A very pleasant park, with lovely rose and other gardens and shade trees, runs along the Pisuerga if you grow weary of city turmoil and Valladolid's past.

Around Valladolid

Not far from Valladolid, once you beat your way clear of the industrial suburbs and the acres of flats that bespeak the city's recent prosperity and attraction for migrants, are several places to visit.

Simancas Town and castle stand some 10 km west of Valladolid on the road to Tordesillas. The town goes back to the Roman Septimanca. The Muslims built a small fortress, but the first subsequent mention of Simancas comes in the *Chronicle of Alfonso III* of 883 which says it was captured by Alfonso I. It fell finally in 899 to Alfonso III who repopulated and fortified it as one of the strategic points in the Duero defence line.

In July 939 Ramiro II of León inflicted such a stinging defeat on 'Abd al-Rahman III near Simancas that the caliph never again took the field in person against the Christians. His son al-Hakam II destroyed the town in 963 along with Osma, and Clunia and Almanzor gave it a few swipes, but then things calmed down and Simancas was left in peace.

The present castle was built in the 15th century by the Enríquez family, dukes of Medina de Rioseco and hereditary Admirals of Castilla, who gave it to the crown in 1480. Only the outer defences date from that time; Philip II turned Juan de Herrera loose on it and he transformed the old military structure into its present state. Don Antonio de Acuña, the troublesome bishop of Zamora and constant agitator during the Comunero uprising, was held prisoner here from 1521 until his murder in 1526 at the instigation of his gaoler, Rodrigo Ronquillo. Acuña's tale will be told when we reach Zamora (pages 249–50).

From the reign of Charles I (or Emperor Charles V), the castle has held the Spanish state archives. Prior to the 16th century, the court was itinerant and state papers were stuck here and there in castles or monasteries, or simply taken home by nobles when they were relieved of their high offices. Keeping track of treaties and other such documents must have been exceedingly difficult. At the urging of his secretary, Francisco de los Cobos, Charles put an end to this disorderly state of affairs in 1545 by depositing state papers at Simancas.

Documents relating to the Americas were sent to Sevilla in 1783, a good thing because the French did a great deal of purely wanton damage in 1809. They also removed everything to do with French diplomacy, though I have been told that many of these documents were returned to Franco by Petain. Among the documents preserved in the existing collection are the marriage contracts of Ferdinand and Isabella and of Philip II and Mary Tudor. The castle is not open to the public.

From the bluff beyond the large church is a fine view over the Duero valley. A seventeen-arch bridge crosses the Pisuerga and the road leads to the village of Pesqucrucla, beyond which the Pisuerga meets the Duero. An old saying has it that 'Duero tiene la fama y Pisuerga lleva el agua' ('The Duero has the fame; the Pisuerga carries the water').

Fuensaldaña A few kilometres north of Valladolid is FUENSAL-DAÑA CASTLE, in the village of the same name, with a magnificent *torre de homenaje* (keep). The castle was built in the 15th century by Alonso Pérez de Vivero, he of the Vivero Palace in Valladolid where Ferdinand and Isabella were married. The keep straddles the walls at one side of the rectangular fortified enclosure, a typical feature of castles built in flat open country. It is now the seat of the Cortes of the Autonomía de Castilla y León.

Between Valladolid and Fuensaldaña is the last leg of the CANAL DE CASTILLA that for some distance parallels the right bank of the Pisuerga before joining it at Valladolid. This is the southernmost branch of a network of canals that was dreamed of from the time of Charles I, but undertaken in a serious way only in the reign of that industrious monarch Charles III (1759–88). Work on the main canals continued into the middle of the 19th century.

The purpose was to open up the Tierra de Campos to irrigation and to the outside world, including the ports of the north coast that heretofore had been accessible only by primitive carts. Grain could now be moved more easily to market and the canals facilitated transportation in general in days when overland travel was a hard business. Some 230 miles of canal now exist, the sides of well-fitted stone, crossed by neat bridges. The stonework and the engineering are impressive, even though the canal system did not fulfil the grandiose hopes that inspired it. The railways usurped many of those functions.

Trigueros del Valle A few kilometres north of Fuensaldaña is Mucientes, with only scraps of its castle remaining, from where a very pretty road runs northeast via Cigales to Trigueros del Valle. The rolling country sloping down to the Pisuerga valley is covered with fields and vineyards and the industrial plants lining the Valladolid–Palencia road in the Pisuerga valley are too far away to spoil things.

The ruined castle appears across the fields, dominating the present village. Substantial portions remain of both the outer precinct walls and towers and those of the inner precinct. The shattered keep occupies the middle of the north wall. There is a well in the middle of the inner court.

Its history is imperfectly known, but it seems to have been built in the 14th century and remodelled, according to a plaque by the entrance, in 1435. At the time of the Comunero uprising, the local citizens attacked the castle, expelled their lords and wrecked the place. It never recovered.

PALENCIA PROVINCE (SOUTHERN)

Before continuing westwards along the Duero, I want to go up the valley of the Pisuerga to nearby Palencia Province to look particularly at some Visigothic remains.

A major road, the N-620, connects Valladolid to Palencia, following the valley of the Pisuerga River. For much of its length the road is lined with factories and other buildings that do nothing for the scenery but do attest to Valladolid's success in attracting foreign investment. At Venta de Baños the Palencia road veers off left while the N-620 continues to Burgos.

History The province stretches far north of its capital city, its

Coca (Segovia) The castle of Coca was begun about 1448 by Alonso de Fonseca, bishop of Ávila, archbishop of Sevilla. The Fonsecas, prominent ecclesiastics, were loyal supporters of Isabella in her struggle for the throne. Their castle is a superb example of Mudéjar brick architecture. The Mudéjar, Muslims who remained after the Christian reconquest, were masters of brick construction.

Coca (Segovia) The main entrance to the Fonseca castle is dominated by the massive keep. The elaborate brickwork and crenellations testify to the craftsmanship of the Muslim Mudejars. At the time it was built, castles were losing their primarily military functions and becoming comfortable residences.

Coca (Segovia) The keep of the Fonseca castle occupies one corner of the inner enceinte following the tradition of early medieval castles built on level terrain. The round corner towers and the intermediate pairs of bartizan turrets make a striking display.

Coca (Segovia) The bartizan turrets on the inner walls of the Fonseca castle show the predominant characteristics of the castle's construction: the use of wide bands of mortar between the brick courses and a herringbone pattern at the base of the turrets. The detailing of the brickwork is extraordinary.

Peñafiel (Valladolid) A castle has stood on this lofty ridge commanding a strategic crossing of the Duero river since at least the 10th century. Fiercely contested by Muslims and Christians, it fell finally to the latter in 1013. The present castle dates mainly from the end of the 13th century. It is one of the better castle views in the valley, looking from town like a great white ship heading north.

Peñafiel (Valladolid) The Convento de San Pablo was built as a palace by Alfonso X in the 13th century and it was here that his nephew Don Juan Manuel deposited his famous library. The building is a wonderful mix of styles; to the right of the intricate early 14th-century Mudéjar brick *cabecera* featuring horseshoe arches is the 16th-century Renaissance apse.

Valbuena de Duero (Valladolid) The monastery was founded in 1143 in a pleasant setting amidst (at least now) vineyards on the north bank of the Duero. The principal cloister, shown here, consists of a 13th-century lower range – with strong Gothic touches – on top of which was added in the 16th century a classical Renaissance range.

Valladolid (Valladolid) The Colegio de San Gregorio in Valladolid is a triumph of Hispano-Flemish architecture. The complex was built at the end of the 15th century when many artists from the Netherlands and Burgundy were working in Castile and influencing local artists. San Gregorio houses the Museum of Religious Sculpture that contains works by some of the most important sculptors of the burgeoning Renaissance.

Valladolid (Valladolid) The entrance hall to the Diputación Provincial, originally a private palace where Philip II was born in 1527, is lined with modern azulejo (tile) scenes. This one depicts the terrible fire of 1561 that destroyed the centre of town.

Valladolid (Valladolid) Of the church of San Martín, only the 13th-century tower remains, a splendid example of Romanesque tower-building.

Valladolid (Valladolid) The Colegio Mayor de Sta Cruz was the first major Renaissance structure in Spain. It was founded in 1483 by Don Pedro González de Mendoza, cardinal-archbishop of Toledo.

Simancas (Valladolid) Near this ancient fortification outside Valladolid the caliph of Córdoba, 'Abd al-Rahman III, was soundly defeated in 939. That turbulent prelate Antonio de Acuña, bishop of Zamora and rebel against Charles V, was held here for five years until murdered in 1526. Philip II had Juan de Herrera (builder of the Escorial) remodel the 15th-century castle into a comfortable residence.

Fuensaldaña (Valladolid) This castle was built in the 15th century by Alonso Pérez de Vivero, who hosted the secret marriage of Isabella and Ferdinand in 1469 at his Valladolid palace. The unfortunate nobleman later fell foul of court intrigues and was flung to his death from a window.

northern boundary resting on the Cantabrian mountains. In the north are marvellous Romanesque churches, but they lie beyond the scope of this book.

Palencia and adjacent León Province take us back to the earliest years of the Reconquista. The repopulation of the region between the Pisuerga and Cea rivers was tentatively under way by the late 8th century; the earliest known *fuero* (municipal charter) is that granted to Brañosera (in the mountains northwest of Aguilar de Campóo) in 824.

The Cea and Pisuerga rivers embrace much of Palencia Province and, in the south, a large part of Valladolid Province. This is the TIERRA DE CAMPOS, stretching west and north of the Pisuerga and Duero. It is grain country, for centuries the bread basket of Castilla and of Spain. The fields roll on and on seemingly without limit. In the late winter and spring the land is green as far as the eye can see; in the summer, it is a yellow of peculiar intensity. The number of whizzing grasshoppers that the yellowing fields produce can only be appreciated by driving through them.

This heartland of Old Castile should be seen. The vastness is almost overwhelming and the isolation of the little villages is striking.

The area is thick with castles, built either during the long-running struggle for possession between León and Castilla (which were not united permanently until 1230) or during the civil strife that plagued the 14th and 15th centuries when the nobility often grew more powerful than the monarchy.

The region east and south of Palencia is known as the Cerrato, also grain country. It is watered by the Esgueva River whose valley makes for a pleasant drive.

Between Valladolid and Palencia

Dueñas The first town of any consequence along the highway is Dueñas, behind old walls pierced with gates. It is an ancient town, one of the centres of the Visigothic Campo Gótico, and it was reoccupied under Alfonso III at the end of the 9th century.

We have previously encountered the seventeen-year-old Ferdinand of Aragón on his secret dash across Castilla in 1469 to meet and marry Isabella of Castilla. We met him at El Burgo de Osma (Soria) and then at the castle of Curiel (Valladolid). Here at Dueñas he rested before going on to Valladolid to meet Isabella. According to William Prescott:

> Arrangements were then made for an interview between the royal pair, in which some courtly parasites would fain have persuaded their mistress to require some act of homage from Ferdinand, in token of the inferiority of the crown of Aragon to that of Castile; a proposition which she rejected with her usual discretion.[6]

Dueñas, now a small agricultural community, was a family fief of Alfonso Carillo de Acuña, archbishop of Toledo and partisan of Isabella, and it was to this little town that the young couple retreated for safety in 1470. They held only Medina del Campo and Ávila against the forces of Enrique IV who had given no sign of approving their marriage. Here they set up their small court, short of money and support, and here in October 1470 was born their first child, the Infanta Isabel.

The main interest now is 13th-century STA MARÍA, the church with the tower at the top of a broad flight of stairs. It has been totally remodelled; the only original elements are the windows in the apse. Inside are interesting tombs of the counts of Buendía, a rather nice title.

On the right wall, near the altar, is the tomb of Don Lope Vázquez de Acuña, who won famous victories against the Moors of Granada in 1489. He was an uncle by marriage of Ferdinand. Across the nave is a charming tomb of a young knight kneeling at a prie-dieu, hands clasped in prayer, while behind him stand two sorrowing pages, one holding the youth's helmet, the other his sword. Behind the altar is a fine retablo of scenes from the life of Christ.

Leaving Dueñas, you cross the Canal de Castilla. Look for signs to Venta de Baños, to the right. Where you turn off the main road for that town, on the right stands the monastery of San Isidro de Dueñas, or LA TRAPA, so called because since 1891 it has housed French Trappists (Cistercians of the Strict Observance). It was originally a Benedictine foundation of the early 10th century. Once again, as at Silos, French monks repopulated the monastery, deserted since the disentailment acts of the 1830s. It is a working monastery and is thus closed to the public.

Baños de Cerrato At Venta de Baños, a railway centre of no visible charm, you have to thread your way through and around rail yards in search of the sign to Baños de Cerrato to the right of the main road. Coming from the south, the road is not well marked; crossing the tracks, you turn abruptly right and you will see the sign. You then pick up signs to the Visigothic church of SAN JUAN DE BAÑOS, at the edge of the village.

The church was built by King Reccesuinth in 661. The date (ERA 699) is on a stone set into the triumphal arch between the nave and the sanctuary. San Juan is the second Visigothic church we have seen, the first being Quintanilla de las Viñas (Burgos). This is far better preserved, though not all we see is of the 7th century. The odd trapezoidal floor plan, wider at the east end than at the entrance, is original, as are the entry porch with its horseshoe arch portal, the arcades that divide the church longitudinally and the walls above them, the main chapel or sanctuary and the interior walls of two lateral chapels which themselves have disappeared. The outer walls of the church date from the 10th and 11th centuries. The belfry was added in 1865.

Like other Visigothic churches, San Juan originally had three separate rectangular apses with open spaces between them. Two Gothic chapels were intruded into the spaces in the 15th century (note the ribbed vaulting) and the two original lateral chapels disappeared some time after the 17th century. On the exterior can be seen the beginning of the springing of the barrel vaults that once covered the original chapels and the band of typically Visigothic carving identical to that which runs around the inside of the present capilla mayor.

The internal arches are horseshoe, as is the vaulting of the capilla mayor. The horseshoe profile of the triumphal arch is carried the depth of the chapel. The eight columns and capitals are Roman, taken from the ancient baths; the capital on the northeast, next to the capilla mayor, has been dated to the 4th century. Above the triumphal arch is the famous inscription, difficult for the amateur to make out, with King Reccesuinth's name and the date. The horseshoe arch also appears in the little windows.

Architectural historians have pointed out similarities between San Juan and other Visigothic churches in Spain and 5th- and 6th-century churches in Syria. The rectangular east end was common in Syrian churches. A colony of Syrian merchants was established in

Narbonne (southern France) from early in the 6th century, the Byzantines occupied southeastern Spain in mid-century for some seventy years and Spanish pilgrims are known to have visited the shrine of St Simon Stylites north of Aleppo.

Palencia

A short distance farther along, on the Río Carrión, is Palencia, capital of the province, a town of 82,000. It is an important agricultural centre standing as it does amid the vast grain fields of the Tierra de Campos.

History Palencia, Roman Pallantia, was previously the chief city of the Vaccaei who bitterly resisted the Roman advance. It was the centre of an important agricultural area, especially in the 3rd century when food shortages threatened the empire. Several villas have been uncovered from those years, including 'La Olmeda' at Pedrosa de la Vega (near Saldaña, northwest of Palencia) which has absolutely spectacular mosaic floors in every room.

Palencia retained its importance under the Visigoths and a bishopric was established very early on. After the Muslim invasion, the site lay desolate for over 300 years, not to be restored till the early 11th century. The repopulation of the lands between the Pisuerga and the Cea rivers had begun long before that, however, and proceeded apace in the 9th and 10th centuries, with the kings charging various counts with the task of resettling specific areas.

Wishing to curb the rising power and ambitions of Fernán González of Castilla, Ramiro II of León (930–51) granted the lands between the Pisuerga and the Cea to Fernando Ansúrez, count of Monzón. (The Ansúrez castle at Monzón, just north of Palencia, was rebuilt in the 15th century and has recently been reincarnated as a hotel.) This touched off a running feud and the possession of these lands was disputed between León and Castilla for generations. They did not become Castilian for good until early in the 13th century. The Ansúrez remained formidable foes of Castilla; Pedro Ansúrez founded Valladolid in 1072, as we have seen, and the family endured till the beginning of the 13th century.

A Tour of the Town Palencia's 14th-century CATHEDRAL was

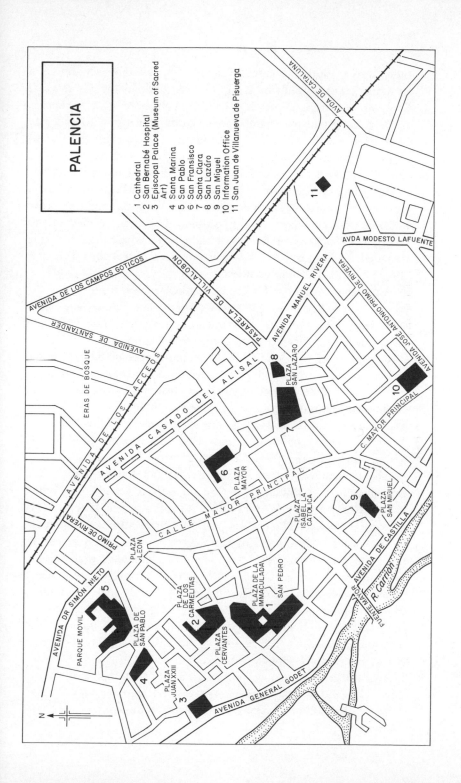

PALENCIA

1 Cathedral
2 San Bernabé Hospital
3 Episcopal Palace (Museum of Sacred Art)
4 Santa Marina
5 San Pablo
6 San Fransisco
7 Santa Clara
8 San Lazáro
9 San Miguel
10 Information Office
11 San Juan de Villanueva de Pisuerga

built over a Visigothic crypt of about 673, all that remains of a structure probably built by King Wamba (672–80) for the relics of San Antolín, an early French martyr, brought here from Narbonne. It is supposed that the chamber once stood above ground and may have been the lower floor of a martyrium, wrecked during Almanzor's attacks at the end of the 10th century. Archways on either side of the crypt may once have been windows or portals.

According to legend, in 1034 King Sancho el Mayor of Navarra, Aragón and Castilla was in hot pursuit of a boar that ran into a cave in which was an image of San Antolín. The saint reacted to this intrusion by paralysing the royal right arm, whereupon the king repented of his rashness and ordered the construction of a new church. A new Palencia grew up around it.

A rather incongruous Plateresque staircase leads from behind the coro to a low barrel-vaulted chamber with three immensely heavy transverse arches, part of Sancho's 1034 structure. The vault and arches spring directly from the floor; there are no side walls.

Beyond is the cave of San Antolín, the chapel of King Wamba, which was rediscovered only a century ago. At the east end are three slender horseshoe arches resting on two heavy columns with Corinthian-inspired capitals and purely Visigothic impost blocks. The bases are inverted Doric capitals. The excavators dared not go beyond the three arches, according to the sacristan, for fear of disturbing the underpinnings of the present cathedral.

The present cathedral, begun in 1321, all but obliterated the Romanesque one. Building went on till 1516, although the cloister, the work of Juan Gil de Hontañón, had to be rebuilt after the 1755 Lisbon earthquake. The earliest part of the structure is the splendid Gothic chevet, with five radiating chapels and flying buttresses. In 1425, the then bishop decided to go for something grander and extended the building westwards, creating a second transept and a second, much grander, capilla mayor. The vault styles thus move from the quadripartite rib vaults of the original apse and the five chapels of the ambulatory to the sexpartite vaulting of the later aisle bays to the complex lierne vaulting of the lofty nave vaults. Generous clerestory windows admit welcome light.

Two transepts mean two portals on each of the north and south sides. Those on the south, including the elaborate Puerta del Obispo, flank a rather military-looking tower of the 15th century.

In the old capilla mayor are the wall tombs (left) of Doña Urraca (d. 1189), Queen of Navarra, daughter of Alfonso VII of León and Castilla, and (right) of Doña Inés de Osorio (d. 1492), a generous benefactor who made possible the 15th- and 16th-century expansion.

The new capilla mayor contains an outstanding retablo with paintings of the life of Christ by the Flemish painter Juan de Flandes (d. 1519). (The two paintings in the top register have been attributed to another hand.) Juan came to Castilla before 1496 to work for Isabella who was partial to Flemish painting. He worked also in Salamanca and spent the last ten years of his life in Palencia. These cathedral paintings are thus the culmination of his life's work. The man in black in the centre of the Burial of Christ (bottom register, right of centre) may be the artist himself.

The capilla mayor and the coro have fine rejas, those stupendous wrought-iron and gilt screens that embellish most cathedrals in Spain and effectively prevent interested visitors from getting anywhere near the treasures inside.

Note also the splendid Renaissance *trascoro* (rear wall of the choir), possibly by Simón de Colonia. It was begun under one bishop of Palencia, Alonso de Burgos, whom we met in Valladolid at San Pablo and San Gregorio, and completed under his successor, Juan Rodríguez de Fonseca, whose tomb we saw in Coca. On the right is depicted Bishop Ignatius of Antioch, fed to the lions by his flock who held him responsible for an earthquake in 115 AD.

The cathedral museum off the cloister contains Brussels tapestries and an early El Greco of San Sebastián.

UNIVERSITY Not a trace remains of the university founded early in the 13th century by Alfonso VIII of Castilla. It grew out of the schools established early in the 12th century which made Palencia a major centre of learning in Castilla. Domingo de Guzmán, founder of the Dominican Order, studied at the cathedral school 1185–95. He established the second of his preaching houses in Castilla at Palencia in 1220.

Alfonso VIII elevated the school to the status of a university about 1210 and brought professors from Paris and Bologna. Despite royal and papal support, the university suffered severe financial problems and did not last a century. It was supplanted by that of Salamanca, founded by Alfonso VIII's cousin, Alfonso IX of León.

CHURCHES Palencia is a pleasant city to wander about in. Of the other churches, SAN PABLO (north of the cathedral) is interesting, with good tombs in the capilla mayor. The couple on the left have their little dog with them.

SAN MIGUEL, further south, has a rather odd 13th-century tower.

In a park at the southeast corner of town stands, rather forlornly, the little early Romanesque church of SAN JUAN, re-erected here some years ago after its village of Villanueva de Pisuerga, further north, was inundated by a reservoir. It has a fine deep portal of six archivolts and good windows.

There is also an Archaeological Museum in Palencia but it has not been open for years and no one seems to know when it might be again.

Tierra de Campos (I)

The Tierra de Campos stretches westwards from Palencia Province into that of Zamora. There are several possible routes, from Palencia (covered here) or from Valladolid or Tordesillas (covered below).

From Palencia, take the N-610 and the C-612 towards Medina de Rioseco and turn south at Torremormojón for Ampudia. They are many dovecotes in these parts, large round structures of mud brick with red tile roofs.

Torremormojón To the left of the road, crowning a rise, is a ruined 14th/15th-century castle. A castle has stood there since the 12th century, if not earlier. The village itself has a PARROQUIA with an extraordinary early 13th-century tower in almost mint condition. Horizontal mouldings sharply define the nine stages of the tower, the top six of which are slightly set back as they rise, with slender columns at the corners. One, two and finally three openings pierce these upper stages. The church is clearly visible from the road, but I suggest you go into the village and park next to the tower to appreciate it fully.

The royalist force driven from Ampudia by the Comunero leaders Padilla and Acuña took refuge here, only to be expelled a few days later. Town and castle were sacked.

Ampudia Approaching the village, 5 km south of Torremormojón, you can see from afar the enormous 18th-century tower of the parroquia, known as LA GIRALDA DE CAMPOS (after the more famous Giralda in Sevilla).

The 14th–15th-century CASTLE on a rise to the south of town has stout square corner towers, the largest of which is the keep, a curtain wall with round turrets, a moat and bridge. It was built on the site of a 12th-century castle that formed part of the dowry of Alfonso VIII's daughter Berenguela when she married Alfonso IX of León in 1197. The marriage was an attempt, unsuccessful, to settle the rivalry between the two royal cousins for these border lands.

In 1521, in the closing months of the Comunero revolt, Ampudia experienced a famous double siege. The royalists had managed to overcome the Comunero garrison, but were then themselves besieged by Juan de Padilla and the battling bishop of Zamora, Antonio de Acuña. After four days, the royalists capitulated and withdrew to Torremormojón.

The castle is now in private hands and has been splendidly restored. It commands fine views of the valley. From Ampudia a road runs east to Dueñas.

Valoria del Alcor The village lies just south of Ampudia with its church of SAN FRUCTUOSO up on the *alcor* or hill at one side of the village. The single nave, apse and tower date from the 12th century; the gallery on the south side is probably earlier. Such a Segovian gallery is rare in these parts. The arches, now blocked up, show clear *Mozarab* influence. The portal at the east end of the gallery has four capitals, badly deteriorated, one with odd little figures with tiny bodies and huge heads. Benches by the church provide repose and views over the village, hills and fields.

Belmonte de Campos This castle, west of Ampudia, is perhaps more easily reached from Medina de Rioseco (Valladolid), but since it is in Palencia Province I include it here. The castle stands on a slight rise among fields that sweep away north of Medina de Rioseco. The only significant piece remaining is the gigantic keep which has four corner bartizan turrets between which machicolations run along the walls. The tops of the bartizans are also machicolated. The walls have rather out-of-place-looking crenellations. An elaborately framed window with a balcony on the south side overlooks the countryside.

Belmonte was built perhaps as late as the early 16th century (which may explain the Renaissance flavour of those crenellations) by Juan Manuel de Nájera, a favourite of Philip the Handsome, Juana's husband.

Belmonte is a bit out of the way, but it is a very short drive north of Medina de Rioseco, a mildly interesting old town, and it is certainly spectacular, especially in contrast with the tiny agricultural village at its feet.

Montealegre Turning west (back into Valladolid Province), you come to the truly formidable castle at Montealegre. This very hilly region just west of the Pisuerga is known as the Montes de Torozos, and the castle of Montealegre stands on the edge of a ridge, lord of all it surveys. The powerful Meneses family built a castle in the 12th century; the present one dates from the late 13th or early 14th century. Along with Torremormojón, Ampudia and Belmonte, Montealegre formed a defensive Castilian cordon against León.

At the four corners are three enormous square towers and one even larger pentagonal mass, facing the village. Round towers rise in the centre of each side. Over the sole entry are machicolations from which unpleasantries could be poured or dumped on attackers. The battlemented walls are 18 to 24 m (60 to 80 feet) high and some 4 m (13 feet) thick. It is a truly formidable fortress.

Montealegre passed through some of the most noble hands in the realm and came eventually to the Guzmán, one of whom Philip IV created marqués de Montealegre. His arms are over the portal. It is said never to have been taken by force of arms. Pedro the Cruel (d. 1369) tried to wrest it from his hated tutor and confidant of his mother, Juan Alfonso de Albuquerque, but the king was thwarted by the gallant defence mounted by Albuquerque's wife, Isabel de Meneses, and had to retire. In 1521 the army of Charles V besieged a Comunero force here; the gates were opened by treachery. It has been heavily restored and is now a grain silo, a fate that has befallen many a castle in these parts, but it is better than having them used as quarries. It still preserves its aura of brute strength.

Villalba de los Alcores Heading back towards Valladolid on the local road VA-90, you see to the left across a field the huge block of a castle. The inner precinct wall has eight towers and the hulking torre de homenaje (keep). The village has taken over most of the extensive outer precinct and towers and stretches of wall stick up from among the houses. The castle is entirely surrounded by houses on one side and someone's fenced field on the other.

According to some, it was built by Hospitaller and Templar knights returning from the first Crusade; to others, it is a construction of the 13th century by another of the Meneses family. In the 15th century it fell to the Pimentel counts of Benavente who constructed the mighty wall around the village. In the time of Pedro the Cruel it too was held by Juan Alfonso de Albuquerque.

The funeral cortège of Philip I (d. 1506), husband of the unhappy Juana la Loca, rested here one night on its dolorous progression from Burgos, where he died, to Tordesillas.

The sons of François I of France, the Dauphin and the duke of Orléans (the future Henri II), were held hostage at Villalba for eighteen months after the king's defeat and capture at Pavia (Italy) in 1525. The king exchanged the boys, aged eight and seven, for his own freedom in March 1526, but diplomatic disputes left them in Spanish hands until July 1530. Tiring of the French king's delays in raising the ransom and unkept promises, Charles V transferred the boys in 1528 to, briefly, Villalpando (Zamora), Berlanga de Duero (Soria) and finally Pedraza (Segovia) where they were held under harsh conditions until they were finally released.

From Villalba de los Alcores it is a pleasant run back to Valladolid via Mucientes and Fuensaldaña (see above).

RETURN TO VALLADOLID PROVINCE

South of Valladolid

Southeast of Valladolid, along the border with Segovia Province, are the castle of Portillo (on the N-601 to Cuéllar and Segovia), the town of Olmedo (on the N-403 to the N-VI and Madrid) and the castle of Iscar in the middle. The two castles guarded the southern approaches to the Duero.

Portillo Portillo's castle stands on a bluff with marvellous views over the Duero valley. It is now a *taller* (workshop) for artisans. A strong fortress in the 10th century, the present structure dates from the 15th, a construction of first the Sandoval and then the Mendoza families who raised the torre de homenaje, all 30 m (98 feet) of it, stoutly girt with walls and huge cylindrical towers.

Distinguished prisoners languished within its walls. For several months in 1444–45, Juan II of Castilla was held here by his cousin Juan of Aragón, King of Navarra, who had seized control of the government. He escaped to destroy his enemies at Olmedo in May 1445 with the help of Álvaro de Luna. Eight years later, de Luna was imprisoned in the castle before being taken to Valladolid and executed. Across town, on the other edge of the spur, is a good fortified gate and fragment of wall.

Iscar The road from Portillo to Iscar offers fine views, especially when it drops down into the valley of the Cega with the snow-flecked Sierra de Gredos in the distance. Iscar was one of the places resettled and fortified by Raymond of Burgundy, son-in-law of Alfonso VI, after the conquest of Toledo in 1085.

Arab sources mention Iscar in relation to 'Abd al-Rahman III's campaign of 939. The present 15th-century castle thus stands on earlier foundations atop a very steep ridge. The huge squat keep has three round towers protecting the entrance side and it is surrounded by a ruinous outer line of walls. It looks like a tough climb.

Olmedo This rather prosperous small town retains stretches of its ancient walls, a couple of gates and several fine brick Mudéjar churches in various states of repair. It was the setting for Lope de Vega's 1641 play *El Caballero de Olmedo*, but well before that it had been the scene of two famous battles in the civil wars which racked Castilla in the reigns of Juan II and Enrique IV.

In May 1445 the combined forces of Juan II, the Prince of Asturias (the future Enrique IV) and the Constable of Castilla, Don Álvaro de Luna, routed those of the Aragonese infantes Juan, King of Navarra, and his brother Enrique, Master of Santiago, and a crowd of dissident Castilian nobles. The Master of Santiago died of his wounds, Juan fled to Navarra and Álvaro de Luna moved several rungs further up the ladder of his king's favour. A scant eight years later he had fallen from grace and was executed.

The second battle took place in August 1467 and pitted the forces of Enrique IV against the nobles who had supported the proclamation at Ávila in 1465 of his young half-brother Alfonso (younger brother of Isabella) as king in his stead. Once again, the royalists were victorious.

Olmedo's 13th-century brick Mudéjar churches can be seen on foot from the Plaza Mayor, a long narrow affair with a rose garden and arcades sheltering cafés. Nearby is another rather run-down square on which stand STA MARÍA, containing what is said to be an early work by Alonso Berruguete (whose retablo from San Benito we saw in the Sculpture Museum in Valladolid) and derelict SAN JUAN. In the other direction are the tidied-up ruins of SAN ANDRÉS in a quiet little park and beyond that is SAN MIGUEL. San Miguel was built athwart the walls and its west façade is adjacent to the old gate. Olmedo's caballeros may have disappeared, but it seems a prosperous small town anyway.

West of Valladolid

Tordesillas Westwards from Valladolid, the N-122 runs through fields of grain just north of the Duero. The river has by now been augmented considerably by the waters of the Pisuerga from the north and from the south by rivers which gather the waters flowing from the Guadarrama mountains above Segovia and the Gredos around Ávila. It is thus a respectable river which flows under the bridge at Tordesillas.

You can also reach Tordesillas directly from Madrid via the N-VI. The approach from the south is best; the town stands high on a bluff above the Duero with its church towers and the white bulk of the Convento de Sta Clara. Before the bridge, the road left along the river takes one to the very pleasant modern Parador de Tordesillas with a swimming pool. It is a good base for exploring the area.

Just over the bridge, the road forks, the old N-VI to the left, up the hill and around town, and the street to the right which leads up to the town centre. Best to park there, by the Mesón Valderrey restaurant, or around on the other side of town. Driving in the historic centre is complicated. The little PLAZA MAYOR with its wooden arcades is a bit dusty but it is a well-preserved example of a Castilian town square.

Tordesillas was the site of a fortress by the 11th century at least, but its history is obscure until about 1344 when Alfonso XI built a palace, now the CONVENTO DE STA CLARA, overlooking the river. His son Pedro the Cruel embellished it and in 1363 ceded it to two of his daughters by María de Padilla. They turned it into a convent, but it retained its role as a royal palace. Poor Blanche de Bourbon was held here after her abandonment by Pedro for María de Padilla in 1353.

In 1420 the Infante Don Enrique of Aragón burst into the palace and seized the person of Juan II who escaped thanks to Álvaro de Luna.

Sta Clara's saddest association is with Queen Juana, the unbalanced daughter of Ferdinand and Isabella. She succeeded her mother as queen of Castilla in 1504, but the early death of her husband, Philip of Habsburg, in 1506 tipped her permanently over the edge. She was confined in the convent from 1509 to her death in 1555, though the exact rooms are unknown. In one room her little clavichord has been preserved.

Here she received her son Charles I after his arrival in Spain in 1517. Charles had landed on the Asturian coast in September and it took six weeks for the royal entourage to reach Tordesillas. Juana remained, in theory anyway, queen until her death, which must have caused Charles at least some disquiet. His chambers at the monastery of Yuste (Cáceres) to which he retired on his abdication in 1556 were and still are hung in black in her memory.

Pedro the Cruel's Mudéjar artists worked the same magic at Sta Clara, though on a much smaller scale, that they did in the Alcázar in Sevilla. The façade, a lovely small patio, a chapel and the baths remain of Pedro's palace. The former portal, blocked up now, has a particularly fine Mudéjar doorway and *ajimez*, that slender twin window effect beloved of the Moors.

The tour is obligatory, but it is an interesting one. The central patio and adjacent chapel are tiled and stuccoed in typically Mudéjar fashion and there are several other good rooms. The chapel has a lovely dome. You are conscious of nuns rustling in the background off the cloister; Sta Clara is still a working convent.

The church, the former throne room of Alfonso XI and Pedro, has a superb and unusually lofty gilded *artesonado* ceiling over the eastern end. The church is not part of the tour and is not always accessible. On the south side of the nave is the impressive Saldaña Chapel of 1432, built by the Vivero of Fuensaldaña. Juana's remains lay here from 1555 to 1557 when she was taken to rest finally with her parents and husband in the Capilla Real in Granada. The church was severely damaged during the Civil War of 1936–39, but has been beautifully restored.

Queen Isabella made Tordesillas her headquarters during the war in 1475–76 against Alfonso V of Portugal, supporter and would-be husband of her rival for the throne, Juana la Beltraneja. Isabella held the home front while Ferdinand commanded the army.

The Treaty of Tordesillas was signed in Sta Clara in June 1494. Brokered by Pope Alexander VI, the treaty divided the New World between Spain and Portugal.

Napoleon lodged at Sta Clara on Christmas Day 1808, shortly before his return to Paris, having dashed from Madrid to force the retreat of Sir John Moore to La Coruña.

Tordesillas was a centre of the Comunero rising against the first Habsburg king Charles I, shortly after his election as Emperor Charles V. After a meeting of representatives of the rebel towns at Ávila, their troops seized Tordesillas in September 1520 and in October the revolutionary junta sent a list of demands to the absent King-Emperor that included the demand that 'the King should live in Castilla, that he should bring no Flemings or Frenchmen nor natives of any other country to fill the posts in his household, and that in everything he should conform to the customs of the Catholic Sovereigns Don Fernando and Doña Isabel, his grandparents'.[7]

The revolt was primarily an urban affair which united all classes, especially after the wanton burning of Medina del Campo by the royalists in August 1520. Charles had left for Germany in May and his regent in Castilla during his absence was Adrian of Utrecht, the future Pope Adrian VI.

In time, the movement fell apart. As it grew more radical, the aristocracy began to desert and factional strife weakened the common effort. In the end, a royalist army crushed the Comunero forces at Villalar between Tordesillas and Toro, on 23 April 1521. Their leaders, including Juan de Padilla of Toledo, the original mover in the revolt, and Juan Bravo of Segovia, were captured and executed.

Also overlooking the river from the bluffs on which the town stands is the massive 15th-century-and-later church of SAN ANTOLÍN (entrance at the top of a flight of stairs), now a museum of religious art taken from churches in the vicinity. The spacious church has a single nave. Its most outstanding feature is the sumptuous Alderete Chapel containing the 1550 alabaster tomb of Don Pedro de Alderete, Commander of the Order of Santiago.

Tierra de Campos (II)

The Tierra de Campos north of Tordesillas offers several important sites. I describe them in order from east to west, without paying too much attention to which roads to take. Wamba, Torrelobatón, San Cebrián de Mazote and Urueña lie east and north of the main N-VI; on the main road is Mota del Marqués; to the south are Tiedra and Villalonso. The roads are good. A full petrol tank is advisable.

Wamba The village has the distinction not only of having a fine Mozarab church but of being perhaps the only village in Spain beginning with a 'W'. Some say that Wamba is identical with Gérticos where King Reccesuinth (653–72) died and was buried and his successor Wamba (672–80) elected.

The Visigothic magnates were determined to prevent any member of the late king's hated family from coming to the throne and they offered the crown to an elderly noble, Wamba. No fool, Wamba demurred, pleading age and infirmity, whereupon one of the nobles drew his sword and threatened the unhappy man with instant decapitation. Wamba fell into line and went off to Toledo to be crowned.

His short reign was reasonably successful, but one day in 680 he fell into a deep coma, induced, it is said, by a powerful narcotic administered by his enemies. In his unconscious state, he was tonsured, robed in penitential garb, and given final unction. Wamba recovered, but it was too late. The law forbade tonsured men to rule, so the poor old man was hustled off to a monastery where he ended his days, not long after. The bishop of Toledo has been accused of being behind the conspiracy.

To return to the present, STA MARÍA DE WAMBA or NUESTRA SEÑORA DE LA ASUNCIÓN, was built 928/948, but of that church only the apse and crossing, the north wall and part of the south remain. The church passed in the late 12th century to the Knights Hospitallers who rebuilt the nave. An inscription on the tympanum over the door gives the date as ERA 1233 or AD 1195.

The 13th-century Romanesque portal has interesting capitals and other decorative motifs and is surmounted by a row of corbels with human faces. The tower was originally higher, but has been cut down to one storey.

The interior of the cabecera with three apsidal chapels presents a fine display of horseshoe arches. The horseshoe profile is carried the depth of the chapels. It is obvious where the 10th-century Mozarabic work stops and the early 13th-century nave and aisles begin. The columns are unusual: built up of rectangular blocks with round members attached. The final stage of transformation later in the 13th century was to raise the roof high above the capitals of the columns by means of sharply pointed arches, thus permitting windows.

Of the various capitals, the most unusual are the one to the left of the triumphal arch showing the Paschal Lamb (left) and (right) a man eating an enormous slab of meat, post Lent. On the right side is a scene of the Weighing of Souls with a demon grabbing the one heavy with sin. On another, a horse appears to be fighting an elephant.

In what remains of the cloister, on the north, are two rooms filled to the vault springing with neatly stacked human bones. Many of the skulls show signs of violent deaths. In the yard is a stone sarcophagus purported to be that of Reccesuinth. The custodian also made the point, proudly, that although the church has been cleaned up and put into good shape, it has not been restored as in the case of San Cebrián de Mazote (see below).

Torrelobatón The 15th-century keep of the castle looms up far in the distance as you approach along the valley, the best view being from the south coming up the road from Tordesillas to Medina de Rioseco (C-611).

The original date of construction is unknown, but early in the 14th century Alfonso XI took possession of it from Don Juan Núñez de Lara y de la Cerda, a scion of one of the oldest Castilian families; his mother was descended from Alfonso X. The castle took its present shape in the 15th century under the Enríquez, dukes of Medina de Rioseco and Hereditary Admirals of Castilla.

The square castle has round towers at three corners and a keep 45 m (148 feet) high at the fourth, facing what was then the village which it presumably awed. The upper part of the three-storey keep has eight fine round corner turrets and slender bartizan turrets in the middle of each face. They rest on brackets and are rather unusual. An outer line of fortifications have all but disappeared. The castle has been restored and is used as a grain silo, a useful if humble role for such a noble pile.

In 1521, the Comunero leader Juan de Padilla besieged Torrelobatón for six days and managed to wrest it from its royalist defenders after a ferocious fight. Only two months later, the forces of Juan de Padilla and Juan Bravo, he of Segovia, marched from Torrelobatón to their defeat at Villalar and the extinction of the Comunero cause. When the castle was repaired on the orders of Charles I, the machicolated parapet was given an inward curve at the top and the crenellations were removed so that grappling irons could not take hold.

San Cebrián de Mazote Further west is the church of San Cebrián de Mazote, in the village of the same name, one of the finer Mozarab churches extant. The custodian lives down the street and around the corner and she is most welcoming, as is usually the case.

San Cebrián was built prior to 916 by Mozarab monks fleeing from Córdoba, invited to settle in the north by Ordoño II of León. It was beautifully restored in the 1930s. Next to the church are the substantial remains of the Dominican convent founded in 1305 and suppressed in 1837. The belfry was added in the late 18th century.

The interior is wonderful. The tall nave is separated from the aisles by arcades of five horseshoe arches that rest on twelve antique marble columns with Corinthian, Visigothic and other capitals. To the left of the crossing and over the splendid ballooning triumphal arch are traces of arches with alternating red and white voussoirs, similar to those in the Great Mosque at Córdoba.

Note also the two finely-worked white marble columns supporting the triumphal arch. The swelling horseshoe arches give a marvellous feeling of lift in the relatively small space. The three apsidal chapels are square and aligned, a Visigothic characteristic. The ensemble is topped off by a painted wooden ceiling. The sense of space and rhythm is invigorating and I found it one of the most powerful of the Mozarab churches we saw in Spain.

North of San Cebrián is the monastery of LA SANTA ESPINA,

originally Cistercian, founded by Doña Sancha, sister of Alfonso VII, in 1147. The present buildings are from the 17th and 18th centuries. Only the 12th-century chapter house survives of the original monastery.

Urueña The walled village stands a short distance northwest of San Cebrián. The best approach is from the south when the whole line of the fortifications – the castle on the right, the line of walls, a gate – appear before you from the edge of the valley opposite.

Descending into the valley, stop at the ERMITA DE LA ANUNCIADA, or Sta María de Urueña, a Lombard Romanesque edifice, unique in these parts, with an octagonal drum and cupola over the crossing and three semi-circular apses. The exterior is decorated with the blind arcading that is standard in early Lombard churches and is common in Cataluña and Aragón. The supposition is that it was probably built towards the end of the 11th century by Catalan monks sent into the territory during the reign of Sancho el Mayor of Navarra who first introduced Cluniac reforms into his realm which included Castilla.

The well-proportioned cubes and curves of the east end make for a striking play of light and shadow; obviously the work of a master builder. It has a fortress-like air and was once walled, as befits such an isolated building. The windows are small, few in number and high up; the only doorway is at the west end, under an arcade.

When you continue on up the other side of the valley to Urueña, you find the castle is in ruins, surrounded by farm machinery and junk. A very narrow gate behind the church admits to the village which is hidden from sight behind the ramparts. These are among the best preserved in the province, dating from the 14th century.

Urueña was probably built in the reign of Alfonso VII (1126–57) as a frontier fortress between the as yet not united kingdoms of León and Castilla. The village sits on the edge of a bluff overlooking a vast landscape of field and valley. The view is extraordinary.

For all its present air of abandonment, Urueña has had a past, mostly as a prison, though Pedro el Cruel's one true love, María de Padilla, lived here for a while. Among other prisoners in the castle were two unsuccessful claimants to the throne of Aragón when the ancient royal line died out in 1410: Jaume II, count of Urgel, and Don Fadrique de Luna, bastard son of the last king of Sicily, both from cadet lines of the Aragonese royal family. The successful claimant was Fernando de Antequera, younger son of Juan I of Castilla, crowned in 1412 as Fernando I.

Enrique IV granted Urueña and nearby Tiedra (see below) to his favourite Pedro Girón, Master of Calatrava, whom he created count of Urueña in 1459. Enrique IV also bestowed the castle of Peñafiel on Girón, as we have seen, and the family built the castle of Jadraque (Guadalajara) about the same time. The 2nd count was a firm supporter of Isabella. The 5th count was created duke of Osuna by Philip II; the 9th duke and his family were painted by Goya and may be seen in the Prado. The Girón are an example of the new nobility that arose under the last of the Trastámara kings; the descendants of these families still hold possessions all over Spain.

Urueña's records and half its houses were destroyed in a fire in 1876.

Villagarcía de Campos The C-519 from Medina de Rioseco to Toro passes just to the west of Urueña. A slight jog to the right brings you to the village of Villagarcía de Campos whose castle, or what remains of it, is right on the road. The two remaining gates are lofty enough to ride a horse through without stooping. There is little to see other than the shattered keep, but the castle had its hour of fame.

In the mid-16th century its proprietors were Don Luis de Quijada and his lady Doña Madalena de Ulloa. To their care in 1554 was entrusted the illegitimate son of Emperor Charles V, the future Don Juan of Austria (1545–78), to be raised in ignorance of his birth. In his will, the king-emperor recognized the boy as his son and in 1559 Philip II recognized him as a member of the royal family. Don Juan went on to great things. He commanded the fleet that defeated the Turks at Lepanto in 1571 and in 1576 was appointed governor-general of the Netherlands, in which post he died after a troubled tenure of office. It was the eve of the Dutch revolt against Spanish rule. The castle was left in ruins by the French in 1810.

The parroquia of Villagarcía has an unusual brick tower.

Heading on towards Medina de Rioseco, you pass, on the left, the scant remains of the castle at TORDEHUMOS, largely dismantled by Charles I for its part in the Comunero revolt. It played its role in the defence of Castilla and was owned by men of distinction, but too little remains to detain us.

Medina de Rioseco   The town has a ruined castle and stretches of its ancient walls. The main street is arcaded, with nice old houses. The large hall church of STA MARÍA DEL MEDIAVILLA (1490–1520) has a giant tower of 1738. It was in a complete state of restoration when I last saw it. In the northeast corner of town is Santiago, past which you find the road north to Belmonte de Campos (see page 217). Medina was the seat of the Enríquez family, from 1405 Hereditary Admirals of Castilla, created dukes of Medina de Rioseco by Charles I in gratitude for their aid against the Comuneros. The mother of Ferdinand of Aragón, husband of Isabella, was an Enríquez.

Villavelid   This small agricultural village, tucked into a fold in the hills, is at the end of a spur off the C-519 heading south towards Toro (turn left coming from Urueña). There is no particular point in going there save for the extraordinary contrast, which you see so often in these parts, between the pathetic remnants that now confront you and what must once have been a substantial town with a huge castle and two giant churches. So many castles and churches in the meseta were built or rebuilt in the late 15th or early 16th centuries when Castilla was rich, after which the whole region slid into an irreversible decline. What was left of the population after emigration to America, European wars, famine, plagues and so on huddled in their shrunken towns as the symbols of their past greatness decayed around them.

On the edges of Villavelid are two large churches, the one on the right all but roofless and collapsing, that on the left in only marginally better shape, and looming over the lot the ruins of a castle of singularly brutal aspect. That it is built of black stone doesn't help. The massive keep is square and unadorned; part of the wall and one corner tower have collapsed into the moat. It was built probably in the 14th century; almost nothing is known of its owners.

Mota del Marqués   It is a quick run on to Toro, but let us make one more stop. On the N-VI south of Urueña is Mota del Marqués: the village, a huge church, a ruined church higher up and at the top the great stump of a keep with a hole punched in one of the three remaining sides. The Teutonic Knights are known to have built a house here in the 13th century, but its exact location is unknown. The town acquired its present name in the 17th century when it came into the hands of the marquises of Ulloa. The huge hall church, SAN MARTÍN, was built about 1540 by Rodrigo Gil de Hontañón. Hall churches were designed to allow as many worshippers as possible to view the altar, thus marking a sharp turn away from enclosed monastic churches, designed primarily for the cloistered community.

Tiedra Just west of Mota del Marqués, on the C-519, are two castles, at Tiedra and Villalonso. The latter is actually just over the border in Zamora Province, but it fits here.

The 13th-century CASTILLO DE TIEDRA stands on a hill at one side of the village. The brooding keep rises four-square from the centre of an irregular polygon of massive crumbling walls. There was a fortress on the site as early as the 11th century and Tiedra was one of the properties Sancho II proposed giving to his sister Urraca in 1071 in exchange for Zamora which she held. She was not tempted; her heroic opposition to her brother is told in the chapter on Zamora.

Tiedra had several royal owners and became entangled in the 15th-century strife between the Castilian and Aragonese branches of the Trastámara dynasty. The lordship of Tiedra was held by the infante Don Sancho, count of Albuquerque, brother of Enrique II, and passed to his daughter Leonor who married Fernando de Antequera, younger son of Juan I of Castilla, who became king of Aragón in 1412. Two of their children, Juan and Enrique, made life hell for their cousin Juan II of Castilla who finally seized Tiedra from them and granted it to his favourite Álvaro de Luna.

After the execution of de Luna in 1453, Juan II bestowed Tiedra and Urueña on Don Pedro Girón, Master of the Order of Calatrava. Tiedra remained in the hands of the Girón dukes of Osuna into the 19th century.

Villalonso This castle, a short distance south towards Toro, is more dramatic than Tiedra. It comes into view in the distance across the fields, standing on a slight rise a bit to the left of the tiny village. A rural road runs to the village.

Traces of an outer line of fortifications surround the walls of the inner enceinte which has cylindrical corner towers and elegant bartizan turrets in the centres of the walls on three sides. The north wall is straddled by the torre de homenaje, as is typical of castles built in open country. The enceinte is empty; the keep a hollow shell, though the supports for several wooden floors are visible. It was built by Juan de Ulloa, governor of Toro castle under Enrique IV and a partisan of la Beltraneja, Isabella's rival for the throne, who surrendered it to Isabella in 1473.

There is no track to the castle; you must walk across the field. The mud in wet weather is of a singular viscosity.

South of Tordesillas

South of Tordesillas are three closely linked ancient towns: Arévalo, Madrigal de las Altas Torres and Medina del Campo. The first two are actually in Ávila Province and will be discussed in Chapter 9, but the three should be seen together. They are easily reached from Tordesillas and are accessible from Madrid via the N-VI.

These old market towns were once important centres of commercial activity. Each had a royal palace and they were linked particularly with Queen Isabella. She was born in Madrigal de las Altas Torres in 1451, spent her childhood until about the age of ten in Arévalo and died at Medina del Campo in 1504. Her brother Alfonso was born in Arévalo in 1453, only to die fifteen years later at Ávila, having been proclaimed king in 1465 by dissident nobles in opposition to his half-brother Enrique IV.

Medina del Campo This ancient town stands 25 km south of Tordesillas on the N-VI. In the Middle Ages it was *the* market town of Castilla and the huge PLAZA MAYOR bears witness to its former importance.

It was taken from the Muslims by Alfonso VI in 1077. A century later, Alfonso VIII gave it to his bride, Eleanor Plantagenet, daughter of Henry II of England, and it passed in time to Leonor de Albuquerque (known as 'la Ricahembre de Castilla' – the Rich Lady of Castilla) who, as noted previously, married her cousin Fernando (younger son of Juan I of Castilla), co-regent of Castilla during the minority of Juan II, elected king of Aragón in 1412 after the extinction of the ancient royal line.

Fernando had been born in Medina del Campo as were his sons Alfonso V of Aragón, Juan II of Navarra and Aragón, and Enrique, Master of Santiago. Juan and Enrique tried for years, and occasionally succeeded, to control Castilla during the reign (1406–54) of their feeble cousin Juan II of Castilla. Their power was based on their vast holdings in Castilla (Juan II of Aragón inherited Medina from his father) and on the support of the minor Castilian nobility who bitterly resented the efforts of Álvaro de Luna, Juan II's chief minister, to strengthen the power of the monarchy. Medina del Campo often found itself in the middle of the wars between the cousins.

The efforts of Leonor and Fernando brought much prosperity to Medina del Campo. After her husband's death in 1416, Leonor saw to the organization on a regular basis of the annual trade fair that made the town so famous and attracted merchants from all over Europe. Here the taxes owed the crown on the great flocks of sheep owned by the Mesta were collected and the raw wool sold or exchanged for the products of the north. It thus became an important monetary exchange centre and, after 1450, Medina was the financial capital of Castilla.

The Catholic Kings were very close to Medina del Campo. The town had been granted to Isabella by her brother Alfonso during his brief 'reign' (1465–68) in opposition to Enrique IV, and the latter subsequently confirmed the grant. Isabella used it as her base for assembling the finances and provisions for the campaign against Granada and in February 1482 the queen issued the summons for her nobles and their armies to assemble at Medina before marching south.

To Medina del Campo in the spring of 1488 came an embassy from Henry VII of England to negotiate with Ferdinand and Isabella for the betrothal of their three-year-old daughter Catalina to Arthur, Prince of Wales. The Treaty of Medina del Campo promised mutual aid and defence, primarily against the French, and provided for the marriage. The wedding did not take place until November 1501; the sickly Arthur died in 1502, thus setting in train the unhappy adulthood of Catherine of Aragon, who in 1509 married the dead prince's brother, Henry VIII.

A notable citizen of Medina del Campo was Bernal Díaz del Castillo (1492–1584) who sailed for the New World in 1517 and two years later marched with Cortés into Tenochtitlán, the Aztec capital. He witnessed much in his career and very late in his long life wrote his *Historia Verdadera de la Conquista de la Nueva España* (*True History of the Conquest of New Spain*). It is a vividly written tale. The old soldier ended his days, aged ninety-two, in Guatemala, and was buried in the crypt of the cathedral in Antigua Guatemala.

In August 1520, during the Comunero uprising, Medina was put to the torch by the troops of the new king Charles I. The disaster discredited the government even further and spurred the Comunero leaders to more radical action. It also was the beginning of the end for the town's prosperity.

The economic and social ills of the late 16th and 17th centuries brought Medina del Campo yet further down from the high place it had so long enjoyed. The population steadily dwindled and many towns and villages in the vicinity were depopulated entirely. Of the 3,000 households recorded in 1570 only 650 remained in 1646.[8]

The remains of the palace where Isabella died in 1504 stand in one corner of the broad Plaza Mayor. It is odd to realize that, given her travels the length and breadth of the country, she died only 26 km from where she had been born. The extent to which she got around is indicated by the birthplaces of her children: Isabel at Dueñas (1470), a stillborn son at Toledo (1475), Juan at Sevilla (1478), Juana at Toledo (1479), María at Córdoba (1482) and Catalina at Alcalá de Henares (1485).

The large brick Colegiata de San Martín anchoring the southeast corner of the plaza dates from the 16th century. Between it and the old palace is the 17th-century Casa Consistorial. San Miguel, classical brick Mudéjar, at the other side of the plaza, stands on the site of a mosque.

CASTILLA DE LA MOTA This huge castle dominates the town from a hill to the northeast. Its origins are remote. Parts date from a reconstruction by Alfonso VIII at the end of the 12th century, making it one of a chain of castles defending Castilla against the ambitions of his jealous cousin Alfonso IX of León. Further remodelling took place in the middle of the 15th century under Juan of Navarra (and later of Aragón), who owned Medina as we have seen, and again under Isabella and Ferdinand. Their architect Alfonso Nieto was assisted, the records show, by the architects Abdallah and Ali de Lerma.

The present structure, an irregular quadrilateral built of concrete faced with ruddy brick, rises from within a moat. A curtain wall with round crenellated towers surrounds the outer precinct, then come the lofty walls of the castle proper and finally the mighty late 15th-century keep (35 m/115 feet), one of the noblest in Castilla. The keep is topped with machicolations and eight turrets. The castle has been beautifully restored and is now a school; you can visit the central patio and some of the rooms.

Standing now in this quiet place, with an elderly keeper and a few students drifting about, the clack of a typewriter sounding from a window, it is difficult to visualize the dramas that the walls have seen.

La Mota was contested in the 15th century by Juan II of Castilla and his minister Álvaro de Luna and the infantes de Aragón, Juan of Navarra (who held La Mota on several occasions) and Enrique. In 1441 Juan of Navarra actually managed to seize the castle with the king inside.

In the rebellions which rocked the last years of Enrique IV's reign, La Mota was held by the opposition who in 1465 declared Enrique deposed in favour of his half-brother Alfonso, Isabella's brother. Three years later, when peace was restored after Alfonso's death, Enrique bestowed La Mota on Isabella, only to take it away when she married Ferdinand.

La Mota next passed to Alonso I de Fonseca, archbishop of Sevilla (and builder of Coca in Segovia Province), whose powerful clan staunchly supported Isabella. Meanwhile, the unhappy inhabitants of Medina del Campo had seen their prosperity wrecked by years of conflict. In 1473 they rose up against the Fonseca and besieged them in the castle. Riding to the rescue of this family of worldly prelates came the duke of Alba who dispersed the besiegers and took the castle, presenting it finally to Ferdinand and Isabella in 1475.

Between the inner and outer walls of the castle was played out on a frigid November night in 1503 the latest of the long succession of personal tragedies to afflict Ferdinand and Isabella. The deaths of their only son Juan in 1497, of their eldest daughter Isabel, Queen of Portugal, in 1498, and of her infant son, Miguel, the Catholic Kings' grandson, heir briefly to the crowns of Portugal, Aragón and Castilla, in 1500, left Juana as heiress to the Spanish kingdoms. It was thus vital to get her back from the Netherlands where she had gone to wed Philip of Habsburg in 1496. Relations between the couple were poor, despite the birth of two children (Isabel in 1498 and Charles in 1500), and Juana's erratic behaviour did not improve the situation.

Juana and Philip arrived in Spain in January 1502. Philip did not impress his parents-in-law. After the Cortes of Castilla had taken an oath to the pair as princes of Asturias and heirs to the throne, Ferdinand and Isabella wanted him back north as much as they desired to keep Juana in Spain.

Philip returned to the Netherlands, leaving behind a distraught and pregnant Juana who gave birth to her second son, the future Emperor Ferdinand I, in March 1503. She then redoubled her efforts to rejoin her husband, rebuffing all her mother's efforts to interest her in the inheritance that would one day, probably soon, be hers.

While Ferdinand was in Aragón tending to a French threat, Isabella fell ill, thus making her even more determined to keep Juana in Spain. In August she took her to Segovia and in November sent her to Medina del Campo, hoping the annual fair would distract her. Philip wrote constantly urging Juana to rejoin him and she prepared to leave. When Isabella sent Juan Rodríguez de Fonseca, bishop of Córdoba, to dissuade her, he found her between La Mota's inner and outer gates. She refused to return to her apartments, at which point the bishop had the gates closed and went for the queen. Juana remained outdoors the whole freezing night, taking refuge in a shed.

The queen came from Segovia in two days and at length persuaded her daughter to go back inside the castle. In the end, Isabella gave in. In exchange for Philip's promise to send the child Charles to Spain, she allowed Juana to depart. Juana reached the Netherlands in May 1504. Relations between her and Philip deteriorated further. Charles was not permitted to go to Spain (and did not go till 1517). It was all too much for Isabella who took to her bed in the palace on the square in Medina del Campo where she lingered until 26 November 1504. Ferdinand was by her side at the end.

The Catholic Kings turned La Mota into a state prison. One of the first inmates was Cesare Borgia, son of Pope Alexander VI. The Borgias came from Borja, in the Ebro valley, from where they moved to Valencia and hence to Rome. Aragón was mopping up the kingdom of Naples at this point and Cesare fell into Spanish hands in 1504. Fernando sent him to Spain where he was clapped into La Mota. He managed to escape in 1506 and fled to Navarra (ruled by his brother-in-law), to be slain in battle soon after.

Another prisoner, among many of note, was Hernando Pizarro, brother of Francisco, who languished here for twenty years (1540–60) for his murder of Diego de Almagro in Peru.

Juan II and Enrique IV ordered that the state papers of the crown of Castilla be gathered at La Mota, a process continued by Fernando and Isabel. It was this collection that was ultimately moved to Simancas by orders of Charles I who established there the first real state archives.

Rueda About halfway between Medina del Campo and the Duero, in the Tierra de Vino just off the N-VI, is Rueda, centre of an important wine-producing area. Attracted by the crowd we saw from the road one day, we stopped to find a grape harvest festival (*vendimia*) in progress featuring a marching band, a festival queen, speeches and what was billed as the biggest paella in the world. They were heating the oil in the gigantic pan, but unfortunately the cooking was not due to start for several hours and we had to get back to Madrid.

The façade (1738–47) of the imposing parroquia, LA ASUNCIÓN, is the work of one of the Churriguera clan, Alberto (1676–1750), who had earlier designed the Plaza Mayor in Salamanca. The portal, between two cylindrical towers, is dedicated to the Assumption of the Virgin. The swooping curves pile up to the Holy Trinity at the top, outlined against the sky.

Pozáldez On another occasion, attracted by a notice we had seen in a bar, we drove to this village deep in the country southeast of Rueda to see an *encierro*, sort of an amateur bullfight. Young bulls are let loose in a corral, often constructed in the plaza mayor, and young would-be toreros get a chance to show their bravery and budding skills. No weapons are used; the boys and young men taunt the bull which then charges, or just looks confused, and everyone scrambles out of the way. The townsfolk gather around, music blares, soft drinks and beer flow, there is much gossip and chatter and a good time is had by all.

Pozáldez is dominated by SAN BOEL, a huge brick Mudéjar church with a particularly fine apse, adorned with tall blind brick arches rising the full height.

West to Toro

Beyond Tordesillas, the Duero curves southwest and then north to Toro, while the not particularly interesting main road (N-122) runs straight across the meseta. A detour south will bring you to San Román de Hornija, a formerly Mozarabic church founded in the early 10th century but completely rebuilt in the 18th. It possesses only fragments of its Mozarab past, a couple of capitals and a column or two.

The valley road south of the Duero is longer, but the scenery is lovely. From the Salamanca road, turn off right for Pollos and Castronuño. Steep bluffs line the north side of the valley, fading back in gentle steps from the river. South, all is flat though one can occasionally see the distant edge of the meseta. Mostly fields; some vineyards; groves of pines with tall bare trunks and puffy tops.

Castronuño sits on a bluff which forces the Duero to turn northwest. Alfonso V of Portugal, champion of Isabella's rival Juana la Beltraneja, took refuge here after his defeat at the hands of Fernando near Toro in 1476. A dam just below the town creates a good-sized lake from which canals lead off to irrigate the valley floor. A short distance beyond, Toro comes in sight on its reddish-brown cliffs and we leave the Province of Valladolid for that of Zamora.

Notes

1. D. Juan Manuel de Peñafiel, *El Conde Lucanor* (Austral, Madrid, 1947), Anteprólogo.
2. Richard Ford, *A Handbook for Travellers in Spain* (London, 1966), p. 931.
3. Henry Swinburne, *Travels through Spain in the Years 1775 and 1776* (London, 1778), p. 412.
4. Ford, *Handbook*, p. 938.
5. See J. H. Elliott, *The Count-Duke of Olivares* (New Haven and London, 1986), pp. 203ff, for details of this complicated and amusing episode.
6. William H. Prescott, *The History of the Reign of Ferdinand and Isabella* (Philadelphia, 1873), Vol. I, p. 205.
7. J. H. Elliott, *Imperial Spain, 1469–1716* (London, 1970), p. 153.
8. Marcel Defourneaux, *Daily Life in Spain in the Golden Age* (Stanford, 1979), p. 92.

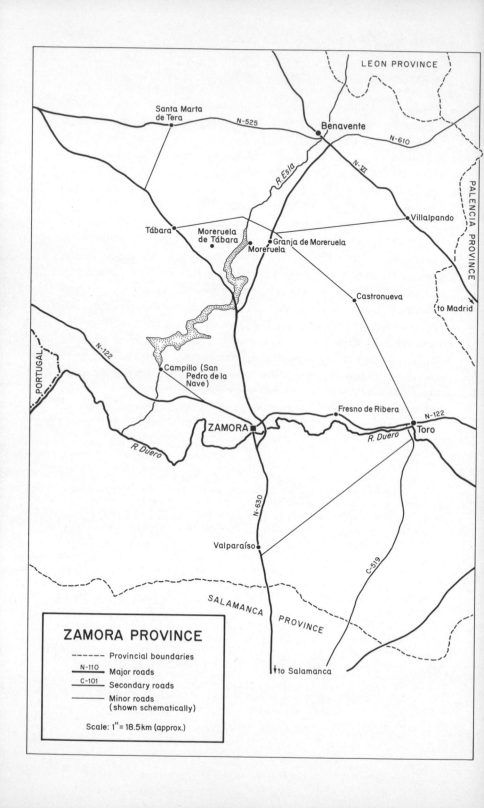

LEON PROVINCE

Santa Marta de Tera

N-525

Benavente

N-610

R. Esla

PALENCIA PROVINCE

N-VI

Villalpando

Tábara

Moreruela de Tábara

Granja de Moreruela

Moreruela

Castronueva

to Madrid

N-122

PORTUGAL

Campillo (San Pedro de la Nave)

Fresno de Ribera

N-122

ZAMORA

R. Duero

Toro

R. Duero

N-630

C-519

Valparaíso

SALAMANCA PROVINCE

to Salamanca

ZAMORA PROVINCE

- - - - - Provincial boundaries

N-110 ───── Major roads

C-101 ───── Secondary roads

────── Minor roads (shown schematically)

Scale: 1" = 18.5km (approx.)

8

Zamora Province

Approaches

The most direct route to Toro and Zamora from Madrid is the N-VI to Tordesillas where you turn west on the N-122. You can also leave the N-VI at Medina del Campo and take the C-112 west across country via Nava del Rey and Alaejos to Castronuño, where you catch up with the route described at the end of the Valladolid chapter. This affords a good view of Toro coming from the south.

History

We are now in the ancient kingdom of León that developed after the reoccupation of that former Roman legionary camp in 856 and the transfer of the capital of the Asturian kings from Oviedo to León in 914. Repopulation of the lands north of the Duero proceeded apace with settlers coming as usual from northern Spain and from beyond the Pyrenees. The territory of León extended originally to the Pisuerga River, beyond which lay Castilla, but the border lands were disputed for centuries, with León usually losing out to its more powerful former satellite. More historical details are given under the entries for Toro and Zamora.

Toro

The Duero is deflected west again at Toro by the bluffs on which the town stands. Shortly before the C-112 reaches the modern bridge, a somewhat paved lane goes off to the right and runs along the river to the old bridge of twenty-two arches, built in the 12th–13th centuries. Below the bridge is a weir over which the river rushes with a pleasant roar. There is a fine view of the Colegiata and the scant remains of the castle.

The modern road crosses a bridge downstream and swings wide around the base of the cliffs and up to the top of the escarpment where you turn right on the N-122 for Toro. For the centre of town, keep going till you see the 'Centro Ciudad' sign pointing through the 18th-century clock-tower gate in the now-vanished wall. That street, if it is not closed to traffic, leads straight to the Plaza Mayor.

History Toro is an ancient town, possibly the Arbukala of the Vaccaei tribe who were conquered by Hannibal in 220 BC but survived to trouble the Romans. The modern name may derive from the bull totem of that Celtiberian people. After the Muslims had been rolled back a bit, Alfonso III repopulated the town in about 910.

Fernando III el Santo, was crowned king of León in Toro in 1230 and his wife Beatrix of Swabia died here. Enrique II, first of the Trastámara line, summoned his first Cortes here in 1369. Juan II was born here in 1404, but the town was to have greater significance for his daughter Isabella.

As we have seen, Isabella had a rival for the succession in Juana la Beltraneja, supposedly the daughter of her half-brother Enrique IV, but more likely of the queen's close friend, the courtier Beltrán de la Cueva. La Beltraneja's supporters arranged her betrothal to Alfonso V of Portugal who was feeling peeved in any case over his earlier rejection by Isabella.

Alfonso invaded Castilla in May 1475, backed by a number of dissident Castilian nobles. Isabella made Tordesillas her headquarters, while Ferdinand moved to secure the loyalty of Salamanca, Toro and Zamora. Alfonso reached Arévalo in July and both Zamora and Toro went over to him, a serious blow for the young monarchs.

Intrigue seethed as troops marched. Zamora swung back to Isabella's cause. The Portuguese crown prince arrived with reinforcements and in March 1476 the rival armies met at Peleagonzalo, a few kilometres southwest of Toro. Ferdinand was victorious in this 'last major contest in Castile to be decided by light cavalry and the

Torremormojón (Palencia) In the Tierra de Campos, vast fields of grain that sweep north and west of Valladolid and Palencia, stands the parochial church of the village of Torremormojón. Its remarkable 13th-century tower is in virtually pristine condition with beautiful detailing from bottom to top.

Palencia (Palencia) The crypt of Palencia cathedral is part of the church built around 1034 by Sancho el Mayor of Navarre, Aragon and Castile on the site of a Visigothic church of 673. The ancient church was rediscovered when a boar the monarch was hunting ran into a cave, in actuality the long-hidden hermitage of San Antolin who promptly paralysed the royal arm for the rude intrusion. Sancho founded a new church – and recovered the use of his arm. The former cave is the apse of the crypt.

Ampudia (Palencia) The present castle of this village of the Tierra de Campos dates from the 14th/15th century. In 1521, during the Comunero uprising against Charles V, the rebel-held castle was rescued from a royalist siege, forcing the king's army to withdraw to nearby Torremormojón.

Belmonte de Campos (Palencia) Over this tiny agricultural community, north of Medina de Rioseco, loom the remains of its castle. The huge keep commands a view over the endless fields. The castle was remodelled in the 16th century which may explain the slightly incongruous Renaissance-looking crenellations atop the mighty walls.

Tordesillas (Valladolid) The Convent of Sta Clara dominates the town. Alfonso XI founded a palace here that was embellished by his son Pedro the Cruel, a devotee of Muslim art. His artists worked the same magic here as they did on a much larger scale in the Alcázar in Sevilla. The Muslim architectural themes of the building, shown here, testify to Pedro's enthusiasm. He ultimately gave the palace to his two daughters who turned it into a convent (which it still is). The unhappy Queen Juana, unbalanced daughter of Ferdinand and Isabella, was immured here from 1509 to her death in 1555.

Sta María de Wamba (Valladolid) The present church was built in 928/948 and is named after the Visigoth noble Wamba, who became king in 672. The apse, crossing, north wall and part of the south wall remain from that structure which was extensively remodelled by the Knights Hospitaler in the late 12th/early 13th century. The transition, including the raising of the height of the nave, is clearly visible in the interior. The ballooning horseshoe arches of the 10th century portion are striking.

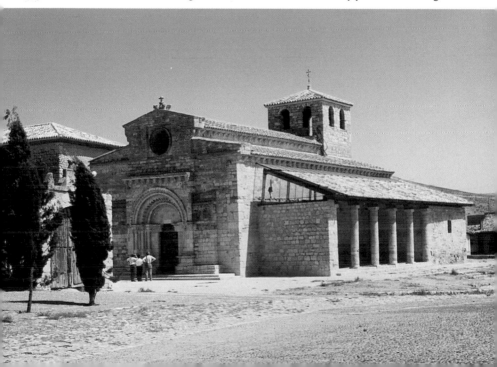

Torrelobatón (Valladolid) The castle here is another fortress of the meseta, the central plateau of Castile. Three round towers fix each corner and on the fourth is the massive keep 45 m. (148 ft.) high. It can be seen for miles coming across the flat country. Its origins predate the 14th century; it was put into its present shape in the 15th. In 1521 the Comunero leader Juan de Padilla managed to take it after a six day siege but was defeated and executed by Charles V soon after. The king had the crenellations of the castle removed and the parapet curved inward so that grappling irons could not take hold.

Villalonso (Zamora) This castle, as with all those castles in the open meseta, has stout cylindrical corner towers, with the keep straddling the north wall. The castle predates the 15th century and was held by partisans of Isabella's rival for the throne of Castile. They surrendered it to her in 1473.

Villalonso (Zamora) A closer view of the castle shows the scant remains of an outer line of fortifications, long vanished. There is no track to the castle, which is now reached only through a ploughed and planted field.

La Mota, Medina del Campo (Valladolid) The castle, dominating this ancient market town, was founded in the 12ᵗʰ century as a Castilian defence against León. The majestic keep, 35 m. (115 ft.) high, was added in the 15ᵗʰ century. Here, in the freezing winter of 1503, was concluded the tragic drama of Queen Isabella and her daughter Juana. The gravely disturbed young woman was stopped in the courtyard attempting to flee to her husband in the Netherlands and refused to take shelter inside. Her mother was summoned from Segovia and managed to bring the distraught Juana under control. It was all too much for the ailing queen who died less than a year later.

Toro (Zamora) The Duero, crossed here by a 12ᵗʰ/13ᵗʰ century bridge of 22 arches, is dominated on the bluffs above by the Colegiata de Sta María and, to the right, the scant remains of the castle.

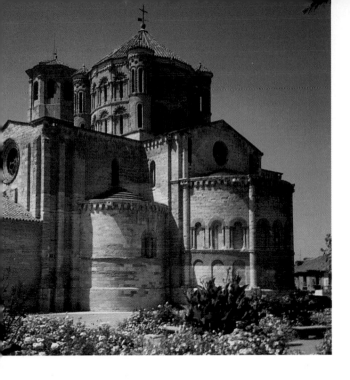

Toro (Zamora) The Colegiata de Sta María is the glory of Toro. The church was begun in about 1160, the last built of a remarkable trio of domed churches of which Zamora and Salamanca were the first. From this eastern angle the full impact of the ensemble, the curves and blocks of rich tawny stone with all the fine detailing, can easily be seen.

Toro (Zamora) The cupola of the Colegiata de Sta María is a marvellous piece of work. The drum supporting it and the interior dome consists of two tiers with 16 windows each, letting a flood of light into the church, unusual for Spain. The drum was an architectural innovation from Zamora Cathedral.

Toro (Zamora) The Colegiata de Sta María has three portals of which this, the 13th century Portada de la Majestad at the west end, is the finest and, with the survival of the polychrome, one of the most remarkable such portals in Spain. In the 14th century a second church was built by extending the nave of the Colegiata and this magnificent portal served as the altar retablo, thus preserving it.

Toro (Zamora) The church of San Salvador is the finest of several late 12th-/early 13th-century brick Mudéjar churches in Toro. It exhibits the tall blind arcades and detailed brick work that distinguish Mudéjar construction.

individual valor of nobles and kings'.[1] The Portuguese broke and
Alfonso took refuge in Castronuño. The fortresses of Zamora and
Toro surrendered to Ferdinand soon thereafter. Alfonso gave up the
game and died in 1480; la Beltraneja retired to a Lisbon convent
where she died in 1530, aged sixty-eight.

In January 1505, after Isabella's death, Ferdinand summoned a
Cortes at Toro. Isabella's legal successors in Castilla were her daughter
Juana with her husband Philip of Habsburg who were at the time in
the Netherlands. The Cortes took the oath to Ferdinand as temporary
ruler and agreed that if Juana be deemed incurably ill, which she
showed every sign of being, he should be regent.

When the pair reached Spain in the spring of 1506, the two men
agreed that Juana was incapable of ruling. Ferdinand turned over
the sole rule to Philip and left for Aragón. Less than three months
later, Philip was dead. Juana became totally unhinged and in August
1508 ceded her rights to her father and was retired to Tordesillas.

When in 1520 the towns of Castilla, the Comuneros, rose against
her son Charles I, who had succeeded his Spanish grandfather in
1516, Toro sided with them. Charles defeated the Comuneros at
Villalar de los Comuneros, east of Toro, the next year.

During the Peninsular War, in the bitter cold of December 1808,
Sir John Moore began his famous retreat from Toro in the face of
superior French forces. The ghastly ordeal ended in Moore's death
before La Coruña (Galicia) in January. In May 1813, 100,000 British
troops gathered in Toro under Wellington's command and from here
Wellington launched the final campaign which expelled Napoleon's
armies from Spanish soil after five terrible years.

Richard Ford visited Toro in 1831 and reported a population of
9,000; it has just under 10,000 now. In 1838 it lost its status as a
provincial capital, its province being merged with Zamora, to which
fact can doubtless be attributed its present pleasant aspect.

A Tour of the Town Toro's collegiate church, COLEGIATA DE
STA MARÍA LA MAYOR, begun about 1160 and completed some
eighty years later, is the town's glory. From the park to the east, a
fine view may be had of the three curved apses and the contrasting
blocks of the transepts with their pediments, all mounting up to the
two-tiered drum of the cupola with four side turrets. The church is
built of a particularly warm tawny yellow stone. The uninteresting

modern roof replaces what was probably a more imaginative topping. The caps of the four side turrets are also modern.

With Sta María, we come to the last built of a remarkable trio of cupolas (*cimborios*) on our itinerary, the other two being at the cathedrals of Zamora and Salamanca, built earlier in the 12th century. The art historian Bernard Bevan, who is far from alone in rhapsodizing over the cupolas, calls them 'one of the most interesting and beautiful features of all Spanish Romanesque'.[2]

Architectural historians seem to agree, however, that the builder of Toro backed away from the creative burst of originality that inspired Zamora and then Salamanca. Since Zamora was the first built, I shall save further discussion of the cupola phenomenon till we reach that town.

The interior has three bays. There is no *coro* (choir). It appears that there may have been two builders, the second of whom took over the vaulting of the nave and the construction of the cimborio. The side aisles have heavy ribbed vaulting, sexpartite in the two western bays and quadripartite in the bay before the stubby crossing. The nave and crossing are barrel vaulted with transverse arches. Look, however, at the massive composite piers; on the nave side there are members to support ribs, but no ribs were built. The arches of the vaults are pointed, a sure harbinger of the Gothic style.

Of the capitals, the most interesting are those before the *capilla mayor*: on the left Daniel and lions, on the right a knight bidding farewell to his lady.

The ribbed dome is raised aloft by the two-tiered drum, the thirty-two windows of which admit generous quantities of light, not something often found in Spanish churches.

The south (river) side has a relatively simple portal surmounted by a small, deeply recessed rose window; on the north side, facing the square, is the wonderful principal entrance; and at the west end is a truly spectacular portal.

The outermost archivolt of the north portal, surrounded by a decorative band, supports the twenty-four Elders of the Apocalypse holding a great collection of musical instruments. Two on the left are sharing an instrument which rests across their laps. At the apex are Christ, the kneeling Virgin and a crowned figure. The second archivolt is doubled with a design of large leaves and flowers. The third is lobed and within the lobes are angels, wings at the ready;

Christ occupies the apex. The broad flat inner archivolt is also lobed, with an angel sheltering under every other lobe. The inner arch rests on solid jambs; the other three on triple clusters of columns with sculpted capitals. Above is a handsome round window. Up on the wall to the right is carved what may be a bishop.

The west portal of the colegiata, the PORTADA DE LA MAJES-TAD, is a polychromed Gothic work of the middle 13th century. It has recently been meticulously restored (with financial support from an impressive roster of donors public and private, national and international) and it is glorious.

A lovely Virgin and Child occupy the central column of the double portal; brackets in the upper corners of the two doorways hold musicians; the one on the far left is lustily blowing a double pipe.

On either side stand four large figures, comparable to those at El Burgo de Osma and Burgos. It is said that Fernando III sent a sculptor from Burgos to execute the work as a reward for Toro's recognition of him as king of León, the first town to do so. King David with his harp is the first on the right. Christ crowns the Virgin in the tympanum, while angels with censers hover overhead; below, the lintel depicts her death.

The seven archivolts are jammed with angels, prophets, apostles, saints (men on one archivolt, women on another), and musicians. Scenes from the Last Judgment occupy the wide outermost band; Christ occupies the peak while the saved rise up as usual on the left while the damned descend to demons on the right. The colours are really quite remarkable.

The portal was preserved because the nave was extended in the 14th century to form a chapel. This was further converted in the 17th century into the church of Santo Tomé for which the portal served as the *retablo*. Its vaults collapsed in the 18th century and only the high outer walls remain.

A stroll east of Sta María along the edge of the escarpment leads to the scant remains of the castle. It may date from the days of Doña Elvira, daughter of Fernando I, to whom he left Toro in 1065. She was dispossessed in 1071 by her brother Sancho II. The keep and most of the rest were razed in the last century.

PLAZA MAYOR Let us return to the Plaza Mayor, with the 18th-century *casa consistorial*, dating from the days when Toro was a provincial capital, on the south side. The Tourist Office is housed here. Across the plaza is the church of SAN SEPULCRO, retaining only half its Romanesque west front. Built for the Knights of the Holy Sepulchre, the church passed in the 15th century to the Hospitallers, later the Knights of Malta.

From the Plaza Mayor, the main street runs straight to the Torre del Reloj (Clock Tower) of 1719, pierced by an arch. In season, tables from the cafés that line the street and the plaza spill outside and you can refresh yourself under bright umbrellas. The east side of the street and of the Plaza Mayor retains its arcades.

MUDÉJAR CHURCHES Of the other churches in Toro, San Lorenzo el Real, San Salvador de los Caballeros and San Pedro del Olmo date from the late 12th or early 13th centuries and are fine examples of brick Romanesque-*Mudéjar*. The example of the Colegiata was not repeated.

The Mudéjar, it will be remembered, were Muslims who stayed behind after the reconquest. The churches they built for their Christian lords are very common in central and western Castilla y León where brick was easier to come by than stone. They have high rounded apses, adorned externally with tall blind arcades and decorative brickwork under the eaves and elsewhere. Narrow window slits break the smooth surface of the panels framed in the arcades.

At SAN LORENZO, a couple of blocks east of the casa consistorial, two tiers of blind arcades run round the building. It is a most satisfactory ensemble, but even more so is the marvellous triple apse of SAN SALVADOR DE LOS CABALLEROS, west of the casa consistorial (follow the Calle de la Judería and bear left or take the Calle de Caballerizos del Conde from the northwest corner of the Plaza de la Colegiata). The tall arcades of each apse reach from the base to the elaborate brickwork beneath the eaves, broken only by narrow window slits with little arched frames. It is a stunning building. The Caballeros of the title were the Knights Templar.

A street north from San Salvador leads to SAN PEDRO DEL OLMO. Only a portion of the *cabecera* is visible, thanks to a high blank white wall built up against it, but it exhibits the typical characteristics of its sister churches.

Zamora

The ZA-713, a good local road, runs northwest through fields of grain and farmland to Moreruela and on to Benavente from where it is an easy drive to Zamora as described below. The loop makes an interesting alternative to driving straight from Toro to Zamora.

We pick up the N-122 again, heading west along the escarpment on the north bank of the Duero, with occasional views over the valley. It is a lovely drive. The wheat-growing region north of the Duero from Tordesillas to the Río Esla, west of Zamora, is known as the Tierra del Pan, while to the south of the river lies the Tierra del Vino. Toro is noted for its red wines. At Fresno de la Ribera there is an exceptionally fine view of the river and its valley.

And so we come to Zamora, a most agreeable town. With some 68,000 inhabitants, it is the second largest town along the Duero in Spain. It has a splendid cathedral, no fewer than nineteen churches of the 12th century or earlier, a first-rate Visigothic church and the ruins of a great Cistercian monastery nearby and a good parador right in the middle of the old town, installed in a 15th/16th-century palace, with a large swimming pool.

Every church or monument has the *horario*, the hours of opening, clearly posted and when the doors open promptly, there to greet you and show you around is a knowledgeable, cheerful and very helpful lady. Zamora gets top marks in the tourist-friendly division. Be warned, however, that this admirable system collapses in the winter. Then you should visit the Tourist Office in the Calle de Santa Clara (main street) for information.

History The parador faces a small park in which stands a bronze statue of a warrior, arm outthrust, dagger at the ready. The Lusitanian chieftain Viriatus, 'Terror Romanorum' according to the inscription, led the Romans a not so merry chase from 146 to 138 BC. Says the *Cambridge Ancient History*, 'Viriatus was the greatest leader of their own nation whom the Iberians ever possessed – and obeyed. To maintain his leadership for fully eight years (146–138) was an extraordinary feat [given tribal rivalries and an endemic lack of discipline] ... Both in strategy and tactics he surpassed his Roman adversaries.'[3] The Roman commander finally bribed three of his companions to assassinate him.

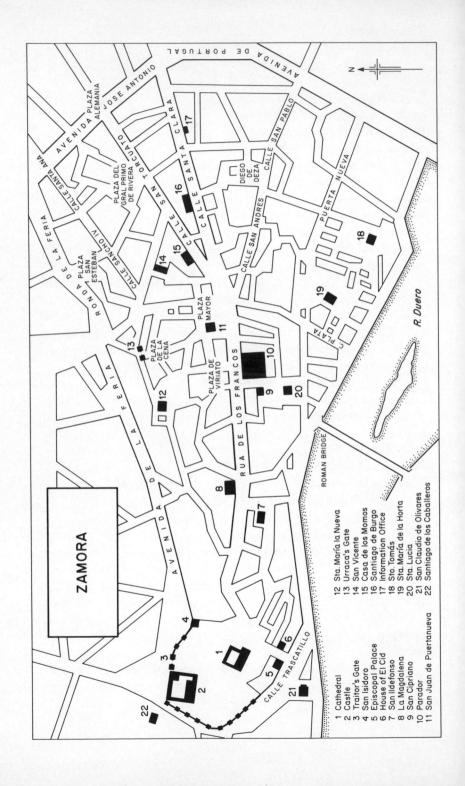

ZAMORA

1 Cathedral
2 Castle
3 Traitor's Gate
4 San Isidoro
5 Episcopal Palace
6 House of El Cid
7 San Ildefonso
8 La Magdalena
9 San Cipriano
10 Parador
11 San Juan de Puertanueva

12 Sta. María la Nueva
13 Urraca's Gate
14 San Vicente
15 Casa de los Momos
16 Santiago de Burgo
17 Information Office
18 Sto. Tomás
19 Sta. María de la Horta
20 Sta. Lucia
21 San Claudio de Olivares
22 Santiago de los Caballeros

The long historical memory of the Spanish is striking as are the allusions to past events which are readily understood. In the summer of 1991, there was some switching of party loyalties at a political meeting in Salamanca, bringing from Manuel Fraga, President of the Xunta of Galicia, the comment that what had occurred was 'the greatest treason known since the times of Viriato'.

A major Roman road, the Via Plata, ran from Mérida (Emerita Augusta) to Zamora where it split, one branch running east to Zaragoza (Caesaraugusta), the other northwest to Astorga (Asturica Augusta). The lands of Zamora formed part of the Visigothic kingdom and in time fell to the Muslims.

Though occupied briefly by Alfonso I of Asturias, Zamora lay in the middle of the no-man's-land that the king created as a buffer zone. Not until 893 did Alfonso III take the town permanently. He repopulated it with *Mozarab* refugees from Toledo and restored its ancient bishopric. Caliph 'Abd al-Rahman III besieged it in 939; it was relieved by Ramiro II only after a ferocious battle. It was then that the mighty walls arose.

Zamora's commanding position made it a natural fortress and it was the westernmost anchor of the Duero frontier. This position is immediately apparent looking at it from across the river, opposite the cathedral. Such was the strength of its walls that it was known as 'Zamora la bien cercada' ('Zamora the well-girt') and the proverb arose: 'A Zamora, no se ganó en una hora' ('Zamora wasn't won in an hour'). The walls remained in reasonably good shape, with twenty of the original twenty-six towers intact, until the middle of the 19th century when large sections were demolished in the name of progress. Further damage was done as late as the 1960s.

The walls did fail against Almanzor in 987, but Fernando I (1037–65) rebuilt them and the town. Zamora was the scene of stirring events in the fratricidal war that broke out after Fernando's death. By the 13th century, these had been woven into the epic *El Cerco de Zamora* (*The Siege of Zamora*), which tells the tale of Fernando's division of his realms between his children, Sancho II's efforts to seize the whole inheritance, his sister Urraca's defiance and defence of Zamora, his murder by treachery in 1072 and the final triumph of his brother Alfonso VI. The tale is worth telling.

Fernando divided his realm between his sons Sancho (Castilla), Alfonso (León) and García (Galicia) and his daughters Urraca and

Elvira (Zamora and Toro respectively). Sancho, however, wanted the entire inheritance for himself and as soon as the brood's mother, Queen Sancha, the last of the old Asturian line, died in 1067, all hell broke loose.

Sancho drove Elvira from Toro in 1071, teamed up with Alfonso to oust García who fled to Sevilla, then seized León and imprisoned Alfonso, who escaped and fled to Toledo. Note that both princes took refuge with Muslim rulers. Hugh, Abbot of Cluny, intervened to secure Alfonso's release from Sancho's clutches, which may explain in part Alfonso's subsequent partiality for the Cluniac cause.

Sancho II was crowned king at León in January 1072 and his father's realm was reunited. Almost. Urraca of Zamora proved a tougher nut to crack.

Standing before the walls, Sancho said, according to *El Cerco de Zamora*: 'Behold how mighty is Zamora; the city can be taken, I believe, neither by Moors nor Christians. If I can get my sister to give it to me for money or in exchange [for other lands], I can consider myself lord of Spain.'[4]

The town shut tight its gates and rallied round Urraca who refused to accede to her brother's demands which were conveyed to her by Rodrigo Díaz el Vivar, the future Cid, at the time in Sancho's service. When Rodrigo recited Sancho's demands, Urraca cried out: 'I pray that the earth will open and swallow me, so that I may no longer witness these disgraceful events.' But, she added, ominously: 'I am a woman and full well does my brother know that I cannot fight against him, but I will have him slain, either secretly or in the sight of all.'

Sancho settled down to a prolonged siege. When life inside the walls had become desperate, Urraca summoned a council to discuss the situation. A knight named Vellido Adolfo rose and proposed to save the city. The queen agreed and Vellido Adolfo laid his plans carefully.

He made his way to Sancho's camp where he swore fealty to the king and undertook to show him a weak spot in the defences. The two rode out beneath the walls where Vellido Adolfo treacherously slew the king. He galloped back to the city through the gate which is called to this day the Portillo de la Traición or Gate of Treason.

Vellido Adolfo is not remembered as the saviour of Zamora, but rather for his treacherous murder of the king to whom he had sworn allegiance. Actually, however, it seems that most of the story is pure invention, though indeed the king was slain by a Zamoran who surprised him in his sleep. Chronicles of the 12th century make no mention of Vellido Adolfo. But this 13th-century tale enabled the Castilian author to remind his audience how Castilla and its rightful king were wronged by the machinations of Alfonso of León and Urraca. Castilla and León had been united only in 1230 and resentment still rankled in at least some Castilian breasts.

Sancho fell on 7 October 1072. Urraca managed to get word to her brother Alfonso in Toledo and his escape from the clutches of his Muslim host forms the final part of *El Cerco de Zamora.*

Alfonso VI (1065/72–1109) was crowned king of León and Castilla at Burgos, thus reuniting the two kingdoms (for eighty-five years). Urraca retired from Zamora and went on to a quieter life as abbess of Covarrubias (Burgos), a post she held till her death thirty years later.

Under Alfonso, the town continued to grow with the help of Cluniac monks and the king's Burgundian sons-in-law and by the time of Alfonso VII (1126–57) the resettlement of the region was complete. Alfonso VII encouraged the Cistercians to come to Spain and at Moreruela, north of Zamora, we will visit one of their earliest houses in the peninsula.

By the 13th century, with the frontier established well south of the Duero, Zamora entered upon a long period of decline which helps to explain why it has such a wealth of Romanesque art still intact. The modernizers of the 16th century, let alone those of the 18th and 19th, did not find Zamora worthwhile and, although much has been destroyed by 20th-century developers, a rich legacy remains.

In the 15th century, Zamora was again embroiled in the affairs of Castilla. On the death of Enrique IV in 1474 and the proclamation of Isabella as queen, Zamora harboured supporters of her rival Juana la Beltraneja. When the latter's betrothed, Alfonso V of Portugal, invaded Castilla in 1475, Zamora went over to him. Ferdinand was besieging Zamora when the Portuguese forces reached the opposite bank. At this critical juncture, support from towns and nobles flowed to Ferdinand and in the end Alfonso V went down to defeat at Ferdinand's hands at Peleagonzalo, near Toro.

When the Comuneros rebelled against Charles I in 1520, the bishop of Zamora, Antonio de Acuña, a man of immense ambition, was a vigorous supporter of their cause. Acuña was the last of the warrior-bishops of Castilla. He had persuaded the pope to appoint him to Zamora in 1507, a move which met with fierce opposition, especially after he marched on Zamora and seized his bishopric by force. He and the city fathers fell to constant feuding.

Acuña put himself at the head of the Zamora Comuneros, seized the fortress, threw the *alcalde* Rodrigo Ronquillo into prison, drove out several notables (including the count of Alba y Aliste, proprietor of the palace which is now the parador) and with some 300 armed clerics seized a number of surrounding towns. Finally expelled from Zamora, early in 1521 Bishop Acuña led 2,000 troops to Valladolid to join the wider movement. The Comunero forces were routed near Toro in the spring, but not before Acuña had marched on Toledo where he persuaded the people to proclaim him archbishop.

Bishop Acuña fell into royalist hands in 1521 and was incarcerated at Simancas. While attempting to escape in 1526, he slew the governor of the fortress. He was recaptured and the king placed Ronquillo (who had been liberated from Zamora) in charge of the proceedings against him. Ronquillo wasted no time in taking revenge on his former captor and had the turbulent prelate murdered.[5] The ecclesiastical authorities absolved him of the murder and he lived on to 1545.

None of this arrested the continuing decline of Zamora. Far from the centres of power, sunk in the poverty that began to afflict Castilla from the 17th century on, the population drained away by famine, plague and migration, the town drifted on. Travellers' accounts all attest to its low state. By 1830, after the Peninsular War, the population was fewer than 10,000. There were those, however, with rosier glasses. Edward Hutton, visiting early in this century wrote: 'The world has forgotten Zamora for many a city less fair, for many a vision less lovely; but few find her out in her ruins and her solitude.'[6] He rhapsodizes over the river, the lush valley, the vineyards, the flowers. It is still a lovely spot.

However much medieval architecture was thus preserved, Zamora's stagnation was not necessarily a good thing. The agricultural poverty endemic in Castilla and León gravely affected the towns of the meseta and Zamora was still in a bad way even as late as the mid-1930s. The boom of the 1960s and 1970s finally brought Zamora around.

A Tour of the Town Let us start at the westernmost point of Zamora where the remains of the so-called CASTILLO DE URRACA and the famous walls overlook the lower town and the valley of the Duero. The earliest extant portions of the walls go back to the 9th century and Alfonso II, but most of the fabric is the work of the 12th and 13th centuries. The castle itself, despite its name, was actually built by Urraca's father, Fernando I, on what remained of the fortress of Alfonso II. Philips II and III remodelled it extensively in the 16th and 17th centuries.

A few of the ancient town gates survive. South of and below the cathedral is the PUERTA DEL OBISPO, the Bishop's Gate, and next to it the so-called CASA DEL CID, an 11th-century structure. The gate and house command fine views of the valley and the seventeen-arched medieval bridge over the Duero.

On the other side of the cathedral, below the church of San Isidro, is the PORTILLO DE TRAICIÓN through which Vellido Adolfo rode on his fateful mission. It is a steep drop; he must have been a fine horseman. A bit further along stood until 1925 the Puerta del Mercadillo (or del Carmen) and the reputed house of Don Arias Gonzalo, alcalde of Zamora at the time of the famous siege; fragments remain.

Where the streets of Sta María la Nueva and Feria meet the modern ring road below the northern walls is the much restored PUERTA DE DOÑA URRACA, just inside of which are remnants of the fortified palace of the queen.

CATEDRAL DE SAN SALVADOR Dominating the western end of the old walled city, which occupies a long narrow ridge, is the cathedral, one of the more interesting early cathedrals in Spain, along with its sisters in Salamanca and Toro.

The see of Zamora was created only after the reoccupation of the town by Alfonso III in 893; it remained vacant for over a century after the raids of Almanzor at the end of the 10th century. In 1102, the Cid's right arm, the warrior-bishop Jerónimo (Jerôme de Péri-gord), dispossessed of his see of Valencia by the Almoravids, was named bishop of Salamanca, Zamora and Ávila.

On his death in 1120, a struggle broke out for the control of Zamora involving several ambitious prelates, most particularly Diego Gelmírez, metropolitan of Santiago de Compostela, the French Cluniac Bernard, metropolitan of Toledo, and several popes, not to mention the kings of Portugal and León who resented foreign meddling in what they viewed as their affairs. It was only after many years and much ecclesiastical acrimony that Zamora was finally assigned to Compostela.

The cathedral was begun about 1151 and consecrated in 1174, a remarkably short space of time. The late 15th-century Gothic cabecera and the huge early 17th-century porch on the north (entrance) side have spoiled the original Romanesque effect. The massive square tower, its bulk relieved by the three ascending bands of arched openings flanked by slender columns, was built early in the 13th century.

An ancient problem was how to place a round dome over a square space. The earliest solution was to throw small arches (squinches) across the corners of the square to form an octagon. The ultimate solution, however, lay in the development of pendentives, concave triangles that fill the curved spaces between two opposing pairs of arches at the crossing of the nave and transept. The pendentives form the upper half of what would be a sphere were not the sides cut away by the planes of the four arches and the top sliced off. On the circular rim thus created, the dome can easily be reared.

Pendentives first appeared in 6th-century Hagia Sofia in Constantinople, reaching Italy in the mid-11th century with St Mark's in Venice and southern France in the early 12th century with the cathedrals of Angoulême and Périgueux. The Spanish architects went one better. On the circular base created by the pendentives, the builder of the cathedral of Zamora raised a circular drum pierced by windows, on top of which he placed the beautiful ribbed dome, the first such built in Spain.

At Zamora there is but one drum, which makes for a rather squat effect when seen from below. The architect of Salamanca thus erected a two-tier drum, lifting the dome higher, and the builder at Toro followed suit. From the windows made possible by the drum light pours into the interior. The drums are buttressed externally by four turrets resting on the piers beneath and, at Zamora and Salamanca, four gabled pavilions.

The architect of Zamora drew elements from Muslim and French sources, combining them in a fresh new way. 'In the whole range of medieval architectural evolution,' wrote one art historian, 'there is not a single instance where this organization of parts occurs in precisely the same manner.'[7]

The *media naranja* (half orange) dome of Zamora has sixteen boldly striped ribs. The sectors between the ribs are deeply convex, another innovation. The rib skeleton was erected first and the spaces between then filled in. It is possible that the builder was inspired by the monastery of Moreruela (see below) where the apse of the capilla mayor is covered by a half dome, the six ribs of which were built first.

The exterior of the dome, buttressed by four round turrets and four gabled dormers, is covered with fish-scale tiles, a Byzantine device that also appears in the cathedral of Angoulême. Given the number of Frenchmen who settled or campaigned in Spain and that Raymond of Burgundy (d. 1107) repopulated Zamora, evidence of French architectural influence is not surprising.

The interior of four bays is notable for the enormous piers supporting the nave vaults which have the first pointed arches in Spain. Three columns attached to each face of the square piers support the doubled transverse arches of nave and aisle bays and the ribs of the vaulting. The aisle bays are covered by groin vaults, the nave by quadripartite ribbed vaults and the transepts by old-fashioned barrel vaults. The simplicity of the capitals may reflect Cistercian influence. They are rather odd: cones topped by crenellations.

The nave is higher than the aisles, with pillars soaring above the tall pointed arcade arches. A kind of clerestory allows for windows.

The original cabecera was demolished in 1506 to build the present capilla mayor; note the fine *rejas* of the apsidal chapels. The western portal was replaced in the 15th century by the Capilla de San Ildefonso with a magnificent Renaissance portal. The *sala capitular* is at the extreme southwest corner. Chapels, also later additions, line the north side of the nave.

The early 16th-century stalls of the coro are notable, if you can get to see them. The arm-rests are wonderfully imaginative and saints, prophets and heros adorn the walls.

The only Romanesque portal remaining is the PUERTA DEL OBISPO (Portal of the Bishop) on the south side facing the archbishop's palace. It is a wonderful creation, with four most unusual archivolts composed of mouldings that look like bolsters or rolls of linen and are of Muslim derivation. The façade is articulated by tall slender shafts, blind arches, rosettes and sculpture, including a lovely Virgin and Child. This harmonious composition inspired other church builders in Zamora.

Go through the cloister (rebuilt after a fire in 1591) to reach the MUSEUM that displays, in a rather crowded way, a collection of superb 15th- and 16th-century Flemish tapestries from the palace of the counts of Alba y Aliste, now the parador. There are Trojan War scenes (one shows Hecuba sinking her white teeth into a Greek shoulder), a series on Hannibal's deeds, and a marvellous coronation of Tarquin as king of Rome. The weavers cleverly labelled all the personages.

SAN ISIDORO   East of the cathedral, across a pleasant park, is San Isidoro (12th century), so called because the relics of the sainted former bishop of Sevilla (d. 636) rested here in 1063 while Fernando I was having them transferred from Sevilla to León. A photogenic stork family occupies the belfry of the otherwise plain church. Just beyond is the Treason Gate.

SAN ILDEFONSO   This church, directly east of the cathedral, was dedicated to the patron saint of Toledo whose remains were brought here to escape Muslim profanation. The relics were lost at the time of Almanzor's raids and not rediscovered until 1260 at which time the Toledanos reclaimed their patron. The church is in poor shape; the blocked south portal was obviously inspired by the Puerta del Obispo of the cathedral.

STA MARÍA MAGDALENA   Near San Ildefonso begins the main street that traverses the length of the old town. The first notable sight is the wonderful south portal of Sta María Magdalena, begun before 1167. The six beautifully carved archivolts, adorned with plant and leaf motifs save for the row of little heads on the outermost, rest on columns with fancifully carved capitals. A fierce feline peers from the middle of the fifth archivolt; an alert human face with a slight smile looks out from the middle of the second.

Above is a rose window and the ensemble is framed by two engaged buttresses. Pilasters rising from ground to eaves divide the semicircular apse into three panels which are further divided into three horizontal sections by mouldings. Observe the detailing of the windows.

The single-nave interior is tall and narrow, with slender engaged columns rising the height of the church. The three panels of the interior of the apse are divided horizontally by two bands of moulding, as with the exterior. On either side of the capilla mayor are curious baldachins reminiscent of those in San Juan de Duero (Soria). In the 13th century, La Magdalena belonged to the Order of St John of Jerusalem (the Hospitallers), as did the Sorian monastery. On the north wall is the canopied tomb of a 12th-century lady whose recumbent effigy is surrounded by busy capitals with humans, birds and beasts.

SAN CIPRIANO Just before reaching the parador, a street to the right leads down to this little square-apsed church (also known as San Cebrián) built in the early 12th century. San Cipriano is one of five churches that antedate the cathedral, the others being San Claudio de Olivares, Santa María la Nueva, Santiago el Viejo and Santo Tomé. All but San Claudio have the square apses characteristic of very early churches, though a few later Zamora churches are square-apsed as well.

The rectangular apse, all that survives of the original building, encompasses three chapels side by side in the Visigothic and Mozarabic tradition. Walk around the church; carved fragments from earlier structures are stuck into the walls. Each of the three chapels has a little window in an arch supported by colonnettes with sculpted capitals and a scene in the tympanum.

The three bays of the interior are separated by enormous transverse arches that spring from low heavy columns. These date from the late 12th century and there were subsequent remodellings. The chapel on the north has a massive baptismal font hewn from a single block of stone.

The central apse is decorated internally with blind arches. The columns supporting the arches of the chapels have sculpted capitals. On the far left, fierce animals worry a little man caught in the middle. On the far right is a bishop with a crozier and other figures. One needs binoculars to make out the capitals of the central chapel.

SAN JUAN DE PUERTANUEVA This fine church, from the second half of the 12th century, stands on the rather uninspiring Plaza Mayor. (The Puerta Nueva or New Gate was opened in 1171.) The tower collapsed in the 16th century bringing down most of the roof, so the rebuilt interior is of that period. From the original structure remain the lovely south portal and rose window, framed between two slender engaged columns rising to the eaves. The three archivolts of the portal are carved with a stylized floral pattern; the two outer rest on pairs of columns. The columns immediately flanking the portal have spiral fluting. San Juan also has a square apse which supports the squat tower, rebuilt.

STA MARÍA LA NUEVA Look carefully at the exterior of the cabecera of this church north of San Juan: the capitals of the little columns flanking the windows and the corbels under the eaves have antic carvings. One little fellow is being pecked by very large birds (this motif recurs frequently); another, clad in a robe tied at the waist by a rope, has his outstretched arms in the mouths of fierce creatures. His expression seems oddly cheerful. The semicircular apse is divided into seven panels by graceful columns and rounded blind arcades.

Only the apse and the south wall with portal survived a fire in 1158, less than a century after the church was built, and thereby hangs a tale: the Trout Mutiny (*Motín de la trucha*). Details vary with the teller; the essence follows.

In the middle of the 12th century, it seems, trout were a delicacy reserved for the nobility. One fine day, a commoner attempted to buy for his lady love a trout which had also caught the eye of a servant of one of the noble families. A fight ensued, the noble servitor was slain and there was civic uproar. The nobles gathered in the church to discuss the situation, whereupon the townsfolk set the place on fire, incinerating those within.

The king launched an investigation and, interestingly enough, did not punish the townsfolk who rebuilt Sta María about 1200. Hence 'la Nueva'. Low down in the north wall, near the high altar, is a curious little vent. Through here, said our guide, the holy images from the altar escaped the flames and took refuge in a nearby sanctuary where they remain to this day. Ah, we said. She shrugged expressively.

The church contains a fine baptismal font from the time of the post-fire reconstruction. A blind arcade of seven arches runs right around it, each arcade framing a scene, including the Baptism of Christ. Traces of Gothic murals appear on the north wall near the capilla mayor and in the sacristy. They are sketched in red and black and some fine heads and faces are still discernible. Somewhat discordant is the recumbent Christ by Gregorio Fernández, that sculptor from Valladolid so fond of hyperrealistic touches.

MUSEO DE LA SEMANA SANTA   Adjacent to Sta María is the Holy Week Museum with a remarkable display of *pasos*, the floats depicting scenes from the Passion, Death and Resurrection of Christ that are carried in procession during Holy Week.

SAN VICENTE   Near the Plaza Mayor rises an attractive early 13th-century tower, about all that remains of the original church, modernized in the 16th and 18th centuries with dreary results.

CASA DE LOS MOMOS   East of the Plaza Mayor, the street bifurcates. To the left is the 16th-century Casa de los Momos with a fine Mudéjar–Gothic façade: a massive arched portal and in the upper register four elaborate *ajimeces* (twinned windows) and an escutcheon. The ensemble is framed in an *alfiz*, that familiar Moorish device still being used at this late date. The house faces a pleasant little park with a charming modern bronze sculpture of a mother and infant.

SANTIAGO DEL BURGO   The right fork, the Calle de Sta Clara, leads to late 12th-century Santiago del Burgo. The interior was reworked in 1820, but the exterior aspects are original. This is another square-apsed church with three naves, the central one being unusually lofty. Against the south wall are five stout engaged buttresses and in the middle is a rather odd portal which looks as though the central shaft of the doorway has been removed, but it was built that way. The portal is surmounted by a small rose window and the remaining three panels have attractive windows.

The north façade resembles the south. The portal has four archivolts composed of what look like little stone pillows. The three archivolts of the west portal, now blocked up, were inspired by the Puerta del Obispo of the cathedral.

The Calle de Santa Clara is lined with residential and commercial buildings, some with glazed balconies. Towards the end of the street is the Tourist Office.

Down the hill is a section of town between the bluffs and the river. Two of its churches are of particular interest.

STA MARÍA DE LA HORTA This late 12th-century church is a wonderful ensemble. The best overall view is from the southeast where a basketball game is likely to be in progress. The church was for centuries the Castilian headquarters of the Knights Hospitallers or of St John of Jerusalem (and eventually the Knights of Malta) whose archives were kept on the second floor of the tower.

Sta María originally had a single nave and a rounded apse. A gallery was added to the south side and that was subsequently divided into chapels. Tall engaged columns divide the apse into three large panels and two small, each of which has a particularly fine window. Note the detailing of the eaves around the church. The main entrance is in the west front, next to the stout square tower. The church was restored in the 1970s.

SANTO TOMÉ This nearby church was founded perhaps as early as 1106. The structure has been stabilized, but it is in worse shape than its neighbour. Of the original building only the three square apses and the north wall remain; the rest is 18th century, when the nave and two aisles were replaced by a single nave. The windows, the carvings on the corbels of the apse and the moulding courses are particularly worth noting, as is the battered north portal. The three apsidal chapels open on to the nave through horseshoe arches.

SAN LEONARDO In the same *barrio* is early 13th-century San Leonardo, but it is in such terrible shape that the last time I was in Zamora it had a 'For Sale' sign on it.

Slightly to the west stands the PALACIO DEL CORDÓN, the future Museum of Zamora. Its fine façade has noble escutcheons and an enormous Franciscan rope with loops and knots in the shape of an alfiz around the portal.

SANTIAGO EL VIEJO Outside and below the castle walls at the western end of town are two other churches. Tiny Santiago el Viejo is visible from the walls in what was once a meadow across a stream. It was founded in the mid-12th century, perhaps earlier, and has a very plain rough exterior. According to legend, the Cid was knighted here, but since he died in 1099, this is not likely. The key to Santiago is at San Claudio de Olivares in the barrio of the same name below the Puerta del Obispo.

SAN CLAUDIO DE OLIVARES The north portal retains traces of polychrome. This is perhaps the oldest of the five pre-cathedral churches. The sculptures are badly eroded, but the outermost of the four archivolts carries a zoo of animals, real and imaginary. The inner archivolt is unadorned save for a nice Agnus Dei. The cornice above rests on corbels carved with human and animal heads. The interior is said to have marvellous capitals. The nave is so broad that the barrel vault pushed out the walls and fell; only the apse vault is original.

PUENTE DE PIEDRA The Stone Bridge crosses the Duero on seventeen graceful arches. It was constructed in the 12th and 13th centuries, with repairs in the 16th and 17th. The defensive towers at either end were pulled down early in this century. It is pleasant to walk out and look back on the town. A short distance downstream are the remains of the 11th-century bridge built on the site of the Roman bridge that carried the Via Plata from Mérida (Emerita Augusta) to Astorga (Asturica Augusta). The bridge was thus a major strategic asset.

North of Zamora

Moreruela The ruins of the Cistercian monastery of Moreruela lie some 40 km (25 miles) north of Zamora. Take the N-630 towards Benavente to Granja de Moreruela where a road leads off 3.5 km to a gate in a fence. The ruins are visible to the right in a thick grove of trees along the river bank.

There is often a sense of adventure and real discovery in visiting ruins in Spain. In England, lovely Cistercian abbeys, castles and stately homes stand in the midst of neatly cropped lawns, with flowering shrubs and the like, and a tuck shop for refreshments when you are done. France and Italy also have their monuments reasonably well tidied up. Not so in Spain. Castles, except for the domesticated ones, stand on lonely barren windswept crags, often requiring a rugged climb. Churches and monasteries can be abandoned in the brush, sometimes occupied by domestic animals. Moreruela is no exception.

The monastery originated on the opposite side of the Río Esla in Moreruela de Tábara where the monastery of Santiago de Moreruela was founded in the 10th century by Ordoño II with Mozarab refugees from al-Andalus. (Others prefer the end of the 9th century under Ordoño's father, Alfonso III.) This was destroyed by Almanzor and though the church was rebuilt, only fragments remain, embedded in the present church of San Miguel Arcángel (see Moreruela de Tábara, below).

Alfonso VII (1126–57) was an enthusiastic promoter of the Cistercians and when the monks of the old abbey embraced the Cistercian reforms, the king saw to the founding of a new monastery on a site east of the Esla. St Bernard of Clairvaux himself sent monks to help with the new house.

This was not just a pious move on Alfonso's part. His actions go to the heart of the important role the Cistercians played in rebuilding Spain. The king had to colonize the empty Duero valley and restore economic activity. The Cistercians had demonstrated their effectiveness in this sort of enterprise in France and elsewhere. Writes Sr Enríquez de Salamanca:

> By the end of the [12th] century and even more in the following, Moreruela had extended its domain enormously, primarily through royal donations, private gifts, and papal exemptions, as well as by purchase and exchange, throughout the northern part of the present province of Zamora and even the north of Portugal. Donated villas were transformed into farms [granjas] ... making new areas habitable and systematically bringing them under irrigation.[8]

By 1168 the task of building was all but finished. The work was in the hands of a Mozarab known as Petrus Mori, Peter the Moor, and the building was to influence other monasteries and churches further afield in Spain. There is virtually no decoration, in keeping with the strictures of St Bernard. The beauty of Moreruela rests in its mass and proportions and in the marvellous chevet with seven radiating chapels which is all but intact.

Two tremendous piers with engaged columns support the triumphal arch in front of the capilla mayor. Eight huge cylindrical columns separate the chapel from the ambulatory and support the vaults. The five arches sustaining the chapel's beautiful ribbed half dome are pointed, in contrast to the rounded windows above them.

The two arches on either side are also rounded. The slightly pointed arches and the vaulting of the aisles signal the approach of the Gothic style.

The construction of the apse of the capilla mayor may have influenced that of the dome of the cathedral of Zamora. The six ribs converging at the keystone, which rest on corbels above the spandrels of the arches, were put in place first as a frame on which to build the half dome itself.

Ambulatories were originally developed in response to the needs of pilgrims for more space and more chapels in which to worship more relics, but since Cistercians opposed relics and rich reliquaries and settled far from the beaten track, they abandoned the ambulatory. For some reason, the practice was revived at Moreruela, with stunning results. There are seven rounded chapels, with one tiny one at the end of each crossing. Elsewhere, such as at Sta María de Huerta (Soria) the cabecera is rectangular, the chapels open directly off the arms of the transepts, and only the capilla mayor is sometimes semicircular.

The façade of the south transept, the north wall of the church up to and including the clerestory windows, and the vaults of the north transept remain intact. The 16th-century cloister, on the north side as at Huerta, has all but disappeared, but the chambers off the east gallery still stand, including the square chapter house with a roof of nine vaults and a refectory with enormous low piers supporting a series of mighty arches, slightly pointed, and vaults.

Go around the monastery to view the exterior of the chevet. It is a wonderful arrangement.

The disentailment of the monasteries in 1835–36 and the expulsion of the monks exposed Moreruela to the depredations that afflicted most such establishments in Spain. Much of the damage to Moreruela occurred early in this century when stone was removed to build, among other things, the parish church of La Granja. Let us rejoice in what is left.

Benavente This interesting and lively town has two very good churches. It commands the confluence of three rivers, the Esla, the Cea and the Orbigo and was an important pre-Roman site. Destroyed in the Arab invasions, it was resettled under Fernando II of León in 1164.

SANTA MARÍA LA MAYOR Also called Santa María del Azoque, the church stands in the middle of a bustling square (*azoque* comes from the Arabic *al-suq*, the market). It is a splendid building begun in the reign of Fernando II (1157–88), from whose time date the unusual cabecera of five apses and portions to the west. There is evidence that the builders of Moreruela worked here as well. Construction continued under Sancho IV (the crossing, the vaults and the pillars of the nave) a century later, but the church was not ultimately finished until the 16th century.

The cabecera consists of five curved apses with superb detailing around the windows and on the cornices. The three beautifully carved archivolts of the south portal rest on pillars; the inner archivolt depicts human and animal figures representing Eve (on the left), the Four Evangelists, Adam and a praying figure. On the tympanum are the Lamb of God and four cheerful angels in flight. The north portal has four archivolts of lovely geometrical and floral design, also crisply done. The interior is remarkable for the elaborate zig-zag carvings on the arches of the crossing and the apses.

SAN JUAN DEL MERCADO The second church is a short walk away, near a rather dispirited plaza mayor, and is notable for the tympanum of the south portal. The scene depicted is the Adoration of the Magi, who approach from the left. The Virgin and Child occupy the centre and off to the right by himself is poor Joseph, resting his head on his right hand and looking out of it all. On each side of the portal are three beautifully carved column figures of prophets (barefoot).

Sta Marta de Tera Twenty-seven km west of Benavente on the N-525 is a village that takes its name from the church of Sta Marta de Tera, one of the finest we shall see, anywhere. The church is on a small square to the left as you enter town. Below the bluff on which it stands, the Río Tera flows to join the Esla south of Benavente.

The church is all that remains of a monastery founded in the 10th century and long under royal patronage. The present church was begun in 1077 and is the oldest in the province. Alfonso VI established an abbey of canons regular that survived until the 16th century. The monastery was famed for curing the halt and the lame, the blind and the deaf and for driving out demons. Its fortunes were secured when Alfonso VII came to be cured of ailments in 1129 – and was.

Sta Marta is in the shape of a Latin cross, very rare in these parts, with a rectangular apse. The exterior is brilliant. Walk around the church (which means clambering through the local cemetery). The building is wrapped by horizontal bands of chequered moulding (technically known, I believe, as billet moulding) that are matched inside by similar mouldings. Each of the windows of the apse (two or which are blind, but were obviously included for the artistic effect) and transepts is flanked by little columns with sculpted capitals and the mouldings tie them all together to make a supremely successful ensemble.

The principal portal is on the south (river) side. It is flanked by two superb 12th-century sculptures, that on the left being Santiago himself, with pilgrim's staff, purse and scallop shell.

You enter now through the north transept door. The nave was reworked late in the 12th century and the three bays have groin vaulting with pointed transverse arches as contrasted with the original barrel vaulting of the apses. The bands of chequerboard moulding are as striking inside as out.

There are some wonderful capitals. To the left of the window in the capilla mayor is the Sacrifice of Isaac. On the right are David, with harp, and King Saul. The capital on the left of the triumphal arch shows a soul in a mandorla being lifted up by two angels; at the March and September solstices this capital is struck by rays of the sun shining through the little round window in the east wall.

Sta Marta is one of the finest Romanesque churches I saw in Castilla y León. The detail is fascinating. The door was open when I arrived and I found the priest in the sacristy with a group of students whom he quickly abandoned for my sake. He could not have been nicer and I urge you to persevere and find him if the door is closed when you arrive.

Tábara From the square by Sta Marta, a pleasant local road runs south through hills and farmland to join the N-631 and so to the village of Tábara. On the left is a church tower of dark stone and striking design.

Where this tower now stands once rose the tower of the famous late 9th-century Mozarabic monastery of SAN SALVADOR DE

TÁBARA founded under the auspices of Alfonso III. San Salvador had a noted scriptorium in which were made several copies of the *Commentaries on the Apocalypse* or the Book of Revelations of St John, compiled in 776 by Beato de Liébana.

Beato was a monk, possibly the abbot, of the monastery of San Martín de Turieno, now Santo Toribio de Liébana, at Potes in Cantabria. He popularized the legend that Santiago, the Apostle St James the Great, had preached in Spain and taken the land under his protection. He was also a fighter against the heresies of the day.

His *Commentaries* was a compilation of writings of the Church fathers and other divines on the last book of the New Testament. Revelations predicts the ultimate triumph of the Church over false prophets and enemies of the faith, a description which fitted the Muslims as well as assorted heretics of the age. Beato's work was copied and illustrated by the best monk-artists of succeeding generations and was widely disseminated. Thirty-five copies are extant, twenty-six of them illustrated. Three stemmed from Tábara.[9]

The oldest extant copy was made in about 945 by a monk named Maius who states in the colophon appended to the text that the work was commissioned by the abbot of San Miguel de Escalada, east of León, refounded in 913. This copy was acquired by the Morgan Library in New York in 1919.

Maius established a workshop at Tábara. When he died in 968, while working on another copy, a monk named Emeterius finished the job with his colleague Senior. This copy, the *Tábara Beatus* of about 970, is in the Archivo Histórico Nacional de Madrid. A famous illustration shows Emeterius and Senior working away at their desks in the scriptorium, next to the five-storey tower of the monastery which is aglow with bright tiles. In an adjacent room, a monk is cutting pages of parchment. The tower has horseshoe windows, ladders connecting the floors, a balcony around the top floor and two little bell turrets. Men are climbing the ladders and one fellow on the ground floor is pulling on the bell ropes. Here in this tower, wrote the monk in his colophon, 'Emeterius has been seated bent over his task for three months, leaving all his fingers crippled with the labour of the pen'.

The third copy, written by Senior about 975 with Emeterius and a nun named Ende, has been in the possession of Girona Cathedral since 1078.

The Silos Beatus in the British Museum was completed at the monastery of Santo Domingo de Silos (Burgos) in 1091.

San Salvador was destroyed by Almanzor. The Romanesque church of which this tower and some other fragments survive was built about 1137. The church itself has undergone various reformations, the latest in the 18th century.

Moreruela de Tábara This village, a short distance southeast of Tábara, was the site of the monastery of Santiago de Moreruela founded by Mozarabic monks at the end of the 9th century under Alfonso III (or slightly later by Ordoño II). It too was wrecked by Almanzor. The dates of its re-establishment are uncertain, possibly around 1132, but in any event the monks were invited by Alfonso VII to take up a new site on the other side of the Esla where they founded the monastery of Moreruela.

The present church of San Miguel Arcángel dates from the latter 12th century, but it was remodelled almost totally in the 18th century.

This is very hilly country, the Sierra de Culebra, and the drive back to Zamora is scenic, with occasional views of the reservoir of the Esla that fills the gorges for miles. Another scenic drive crosses the northern part of the gorge between Tábara and (just north of) Granja de Moreruela.

West of Zamora

At Zamora, we pick up the N-122 again which runs west to Portugal. Our goal is one of the most fascinating Visigothic churches remaining.

San Pedro de la Nave Some dozen kilometres west of Zamora, turn right to Campillo (signposted). The road to San Pedro de la Nave peels off left after a while. Fields of wheat stretch in every direction, valleys add variety to the landscape and from time to time there are views of the valley of the Río Esla, now filled with the waters of an enormous reservoir.

The village comes suddenly into view, a few houses in a fold in the hills, with the stubby square tower of San Pedro plainly visible on a slope beyond. The road goes down the hill to the middle of the village where, at an ugly brick house containing a machine shop, you turn right up the hill to the church. If there is no one there, go back to the village centre; to the left of the machine shop a lane leads straight to the house of the woman who holds the key.

San Pedro de la Nave dates probably from the end of the 7th century, in the reign of King Egica (687–701), though the first documentary reference to it is not until 907. Some scholars place it after the repopulation of Zamora in 893/902, but Bevan notes that the fine reddish-yellow sandstone of which the church is built came from a quarry some distance away on the other side of the river.[10] The only bridge capable of supporting such loads was the Roman bridge, destroyed in the early 8th century and still in ruins in the 10th.

Due to its remote location, San Pedro did not come to public attention till 1870. It stood originally on a site now flooded by a reservoir and was moved stone by stone to Campillo in 1932.

The church is solidly built of finely dressed stone, a Visigothic characteristic, as we have seen. The only external ornamentation consists of decorative bands on the impost blocks of the portals at the ends of the two transepts. There are little slit windows around the church; note especially the ajimeces (twinned windows) on the faces of the transepts. That on the west side of the north transept has a little column dividing the windows, with a tiny capital carved with grapes.

The church may have fallen into disrepair and been restored about 900 when the Christians retook the area. The full weight of the crossing rests on the walls, not on the columns, possible evidence of rebuilding. The western end of the church seems to have collapsed in the 12th century and the stubby three-aisled unadorned nave dates from the ensuing reconstruction. The two lateral aisles end in walls where the transepts cross the nave, walls that are pierced on either side with twinned horseshoe arched apertures of considerable size. From here east, the structure is pure Visigothic.

The horseshoe arch is used throughout. The triumphal arch, at the entrance to the capilla mayor, is particularly fine. Its voussoirs are alternately of red and tawny stone, just as they are in the Great Mosque of Córdoba. The arch rests on columns with trapezoidal capitals and squared-off impost blocks, carved with typically Visigothic motifs. On either side of the chancel are two chambers. Despite the solidity of construction, considerable light comes through windows high up in the chancel and in the tower over the crossing.

The trapezoidal capitals at the crossing are remarkable. Scenes do not generally appear carved on capitals before the Romanesque period, yet here they are. The background has been cut away, leaving the scenes in low, flat relief.

In the southwest corner is the Sacrifice of Isaac, with saints Peter and Paul occupying the two sides; in the northwest, Daniel in the lions' den on the face of the capital, flanked by saints Thomas and Philip. Inscriptions tell you who is who. Birds occupy the two eastern capitals. The bases of the columns are also carved, though only that on the southeast is still in decent condition. All around the interior at the level of the impost blocks is a band of typically Visigothic ornamentation: interconnected circles of rope or vines with birds, animals, masks, bunches of grapes, rosettes, spirals, leaves, stars and so on – all good Syrian designs, as several authors have noted. Georgiana King also observes that Saints Philip and Thomas were Arabs, giving another clue to the origins of the design elements in San Pedro.[11]

San Pedro is one of the best Visigothic churches extant. The setting is evocative; the deep gorge of the Esla is visible on the north and west; the meseta stretches away in all directions.

And Westwards Beyond Zamora, the Duero has fallen into the hands of man. The Río Esla, flowing down from above León, joins the Duero west of Zamora, but their waters have been impounded by a dam and three more dams block the Duero between Zamora and the Portuguese frontier some 35 km (22 miles) away, part of Spain's electric power grid.

The Duero has now begun to cut its way down from the meseta to the sea and on turning south at the border enters the Arribes del Duero, a gorge which for 112 km (70 miles) marks the international frontier. In this stretch, the Duero is joined by the Río Tormes coming down from Salamanca and the Gredos Mountains southwest of Avila. The Tormes, too, has been dammed, just short of its junction with the Duero, and an enormous reservoir created.

Before going to Salamanca and the border, let us backtrack and go to Ávila. If you prefer to go to Salamanca first and return to Madrid via Ávila, the N-630 Zamora–Salamanca runs virtually straight dully across the meseta for 62 km (40 miles). Equally good roads run from Toro and Tordesillas; the landscape is much the same. Perhaps 25 km along the N-630 is a small brown sign saying 'Valparaiso' and just beyond that a monument to Fernando III el Santo, conqueror of Córdoba and Sevilla. Here stood the Cistercian monastery of Valparaiso, now all but vanished, where the future king was born in 1199.

Notes

1. Peggy Liss, *Isabel the Queen* (Oxford, 1992), p. 127.
2. Bernard Bevan, *A History of Spanish Architecture* (London, 1938), p. 64.
3. *Cambridge Ancient History* (Cambridge, 1952), Vol. VIII, p. 316.
4. Quotations and story are from 'El cerco de Zamora' in Rosa Castillo (ed.), *Leyendas épicas españoles* (Madrid, 1987).
5. J. H. Elliott, *Imperial Spain, 1469–1716* (London, 1970), pp. 157–8, tells the Acuña story.
6. Edward Hutton, *The Cities of Spain* (London, 1906) p. 54.
7. Carl Kenneth Hersey, *The Salmantine Lanterns: Their Origins and Development* (Cambridge, MA, 1937), p. 5.
8. Cayetano Enríquez de Salamanca, *El ruta románico en la provincia de Zamora* (Madrid, 1989), pp. 94–5.
9. The three Tábara copies and others are discussed in *The Art of Medieval Spain* (Metropolitan Museum of New York, 1993), pp. 153–60, 289–93, and 300–3. The introduction to the Morgan Library's facsimile edition of its Beatus (*A Spanish Apocalypse*) contains much information on the *Commentaries* and its copiers, as well as superb reproductions.
10. Bevan, *A History of Spanish Architecture*, p. 13.
11. Georgiana G. King, *Pre-Romanesque Churches of Spain* (New York, 1924), p. 55.

9

Ávila Province

The Sierra de Guadarrama covers the eastern part of the Province of Ávila, separating it from the Comunidad de Madrid; the Sierra de Gredos covers the southern half. North and west, the province extends into the meseta. The weather can be bitterly cold in winter; at 1,130 m (3,710 feet) Ávila sits on a rocky height at a bend in the Río Adaja and is the highest provincial capital in Spain. The wintry winds whistle around the ancient walls and old granite buildings.

Approaches

Leaving Madrid on the N-VI to the northwest, you can take the A-6 toll road (*peaje*) through the Sierra de Guadarrama tunnel or stay on the N-VI and climb over the Puerto de Leones (the Pass of Lions). A third alternative is via the C-505 and San Lorenzo de El Escorial. This very scenic route affords views of (or enables you to visit) the monastery of Philip II.

From the N-VI or A-6, exit at Villacastín (80 km/50 miles from Madrid). It is a short run from there to Ávila across a wild landscape strewn with enormous grey granite boulders. The approach from the east or north is not very interesting because the modern town shields the old walled town. The classic view is from across the Río Adaja, on the road to Salamanca, and another good view can be had coming up the long valley that stretches south from the city.

To reach Arévalo and Madrigal de las Altas Torres in the northern part of the province, continue on the N-VI.

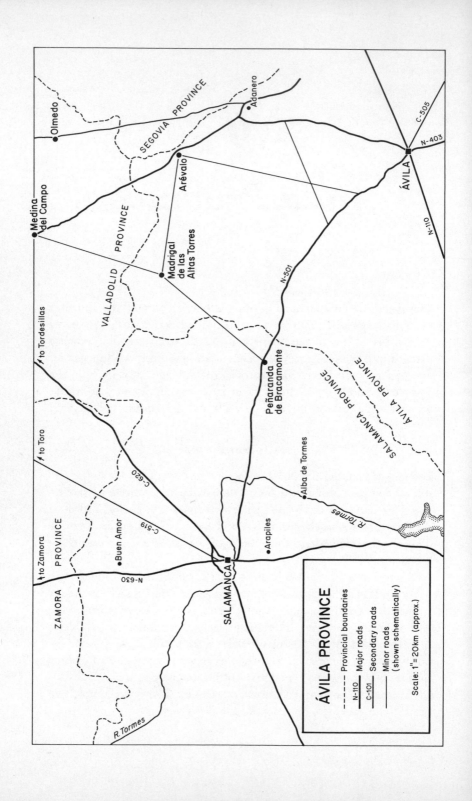

ÁVILA PROVINCE

Provincial boundaries
N-110 Major roads
C-101 Secondary roads
Minor roads
(shown schematically)

Scale: 1" = 20km (approx.)

If you approach Ávila from the north, I recommend the provincial road AV-802 from Arévalo. The country is undulating, with the mountains ahead, and the road runs through pine and other forests alternating with sweeping fields. This was and remains agricultural land.

Ávila

History There was a Celtiberian settlement on the site and from that period date the massive granite bulls and boars which can be seen here and there in the city and the province. They were probably totemic figures marking the tribe's territory. Known by the Romans as Avela, the town was the seat of a bishopric very early on. One of its bishops achieved a considerable measure of notoriety.

The early centuries of Christianity were roiled with controversies over the precise relationship between the members of the Trinity and their natures. In 380, Emperor Theodosius I decreed the orthodoxy of the Roman credo and condemned adherents of all other creeds as heretics, subject to punishment. The first victim of the emperor's edict was Priscillian, bishop of Avela 381–85.

Priscillian was a proponent of extreme asceticism, not in itself particularly disturbing, but he also renounced marriage which did create a stir. Critics of the bishop and his followers accused them of Manichaeanism, a set of eastern beliefs associated, wrongly, in the West with magic and sorcery. None other than St Jerome condemned Priscillian in the strongest terms.

In due course, the orthodox party in Hispania appealed to the emperor against these supposed schismatics. The bishop also appealed, but in the end he was burned alive at Trier in 385 on the orders of Magnus Maximus, co-emperor in the West. Priscillian was thus the first to be condemned and punished by the secular authorities for a purely religious offence. That Theodosius, Priscillian and Maximus were all Spaniards makes the tale all the more poignant considering the later contributions of Spain to the annals of religious persecution for the sake of state-approved orthodoxy.

What was left of Avela at the time of the Muslim invasion fell into the buffer zone created by Alfonso I between Asturias and al-Andalus in the middle of the 8th century. It was taken and repopulated in 940 under Ramiro II, but later in the century it suffered the raids of Almanzor.

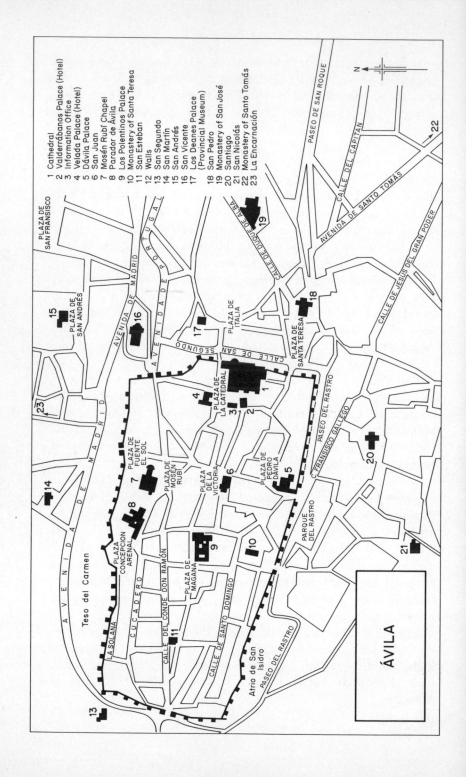

ÁVILA

1 Cathedral
2 Valderrábanos Palace (Hotel)
3 Information Office
4 Velada Palace (Hotel)
5 Dávila Palace
6 San Juan
7 Mosén Rubí Chapel
8 Parador de Ávila
9 Los Polentinos Palace
10 Monastery of Santa Teresa
11 San Esteban
12 Walls
13 San Segundo
14 San Martín
15 San Andrés
16 San Vicente
17 Los Deanes Palace
   (Provincial Museum)
18 San Pedro
19 Monastery of San José
20 Santiago
21 San Nicolás
22 Monastery of Santo Tomás
23 La Encarnación

Zamora (Zamora) This ancient fortress town stands on an easily defensible bluff above the Duero. Its Puente de Piedra (the Stone Bridge) of 17 arches dates from the 12th/13th centuries. Zamora's medieval walls were famous for their strength and durability.

Zamora (Zamora) The town's Cathedral was built 1151-1174, though much altered in the 16th century and later. Visible here over the uninspired 17th-century porch is the top of the cupola, the first built of the trio that includes Salamanca and Toro. To the left is the early 15th-century apse; on the right is the massive early 13th-century tower.

Zamora (Zamora) The cupola and interior dome of Zamora Cathedral constitute an architectural landmark. The use of pendentives for the transition between a square crossing and a round dome was introduced in Constantinople and spread to southern France. The Spanish innovation was to elevate the dome on a drum and admit light through, here, 16 windows. Externally, however, the ensemble has a rather squat appearance, which is why the builders of the later Salamanca and Toro cupolas used two-tiered drums. The fish scale tiles are also of Byzantine derivation.

Zamora (Zamora) The mid 12th-century church of Sta María Magdalena is one of the finest of the town's 20 medieval churches. The portal is splendid; this is a detail of the right side. The capitals of the columns supporting the archivolts are richly carved with mythological figures, fronds and leaves.

Zamora (Zamora) The Puerta del Obispo (Gate of the Bishop) is the sole remaining Romanesque doorway at the Cathedral. It is a remarkable assemblage of details, with the unusual archivolts resembling rolls of linen. They are of Muslim derivation. Two slender columns divide the facade into three vertical panels; bold mouldings define three horizontal sections.

Zamora (Zamora) Storks in Spain seem to favour ecclesiastical buildings on which to construct the nests to which they return every year after summering in Africa. They are rarely seen on secular buildings. This nest is atop the church of San Isidoro. Storks make odd clattering noises with their beaks and at sunset can be seen circling around till they settle down for the night. Spanish villagers are very protective of the birds.

Moreruela (Zamora) The ruins of this Cistercian monastery north of Zamora, from the mid 12th century, have left exposed the apse and part of the north transept. The monastery was not only the centre of a spiritual revival but played a crucial role in bringing empty lands back into cultivation and introducing advanced agricultural techniques pioneered by the Cistercians in Burgundy.

Moreruela (Zamora) This view inside the ruined apse of the monastery shows the transition between the rounded arches of the Romanesque and the early hints of Gothic pointed arches introduced by the Cistercians. The ribs of the half dome of the apse spring from ornamental brackets at the moulding line rather than from the ground.

Moreruela (Zamora) The graceful columns of the entry arch to the apse of the monastery and the stout columns of the apse itself have capitals completely devoid of carving. The Cistercians believed in simplicity. One of the powerful transverse arches supporting the vault of the north transept is also visible.

Benavente (Zamora) The four archivolts of the north portal of Sta María del Azoque are carved with geometric designs and flowers and are supported by columns with elaborately carved capitals. The portal is a splendid example of late 12th-/early 13th-century Romanesque sculptural mastery.

Benavente (Zamora) Sta María del Azoque, dating from the late 12th/early 13th century, is the principal church of this town. Shown here is the rich carving on the right side of the north portal, with beasts both real and imagined adorning the capitals of the columns.

Sta Marta de Tera (Zamora) All that remains of a famous monastery founded in the 10th century, this is the oldest surviving church in the province, begun in 1077. The monastery had a reputation for healing the sick and when King Alfonso VII was cured of what ailed him in 1129, its success was assured.

Sta Marta de Tera (Zamora) Sta Marta is near the pilgrimage road to Santiago de Compostela as demonstrated by this 12th-century figure of Santiago, St James the Great, flanking the south portal.

Sta Marta de Tera (Zamora) This detail of the central apse window of Sta Marta de Tera shows the bold carving of the fanciful creatures on the capitals and of the bands of moulding.

The town owed its rebirth to the tireless Raymond of Burgundy (d. 1107), husband of Urraca, daughter and eventual successor of Alfonso VI. After the capture of Toledo in 1085, Alfonso VI entrusted Raymond (Raimundo de Borgoña in Spanish) with the defence of the new frontier. He created a chain of fortresses from Segovia through Ávila to Salamanca and repopulated these towns and, in this sector, the area to the north including Arévalo and Madrigal de las Altas Torres. Commanding the valleys and passes that led from the meseta down to Toledo, Ávila was a particularly important stronghold. Among the many settlers who responded to his call were French knights; hence the sobriquet 'Ávila de los Caballeros'.

As elsewhere (especially Segovia and Salamanca), the new settlers came from many different places and grouped themselves in *barrios* around their parochial churches, both inside the walls and out. There were some nineteen churches by 1250. Thus it was that the 12th-century Moroccan geographer al-Idrisi remarked of Ávila as he did of Segovia that it was nothing more than a collection of villages.

Raymond's most stupendous visible achievement is the city walls begun in the last decade of the 11th century, although it is now held that much of the existing circuit dates from the second half of the 12th. Eighty-eight stout towers punctuate the roughly rectangular circuit, 2.5 km or more than a mile and a half in circumference, pierced by nine gates. The Muslim menace was far from extinguished when they were built. The effect of these mighty fortifications is best appreciated from the belvedere across the Río Adaja.

Ávila's key position on the most westerly of the *cañadas* or highways for the huge flocks of sheep migrating seasonally from the mountains of the north to winter pastures in the south made it a natural centre for the wool industry.

In the struggle for the succession to Enrique IV, Ávila was the scene of dramatic happenings on 5 June 1465. William Prescott, drawing on a contemporary account, tells the story of how the faction of the nobility opposed to Enrique deposed him in favour of his half-brother Alfonso:

> In an open plain, not far from the city of Ávila, they caused a scaffold to be erected, of sufficient elevation to be easily seen from the surrounding country. A chair of state was placed on it, and in this was seated an effigy of King Henry, clad in sable robes and adorned with all the insignia of royalty, a sword at his side, a sceptre in his hand,

and a crown upon his head. A manifesto was then read, exhibiting in glowing colors the tyrannical conduct of the king, and the consequent determination to depose him ... The archbishop of Toledo then, ascending the platform, tore the diadem from the head of the statue; the marquis of Villena removed the sceptre, the count of Plasencia the sword, the grand master of Alcantara and the counts of Benavente and Paredes the rest of the regal insignia; then the image, thus despoiled of its honors, was rolled in the dust, amid the mingled groans and clamors of the spectators. The young prince Alfonso, at that time only eleven years of age, was seated on the vacant throne, and the assembled grandees severally kissed his hand in token of their homage; the trumpets announced the completion of the ceremony, and the populace greeted with joyful acclamations the accession of their new sovereign.[1]

Joy was short-lived. Three years later, young Alfonso was dead. His sister Isabella succeeded when Enrique IV died in 1474.

Ávila took part in the Comunero revolt against Charles I, the emperor Charles V, in 1520. In August 1520, after the towns failed to receive satisfaction from the new king in answer to their petitions, representatives of Ávila, Toledo, Salamanca and Madrid met in Ávila. From there, Juan de Padilla of Toledo led the troops of the four towns to Tordesillas, setting in train the revolt which was crushed less than a year later near Toro.

Ávila was the birthplace of Teresa Sánchez de Cepeda y Ahumada (1515–82), Santa Teresa de Ávila (or de Jesús), an altogether indefatigable lady whose ubiquitousness is attested by plaques on buildings in an astonishing number of Spanish towns. She joined the Carmelite Order at the age of twenty. Her mission became the reform of the Order and the establishment of the Barefoot (Descalzas) Carmelites.

The visions and mystical experiences for which she became famous began when she was in her forties. She travelled all over the country establishing convents and monasteries where the reformed Carmelites could live stricter and more contemplative lives. Teresa died in Alba de Tormes (Salamanca), where she is interred, and was canonized in 1622, along with her fellow Spaniards Ignatius Loyola and Francis Xavier and the Italian Philip Neri, in a sumptuous quadruple ceremony orchestrated by Pope Gregory XV.

Her friend and fellow mystic, San Juan de la Cruz (1542–91), was born at Fontiveros, northwest of Ávila; he lies now in Segovia.

Ávila began to go downhill with the accession of the Habsburgs in the 16th century and the establishment of the court at Madrid. The expulsion of the Moriscos, descendants of those Moors who had converted in the time of Ferdinand and Isabella, in 1609 brought economic ruin. The population gradually declined to only a couple of thousand.

When Joseph Townsend passed through Ávila in 1786 he noted that there were only a thousand houses or one-sixth of its former population. He also commented, rather tartly, that the shrinkage of the population did not seem to have diminished the number of churches and convents.[2]

Richard Ford came half a century later, after Napoleon's troops had done their usual worst, and remarked on the town's decay. In the 1850s there were still but 4,000 inhabitants. And as late as 1954, H. V. Morton noted the large uninhabited areas within the walls from which, he wrote, 'you can see how the old city has shrunk like an invalid in a suit that has become too large for him'.[3]

The modern population, now 50,000, lives mostly in the modern town outside the walls. Tracts within the walls seem uninhabited even now, especially on the west side which slopes down to the river although of late there has been a burst of construction activity.

A Tour of the Town The best view of the walls is from the BELVEDERE marked by four classical columns just across the Río Adaja and up the hill on the Salamanca road (N-501). The sun is right by mid-afternoon.

There are walks along and atop the walls and the old walled town is full of mansions and escutcheons, churches and convents. The small Plaza Mayor, known as the Plaza del Mercado Chico (or Plaza de la Victoria) with the *ayuntamiento* on one side and the church of San Juan, originally Romanesque, on the other, is attractive. Both church and plaza were renovated in the 16th century.

If you are lucky, you can find a place to park by San Vicente outside the walls and do the rest on foot.

SAN VICENTE Cluniac monks came along with Raymond of Burgundy and the church of San Vicente soon rose on the site where, it was said, the patron saint and his two sisters, Cristeta and Sabina, had been martyred by the Romans in 303. The original church had

been destroyed by Almanzor; rebuilding was delayed until the repopulation of the 1080s. Work began as usual at the east end, so the
cabecera dates from the late 11th/early 12th century; the principal
parts of the nave, the vaulting and the west portal from the second
half of the 12th century. Work continued into the 14th and even 15th
centuries.

Entrance is usually from the south porch. The sculptures flanking
the portal, by different 12th-century hands, are outstanding. On the
left is the Annunciation with an exceptionally beautiful Archangel
Gabriel. The Virgin seems startled as she turns to him. Opposite are
Santa Sabina in an elegantly embroidered robe, San Vicente and a
seated king. The foliated carving and rosettes on the impost blocks
and archivolts are beautifully rendered, as are the beasts occupying
the capitals.

The lofty interior consists of a nave of six bays, two aisles, a
transept and three apsidal chapels. The transition from Romanesque
to early Gothic is apparent in the vaulting: the transept is barrel
vaulted, the aisle bays have groin vaults and round-headed arches.
The arches of the nave, on the other hand, are pointed, the nave is
divided horizontally into arcade, blind triforium and clerestory and
there are a number of windows, all typical of Gothic. This shift is
due to a Burgundian, one Fruchel (d. 1192), who took over the works
in the middle of the 12th century after a half-century hiatus in
construction.

The lantern over the square crossing rests on an octagon formed
by small squinch arches. Some of the carved capitals are very fine.

The remarkable cenotaph of the three martyred saints stands in
the crossing just to the right of the *capilla mayor*. The cenotaph dates
from the late 11th century; the base and canopy are from the 15th. It
is in the form of a church with a high central nave under a pitched
roof and two aisles. The actual relics of the saints were removed to
León in 1065.

The end of the cenotaph nearest the altar shows the Three Kings
bearing gifts to the Virgin and Child; below, left, the kings are riding
to Bethlehem and, right, the three are tucked up in bed with an
angel warning them to avoid Herod on the way home. The west end
shows Christ in Majesty with the bull of St Luke and the lion of St
Mark.

The wonderful scenes on the sides relate the history of the saintly trio. The story begins on the north side with Vicente and his sisters before the Roman governor Dacian (time of Emperor Diocletian who ordered a persecution of the Christians in 303) who orders them to worship the gods. The idols crumble in the face of their faith and the trio flee, pursued by soldiers.

The opposite side shows their fate: (1) San Vicente and his sisters being stripped naked by the mail-clad soldiers; (2) being tortured on the wheel and dismembered; (3) their burial, with their souls in the form of children being wafted up to heaven to be welcomed by the hand of God. Note the soldiers pressing down hard on the top of the coffin. The next two scenes require explanation.

According to legend, the saints' bodies were thrown to the dogs. When a Jew paused to mock, a snake jumped out of a hole and bit him. (He and the snake are depicted.) The Jew was converted on the spot and here he is, first praying to God and then working hard in a carpentry shop on three proper coffins for the martyrs. The snake hole is said to be in the crypt below the church.

The west portal, enclosed in a lofty porch, is a magnificent but badly deteriorated ensemble with Christ in Majesty on the central column, flanked by prophets and saints. It is later in date than the south portal. From the street, there is a good view of the outside of the cabecera with its three tall slender apses, nicely detailed. The ground drops off here, so the apses appear unusually tall.

SAN ANDRÉS North of San Vicente is 12th-century San Andrés with interesting portals, a pleasing triple apse, and carved corbels. It is one of the earliest churches in Ávila.

CATEDRAL DE SAN SALVADOR Across the way from San Vicente is one of the city gates. Turn left inside and walk along the narrow Calle de Tostado to reach the cathedral. Or, walk through the rose garden outside the walls to the gate next to the massive apse of the cathedral imbedded in the walls. A plaza extends in front of the cathedral, marked off by posts on which stand battered lions holding in their mouths loops of the chain that encloses the precinct.

The north portal, the Portada de los Apóstoles, is a 13th-century survival which stood originally at the west end, but was moved around here in the 15th century by Juan Guas who created a new west portal. The best preserved portion is the tympanum which depicts

Christ in Majesty flanked by angels, some carrying the instruments of the Passion. The Coronation of the Virgin occupies the apex. Angels, the Elders of the Apocalypse and so forth occupy the five archivolts.

The customary entrance to the cathedral is through what is left of Juan Guas's 15th-century portal, totally revamped with uninspiring results in the late 18th century. It is flanked by two towers and by *maceros*, wild men bearing maces.

The original church on the site, founded by San Segundo, first bishop of Avela in the 7th century, was destroyed in the Muslim invasion. The present cathedral was begun about 1157 on land given to Bishop Sancho (d. 1181) by Alfonso VIII in gratitude for that prelate's protection in 1163 against the designs of his uncle Fernando II of León when he was still but a child. The same Fruchel who was master of works at San Vicente also worked here, beginning with the east end as usual. From any direction, the cathedral has a military air, especially that formidable battlemented apse protruding from the walls.

The cathedral exhibits a mixture of Romanesque and Gothic details, reflecting changes in styles and techniques over the long period it was under construction. It is rather squat but lofty in comparison to the width of the early 13th-century nave and aisles, divided into three bays with quadripartite vaulting. The crossing, which may be of the late 13th century, has sexpartite vaulting. The capitals are plain, suggesting Cistercian influence.

The powerfully fortified outer layer of the apse, which protrudes from the walls, was added later in the 13th century, along with the cloister and other dependencies and the Portada de los Apóstoles. Work continued into the 15th century when Juan Guas was master of works (1471).

The cathedral is flooded with light in contrast with most Spanish churches. The brilliantly polychromed shafts and pillars on the right, at the crossing, are presumably restored, but give a good idea of the original look. The magnificent walnut *coro* and stalls are also 16th-century work, by a Dutch master.

A double ambulatory flows around the capilla mayor in the huge apse. It and the radiating chapels, the work of Fruchel, are embedded in the thickness of the walls. The remains of San Segundo have lain since the 16th century in a chapel on the south side of the ambulatory.

The paintings of the life and passion of Christ on the splendid retablo in the capilla mayor were begun by Pedro Berruguete (d. 1504) and completed by Juan de Borgoña (d. 1533).

At the back of the capilla mayor is the 1518 sepulchre of Alonso Fernández de Madrigal (d. 1455) who was professor of moral philosophy and scripture at the University of Salamanca when he was named bishop of Ávila in 1449. He was short, fiery and known as el Tostado from his dark complexion. He even had the temerity to disagree with the Inquisitor Torquemada. The bishop was a prodigious writer throughout his life and is depicted, mitred and robed, thoughtfully writing in a large tome. Behind and above him is a scene of the Adoration. It is a very fine piece of work.

Enter the recently restored 14th-century cloister through an antesacristy and a sacristy which have notable 13th-century eight-rib vaulting. The two rooms hold the usual ecclesiastical treasures and two not so usual: a sumptuous alabaster retablo and a silver reliquary, both 16th century.

SAN SEGUNDO This little church stands below the walls, down by the river. Getting across traffic on the road can be tricky, but it is worth the effort. The custodian lives in the house next door; ring and she will appear.

According to legend, San Segundo was one of the 'Siete Varones Apostólicos' (seven male apostles) who came from North Africa to spread the new faith in the peninsula. Segundo founded the see of Avela. All memory of him having faded with the passage of time, the Romanesque church built over the ruins of his shrine was dedicated to San Sebastián and Sta Lucía. Not until 1519 when the church was being remodelled were the tomb and relics of the founder saint discovered and the dedication changed.

The two lateral arches separating nave from aisles date from the 16th-century remodelling. Note the pairs of holy water stoups on each supporting column carved from a single block with the drum of the column, an unusual arrangement.

The apse is original, preserving very fine capitals. The one to the left of the triumphal arch depicts three women, one with a wimple and a tender smile. Opposite is a winged griffin. The south portal and portions of the walls are also original.

The showpiece of the church is, however, the resplendent alabaster tomb (1573) of the saint by Juan de Juni whose work we have encountered in Valladolid. It is remarkably out of place, but it is certainly a work to be noticed.

To the right of the sanctuary is a figure of a lady with a huge pair of pliers hanging from her girdle and a large tooth in her left hand. She is St Apollonia, patron saint of dentists. A 3rd-century martyr of Alexandria, her teeth were knocked out by her tormentors and here she is.

SAN ESTEBAN Once back across the street, pass through the Puerta de Puente and walk up to a small square on which stands the first church built after the 11th-century repopulation. Traces of the Visigothic church that stood on the site remain; one is shown stone pulpit steps. The cabecera, north wall and part of the south wall with the portal of Romanesque San Esteban have survived.

The capitals in the apse are notable and rather odd. To the left of the triumphal arch is a huge bat; opposite, a fierce owl and another bird of prey. On those behind are fronds with a crude head on the left and a crucifixion on the right.

The considerable polychrome remaining in the apse is said (by the nuns in charge) to be original. The *artesonado* ceiling has been repeatedly restored over the years; what you see is largely 16th century.

SAN PEDRO From the impressive PUERTA DE ALCÁZAR to the south of the cathedral you pass from the walled town into the Plaza de Santa Teresa (or Plaza del Mercado Grande). The *alcázar* itself has vanished, leaving only this gate and the adjacent strongly fortified tower. A statue of the saint stands in the middle of the plaza.

At the far end is the church of San Pedro, begun in the first half of the 12th century and consecrated by the end of the century, though construction continued into the 15th. The interior is rather heavy, with huge composite piers supporting the massive quadripartite ribs of the five bays. The ribbing of the lantern dome is unusual as are the squinches. For a good view of the lovely triple-apsed cabecera, go around the back outside. A rose window adorns the west front.

CONVENTO DE SANTO TOMÁS Further down the hill to the right

of San Pedro is the monastery of Santo Tomás, built between 1482 and 1493 thanks to the generosity of Doña María Dávila, widow of the royal treasurer and a member of an Ávila clan whose mansion stands in a street just inside the southern city walls, west of the cathedral. The lady had the support of the Inquisitor Torquemada and the monastery benefited from the confiscated properties of Jews and heretics.

Ferdinand and Isabella took a great interest in Sto Tomás and chose it as the burial place of their only son, the Infante Don Juan, who died in 1497 at the age of nineteen while a student at Salamanca. The lovely tomb with a recumbent effigy of the young prince, by a Florentine craftsman (1512), stands in front of and below the high altar.

The death of this promising young man was a national catastrophe and he was widely mourned. His death, followed by the deaths of his older sister Isabel, queen of Portugal, and then of her infant son, threw the succession to the unstable Juana and her husband Philip of Habsburg.

The high altar is elevated in a gallery across the nave, an arrangement unique in Spain. Behind the altar stands the sumptuous retablo with paintings of the life of St Thomas Aquinas by Pedro Berruguete (fl. 1477–1504) whose work also adorns the cathedral. Other than the several paintings, note the supremely Gothic pinnacles and detailing.

The coro is elevated on a tribune at the west end of the single-nave church.

The monastery also holds the tomb of the Dominican friar Tomás de Torquemada (1420–98), the first Inquisitor General. The current Dominican inhabitants have installed a little museum of East Asian art and artefacts in the monastery. Some of the present group have served in Macau and the Philippines. The elderly friar said they had installed the exhibition to show the locals that there were worlds out there beyond Spain.

The convent has three cloisters, each of two storeys. You enter the rather small and plain Claustro del Noviciado. The second, the Claustro de Silencio, is very fine; the frieze between the two storeys bears the arms of Ferdinand and Isabella. The third, largest and most splendid, the Claustro de Reyes, contains the royal apartments where the Catholic Kings lived when in residence. In the second and third cloisters, the predominant decorative motif is a ball design that must have driven the sculptors crazy and is rather monotonous. From this cloister a flight of stairs enabled the monarchs to reach the elevated coro.

FOUNDATIONS CONNECTED TO STA TERESA These include the CONVENTO DE STA TERESA just inside the gate in the south wall which bears her name. It was built on the site of the house where she was born. Outside the walls (due east of the cathedral, northeast of San Pedro) is SAN JOSÉ, the first convent she founded (1562); the church proper dates from 1615. Some sixteen nuns are now in residence. The visitor is shown cells with memorabilia of the saint. One is a mock-up of her own cell. To the north is LA INCARNACIÓN where she lived for a number of years.

PALACIO DE LOS DEANES This handsome palace, on a square between San Pedro and San Vicente, houses the provincial museum which has a small but very interesting archaeological collection.

La Moraña

North of Ávila, once out of the mountains and back in the broad meseta, stretches the region known as La Moraña after the Moors who remained there after the Reconquista had rolled over them.

Since the days of the Visigoths, this has been a rich agricultural region. Following his conquest of Toledo in 1085, Alfonso VI turned to the repopulation of the zone south of the Duero which had been practically deserted in the bleak years of the 8th and 9th centuries. He had to bring the land under cultivation and open communications between the old settled areas north of the Duero and the lands of Toledo. The task was entrusted to Raymond of Burgundy who recruited settlers from Burgos, La Rioja, León, Palencia, Portugal and the mountains and coast of the north as well as *Mozarabs*, *Mudéjars* and Jews.

The fields still stretch to the horizon on all sides and scattered thinly across the landscape are small agricultural villages of great antiquity. Judging from the size of the enormous new grain silos at the railway siding just outside Arévalo, production must be substantial.

The two principal towns are Arévalo and Madrigal de las Altas

Torres. As isolated as these towns appear now, in the Middle Ages they lay on one of the great trade routes of Castilla, connecting the south with Medina del Campo and its trade fairs and, beyond that, to the north coast. One is struck by the huge size of the plazas, the size and number of churches and the remains of impressive defensive walls and castles – all bespeaking a grander and more vibrant past.

Arévalo The town is just inside the northeast corner of Ávila Province. The N-VI goes east of town, providing a good view of its churches and the castle on the outskirts. During the day, Arévalo looks rather crumbly; at night, thanks to some inspired lighting, it looks absolutely magical. A very pleasant local road also runs to Arévalo from Ávila.

Arévalo is a Mudéjar town, built of brick, strategically located at the confluence of two rivers and defended by deep gorges. In 1454, on the death of Juan II, it belonged to his second wife, Isabel of Portugal, who retired here with her two young children, the future Queen Isabella and Alfonso. Isabel of Portugal was reclusive if not mad, an affliction that descended to her granddaughter Juana, and the young princess had a difficult ten years before her step-brother Enrique IV called her to court in 1461. Her biographer Peggy Liss notes that these ten years were the longest she lived anywhere. Enrique IV granted Arévalo to one of his supporters in revenge for Isabella having married Ferdinand; she did not get it back until 1480 after that lord's death. Isabel of Portugal remained in seclusion in Arévalo till her death in 1496.

By Isabella's reign, wool had become the chief export of Castilla. She and Ferdinand promoted foreign trade and encouraged this most profitable domestic product. In 1492, they confirmed the privileges of the *Mesta*, the sheep-owners' association founded by Alfonso X in the 13th century, that had been generous in its financial support for the crown during the long wars against Granada. Castilian wool became a staple of trade with Flanders, Brittany and England and the crown collected revenue on all sales and on the seasonal migration of the vast flocks of sheep that numbered some 3 million by the end of the century.

Decline set in with the Habsburg monarchs and their expensive foreign entanglements, inflation caused by the glut of treasures from America, plague and the drought and famine which have so often seared the meseta. Many villages around Arévalo were all but abandoned by the early 17th century.

After crossing the Río Adaja, you enter the centre of town past the church of EL SALVADOR (early 13th century), completely renovated in the 16th century.

PLAZA MAYOR Turn left at the church of SANTO DOMINGO DE SILOS into the Plaza Mayor, a long rectangle, with Sto Domingo at the upper end and shops, restaurants and public buildings around the arcaded sides. Sto Domingo is another Mudéjar Romanesque church, remodelled in the 16th century, a sure sign of prosperity but not good for the preservation of original fabrics. It has some very baroque altars.

On the right side of the Plaza Mayor the double ARCO DE CÁRCEL, one of the few remnants of the old walls, leads to the Plaza Real. However old, this square has been thoroughly and pleasingly modernized with brick and arcades to evoke the ancient flavour. Here stands the ayuntamiento.

You will see a number of good antique shops. One owner said that Arévalo was famous for its 'antigüedades y cochinillo' (antiques and roast piglet). On weekends the place is jammed with visitors (Spanish) buying and eating.

CASTLE At the lower end of the Plaza Mayor, past the restaurant La Pinilla on the left and an antique shop and a Romanesque–Mudéjar church on the right, the street follows the ancient walls and you are soon at the castle, much restored, at the very northern edge of town. The *torre de homenaje* is enormous. Blanche de Bourbon, the ill-fated young wife of Pedro the Cruel, was held prisoner here in 1353 before she was sent off to Toledo and death. The castle has been a silo.

SAN MARTÍN Passing behind the apse of Santo Domingo (not turning into the Plaza Mayor), a twisting street leads past old houses in need of repair but with fine views over the country from their top-floor loggias to the ancient PLAZA DE LA VILLA. It can also be reached easily by foot from the Plaza Mayor via the Arco del Cárcel and the Plaza Real. This large irregular space is surrounded by two-storey, arcaded houses which look to be of great age. They were in terrible decay only a few years ago and are now being rehabilitated.

At either end stand two brick Mudéjar churches of the 12th century. SAN MARTÍN has two fine towers, one against the north crossing, the other at the west end. The former is particularly attractive, with three tiers of blind arches at the bottom, and is known as the Chess Tower (*torre de los ajedreces*) from the decoration of the two upper segments. On its south side is the southernmost example of the galleried porticos of the Segovia type. Ten arches including the entrance rest on simple granite columns, presumably dating from a later modification. The remaining capitals are badly deteriorated.

STA MARÍA LA MAYOR   This church stands at the other end of the plaza. It was a virtual ruin until recently, the roof of the single nave having collapsed during an apparently bungled restoration attempt. It has now been put back together again and looks as good as new. The very handsome apse has three tiers of the typically Mudéjar blind arches. The collapse of the roof brought down plaster and revealed 13th-century frescoes in the apse (still under restoration on my last visit). The church tower surmounts a gate in the old walls.

STA MARÍA DE LA LUGAREJA   Just south of town, across the Río Adaja, are the remains of this Cistercian nunnery founded in 1237. All that is left is the cabecera of the church with three semicircular apses and a huge squat tower over the crossing. Inside the tower is an apparently unsuccessful copy of the famous cupolas raised on pendentives at Toro, Zamora and Salamanca.

La Lugareja is of brick, with tall slender arcades adorning the three rounded apses and the tower, with an occasional narrow window slit. It stands on a high ridge overlooking the river and it is quite a climb to reach it. The fragment stands next to a fenced property which is guarded by several large, loud and unwelcoming dogs.

Madrigal de las Altas Torres   Some 25 km west of Arévalo across the flat fields is Madrigal de las Altas Torres, founded at the end of the 11th century as part of Raymond of Burgundy's settlement of Ávila. The walls of this mellifluously named town once boasted forty-eight strong towers and four great gates. The circuit walls have crumbled, but are still impressive, and the towers are mostly gone or reduced to stumps. The gates remain, as do some stretches of wall, heavily restored. Dominating the centre of town is the enormous brick Mudéjar tower of SAN NICOLÁS DE BARI; the interior was much remodelled in the 16th century.

CONVENTO DE LAS AGUSTINAS Down the hill is the palace where Isabel la Católica was born in 1451, now an Augustinian convent. Just bang on the door, a passer-by advised, and keep banging until a nun opens up. We did and a very jolly plump nun took us around.

Emperor Charles V gave this palace of Juan II to the Augustinian nuns in 1527. They have been there ever since, though there are only a few left. The lovely simple cloister was once part of the summer palace; the nuns now live in what was the winter palace, adjacent.

The church contains the battered base of the tomb of Isabel of Portugal (d. 1496), Queen Isabella's mother, savaged by French troops during the Peninsular War. A number of royals are buried here, including two illegitimate daughters of Ferdinand and the 'last of the Austriacos' (which is what the Spanish always call the Habsburgs), Doña Ana, daughter of Don Juan of Austria the Younger (d. 1679), illegitimate son of Philip IV. The *sala capitular* has a superb artesonado ceiling of unpainted wood.

Upstairs are the bare chambers where Isabella was born. On the wall is a striking double portrait of the young Ferdinand and Isabella. He has a pronounced five o'clock shadow; she is a trifle chubby.

Diagonally across the square from the entrance to the convent is the Hospital de la Concepción, founded in 1443 and reconstructed in the 16th century.

South and West of Ávila

Fertile valleys stretch south of Ávila between the rugged chains of the Sierra de Gredos. The scenery is striking, but we are heading west. Should you, however, be driving south on the N-502 for Talavera, stop at the Puerto (Pass) de Pico north of Arenas de San Pedro where a long stretch of Roman road, in remarkable condition, twists its way up the pass. This was presumably part of the Via Plata from Emerita Augusta (Mérida) to the north.

Turning west from Ávila, the N-501 runs through rocky hills which gradually give way to the flat plains of Salamanca. Just across the provincial line is Peñaranda de Bracamonte whose appearance does not do justice to its poetic name.

Notes

1. William H. Prescott, *The History of the Reign of Ferdinand and Isabella* (Philadelphia, 1873), Vol. I, p. 175.

2. Joseph Townsend, *A Journey through Spain in the Years 1786 and 1787* (London, 1791), p. 98.

3. H. V. Morton, *A Stranger in Spain* (New York, 1955), p. 247.

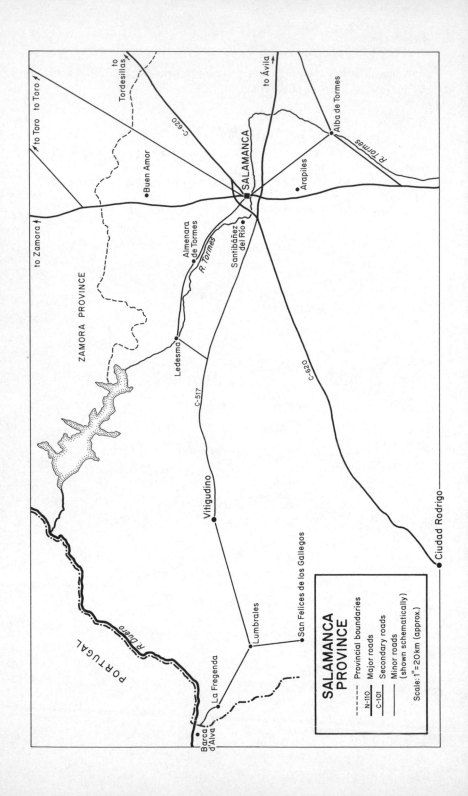

SALAMANCA
PROVINCE

Provincial boundaries
N-110 — Major roads
C-101 — Secondary roads
—— Minor roads
(shown schematically)

Scale: 1" = 20 km (approx.)

PORTUGAL

ZAMORA PROVINCE

to Zamora

to Toro
to Toro
to Toro

to Tordesillas

to Ávila

Alba de Tormes

SALAMANCA

Buen Amor

Arapiles

Almenara
de Tormes

Santibáñez
del Río

R. Tormes

R. Tormes

C-620

C-620

Ledesma

C-517

Vitigudino

San Felices de los Gallegos

Lumbrales

La Fregenda

Barca
d'Alva

R. Duero

Ciudad Rodrigo

10

Salamanca Province

The north of the province is typical meseta country. Further south, hilly pasture land appears where toros are raised and cork trees grow. The Sierra de Gredos borders the province on the east; farther south is the wild and lovely mountain range called the Peña de Francia.

Approaches

You can reach Salamanca from Madrid via Ávila or you can stay on the N-VI to Arévalo and then drive cross-country to meet the N-501 near Peñaranda de Bracamonte. Salamanca is also easily accessible from Tordesillas, Toro and Zamora.

From Ávila, the N-501 runs due west across the plains, crosses the Río Tormes and shortly thereafter reaches the outskirts of Salamanca. The massive tower of the cathedral appears from time to time, but the trees along the river hide the city until you are upon it. Two bridges carry the motor traffic; take the first one.

History

You are now in what was at the time of the Reconquista the *Extremadura leonesa*, the area south of the kingdom of León, across the

Duero, for the reconquest and resettlement of which the kings of León were responsible. When the job was done and the fighting border moved south, the name Extremadura moved south as well to describe the lands bordering Portugal, the modern provinces of Cáceres and Badajoz.

Celtiberian tribes roamed the land and then came the Romans who occupied it (loosely) in the 2nd century BC. The Visigoths left few traces. The Muslims overran the area 712–15, but after the Berber revolt in the mid-8th century and the Arab abandonment of the Duero basin, the Muslims established their forward lines farther south on Coimbra on the (now Portuguese) coast and Coria (Cáceres).

The Christians made preliminary efforts to resettle the Extremadura leonesa area in the late 9th century. The defeat of Caliph 'Abd al-Rahman III at Simancas in 939 enabled Ramiro II and his ally Count Fernán González of Castilla to move into the Tormes River valley and reoccupy Salamanca and Ledesma, but then came the devastating campaigns of Almanzor. Repopulation was not seriously resumed until after Toledo fell in 1085.

The new settlers included warriors, farmers and most importantly pastoralists who owned significant flocks of sheep by the end of the 11th century. Sheep raising was to be a major source of revenue. With Salamanca firmly established, other settlements became possible. Ciudad Rodrigo was first resettled early in the 12th century and developed into a stronghold on the Portuguese border later in the century. The kings of Portugal meddled enthusiastically in the affairs of their Leonese and Castilian cousins – and vice versa.

Salamanca

The town is built of a beautiful tawny reddish-gold stone that is easily carved when first extracted from the quarries, hardening on exposure to air, qualities that have encouraged an exuberant froth of ornamentation on many buildings.

Despite some tacky modern construction of the 1950s and 1960s, Salamanca preserves a wealth of architecture, particularly of the 15th and 16th centuries. It is a fine place for walking and poking about and, of course, for sitting in the Plaza Mayor.

History Helmantiké was an important Celtiberian town, captured

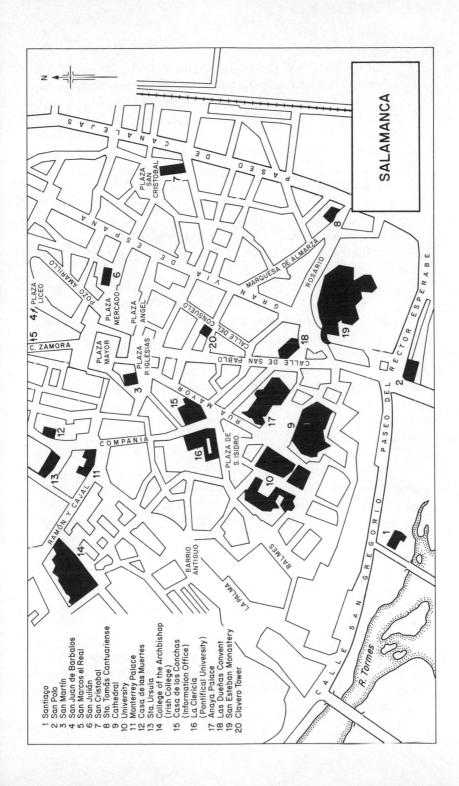

SALAMANCA

1 Santiago
2 San Polo
3 San Martín
4 San Juan de Barbalos
5 San Marcos el Real
6 San Julián
7 San Cristobal
8 Sto. Tomás Cantuariense
9 Cathedral
10 University
11 Monterrey Palace
12 Casa de las Muertes
13 Sta. Ursula
14 College of the Archbishop
   (Irish College)
15 Casa de los Conchas
   (Information Office)
16 La Clericia
   (Pontifical University)
17 Anaya Palace
18 Las Dueñas Convent
19 San Esteban Monastery
20 Clavero Tower

by Hannibal in 220 BC. Roman Salmantika was a stage on the Via Plata between Emerita Augusta (Mérida) and Asturica Augusta (Astorga). Salamanca was a Visigothic bishopric in the late 6th century.

Around 712 the town fell to the Muslims and for some 300 years it lay more or less deserted, though peasants and *Mozarabs* fleeing from persecution in al-Andalus squatted among the ruins. Ordoño I of Asturias reoccupied it in 863, but the town suffered from periodic attacks. Following Caliph 'Abd al-Rahman III's defeat in 939 at Simancas, it was ravaged by Almanzor in 977 and changed hands repeatedly over the next century.

After Alfonso VI took Toledo in 1085, Salamanca formed the western bastion of a new line of defence organized by the king's son-in-law, Raymond of Burgundy, that included Ávila and Segovia. Salamanca guarded the gap between the western flank of the Sierra de Guadarrama and the Sierra de Francia. The Almoravid threat was still very real and Alfonso was taking no chances on what might happen if Toledo fell to them.

Asturians, Galicians, Portuguese and men of the northern coasts arrived as settlers in the years 1101–3, along with French warriors and Cluniac monks. Each group gathered around its own *parroquia* (parish church). Mozarabs and Jews lived each in their own quarters, the *morerías* and *juderías*, around their mosques and synagogues. A stout wall rose to protect them all.

The ancient bishopric of Salamanca was restored in 1102. The first bishop was Jerónimo (Jérôme de Périgord) who had been the companion of El Cid and who had just been ousted from his see at Valencia by the Almoravids. By the time Salamanca received its *fuero* at the end of the century, no fewer than forty-six parroquias had been established. Of these only a dozen, plus the Old Cathedral, remain relatively untarnished by renovators and developers of succeeding generations.

Alfonso IX of León established the university in about the year 1219 to rival that founded earlier by his cousin Alfonso VIII of Castilla at Palencia. The University of Palencia withered after a century's tenuous existence, leaving Salamanca supreme.

Salamanca sided with Isabella against Juana la Beltraneja in the succession struggle of the late 15th century. Isabella and Ferdinand's only son, the Infante Don Juan, died in 1497, aged nineteen, while a student at the university.

The municipal authorities recognized the Habsburg Charles I as king of Spain in 1517, but some of the leading families joined the urban revolt of the Comuneros against the new king. The city was severely punished.

In 1626 a terrible flood carried away half the ancient bridge, destroyed most of the old Mozarab quarter and ruined city life until the 18th century when it revived under the Bourbon kings. But the great days were gone. The court's establishment at Madrid in 1561 drew off the scions of aristocratic families in search of preferment and the population declined steadily.

The Peninsular War delivered the final blow. In 1811 the French destroyed part of the town in order to build fortifications against Wellington advancing from Portugal. Thirteen out of twenty-five convents and twenty of the twenty-five colleges of the university were razed. Wellington besieged the city and on 22 July 1812, the two armies met at Arapiles, a small village a few kilometres south of town. Wellington won an outstanding victory, forcing the French to withdraw from Madrid.

Richard Ford reported in 1832 that the western part of the city 'is now quite a heap of ruins' and that 'a day or two will suffice to see the marvels of ruined Salamanca',[1] for which he gave a population of 14,000. In 1872 Augustus Hare called it a city of ruins and as late as 1904 Edward Hutton sighed over the city, 'so beautiful, so desolate'.

At the outbreak of the Civil War in 1936, Franco's Nationalist forces took control of an arc of territory west and north of Madrid, the heartland of conservative Castilla. Franco established his military headquarters at Salamanca and it was here that the Junta de Defensa Nacional decided to name him Generalissimo and Head of State.

The city is now the second largest in the Autonomía, with some 186,000 inhabitants, and the university has a new lease on life. The boom has taken its toll, however. Speculative development during the 1960s wrought fearful damage. One writer quotes official statistics to the effect that more than 8,000 of the 13,000 buildings erected in Salamanca prior to 1936 have been destroyed.[2] Fortunately, much remains.

A Tour of the Town Salamanca's one remaining Roman relic is the PUENTE ROMANO which spans the Tormes between the two modern bridges. The northern half dates mostly from the rebuilding under Trajan and Hadrian early in the 2nd century. From the southern end is a superb view of the cathedral. Old prints and photographs show horses being washed by the river's edge; now it is more likely to be cars and trucks, but the view is still stunning.

The spectacular examples of 16th-century architecture in Salamanca may cause the visitor to overlook the humbler Romanesque churches. I therefore start the tour with them.

New settlers had founded forty-six parroquias by the end of the 12th century. The northern French had five, including Sta María la Mayor (the Old Cathedral); the Provençals, five; the Cantabrians, six; the Galicians, four; the Portuguese, three; settlers from Toro, five; the Castilians, seven; and the Mozarabs, eleven. A scant dozen survive.

SANTIAGO This Mozarab church of 1145 stands now in some isolation by the Roman bridge. All the other churches in this *barrio*, including San Juan el Blanco which served as the principal church of the town in the days of Muslim domination, were swept away by the flood of 1626. Santiago is one of two surviving examples of brick Mudéjar Romanesque, restored in the 1950s. The elegant triple apse has tall blind arches on the side apses and a two-tier arrangement in the centre.

SAN POLO Nearby, at the Puerta de San Pablo, where the modern bridge reaches the city, stand the tidied-up ruins of San Pablo, or San Polo, a Portuguese foundation of 1112.

STA MARÍA DE LA VEGA Not easy to find in the southeast angle of the city between the peripheral road and the river is what little remains of this church whence came the statue of the Virgin venerated in the Old Cathedral. The monastery was wrecked in the flood of 1626. With scattered, battered and not always matching fragments, five arches of the cloister have been assembled in a room that serves as the chapel for a secondary institution run by the Fundación Rodríguez Fabres. The wrought-iron gate is just beyond the Instituto de Recursos Naturales y Agrobiológia. Access requires contacting the director, an amiable man, but you may not find the effort worth it.

SAN MARTÍN Now outside the southern side of the Plaza Mayor, this was built in the Toro barrio in the middle of the 12th century. It is encased in later buildings and its major interest lies in the north portal, inspired by the Puerta del Obispo of Zamora Cathedral. On the tympanum is a fine relief of San Martín dividing his cloak with the beggar. The central nave collapsed in the 18th century and has been reconstructed.

SAN JUAN DE BARBELOS In the northern part of town are two churches of note. San Juan de Barbelos was founded about 1140 by the Knights Hospitallers in the Castilian quarter. San Vicente Ferrer (d. 1419), that ferocious Dominican who did his level best to whip up anti-Jewish hatred in Castilla at the end of the 14th century and succeeded all too well, preached here. It is a small church, with a single nave and a pleasing apse.

SAN MARCOS EL REAL The second, at the top of the Calle de Zamora on the edge of the old town, is the round church of San Marcos, another Castilian foundation, of 1178. There are other round churches in Spain, but their apses protrude; San Marcos is absolutely round. Three aisles with three apsidal chapels have been fitted neatly inside the circle. Four stout round columns and arches support the vaults. The 14th-century paintings in the apse and on the side walls were discovered only in 1967. The belfry is 18th century.

SAN JULIÁN This church has a fine location down the hill east of the Plaza Mayor, just past the market. On the north side is a pleasant little square, with a couple of cafés. San Julián, another church of the Toro settlers, was begun in 1107, but of the original structure only part of the north wall, with the portal, and the base of the tower remain. The church was completely rebuilt in the 16th century.

The portal's three archivolts have geometric and floral patterns, surrounded by an elegant band of outcurving fronds. Above, under a cornice, four of the five remaining corbels retain their carvings: two human and one animal head and a frond. Further up on the right, glued against the wall, is an animal, perhaps a lion.

SAN CRISTÓBAL Farther down the hill and across the Gran Vía is San Cristóbal, built in 1145 for the Knights Hospitallers. It has some wonderfully sculpted heads around the cornice, including one Afro-Leonese.

SAN TOMÁS CANTUARIENSE St Thomas of Canterbury was founded by two Englishmen in 1175 in the Portuguese quarter, behind the monastery of San Esteban. Thomas Becket's cult spread through Europe with amazing rapidity; he was slain in 1170 and canonized in 1172. The church's three semicircular apses have good windows, but I do not think it is as graceful as some others. The interior was modified in the 16th century and again in the 18th.

PLAZA MAYOR We turn now to Salamanca's most famous sight. Wrote Joseph Townsend in 1787:

> I had almost hourly occasion to pass through it, and never saw it without pleasure. It is spacious, regular, built upon arches, and surrounded by piazzas. Such a square would be admired even in London, or in Paris; but in a city like Salamanca, where all the streets are narrow, it gives peculiar expansion to the lungs, when you find yourself at liberty to breathe, when light bursts upon you by surprise, and when symmetry unites with greatness in all the objects by which you are encompassed.[3]

The square was designed by Alberto de Churriguera (d. 1750); construction began in 1733. It was completed in 1755 by Andrés García de Quiñones who built the *ayuntamiento* on the north side. Despite the ornate style usually associated with the Churriguera family, Alberto managed here to exercise restraint to good effect.

Four uniform ranges of three storeys above an arcade sheltering shops and cafés surround the plaza. Medallions with the busts of rulers and notables past and present occupy the spandrels between the arches. Tables and chairs spill out into the square in good weather. The lighting at night is a triumph, soft and diffuse. Wide-arched portals give access at several points. The square teems with people at most times, but especially in the late afternoon and evening when a stately procession moves slowly around the plaza. As with other plazas, the tables in the shade in summer or in the sun in cold weather are the most popular and the crowd eddies slowly around the square depending on the time of day.

CATEDRAL DE STA MARÍA LA MAYOR Leaving the Plaza Mayor by the south side and taking the Calle Mayor, you reach the cathedral.

The cathedral of Salamanca is extraordinary, or are extraordinary since there are two of them. This is, I believe, a unique instance of a Romanesque cathedral remaining in use while a new 16th-century Gothic cathedral was built adjoining it. The contrast between the two is one of the delights of visiting the place.

Go around first to the west front. On the left is the façade of the 16th-century Catedral Nueva, in the centre the massive square tower and on the right the humble remains of the façade of the Catedral Vieja, covered up in 1680.

Rodrigo Gil de Hontañón, who became master of works for the Catedral Nueva in 1538, wrapped the ancient tower of the Catedral Vieja in a more stylish one. The wooden belfry was struck by lightning in 1705 and the stone replacement proved to be too heavy. The Lisbon earthquake of 1755 all but finished off the structure and it was recommended that it be torn down and replaced. The Salmantinos were fond of their old tower, however rickety, and called in a French engineer who put a strong stone casing around the entire structure. What we see is thus a Russian doll sort of tower, one inside the other.

The only entrance now to the CATEDRAL VIEJA is from the first chapel on the right of the New Cathedral. From the richness of the 16th-century building, a stair leads down into the cool, rather severe grandeur of another age.

The Old Cathedral was begun early in the 12th century at the initiative of Raymond of Burgundy and Bishop Jerónimo, the right hand of El Cid and bishop of Valencia until its fall to the Almoravids in 1102. It was open for business by 1178. The three apsidal chapels were built first, which accounts for the Romanesque rounded arches and barrel vaulting.

Elsewhere, the arches are pointed and the vaults are quadripartite throughout, between heavy transverse arches. The shift from Romanesque to Gothic was the work of the man who designed the Torre del Gallo (see below) and who learned this new style from Fruchel, the Burgundian who worked at Ávila. The cathedral is in the shape of a Latin cross, with five bays before the crossing, and the nave is sufficiently higher than the side aisles to permit windows. Most of the north side fell victim to the builders of the Catedral Nueva.

The columns of the arcades and the engaged shafts that run up between the bays to support the ribs and arches of the vaults have richly carved capitals with assorted beasts, human heads and foliage. Note the third pier on the left with Samson, long hair streaming, tearing apart the lion. The supporting members and the ribs do not exactly match, an indication that, as at Toro, the builder abandoned Romanesque for Gothic vaulting after the piers were built. The view down the nave is unusually open for a Spanish church because in 1847 the *coro* was removed.

Near the foot of the entrance stairs, in the bottom of the tower, is the CAPILLA DE SAN MARTÍN, founded by Bishop Pedro Pérez (d. 1264) who is buried here. Outstanding are the 13th- and 14th-century tombs and fresco paintings. The fresco on the right, resembling a retablo and retaining remarkably vivid colours, is dated by an inscription to 1262, making it the oldest dated fresco in Spain. An image of the Virgin once occupied the central niche. The fresco of the Last Judgment dates from 1340.

As at Zamora and Toro, the outstanding feature of the cathedral is the two-tiered drum topped by a boldly ribbed dome over the crossing. A handsome moulding separates pendentives and drum. Thirty-two windows illuminate the centre of the church and the retablo of the *capilla mayor*. Sixteen columns rising above the pendentives separate the pairs of windows and support the sixteen ribs of the dome. Slender angels with trumpets, standing on brackets carved with demonic heads, were placed in the point of each pendentive; that on the southeast has disappeared.

The best view of the exterior of the TORRE DEL GALLO or Cock Tower is from the Patio Chico which abuts the east end of the Catedral Vieja and the face of the south transept of the Catedral Nueva. Various structures have been built against the cathedrals and you must thus go around Robin Hood's barn to find the Patio Chico, at the top of a flight of stairs, but the effort is worthwhile. While here, admire also the lovely triple apse of the Catedral Vieja.

The tower was begun about 1160. The builder took the basic design of Zamora and improved on it. The one-tier drum at Zamora is rather squat when seen from below; at Salamanca the builder created two tiers. The four flanking towers rest on the piers of the crossing in the church below. Between the towers are gabled dormers and the conical roof is covered with fish-scale tiles, a southern French feature of Byzantine origin that appears also at Zamora. A bronze rooster, symbol of the Church Vigilant, tops it off.

The enormous glowing RETABLO at the eastern end of the cathedral is the work of the Florentine brothers Niccolò and Dello Delli who were active in Spain in the 1440s. Dello went back to Florence in 1446; Niccolò, known locally as Nicolás Florentino, remained. (He died in Valencia in 1471.) The fifty-three paintings are arranged in five tiers. Against the retablo stands a gilt bronze statue of the Virgin and Child, enamelled and studded with jewels, from the ruined church of Sta María de la Vega (see above). The retablo is surmounted by a powerful Last Judgment in the vault of the apse, also the work of Nicolás.

To the right of the triumphal arch is a nice polychrome bishop. The south transept holds four tombs, three resting on roaring lions. The sculpture is very fine and the tombs preserve their polychrome. Atop the second tomb reposes one Doña Elena (d. 1272); on the front are mourners and two angels lifting up her soul in the shape of a child. Above the fourth tomb are the Three Magi, with a groom holding their three horses while they adore.

The entrance to the CLOISTER is from the south transept. The original 12th-century work was severely damaged by the Lisbon earthquake in 1755 and was rebuilt in 1785 in the neoclassical style. Several chapels off the cloister were used as university classrooms from the 13th century to the 15th when the new university buildings began to rise.

The first cloister chapel on the left is the late 12th-century CAPILLA DE TALAVERA, originally the *sala capitular*, but converted in 1510 to a chapel for the practice of the Mozarabic rite, the ancient liturgy of the Spanish Church to the end of the 11th century. The chapel contains the tomb of Dr Rodrigo Arias Maldonado of Talavera who bought the chapel in 1489. The octagonal chapel has a fine Mudéjar vault with eight arches arranged in parallel pairs. We have seen its like at San Miguel in Almazán (Soria), inspired by similar structures in the Great Mosque of Córdoba. Note the elegant retablo with the lovely Virgin of about 1350.

The chapel also holds the tombs of two of Dr Rodrigo's grandsons, hanged by Charles I in 1521 and 1522 for their part in the Comunero uprising.

In the CAPILLA DE STA BÁRBARA is the tomb of Bishop Juan

Lucero under another fine ribbed vault. Until 1843 the new rector of the university, elected annually, was proclaimed here. Exams were held here until the 19th century. Doctoral candidates sat on the chair between the tomb and the altar with their feet propped up on the tomb for good luck. Professors and divines sat on the benches round the sides. Successful candidates exited in triumph through the main portal of the cathedral while the unsuccessful slunk out of a rear door, hoping to escape the jeers of the crowd.

The next chapels contain the MUSEO DIOCESANO. Among its treasures is the retablo of San Miguel, a 1506 work by Juan de Flandes (d. 1519), one of the first Flemish painters to work in Castilla. We have encountered his last works in the retablo of Palencia Cathedral.

The very large CAPILLA DE STA CATALINA, off the south gallery of the cloister, was and still is used for functions. Between it and the next chapel are columns with some charming capitals.

The CAPILLA DE SAN BARTOLOMÉ or DE ANAYA contains the magnificent tomb of Bishop Diego de Anaya y Maldonado, surrounded by an equally magnificent wrought-iron *reja* of 1514. Others of the family lie around the walls.

Bishop Diego (1357–1437) was tutor to the future Enrique III of Castilla and Fernando I of Aragón and occupied successively the episcopal sees of Tuy, Orense, Salamanca and Cuenca. In 1416 he was sent as Castilla's representative to the Council of Constance which had been called to put an end to the Great Schism that since 1378 had seen rival popes sitting at Rome and Avignon. Anaya argued forcibly for the deposition of the two rival papal lines and the election of a new pope, Martin V, who rewarded him in 1418 with the archbishopric of Sevilla.

Unfortunately, the bishop then fell foul of Álvaro de Luna, the all-powerful favourite of Juan II of Castilla, who supported the rival candidacy of the antipope Benedict XIII, his great-uncle, who insisted obstinately on continuing the Avignon line of popes, thus throwing Spain into ecclesiastical turmoil. Anaya was deprived of his archbishopric in 1423.

He bequeathed his library and possessions to the Colegio de San Bartolomé which he had founded in 1401; after many a rebuilding, it now stands as the 18th-century Palacio de Anaya across the square from the Cathedral Nueva.

You enter the CATEDRAL NUEVA through the north portal.

Above, Jesus enters Jerusalem on an ass and is greeted by people in 16th-century costume, even the curly-headed boy in the palm tree.

The New Cathedral is a gigantic structure, about twice the length of the old church. With the flush of prosperity that accompanied the Catholic Kings, the cathedral chapter decided that Salamanca needed a bigger and better cathedral and invited Antón Egas and Alonso Rodríguez, masters of works respectively at the Toledo and Sevilla cathedrals, to draw up plans for a new building. They met in 1510 and two years later the chapter summoned nine eminent architects, among them Antón Egas, Juan Gil de Hontañón, Juan de Álava, Juan de Badajoz and Alonso de Covarrubias, to review their plans. The plan finally adopted closely resembles that of Sevilla Cathedral.

The first stone was laid, at the west end, in May 1513, with Juan Gil de Hontañón (d. 1526) as master architect. To him succeeded Juan de Álava (d. 1537), then briefly Antón Egas and in 1538 Rodrigo Gil de Hontañón (d. 1577). Work stopped at the crossing in 1584, not to resume until 1714 when Joaquín de Churriguera (d. 1724) became master of works. His brother Alberto (d. 1750), who raised the cupola, succeeded him. The cathedral was consecrated at long last in 1733. The cupola had to be rebuilt after the 1755 earthquake.

The huge rectangular structure has five naves, the two outer ones containing chapels between buttresses, five bays west of the crossing and three east and three rectangular chapels in the apse. At one point the construction of a chevet was considered, but in the end a square apse was built. Complex lierne vaulting covers the bays. An octagonal lantern rises over the crossing.

With construction spread over some 250 years, the architectural styles of the cathedral move from the Gothic to the Renaissance and beyond. Immensely high piers support the arcade and slender shafts rise still further to the elaborate tracery of the vaults. A lovely balustrade runs all around the interior in place of a triforium. The magnificent coro of 1732–38 is by Alberto Churriguera; Joaquín did the stalls (1724). For once, there is enough light to see the stalls and the putti standing along the tops.

Alberto Churriguera also wrought the exceedingly ornate retablo of the central chapel of the apse, behind the capilla mayor, the CAPILLA DEL CRISTO DE LAS BATALLAS. The warrior Bishop Jerónimo lies beneath the altar. Against the retablo is the celebrated crucifix of Cristo de las Batallas, the Christ of Battles, said to have been carried into battle by the bishop when he fought alongside El Cid. The rigid little wooden figure of Christ, with outstretched arms and staring straight ahead, dates probably from the early 11th century.

The west portal by Juan Gil de Hontañón is a Plateresque delight, with two different Adorations over the doors, framed in an intricate setting of carving and curved arches.

UNIVERSITY OF SALAMANCA Opposite the west front of the cathedral is the rear of the University of Salamanca that developed from a cathedral school elevated to university status by Alfonso IX about 1218. The university used the facilities of the cathedral until its own premises were constructed in the 15th century.

Fernando III (1217–52) encouraged the use of Castilian rather than Latin at both Salamanca and Palencia. In 1255, Pope Alexander IV granted graduates of the university the right to teach anywhere in Christendom. The Colegio de San Bartolomé (now the Anaya Palace) was built in 1401 as the first residential student quarters. The first chair of Greek in Spain was established here in 1480. Reflecting the scientific interests of the age, the teachings of Copernicus (d. 1543) were introduced in 1561. Salamanca had become one of the premier universities in Europe by the 16th century, with some seventy professors, 12,000 students and twenty-five colleges and faculties of arts, medicine, law and theology.

The university had four Colegios Mayores, founded between 1401 and 1521. Each had twenty to thirty places and offered divinity, law, medicine and the classical Quadrivium (arithmetic, geometry, astronomy and music). The Colegios Menores taught the Trivium (grammar, logic and rhetoric), the lower tier of the traditional seven liberal arts.

Wealthy benefactors of the early Middle Ages endowed monasteries, but in the 15th century they turned to schools and colleges. The Colegios Mayores were thus aristocratic foundations. At the beginning of the 16th century, there were six in Spain, the four at Salamanca and one each at Valladolid and Alcalá de Henares.

The schools were divided into Escuelas Mayores (theology, canon law, medicine, mathematics, philosophy, languages and rhetoric), Menores (grammar and music), and Minimos (basic studies such as reading and writing).

Decline was nigh, however. During the 17th century, law came to

supersede theology and the humanities as an expanding state bureaucracy demanded more trained administrators. Add to that religious
obscurantism and feuding among the great families, and by the 18th
century the university was in a sad state.

The ravages of the Peninsular War furthered the decline. 'The
splendid collegiate buildings [and] palaces', wrote Augustus Hare in
1872, 'are either in ruins or let out to poor families, with the exception
of San Bartolomé, which is turned into the house of the civil governor, and El Arzobispo, whose beautiful *cinque-cento* buildings are now
given up to the Irish college' with but nine students.[4] The university
did not revive until this century; it now has some 12,500 students.

You have to go around to the front of the university to see the
extraordinarily rich PLATERESQUE FAÇADE of about 1520. The
artist may have come from Italy, or at least been there. The three
tiers are filled with foliage, birds and beasts, heraldic shields and
roundels with expressive and extremely realistic human heads, a
typically Renaissance touch. Each tier has a central focus: in the
bottom tier are Ferdinand and Isabella looking rather pleased with
themselves and surrounded by an inscription in Greek that translates
'The Kings for the University and it for the Kings'. Above them are
the many-quartered arms of the king-emperor Charles I/V and
above them is a (or the) pope.

The portal leads to the ESCUELAS MAYORES, built in the first
third of the 15th century at the instance of Pedro de Luna (d. 1423),
the anti-pope Benedict XIII. Several old classrooms surround the
spacious patio. That with ancient benches and desks was the lecture
hall of Fray Luis de León (d. 1591), philosopher and professor of
theology, who fell foul of the Inquisition and was imprisoned for five
years. On his release, he resumed teaching in his accustomed place
with the words: 'As we were saying yesterday ...'

At the outbreak of the Civil War, Miguel de Unamuno (1864–
1936), one of the great thinkers and writers of the period, and a true
lover of Salamanca, was rector of the university. At a ceremony in
October 1936, he shared the podium with the bishop of Salamanca,
the wife of Francisco Franco, recently appointed Generalissimo, and
General Millán Astray, commander of the Foreign Legion. Astray
gave an inflammatory speech, glorifying the military prowess of
Castilla, while his followers shouted the Legion slogan 'Viva la
muerte' ('Long live death').

Enraged, Unamuno offered a blistering reply in which he said that the military needed not only to conquer (*vencer*) the people, but to convince (*convencer*) them. Only the physical intervention of Sra Franco prevented the general, now shouting 'Muera la inteligencia' ('Death to the intelligentsia'), from falling on Unamuno. The rector was expelled from his post and died in December, shunned by his friends who dared not associate with him.[5]

An elaborately carved staircase leads to the upper floor and the old and new libraries. The old library, a long vaulted chamber with some 50,000 ancient books, may be observed from a glass booth.

Across the street in the Patio de las Escuelas stands a bronze statue of Luis de León and beyond that, in the corner on the left, is the entrance to the Escuelas Menores with an attractive patio surrounded by arcades of the peculiar and rather weak-looking style of arch which evolved in Salamanca.

PALACIO DE MONTERREY The palace, a few blocks west of the Plaza Mayor, was begun in 1539 by Don Alonso de Acevedo, count of Monterrey, according to plans drawn up by Rodrigo Gil de Hontañón. Work was continued by his successors, notably Don Manuel de Fonseca y Zúñiga, 6th count, whom Philip IV made viceroy of Naples.

The best view is from the square beside the palace: three storeys separated by bold cornices, large square towers topped by assorted pinnacles and elaborately carved parapets and a herald's delight of coats of arms. The enclosed gallery on the top floor, a common feature of Renaissance palaces, must have made for pleasant promenading.

The palace was originally planned to surround the area now occupied by the square, but only the north side was ever completed. It was severely damaged by Napoleon's troops.

During his stay in Naples, the 6th count came to know José Ribera (1588–1652), the painter known in Italy as Lo Spagnoletto, who painted for him an Immaculate Conception. To house the painting, Monterrey built the Augustinian convent, LAS AGUSTINAS DESCALZAS, across the park on land originally intended for one wing of the Monterrey palace. It is now part of the university.

CASA DE LAS MUERTES Up the street in the opposite direction is

Ávila (Ávila) The Claustro del Silencio of the monastery of Sto Tomás in Ávila was constructed in the late 15th century with support from Queen Isabella and King Ferdinand who often resided here. Buried beneath a splendid marble tomb in the church is their only son, Prince Juan, who died in 1497, aged 19. The frieze between the two storeys is decorated with Dominican shields and the emblems of the Catholic Kings.

← **Ávila (Ávila)** The church of San Vicente was begun in the late 11th century as Ávila recovered from the depredations of Almanzor. In this 12th-century Annunciation scene on the south portal, the Virgin seems almost startled as she turns to hear the words of Gabriel.

↓ **Salamanca (Salamanca)** The great courtyard of the Colegio del Arzobispo was built around 1520 and represents the collaboration of some of the finest artists of the day. It is a Renaissance triumph. The medallions flanking the columns in the spandrels of the arches bear male and female busts with marvellously expressive faces. The archbishop who founded the college, part of the University of Salamanca, was Alonso III de Fonseca (d. 1534), one of that illustrious family of prelates and art patrons.

Salamanca (Salamanca) The dome of the city's Old Cathedral is known as the Torre del Gallo (Tower of the Cock) from the bronze rooster that tops it, symbol of the Church Vigilant. Begun in about 1160, it closely resembles that of Zamora though the dome here is raised on a two-tiered drum, thus giving it a more commanding stance (obscured now by the overwhelming mass of the Gothic New Cathedral).

Santibáñez del Río (Salamanca) Little remains but this portal and a number of sculpted corbels under the eaves of the roofless 12th-century church of San Juan in a small village on the Tormes river near Salamanca. Six feline faces peer out of the moulding above the arch and below the two birds. The ruin has been stabilized in recent years.

The Duero (Salamanca) The Duero forms the frontier between Spain's Salamanca Province on the right and the mountains of Portugal on the opposite bank. To the left, off the picture, the river turns abruptly west into Portugal.

the early 16th-century Plateresque façade of this lugubriously-named mansion with realistic portrait busts of Archbishop Alonso III de Fonseca (d. 1534) and six of his more worldly-looking relatives. Unamuno died in the house next door.

STA URSULA Across the street is the lofty apse of Sta Ursula with an odd balcony or mirador at its top. In the church is the tomb of Archbishop Fonseca. According to a plaque at his feet, the 'dispersed pieces' of the tomb (dispersed by whom? the French?) were reassembled in 1928 thanks to the efforts of Dr Jacobo Stuart y Falcó de Berwick y de Alba, count of Monterrey and, though it does not say so, 17th duke of Alba. He was, of course, a descendant of James FitzJames, Duke of Berwick, son of James II by Arabella Churchill, who rose high in French service. The family acquired the duchy of Alba by marriage in the late 18th century.

COLEGIO DEL ARZOBISPO West of this area the ground drops off and then rises again to a ridge where stands this college (also called the Colegio de los Irlandeses) founded about 1520 by Archbishop Fonseca as one of the colegios mayores of the university. The Irish priests came much later. The splendid and unusually spacious Renaissance patio is the work of Juan de Álava along with Diego de Siloé, Alonso Covarrubias and perhaps Alonso Berruguete. The heads in the typically Renaissance medallions around the court are marvellous. Fonseca was, of course, archbishop of Santiago de Compostela, but that seems not to have prevented him from lavishing money on Salamanca.

CASA DE LAS CONCHAS This famous 15th-century mansion is on the street from the Plaza Mayor to the cathedral. It has recently been converted to a public library and also houses the Tourist Office. The shells on the façade create a wonderful effect of light and shade. They are the badge of its builder, a knight of Santiago. This treatment was inspired by the Palacio del Infantado in Guadalajara, a major work of Juan Guas (d. 1496). The windows are small and few. Those on the ground floor have elaborate iron grills; the upper stand above carved panels. The good patio contains more of those curious Salmantine arches.

LA CLERICIA Next is this overpowering Jesuit foundation, an example of Spanish baroque. Begun in 1617 it went through several changes of architect, plan and style. The baroque phase began in 1655. The complex was finished in 1750, just seventeen years before the Jesuits were expelled from Spain. It is now the Pontifical University. The central courtyard is imposing.

PALACIO DE ANAYA Facing the Catedral Nueva, across the Plaza de Anaya, is what was originally the Colegio de San Bartolomé, founded in 1410 by Bishop Diego de Anaya. The present building dates from 1765 and is a rare example of neo-classical architecture in Spain. It is still part of the university.

CONVENTO DE STA MARÍA DE LAS DUEÑAS Crossing the plaza, walk down to the bottom of the hill and turn left to the inconspicuous entrance to this Dominican convent founded in 1419. It has a marvellous 16th-century cloister which you view from the upper storey. Men, women and creatures writhe and cry out on the capitals, though some few seem to be keeping their wits when all about them are losing theirs. As in most convents, the good sisters sell sweets (dulces) and other hand-made products.

SAN ESTEBAN The 16th-century monastery, originally founded by the Dominicans in the 13th century, has a stunning façade and a fine cloister. The present church was designed and begun by Juan de Álava (d. 1537); the expenses were borne by Juan de Toledo, bishop of Córdoba and uncle of Fernando Álvarez de Toledo y Pimentel, 3rd duke of Alba (d. 1582), notorious for his savage suppression of the revolt of the Dutch. His tomb is in the church.

The sculptured west front is recessed under a huge arch and consists of three segments: the portal itself, a graphic scene of the stoning of St Stephen (by a Milanese, Coroni), and a Crucifixion. Look at the fellow in the turban reaching for another rock. The pediment and belfry on top do not seem to fit.

In San Esteban in 1486, the professors and deans of the university debated the wisdom of Columbus's plans for his voyage. Finding the plan 'vain, impracticable, and resting on grounds too weak to merit the support of the government', they were dead set against the venture. The Dominicans, led by Diego de Deza (1443–1523), later

Inquisitor General and archbishop of Sevilla, benefactor of San Esteban, were in favour and pressed Columbus's case with Ferdinand and Isabella.

To the right of San Esteban is the entrance to the CLAUSTRO DE LOS REYES, built in 1544 by Juan de Álava. The tall arches of the lower arcade are divided by three slender columns below a stone grill; each of these is matched by two plainer arches in the upper storey. Here too is much writhing on the capitals. Clear signs of the Renaissance are the medallions with heads. A fine staircase leads to the upper storey.

The church has an impressively spacious interior. The coro is elevated at the west end on a huge arch; its paintings glorify the Dominican Order. The retablo at the opposite end can scarcely be ignored.

It was the first major commission (1693) of José Benito (1665–1735), the eldest of the three Churriguera brothers. The retablo has three sections: a monumental base topped by an entablature; a central zone containing the tabernacle flanked by mighty spiralled columns (solomonic they are called) adorned with vines and bunches of grapes; the top portion, curved to fit the vault, centring on a painting of the martyrdom of the patron saint. Hexagonal in shape to fit into the curve of the apse and therefore deep as well as lofty, it is considered the prototype of the style that came to bear the family name.

TORRE DE CLAVERO Strolling back towards the Plaza Mayor, you pass a small park in the far corner of which stands a very military tower with bartizan turrets. This is about all that remains of the 1480 mansion of Don Francisco de Sotomayor, keeper of the keys (clavero) or treasurer of the Order of Alcántara.

Around Salamanca

Alba de Tormes It is a pleasant half-day outing to Alba de Tormes, an ancient town repopulated in the 11th century thanks to the efforts of the indispensable Raymond of Burgundy. His father-in-law Alfonso VI granted it a fuero in 1140 and in time it became the centre for a famous fair which attracted tradesmen and merchants from Castilla and Extremadura.

Just east of Salamanca, a local road turns off south and follows the valley of the Tormes for some distance before suddenly disappearing into a farmyard. If you persevere on the occasionally rather dubious track, you will be rewarded by an ancient castle and miles of glorious landscape and you will eventually reach Alba de Tormes. The more conventional approach is via the C-510 southeast of Salamanca.

A bridge with twenty-two arches crosses the river into town. The most interesting of several brick *Mudéjar* Romanesque churches is SAN JUAN on a corner of the pleasant Plaza Mayor, arcaded and with a central fountain surrounded by flowers. San Juan seems to have been founded late in the 12th century and from that time remain part of the *cabecera* and the lower portions of the walls. Little brick columns with carved capitals adorn the windows of the left apse of the cabecera; the central apse is in the more common brick Mudéjar style with tall, unadorned, blind arches. On a capital to the right of the entrance a singularly unattractive double-bodied monster is chewing on something doubtless unpleasant.

The church now has a single nave in place of the original three. San Juan's treasure is an extraordinary APOSTOLADA, a group of the Twelve Apostles with Christ, in the capilla mayor. The stone figures retain traces of polychrome and date probably from the late 12th or early 13th century. Their provenance is unknown; they were in San Juan by the beginning of this century. The figure of Christ is almost 4 feet high; the Apostles, six on each side, are somewhat shorter.

Nearby is the CONVENTO DE CARMELITAS DESCALZAS, founded by Sta Teresa de Ávila in 1571. She is buried here.

The mighty TORRE DE LA ARMERÍA dominating the town from a hill is the only remaining segment of the castle of the Álvarez de Toledo family, created dukes of Alba by Enrique IV in 1469. The most famous duke of that lineage, the 3rd, Fernando (1507–82), scourge of the Netherlands, we have found buried in San Esteban in Salamanca.

The original castle formed part of the Christian defence system along the Tormes. In the 15th century it fell into the hands of the infamous infantes of Aragón, Juan and Enrique, bitter enemies of Juan II and Álvaro de Luna. When the king finally managed to wrest the castle from them, he granted it in 1429 to the bishop of Palencia, on whose death it passed to his nephew, Fernando Álvarez de Toledo. This count of Alba erected the castle of which only the Torre de la Armería remains; it was wrecked during the Peninsular War. The 4th duke employed as secretary the dramatist and poet Lope de Vega (1562–1635) who lived at Alba de Tormes from 1590 to 1595.

Arapiles A few kilometres south of Salamanca on the N-630 is the village of Arapiles where, on 22 July 1812, Wellington won his great victory over the French under Marshal Marmont, forcing Joseph Bonaparte to abandon Madrid. Beyond the little village the paved road peters out; on a ridge across the fields is a monument to the battle.

Santibáñez del Río Returning to Salamanca, do not cross the Tormes but, from the roundabout, take the N-620/C-517 west. The C-517 peels off to the right and, just a bit further along, turn right on to a small road (signposted Pino de Tormes) that takes you to this crumbling village. Park off the road and cross the stream (sometimes tricky; the stream tends to wander) to the little church of SAN JUAN, only a shell now, but with an extraordinary portal in a richly adorned south wall, rescued from almost total ruin in 1986.

The church dates probably from the second half of the 12th century. The portal is recessed in a rectangular frame. The single flat archway and the impost blocks on either side are beautifully carved with rosettes and floral motifs, while from the richly carved course above the arch peer feline faces. Immediately above the door are two large birds pecking on the head of a hapless man. Above that, and extending the length of the nave, is a cornice with carved corbels. San Juan is well worth the detour.

Buen Amor About 22 km north of Salamanca on the Zamora road, off to the right following a somewhat paved lane, is the CAST-ILLO DE BUEN AMOR built in the 15th century by Archbishop Alonso Fonseca de Quijada. When, or why, the castle acquired this rather non-episcopal name, I am unable to say.

It is now a private residence, and a most attractive one. The old castle walls form a square, on a slight eminence overlooking farm land and pastures, with three corner towers and, on the northeast, the keep slightly detached from the main block. A swimming pool has been fitted into the moat on one side. According to a little sign, you can visit if the family is in residence.

West of Salamanca

Although we did not explore the Portuguese segment of the Duero, I wanted at least to get to the border where the river turns west into Portugal. That point is now our final destination.

Almenara de Tormes Taking the local road that hugs the north bank of the Tormes, this village is the first stop. The church of STA MARÍA was built around 1164. The cabecera was disfigured in the 17th century by the intrusion of awful windows which fit the structure 'as well as two pistols would suit Christ' ('que le sientan como a un Cristo dos pistoles') in Sr Enríquez de Salamanca's pungent phrase.[6]

On the exterior of the cabecera are two bands of almost Visigothic carving: rosettes and animals in roundels. The south portal, under a protective porch, is a triumph. A richly carved frieze resting on sculpted corbels surmounts four simply but gracefully decorated archivolts. The capitals and impost blocks bear floral and animal motifs. The portal on the north side is also well carved; above is a partially destroyed cornice with carved corbels. From the capital on the left, a feline peers from behind palm leaves. The artists of the 11th and 12th centuries must have had fun creating these carvings; they cannot have been totally driven by religious motivations.

Ledesma This well-girt town has guarded the crossing of the River Tormes since the days when it was Roman Bletisama. It stands high on a crag on the south side of the impressive gorge the Tormes has by now cut into the rock of the meseta. Ledesma was taken briefly by Alfonso I in the 8th century, repopulated for a while by Ramiro II in the 10th, and conquered finally around 1158 by Fernando II who granted it a fuero in 1171.

In 1429 it was erected into a countship for the Zúñiga family whom we have encountered in Peñaranda de Duero and Salamanca and who caused Isabella considerable discomfort on her path to the throne. Enrique IV granted it to his favourite Beltrán de la Cueva. Ledesma was finally ceded to Salamanca.

You cross the bridge, go around to the right to the far side of town and make your way upwards. The stout walls date from the time of Fernando II. The arcaded Plaza Mayor is so thickly planted with trees that it is difficult to see STA MARÍA LA MAYOR that dates from the years of repopulation and overwhelms the little plaza. From that era only the west front and the tower remain. Granite is the favoured building material.

What remains of the castle stands on a high point in the middle of town. The irregular-shaped walled enclosure has round tapered towers and a massive pentagonal keep on the side towards Portugal. The north portal is surmounted by an escudo with a mounted knight. Romanesque STA ELENA on the east side of town has some good corbels.

The Frontier The Tormes is dammed below Ledesma. A huge reservoir stretches towards the Portuguese frontier through which runs the boundary between Zamora and Salamanca Provinces. Our way lies to the south, to regain the N-517 and drive on to Vitigudino, an unremarkable agricultural town (with, however, a pastelería serving excellent coffee and pastry). Lumbrales is next, and beyond that a road goes off right to Hinojosa de Duero where there is reportedly a good Romanesque church.

Broad wheat fields and olive groves cover the Castilian landscape here and the rugged mountains of Portugal on the other side of the Duero gorge are visible from some distance away. The N-517 now begins to drop down from the edge of the meseta, curves through La Fregeneda, a prosperous-looking little place, and 10 kilometres further on stops abruptly at the water's edge.

A calm sheet of water extends south, west and east. The Río Agüeda comes up from the south to form the international border for a distance and meets the Duero coming from the north and east. Together they turn due west and begin the final run to the Atlantic. Their progress is interrupted by another barrage further downstream, out of sight.

High up over the Agüeda, a railway bridge carries the line from Salamanca to Porto. In the distance, partially hidden by a fold in the mountains, the red roofs and white walls of the Portuguese village of Barca d'Alva are visible.

The journey is over.

Notes

1. Richard Ford, *A Handbook for Travellers in Spain* (London, 1966), pp. 852 and 857.

2. David Gilmour, *Cities of Spain* (London, 1992), p. 118.

3. Joseph Townsend, *A Journey through Spain in the Years 1786 and 1787* (London, 1791), p. 83.

4. Augustus Hare, *Wanderings in Spain* (London, 1873), pp. 169–70.

5. The story is told by, among many others, Gabriel Jackson in his *The Spanish Republic and the Civil War* (Princeton, 1965), pp. 300–1.

6. Cayetano Enríquez de Salamanca, *El ruta románico en la provincia de Salamanca* (Madrid, 1989), p. 79.

Appendix

Rulers of León and Castilla, and Later of Spain

Kingdom of Asturias

718–37	Pelayo
737–39	Favila
739–57	Alfonso I, the Catholic
757–68	Fruela I
768–74	Aurelio
774–83	Silo
783–89	Mauregato
789–91	Bermudo I, the Deacon
791–842	Alfonso II, the Chaste
842–50	Ramiro I
850–66	Ordoño I
866–910	Alfonso III, the Great

Kingdom of León

910–14	García I
914–24	Ordoño II (Galicia 910–24)
924–25	Fruela II (Asturias 910–25)
925–31	Alfonso IV, the Monk
931–51	Ramiro II
951–55	Ordoño III
955–58	Sancho I, the Fat
958–60	Ordoño IV, the Bad

Kingdom of León		Kingdom of Castilla	
960–66	Sancho I (restored)	c. 930–70	Fernán González
966–84	Ramiro III	970–95	García Fernández
984–99	Bermudo II, the Gouty	995–1017	Sancho Garcés
999–1028	Alfonso V, the Noble	1017–29	García Sánchez
1028–37	Bermudo III	1029–35	Sancho I, el Mayor (Nav.- Arag. 1000–35)
1037–65	Fernando I, the Great	1035–65	Fernando I, the Great
		1065–72	Sancho II, the Strong
1065–1109	Alfonso VI	1072–1109	Alfonso VI
	1109–26 Urraca		
	1126–57 Alfonso VII, the Emperor		
1157–88	Fernando II	1157–58	Sancho III
1188–1230	Alfonso IX	1158–1214	Alfonso VIII
		1214–17	Enrique I
		(1217	Berenguela)
1230–52	Fernando III, el Santo	1217–52	Fernando III el Santo

Castilla y León (permanently united 1230)

1230–52	Fernando III, el Santo
1252–84	Alfonso X, the Learned
1284–95	Sancho IV, the Brave
1295–1312	Fernando IV
1312–50	Alfonso XI
1350–69	Pedro I, the Cruel
1369–79	Enrique II de Trastámara
1379–90	Juan I
1390–1406	Enrique III, the Sufferer
1406–54	Juan II
1454–74	Enrique IV, the Impotent
1474–1504	Isabel I, 'la Católica'
1474–1504	Fernando V (Fernando II of Aragón 1479–1516)
1504–06	Juana (with Fernando as Regent)
1504–06	Felipe I (Philip of Habsburg)
1506–16	Fernando V, King-Regent

House of Habsburg ('los Austriacos')

1516–56	Carlos I (Emp. Charles V 1519–56) (abd; d. 1558)
1556–98	Felipe II
1598–1621	Felipe III
1621–65	Felipe IV
1665–1700	Carlos II

House of Bourbon ('los Borbones')

1701–46	Felipe V (confirmed 1714)
1724	Luís I
1746–59	Fernando VI
1759–88	Carlos III
1788–1808	Carlos IV (abd; d. 1819)
1808	Fernando VII
1808–13	José I (Joseph Bonaparte)
1810–14	Cortes at Cádiz (National Government)
1814–33	Fernando VII (restored)
1833–68	Isabel II (deposed; d. 1904) (María Cristina de Bourbon, Regent 1833–1840)
1868–71	Regency and Provisional Government
1870–73	Amadeo I de Saboya (Savoy) (abd)
1873	First Republic (4 presidents, Feb.–Dec.)
1873–74	Regency & Provisional Government (Jan.–Dec.)
1874–89	Alfonso XII
1889–1931	Alfonso XIII (deposed; d. 1941) (María Cristina of Austria, Regent 1889–1902)
1931–39	Second Republic
1931–1936	Niceto Alcalá Zamora, Pres.
1936	Diego Martínez Barrio
1936–39	Manuel Azaña
[1936–39	Civil War]
1939–75	Francisco Franco y Bahamonde, Head of State
1975–	Juan Carlos I

Glossary

Spanish Terms

ábside	apse
ajimez (-ces)	twinned windows, divided by a column
alcalde/alcaldessa	mayor (m. and f.)
alcázar	castle (usually royal castle in a town)
alcor	hill
alfiz (-ces)	square moulding around doors/windows
alfoz (-ces)	territory surrounding and belonging to a medieval town
almenas	battlements
archivolta	archivolt; moulding around portal
arco apuntado	pointed or lancet arch
arco ciego	blind arch
arco de herredura	horseshoe arch
arco de medio punto	round-headed arch
arco toral	each of the four arches that define the crossing and support the cupola
arco triunfal/de trionfo	arch between nave and sanctuary
artesonado	coffered and panelled wooden ceiling
atalaya	watch tower
auto de fe	act of faith (referring to the trial)
ayuntamiento	town hall
azogue/azoguejo	medieval market place
azulejo	tile
barrio	neighbourhood of a town
bóveda de arista	groin vault
bóveda de cañón	tunnel or barrel vault

bóveda de crucería, o nervadura	ribbed vault (two pointed arches that cross, which the vaulting rests)
bóveda de horno	semicircular vault, like an oven
cabecera	apse (east) end of church
cañada	migratory route travelled by sheep
canecillo	carved corbel or eave bracket supporting the cornice; often sculpted
capilla mayor	main chapel with high altar
carretera	main road; national highway
casa consistorial	town hall (of a large town)
casco antiguo	old, historic section of town
cimborio	cupola or tower above crossing
claustro	cloister
colegiata	collegiate church (not the seat of a bishop, but administered by a chapter of canons)
contrafuerte	buttress
Conversos	baptized Jews
coro	choir (place where services are sung)
Cortes	parliament of Spain (from 'corte' or royal court)
crucero	crossing of transepts and nave; also, entire transept
cuidad	city
culto	service (mass)
cura	village or parish priest (see also párroco)
custodio/-a	custodian (who has the key)
desamortización	disentailment (of religious property)
encierro	amateur bullfight
'en obras'	'in works', under construction (in other words, closed)
Epistola, lado de	right side of church, facing altar
ermita	hermitage
escudo	escutcheon, shield with coat of arms
espadaña	belfry
Evangelo, lado de	left side of church, facing altar
fuero	municipal charter of civic rights
girola	ambulatory around the apse
granja	medieval farm attached to monastery

horario	schedule of opening/closing hours
judería	Jewish quarter in a medieval town
letrado	medieval university-educated bureaucrat
llave	key
maceros	mace bearers
meridional/de meseta	southern
mediodía	central tableland of Spain
Mesta	medieval association of sheep-owners
mihrab	prayer niche (mosque)
modillón	see canecillo
moldura	moulding
morería	Muslim quarter in a medieval town
Morisco	converted Moor or descendant of one
Mozárab, -es	Christians under Muslim rule who adopted their customs, dress, language
Mudéjar, -es	Muslims who remained behind after the Christian reconquest
nervio	rib (of a vault)
oculo	small round window
oriente	east
párroco	parish priest
parroquia	parish church
poniente	west
presbiterio	presbytery, chancel – square area between nave and sanctuary
reja	wrought-iron grill (chapels and coros)
retablo	carved and painted screen behind altar
rollo	elaborate Gothic column often used as pillory
sala capitular	chapter house (of church or monastery)
señorío	lordship
septentrional	northern
sillería	choir stalls
taifa	petty kingom in al-Andalus after end of caliphate of Córdoba
taller	workshop (for artisans)
testero	cabecera
torre de homenaje	castle keep

trascoro	back (west) wall of coro enclosure
vendimia	grape harvest (festival)
verbena	town festival, 'block party'

English Terms

ambulatory	extension of aisle carried around and behind the main altar
apse	eastern (altar) end of church beyond crossing
arcade (1)	series of arches, as in cloister
arcade (2)	lower third of Gothic cathedral nave separating nave from aisles
archivolt	one of a series of concentric mouldings on the face of an arch, moulding around door or window
baldachin	ornamental canopy over an altar
bays	transverse sections of church
blind arcade	arcade flat against a wall surface
calefactorium	warming room in monastery
canon	clergyman observing a Rule (Augustinian, for example) belonging to the staff of a cathedral or collegiate church
chancel/presbytery	area between crossing and main altar; space reserved for clergy and choir, separate from body of church
chapter house	chamber where governing chapter of cathedral or monastery meets
chevet	apsidal complex consisting of high altar, ambulatory and radiating chapels
choir	place reserved for clergy or monks to chant services
clerestory	upper third of Gothic cathedral nave containing the windows
collegiate church	church not the seat of a bishop but governed by a chapter of canons
corbel	block of stone, often carved, projecting from wall to support roof beams or eaves
crossing	where transept crosses nave
drum	cylinder supporting a dome

impost (block)	top stone of pillar from which springs the arch
mandorla	Italian for almond; oval frame or aura that often surrounds Christ or the Virgin in Romanesque art
pendentives	concave triangular sections of sphere placed between upper portions of arches of crossing to form a circle
pier	heavy column, usually square
pilaster	pier affixed to wall face and projecting slightly therefrom
refectory	dining hall of monastery
scriptorium	room in monastery where books were written and illuminated
squinches	small arches across corners of crossing to convert square to octagon
tribune	raised platform at west end of church, for choir
triforium	section of Gothic cathedral between arcade and clerestory
tympanum	triangular or semicircular section above portal, between lintel and arch, usually sculpted
vaults:	
barrel or tunnel	shaped like half a cylinder
groin	intersection of two barrel vaults
lierne	with intermediary ribs from one main rib to another; often curved (Gothic)
quadripartite	two ribs crossing to make four sections
sexpartite	two ribs and an arch crossing to make six sections
voussoir	each of the wedge-shaped stones forming an arch

Bibliography

Books in Spanish

Aub, Max, *Manual de Historia de la Literatura Española* (Mexico City, 1966).

Azcárate, José María, *Arte Gótico en España* (Madrid, 1990).

Bango Torviso, Isidro G., *El románico en España* (Madrid, 1992).

Bernard, Javier, *Castillos de Burgos* (León, 1992).

— *Castillos de Soria* (León, s/f).

— *Castillos de Valladolid* (León, s/f).

El Cantar de Mio Cid (Austral, Madrid, 1990).

Castán Lanaspa, Javier, *El Arte Románico en las Extremaduras de León y Castilla* (Valladolid, 1990).

Castillo, Rosa (ed.), *Leyendas épicas españolas* (Madrid, 1987).

Díez Alonso, Matias, y P. Albano García, *Tierra de Campos* (León, 1990).

Enríquez de Salamanca, Cayetano, *El ruta románico en la provincia de Palencia* (Madrid, 1991).

— *El ruta románico en la provincia de Salamanca* (Madrid, 1989).

— *El ruta románico en la provincia de Soria* (Madrid, 1986).

— *El ruta románico en la provincia de Zamora* (Madrid, 1989).

Iradiel, Paulino, Salustiano Moreta y Esteban Saresa, *Historia Medieval de la España Cristiana* (Madrid, 1989).

Lafora, Carlos R., *Por los Caminos del Románico Porticado* (Madrid, 1988).

— *Andanzas en Torno al Legado Mozárabe* (Madrid, 1991).

Moreno García, Rafael, *Castillos de Palencia* (León, 1995).

Navascués Palacio, Pedro, *Monasterios de España*, Vol. I (Madrid, 1991).

Peñafiel, Don Juan Manuel de, *El Conde Lucanor* (Austral, Madrid, 1947).

Pinilla González, Jaime, *Castillos de Zamora y Salamanca* (León, 1989).

Poema de Fernán González, ed. H. Salvador Martínez (Austral, Madrid, 1991).

Regueras, Fernando, *La arquitectura mozárabe en León y Castilla* (Salamanca, 1991).

Rincón García, Wifredo, *Monasterios de España*, Vols II and III (Madrid, 1991, 1992).

Ruiz Montejo, Inés, *El Románico de Villas y Tierras de Segovia* (Madrid, 1988).

Sáinz Sáiz, Javier, *El Románico rural en Castilla y León* (León, 1991).

Sarthou Carreres, Carlos, *Castillos de España* (Madrid, 1992).

— y Pedro Navascués Palacio, *Catedrales de España* (Madrid, 1990).

Books in English

Aguilar, M. and I. Robertson, *Jewish Spain, A Guide* (Madrid, 1986).

Bevan, Bernard, *A History of Spanish Architecture* (London, 1938).

Braunfels, Wolfgang, *Monasteries of Western Europe* (London, 1972).

Brenan, Gerald, *The Spanish Labyrinth* (Cambridge, 1990; first published 1943).

Brooke, Christopher, *The Monastic World* (New York, 1974).

Cambridge Ancient History (Cambridge, 1952).

Collins, Roger, *Early Medieval Spain: Unity in Diversity, 400–1000* (New York, 1995).

Conant, Kenneth John, *Carolingian and Romanesque Architecture 800–1200* (New York, 1978).

Elliott, J. H., *Imperial Spain, 1469–1716* (London, 1970).

Fletcher, Richard, *Saint James's Catapult: The Life and Times of Diego Gelmírez of Santiago de Compostela* (Oxford, 1984).

— *The Quest for El Cid* (New York, 1990).

— *Moorish Spain* (New York, 1992).

Ford, Richard, *A Handbook for Travellers in Spain* (London, 1966; first published 1846).

Gerber, Jane, *The Jews of Spain* (New York, 1992).

Gilmour, David, *Cities of Spain* (London, 1992).

Hare, Augustus, *Wanderings in Spain* (London, 1873).

Hay, John, *Castilian Days* (Boston, 1871).

Hersey, Carl Kenneth, *The Salmantine Lanterns: Their Origins and Development* (Cambridge, MA, 1937).

Hutton, Edward, *The Cities of Spain* (London, 1906).

Kamen, Henry, *Spain 1469–1714: A Society of Conflict*, 2nd edn (New York, 1991).

King, Georgiana Goddard, *Pre-Romanesque Churches of Spain* (New York, 1924).

Kubler, George and Martin Soria, *Art and Architecture in Spain and Portugal and Their American Dominions 1500–1800* (London, 1959).

Lalaguna, Juan, *A Traveler's History of Spain* (New York, 1989).

Lawrence, C. H., *Medieval Monasticism* (New York, 1989).

Lee, Laurie, *As I Walked Out One Midsummer Morning* (London, 1969).

Linehan, Peter, *History and the Historians of Medieval Spain* (Oxford, 1993).

Liss, Peggy, *Isabel the Queen* (Oxford, 1992).

MacKay, Angus, *Spain in the Middle Ages: from Frontier to Empire, 1000–1500* (London, 1993).

Morton, H. V., *A Stranger in Spain* (New York, 1955).

O'Callaghan, Joseph F., *A History of Medieval Spain* (Ithaca, NY, 1975).

Parkinson, Roger, *The Peninsular War* (London, 1973).

Prescott, William H., *The History of the Reign of Ferdinand and Isabella* (Philadelphia, 1873).

Pritchett, V. S., *The Spanish Temper* (New York, 1954).

Rahlves, Frederick, *Cathedrals and Monasteries of Spain* (London, 1966).

Reilly, Bernard F., *The Medieval Spains* (Cambridge, 1993).

— *The Contest of Christian and Muslim Spain, 1031–1157* (Cambridge, MA, 1995).

Snyder, James, *Medieval Art* (New York, 1989).

Sobré, Judith Berg, *Behind the Altar Table: The Development of the Painted Retablo in Spain, 1350–1500* (Missouri, 1989).

Swinburne, Henry, *Travels through Spain in the Years 1775 and 1776* (London, 1778).

Townsend, Joseph, *A Journey through Spain in the Years 1786 and 1787* (London, 1791).

Webb, Michael, *The City Square* (New York, 1990).

Whitehill, Walter Muir, *Spanish Romanesque Architecture of the Eleventh Century* (Oxford, 1941).

Index of Monuments

General Index